I0622570

Criterion Tuesdays

A Fan's Journey Through World Cinema

Peter Johansson

Naughty Hugo Press, LLC, Olympia

Cover design, back cover illustration by Peter Johansson
Interior format by Polgarus Studios

ISBN: 979-8-9881608-0-9 (paperback)
ISBN: 979-8-9881608-1-6 (hardcover)
ISBN: 979-8-9881608-2-3 (ebook)

Naughty Hugo Press, LLC, Olympia, WA

For Sam,
my filmmate

Contents

Introduction

If I knew how to make sourdough, you probably wouldn't be reading this right now.

Criterion Tuesdays began as a COVID pandemic project. But before we get into that...

Hi. I'm Peter. I don't teach film, I don't have a degree in film studies, I have no legitimate credentials entitling me to write a book about film. By profession, I'm a nurse. My only real qualification is that I love movies, a qualification - if you're reading this book - we probably share.

I have loved movies my entire life. My pre-streaming, pre-internet, pre-VCR, pre-cable youth was spent searching out movies - any kind of movies - on VHF and UHF rabbit-eared television, and often sneaking out of the house and into the movie theater. The arrival of VHS hit me like the Gutenberg Press hit the book world, and in the 1990s I began collecting movies on VHS. Most of these I eventually replaced on DVD[1], and as of this writing in June of 2023,

---

[1] I'd be grateful to anyone who could hook me up with a reasonably priced disc of the 1988 Michael Keaton film, *Clean and Sober*.

The Collection stands at… well, it's a lot. (Why collect discs? I'll get into that at the end of this how-do-you-do.) I have a serious problem. Or I'm awesome. Whatever.

Sooner or later, when you collect movies on disc, you're going to run into the Criterion Collection. The Criterion Collection describes itself as "dedicated to publishing important classic and contemporary films from around the world in editions that offer the highest technical quality and award-winning, original supplements." When you buy a Criterion film, you're getting an edition that's been cleaned up, usually restored, and generally dazzling, which is a particularly great way to watch old films. (They also have a Criterion Channel on which you can stream much of their collection.) The Criterion discs usually come loaded with extras; commentary tracks with filmmakers or film historians, essays, documentaries, trailers, etc. You really are getting the best, truest possible version of the film. The only drawback is the Criterion versions generally end up costing about twice what the usual DVD or Blu-Ray would run. So I typically don't buy a movie from Criterion unless I *really* want the best possible version of it. Or if no one else is carrying it.

Over the years, as I've built The Collection to include international films, silent films, cult, quirky, or independent films, I've picked up quite a few Criterion editions. Usually when I'd acquire one, I'd watch the film, then put it on the shelf. Probably watch it again sometime when the mood hit me. But I never got into all the extras included, and one day it struck me that I really wasn't getting my money's worth out of my Criterion films if I didn't read the essays, rewatch the film with the chat tracks, watch the accompanying interviews, documentaries, *all* the bells and whistles. So I decided once a week - usually Tuesdays - I'd take a Criterion film down off the shelf and do a deep dive into it. Almost like taking a film class.

Thus began my geeky little pandemic project.

Initially, I wrote about my Tuesday movie on Facebook (along with an IMDB link, if it existed, to the film's trailer). It wasn't to lecture, but to encourage discussion. Some of these films I've struggled with (*Limite* immediately comes to mind). Others (like *All That Jazz*) were old friends I felt right at home with. In any case, what I hoped to do was two things: Satisfy an itch I had to talk (write) about films I was learning about. And maybe introduce a friend to a film they might not otherwise see. But Facebook, especially if consumed on a phone, isn't the best place for long essays, and my posts were getting a little windy. So in 2022, I moved my essays over to a blog (criteriontuesdays.com), spiffing up some of the original posts.[2] In the spring of 2023, I had the idea of taking 100 of my favorite essays, and publishing them as a book. This book.

The rules I originally set for myself were to watch every Criterion film I had in alphabetical order, and read/watch *all* the extras that came with it (in at least three films I own, this meant reading the source novel or stories included with the

---

[2] Gradually, I turned to posting essays on Tuesdays, giving myself a week to take in a title, letting it "percolate" while I thought about what I'd write.

film). For a film like *Brazil* this meant watching multiple versions of the film, each with their own commentary track. There are roughly 100 films I own in non-Criterion editions, but which Criterion carries editions of. I decided not to include these since I wouldn't have access to the extra features. Some of these (*The 400 Blows, Bicycle Thieves, Repo Man*) I would eventually like to replace with their Criterion counterparts. Boxed sets (*The Apu Trilogy, A Film Trilogy by Ingmar Bergman*) I would treat as a single entry. The exception to this would be the twelve films that make up Volumes 1 and 2 of *Martin Scorsese's World Cinema Project* (more on this later), which includes *Dry Summer, The Housemaid, Insiang, Law of the Border, Limite, Mysterious Object at Noon, Redes, Revenge, A River Called Titas, Taipei Story, Touki bouki,* and *Trances.* These I felt deserved to be written about separately. So these essays - think of them as "book reports." Each essay is a recap of what I've learned about the film in question from consuming all of the available supplemental materials. Where I've quoted people directly I've been sure to let you know. Sometimes I'll add an insight I've picked up over years of reading about and watching movies, or a personal story. Sometimes I've done a little digging if the historical background to either the film or the story is helpful.

(This would be a good spot for me to throw in a disclaimer: None of these essays reflect the views or opinions of the good people over at The Criterion Collection, or of the filmmakers involved in these films. My blog and this book are wholly unaffiliated with them. I have no official connection with The Criterion Collection, and they do not provide me with any films, or suggest titles in any way. My only relationship with them is as an enthusiastic customer.)

For me, this experiment has had some unexpected benefits. Like a lot of us, I had developed bad movie-watching habits while at home - pausing frequently for bathroom breaks, to change laundry loads, answering texts, etc. Or even scrolling through my phone through a slower section of film. The pandemic had gotten me out of the habit of watching a film in a darkened movie theater uninterrupted, with nothing else competing for my attention. With these films, I made myself darken the room, put my phone out of reach, and focus on what was on screen. I didn't watch these films on a phone or laptop, but from my television, the biggest screen I have. And with many of these films - the older ones especially - I was amazed at how much I had missed. I think we've lost something of the idea of watching a film actively and intentionally - at least I had - and I'm grateful for my Tuesday nights. They made me a better film student.

The films in this book don't really represent an organized canon of world cinema. Mostly, they represent one film buff's biases (as well as the films available to Criterion for release; I suspect that there are many films they'd like to get the rights to that studios are withholding from them). It won't take you long to find out, for example, that I'm a huge fan of both Ingmar Bergman and Akira Kurosawa, so their films are overrepresented here. Which is fine; we're all allowed biases in our own media collections, whether it's the music of Taylor Swift or the novels of Stephen King. But in the past ten years or so, both the Black Lives Matter and #MeToo movements have convinced me - an old white guy - that I need to listen to more of the stories from people who aren't me. Woke? Sure, I'll own that, proudly. It's made me a better person, I think, and opened up a brilliant new world of stories to me. But also, as I made my film collection "public" through the blog, and now this book, I felt a responsibility to expand beyond the typical canon of Western film. Hence, the inclusion of the World Cinema Project films, designed to restore and raise awareness of films and filmmakers that work out of marginalized film cultures. Filmmakers of color, women, LGBTQI+ voices are present in these pages, but remain woefully underrepresented in my film collection, as in popular culture. But I'm trying, and to its credit, I think Criterion is, too.

While we're on the topic, a note about my language in this book. I've tried hard to use gender inclusive terminology, but am sure I've gotten it wrong in spots; please let me know. I've also often replaced the "LGBTQI+" adjective with "queer," not only because it's less cumbersome, but because that's how my queer pals self-refer. Also, titles are capitalized (or not) according to filmmaker preference, and in the case of film titles in Italian or French, according to grammar rules specific to those languages, which capitalize only the first letter of a title (*La dolce vita*, or *Touki bouki*, for example).

႙ ႙ ႙

And now to the question of "Why discs?" Why not just stream these films? Who even buys films on disc anymore anyway?

Well, me, for one. The lesser half of the reason is availability. Films go on and off streaming services all the time, and for some of the older or more obscure films, good luck finding them streaming at all. And as some of us found out with streaming music services, their definition of "buying" a song or album differs from yours and mine. Many of us found out the fine print in agreements with streaming services actually lets us know we were only "leasing" the music we thought we had bought, and that it could be taken away at any time. I don't want the same thing to happen to digital films I purchase, even if it is for a smaller price. Once I have a movie on DVD or Blu-Ray, it can't be taken back, and it can't be altered. Maybe this sounds paranoid of me, but I'm not sure we won't hit a point in this country where electronic media won't be subject to editing to suit the financial, cultural, or political pressures on streaming platforms. By purchasing movies on disc, I know they'll always be available to me, and in exactly the version I bought them in. Sometimes people suggest that equipment to play these films may no longer be available, but I'm gambling it will (at least in my lifetime). Hey, if vinyl can make a return, why not DVDs and Blu-Rays?

But really, it's habit, and a collector's pride. I spent much of my film-collecting life living in rural Pennsylvania, and at that time, reliable streaming just wasn't available, and there's nothing I hate more than pauses in a movie I'm watching. So I got into the habit of buying films rather than streaming them (almost always films I'd seen and wanted to see again). By the time I got to a place where streaming was a reliable option, I already had more than a thousand titles. I figured I was past the point of no return.

But anyone who collects anything knows - whether it's porcelain frogs, baseball cards, souvenir teaspoons, Monets, or anything else - there's a certain amount of pride in tracking down the rare item and displaying it. Book owners know this best of all. I have to admit a certain lift I get from sitting in a room surrounded by hard copies of great (and gleefully shitty!) movies. I remember the day I was finally able to track down a DVD copy of *Faster, Pussycat! Kill! Kill!* Every collector has a moment like that. So sue me. For every obsession someone has that most people can't understand, there's someone out there that says, "That's my cup of kibble right there." *My* kibble is a living room wall-to-wall with movies I love.

ʘ ʘ ʘ

How should you read this book? Cover to cover. In one sitting. While the plaintive cries of family and employers go unheeded.

Just kidding.

Please feel free to surf through the book, sampling as you go. Each essay is designed to stand alone, or refer you to another one if there's pertinent information there. So start with films you've seen, to see if you find anything new, or to see if you agree with my assessment. Use *Criterion Tuesdays* to point you toward films you might want to check out. Hop around. Or, read it cover to cover if you like; I'll bet you learn something new. Over the course of the book, I try to spend a little time defining common terms in film theory, as well as visiting highlights of global cinema history. Hell, use it to fake your way through a conversation about *The Seventh Seal* at a cocktail party. I don't care.[3]

And for the love of Pete (see what I did there?), don't be hard on yourself if you don't recognize these films, or have only seen one or two. Most of my friends haven't. Why would they? It's hard enough keeping up with current popular culture without going skulking around in the past. I'm not here to lecture. I'm here to help, if you're curious about old movies, foreign-language flicks, or "arthouse" cinema.

My goal was to write about movies in clear language, for people who love movies, but don't subscribe to film journals. There is a lot of opaque language in film writing, and I suspect at least some of it is an attempt at gatekeeping, or a desire for the writer to prove they're as smart as the next film writer, or critic. I don't think that helps anyone. A lot of this comes from a career of almost 30 years in nursing, where I've seen both nurses and providers sometimes forget that patients aren't always fluent in medical terminology. I've taken pride in being clear when educating patients. I've tried to make use of my half-educated position here, somewhere between movie buff and film writer to bridge the gap between the two. My goal has always been to welcome people in, not build up another barrier.

Welcome to my book. I hope you have fun here.

---

[3] Well, I care a little. Don't be a poser. And are cocktail parties even a thing anymore? I've never been to one.

8½

Italy, 1963. Directed by Frederico Fellini. 138 minutes, black & white.

8½ is a place to begin.

It's a dive into the deep end. It's hitting the ground running. It's both the best and the worst place to start studying serious film.

Months after watching this I would read about Italian neorealism and Frederico Fellini and the way his films both refute and reflect on what came before him. But at the time of this viewing, I was beginning an experiment, taking the first step of a journey. *8½* became a reality check on my little project. It would probably have been easier to begin with one of the many American films in my Criterion collection, but I'd sworn to do this alphabetically, figuring the randomness would keep me from categorizing or editorializing. Much better to jump in and meet the film where I am and where the film is (to this day I don't look ahead to see what I'll be watching next).

But I made a decision in watching *8½*, a decision that would stick with me throughout this project. I'd start by reading any essays that were included along with the disc, then watch the film, then repeat a day or two later with the commentary track (if any). Then I'd go through the rest of the supplemental materials on the disc. In the case of this first film, I benefited from the accompanying essay, "When 'He' Became 'I'" by Tullio Kezich, and that essay and the film itself became a great launchpad for a journey through world cinema. They both bore a warning to me, and that warning was "You cannot watch these films as a 21st-century American." In other words, I'd have to shift my focus away from Disney, away from the Marvel Cinematic Universe, away from Bruce Willis and Tom Cruise. There's nothing necessarily wrong with those things, but that's not where these films live. They live in a time and place where the audience was expected to meet the filmmaker halfway. You can't view these films passively. They demand your attention and concentration. And if you can offer that, you'll be rewarded.

I'll admit to buying a lot of Italian and French films, especially those of the mid-20th century not because I was hooked on them, but because I thought I should. I also thought, naively, that I could appreciate them without a guide, as if I'd be ready for authentic local Kenyan or Indonesian cuisine on my first day off the plane. They're what I described to my son as "vegetable movies;" films you consume because you know they're good for you. But like vegetables, consume enough good ones, and you start to like the taste. But you still need to acclimate, and I hadn't done that yet.

My problem with Fellini, and with *8½* in particular, was

that I was waiting for a coherent story to be presented to me in a linear fashion. In my defense, that's how movies are generally presented to we Americans. And if (pre-internet) you weren't lucky enough to grow up near a major city or a university campus, you simply would not have had access to anything other than mainstream Hollywood fare. You have to *learn* how to watch films like these, and I didn't have an opportunity for that until well into my adult life. Still, as a former Lit major, I should have known better.

What I found I had to do with *8½* is surrender myself to the film. Let it absorb me, not so much the other way around. Stop trying to demand exposition, and let the film unravel itself in its own terms. Kezich's essay gave me some broad outlines about what the film meant to him, but also where Fellini was as a director: he was tired. He was looking for his next project, and wasn't sure what stories or ideas he had left in him. And since he was, well, Frederico Effing Fellini, the man walked around under a ton of expectations. So *8½* is kind of a film about the making of itself (the title comes from Fellini joking that this film fell between his eighth and ninth films). Having a few hints going in, and not demanding, "Who's that character? What's the relationship? How does this scene explain the plot?" helped me just watch Marcello Mastroianni's performance as a famous film director trying to justify himself, his career, and his place among his peers. Watching Mastroianni move through this film told me more about Fellini's struggles than any plot synopsis could. On a second viewing, I'd recognize which touches were brought by Fellini himself, and the whole film - something I'd seen before (I've seen most of my Criterion films before) - began to gel, really for the first time. I started to get it. I wasn't there yet. But I was on the road to being a better film audience.

It just takes practice, which, as we know, makes perfect. A friend of mine who coaches high school football would clarify, "Perfect practice makes perfect." I'd learn later (oddly, from another Fellini film) that watching these films means watching well; darkening the room, putting away (and silencing) the phone, watching on the biggest screen you have. In other words, duplicating the movie theater experience as closely as possible. That, after all, is how these films were meant to be seen. But here's the thing: I'm really good, for example, at crossword puzzles[4]. I do the Sunday NYT puzzle in the Seattle Times every week in ink, and my friends think that's because I'm smart. But what they don't get is even with something like crossword puzzles, you get better the more you do them. Certain words are repeated, certain patterns emerge, and mostly (I think) repeating the experience over and over again of getting stuck, clearing your head, and approaching the puzzle fresh builds a resistance to giving up. It's absolutely a learnable skill. Same with watching movies. Reading about them helps, and film books and articles have certainly enhanced my understanding. But there's nothing that can replace repetition, simply getting

[4] Not *that* good, as I learned when I was relieved of my lunch money the first time I competed in the American Crossword Puzzle Tournament in 2012.

used to watching a different kind of film in a new way.

And, damn, Marcello Mastroianni is *cool*. Eternally, effortlessly cool. That I picked up right away.

All That Jazz

US, 1979. Directed by Bob Fosse. 123 minutes, color.

Before I get into *All That Jazz*, a confession: I have long nurtured a fundamental prejudice against movie musicals. For years I let people convince me that I was being too uptight, too analytical. After all, I am the only person I know whose blood pressure goes up when watching *Singin' in the Rain*, and not in a good way. But I think the problem was more that I was being fed a very specific, very bland sort of musical comedy; my exposure was usually the lowest-common-denominator stuff they'd throw on television when I was growing up, and the productions the local high school would stage when they wanted to be sure there were parts for as many kids as possible. Given that lack of choice, maybe I (and a lot of other folks I'm sure) could be forgiven for thinking that musicals were just excuses for people to break into song for no reason, sacrificing both good acting and good music in the process. It also didn't help that in a lot of family-friendly musicals, adults would behave childishly. I never liked adults acting like kids in movies or television shows when I was a kid, and I don't think most kids do. We feel safer if we know the adults are actually in control. I think it's why most people of my generation have fonder memories of *Mary Poppins* than we do of *Chitty Chitty Bang Bang*.[5] There's a reason *Mr. Rogers Neighborhood* ran for 31 seasons and *The Banana Splits* for two.

But as an adult, I began to discover more adult musicals. Sure, the annual television broadcast of *The Sound of Music* should have tipped me off that there were less silly types of musicals out there, but that always seemed like more of an "event" than an actual movie. Yet slowly, films like Robert Wise and Jerome Robbins' *West Side Story*, and the 1944 film *Meet Me in St. Louis* began to show me that movie musicals could convincingly tell dramatic stories, too. Or, as in the case of *All That Jazz*, could tell the story of an artist contemplating his work, his relationships, and his own mortality.

Since I'm watching my Criterion films in alphabetical order, *All That Jazz* is the follow-up to last week's *8½*. Interesting that both films are more or less a director telling a story about himself and his art (as well as the way each filmmaker revered, objectified, and abused the women in his life). Roy Scheider

---

[5] Although the James Bond connections to *Chitty Chitty Bang Bang* are astonishing, beginning with the source novel, the only children's book written by Ian Fleming, author of the James Bond spy thrillers. The film is produced by Albert R. Broccoli, who also produced the Bond films. Baron Bomburst is played by Gert Fröbe, better known as Auric Goldfinger in the film *Goldfinger*. And Mr. Coggins, the kindly junkman who sells the heap to Dick Van Dyke to fix up, is played by none other than Desmond Llewelyn, the original Q in the James Bond films. No wonder the car can fly.

plays Joe Gideon, a loose stand-in for director Bob Fosse himself (in a neat bit of trivia on the chat track, I learned that the address on Joe Gideon's dexedrine bottles was actually the address of Fosse's Manhattan apartment at the time). Gideon is in the process of casting a new Broadway production while concurrently editing a film he's directed about a stand-up comic (Fosse had also directed the 1974 film about Lenny Bruce, *Lenny*, starring Dustin Hoffman). Through the stress of it all, along with chain-smoking, drinking, and pills, Gideon finds himself in the hospital facing open-heart surgery. In a stand-out scene in the film, Gideon hallucinates lavish production numbers - directed by himself - and featuring the women in his life, including lovers, a tween daughter, and Jessica Lange as a hovering angel of death.

If it sounds self-indulgent, well... it is, shamelessly so. But it's also amazing to me how well this film has aged. The choreography still looks fresh, and is a major lure (naturally) to this movie. You'd expect that of a Bob Fosse-choreographed film, dancing crisp, sexy, and stylistic. But what draws me to this film repeatedly over time is how well Fosse directs and edits the non-musical parts of the film. There's a repeated motif that separates sections of *All That Jazz*, a montage of Gideon showering, popping pills, taking eye drops, and grimly trying to psych himself in the bathroom mirror with a weary "It's showtime!" all to Vivaldi's Concerto in G. But in this viewing, I noticed that each montage is just a little different, and the pace of these scenes slows as Gideon nears his attack. Fosse also cuts in glimpses - almost but not quite too quick to see - of the impending reality Gideon is desperately trying to keep at bay, not just with his health, but his relationships. It's brilliant editing for any filmmaker, not just a choreographer. And Fosse opens the film with one of the truly iconic scenes in musical films - a largely wordless 8-minute audition scene set to George Benson's "On Broadway."

It's also fascinating to me how well Roy Scheider fits into Bob Fosse's shoes (did I mention that Marcello Mastroianni did *exactly* the same thing with Frederico Fellini just a week before?). Scheider of course was known for his tough-guy roles (as in flicks like *The French Connection* and *Jaws.*) Apparently, he had to sell Fosse himself on his ability to act his story, and he did it by reminding Fosse that he had learned his craft in New York theater, having done his time in musical theater along with many of his peers. It's hard now to imagine Fosse casting anyone else, as Scheider brings a streetwise cop's intensity to both Fosse's work and his disastrous private life. During the aforementioned opening scene? Scheider's body language alone sells the role.

This film is a glorious snapshot of a great American choreographer and director at his peak. And when I finished watching, it immediately sent me to my movie shelves to watch my (non-Criterion) copy of *42nd Street.* It's a 1933 film about a Broadway show that in many ways embodies a lot of the things I always hated about movie musicals. But maybe *All That Jazz* helped me watch *42nd Street* with better eyes, especially in the final scene, when the show's director is too exhausted to enjoy the success in which his cast and producers revel.

The Apu Trilogy

Pather Panchali, India, 1955. Directed by Satyajit Ray. 125 minutes, black and white. *Aparajito*, India, 1956. Directed by Satyajit Ray. 110 minutes, black and white. *Apur Sansar*, India, 1959. Directed by Satyajit Ray. 106 minutes, black and white.

> "Even before he had embarked on his first film, *Pather Panchali* (1955), Ray had written a piece titled 'What Is Wrong with Indian Films?' in *The Statesman* newspaper in Calcutta in 1948 - 'The raw material of the cinema is life itself. It is incredible that a country which has inspired so much painting and music and poetry should fail to move the filmmaker. He has only to keep his eyes open, and his ears. Let him do so.'"

From "Humanism and Hope: The Legacy of Film Director Satyajit Ray" by Sundeep Bhutoria.

My Indian friends have learned to be patient with me. It's taken me years to learn not to ask if they've seen any of the three films of *The Apu Trilogy* (*Pather Panchali,* *Aparajito,* and *Apur Sansar*). They haven't, any more than my American friends have seen *The Searchers* or *The Asphalt Jungle.* Especially if they're under 40.

I'm going to get to *The Apu Trilogy* and director Satyajit Ray in a bit, but first I want to give a little bit of context for Indian cinema. The first thing you should know is that it's not all Bollywood, as that has been a relatively recent development. That I'll get to at the end of the essay.

India has had a film industry for as long as most of the rest of the world; the silent film *Raja Harishchandra*, directed by Dadasaheb Phalke and released in 1913 is generally credited to be the first full-length Indian film. It was generally thought that sound films would toll the death-knell for Indian cinema, since talkies would force the industry to segment into regional language groups; up to 26 regional languages were spoken, 15 of them official (even the majority Hindi language had three distinct dialects). But with the release of Ardeshir Irani's *Alam Ara* in 1931, Indian cinema enjoyed its first huge success. As a musical, domestic audiences probably cared less about rigorously following the dialogue (and perhaps Westerners had overestimated the language barriers among people who had probably become used to negotiating them). It also helped that India had an enormous cultural well to draw movie plots from - a rich 19th-century tradition of folk-music stage drama, themselves based on centuries-old religious myths. From then throughout the war years, Indian cinema thrived on bringing these stories to the screen and producing epic historical films. Music, melodrama, and the supernatural were the norm.

Indian film may have remained in that niche, give or take the occasional outlier, but without exception, national cinemas have thrived under freedom and suffered under censorship. German expressionist cinema was strangled as the studios were bought out by industrialists sympathetic to the growing Nazi party, the great work of Soviet montage cinema was outlawed by Stalin, and American films became bland and obedient to authority under theHays Code.[6] With the end of the British Raj in 1947, Indian cinema seemed to wake up and look around. Without abandoning popular entertainments, Indian filmmakers began to study and converse with what the rest of the cinema world was doing.

Satyajit Ray was one of those filmmakers. Ray had studied art under Hindu poet Rabindranath Tagore. Ray wanted to make a film of the novels of Bibhutibhusan Banerjee (which he had illustrated), and was fascinated by the Italian neorealist films at the time, including Vittorio De Sica's 1948 film, *Bicycle Thieves*. Neorealism was, as the name implies, concerned with capturing daily life as realistically as possible. The films avoided camera effects, stylization, anything that might detract from the real life being filmed. Neorealists stayed away from historical settings, favoring urban streets and interiors. In fact, De Sica

---

[6] For a closer Look at The Hays Code see "Early Hollywood and the Hays Code" by Maria Lewis on the ACMI website.
https://www.acmi.net.au/stories-and-ideas/early-hollywood-and-hays-code/

went so far as to eschew professional actors; the cast of *Bicycle Thieves*, including its two protagonists, were non-actors chosen for their faces. Ray wanted his films to join that conversation. With the encouragement of Jean Renoir (who happened to be in India in 1951 shooting *The River*), Ray put his salary, his possessions, and his wife's jewelry into getting started as a director.

The Apu Trilogy follows the life of Apu, from a child growing up in a rural Indian village, through his university years in the city and into adulthood. These films are intimate, affectionate, and heartbreaking without turning saccharine. Most importantly, they give us an unvarnished look at Indian life and people in both the country and the cities. During *Pather Panchali*, the first of the films where we encounter Apu as a young boy, notice how often Ray brings the camera on his huge eyes. Apu wants to see everything that's going on, and Ray wants us to take it all in with him. There's pride in this kind of filmmaking. As Apu faces change and loss in his life, the lack of cinematic sugar coating allows us to understand how much the Indian people have to shoulder without the help of gods or melodramatic plot twists. As Apu grows, his family sends him to the city for his education, where he finally settles for work as an adult. Likewise, Ray presents the city of Varanasi without artifice or glamorization, and allows his actors to speak to us by quieting his camerawork. But the films are also shot beautifully (Subrata Mitra served as the cinematographer on all three films), proving that "neorealist" didn't have to be a synonym for "boring."

Going through the supplemental reading, I was surprised to discover that Satyajit Ray was not only new to filmmaking, but also a relative stranger to rural India, as he'd been raised in the more urban Kolkata (Terrence Rafferty, in his essay, believes that as a man of the city, Ray may have had a fresh eye for images a director from a rural background may have taken for granted). It may have been Ray's relative youth and inexperience that served him. I can only surmise, but perhaps not being steeped in what Indian cinema was "supposed" to be may have served him well. But what Ray was able to accomplish put Indian cinema on the map. *Pather Panchali* would be instantly recognized as an important film, winning an award for Best Human Document at the 1956 Cannes Film Festival. More importantly, Ray proved to Indian filmmakers who came up later that there was room in India for all kinds of stories, and all kinds of storytelling.

☀ ☀ ☀

Now let's talk about Bollywood, which I'm going to do here only because Criterion doesn't carry any Bollywood films at this writing, so I won't get the chance later. If you know anything about Bollywood films, it's probably from YouTube clips, or the film *Slumdog Millionaire*, which tags a dance number to the closing credits. Bollywood films aren't really "musicals" in the way we think of them in this country, though they usually have music. The general formula for a Bollywood film is said to be, "a star, six songs, and three dances," and that formula - for its biggest and most commercial films - seems to hold true. In fact the star system seems to drive Indian cinema even more than in the US. Also they're long movies, often surpassing the 3-hour mark.

The first thing that struck me in the Bollywood films I've seen is that they're kind of all over the place. The 2009 comedy/drama *3 Idiots*, for example, seems to lurch back and forth from juvenile humor to pathos to heartwarming without warning. Similarly, the 2023 film *Amigos* (which I was lucky enough to catch at my local Pacific Northwest mall theater) seems to spend the first half as a kind of silly romcom before unexpectedly turning into an action thriller in the second half (honestly, the trailer promotes the action side so much that I thought they'd switched movies on me in the first half). But this is not a defect in Indian films; it's a product of design.

While the Indian television industry began broadcasting in 1959, poverty in the country kept most families from owning television sets; until 2007 only half of the households in India had televisions, as opposed to 98% of American homes. So going to the movies was much more a part of the entertainment diet for people who couldn't watch at home. But if you were going to spend your hard-earned cash on a movie, you wanted your money's worth. So Bollywood films made long movies with a "something for everyone" mentality. According to my Indian American friends, when you go to the movies in India, expect a raucous affair. People will be dancing in the aisles, people will be yelling back at the screen, people will go there to have a good time. Moviegoing in India is apparently not a spectator sport. Of course there are serious films in serious theaters for people who are serious about watching a movie. But Bollywood sees no reason to jettison its joyous past, and will always make films for Indians who want to go to the movies for a communal good time.

Who can argue with that?

The Asphalt Jungle

US, 1950. Directed by John Huston. 112 minutes, black and white.

Man, this is a good movie.

The Asphalt Jungle is a heist flick, and a noir, and I've rarely seen either genre done better. There's a plan, dreamed up by the immigrant Doc Riedenschneider (Sam Jaffe) while he cooled his heels for a stretch in prison, and as with any heist flick we begin with our team: the leader (Sterling Hayden), the financier (Louis Calhern), the muscle (James Whitmore), the loyal dame (Jean Hagen) and the femme fatale (Marilyn Monroe, in her breakout role). There are other beats we hit - the planning, the setback, the execution - and as with any heist flick we want to cheer for the crooks, see if this time they can get everything they want, straighten out, and live happily ever after.

But because this heist flick is also fully film noir, we know from the start that ain't gonna happen. Our financier/lawyer is as crooked as they come, and from almost the beginning believes he can play this streetwise crew for chumps (sorry, but a great gangster flick like this gets me writing like this).

He's not fooling us, only himself, dazzled as he is by the money that can get him out of trouble. But one of the two characters that truly own this film (and we'll get to Sterling Hayden's Dix Handley in a minute) is Jaffe's Doc Riedenschneider. He knows better than any of them that the fix is already in; they've chosen their roles in life, and the role of the thief is to make some scores, and get caught once or twice along the way. He won't glamorize it, and he won't pretend he or anyone else is above the game, or immune to its payoffs, good and bad. There's a fatalism running through this film; most of these characters know it won't end well, but they also know they have to play it all out. That's what thieves do. They play it out.

I don't think you'll find a better tough guy than Sterling Hayden. He's a marvel to watch at his peak. Usually when you think of menacing, you think of muscles, but Hayden does it all with the face and the voice. He appreciates Jean Hagen's Doll, probably even loves her, but that's got nothing to do with the job at hand. He's tender toward her when he can afford it, but he can't risk softening up very much or very often. And how can we blame him? Even he knows that his dream of coming home to his family's Kentucky horse ranch is a sap's hope. But he's got to play it out.

It's worth pausing here for a word about "film noir." Film noir is a film genre, but it's also a lot bigger than that. It begins with an apparent contradiction: a French term used initially to describe American films of the 1940s (literally, "dark film"). During the German Occupation of France during WWII, French filmmakers and audiences were cut off from the cinema of the rest of the world, at least from Allied countries. Once France was liberated, French critics were astonished at what many American directors had been up to during the war. They saw films that were much darker than the usual American fare, more cynical about modern life, more urban, more realistic. Maybe it took an outsider to recognize a burgeoning movement in film, or maybe American filmmakers and audiences - disdainful of what they might have considered elite "ivory tower" film study - simply chose not to look too hard at what they were doing. While the term usually describes detective or crime films, it can span across all kinds of genres - there are noir westerns, noir musicals, even noir science fiction. It's a slippery term to define; entire books have been written on it, and it's not uncommon for film writers to kind of throw up their hands and, à la Justice Potter Stewart "defining" pornography, tell us we'll know it when we see it. It's something I'll tackle over the course of several films, but for right now, since we were just talking about Sterling Hayden, let's talk about one aspect: The Antihero.

The worldview of film noir is that society is corrupt, rigged to serve a powerful few. So instead of "heroes," upstanding white-hat men and women sworn to uphold society, we get antiheroes. The antihero is a figure who is a central character in the movie, the audience's guide to the world of the film. Because society is corrupt, the antihero will not side with Authority, but instead will oppose it. Think of Humphrey Bogart's Sam Spade in *The Maltese Falcon*. He won't work with the cops, won't rely on them to help solve his case. There may be a few cops he respects, but it's not because they're authority figures, it's because they're smart enough to know the game is rigged. The antihero, then, won't share in the same moral code as society, but he's never amoral. His moral code is meant to guide him through the reality of a corrupt system. So our antiheroes aren't pleasant men or women, and if they're not openly defying societal norms, they're at least disdainful of them. But I'd argue that the antihero's moral code is *more* important to him, because it's all he's got to rely on. For Sterling Hayden's character in *The Asphalt Jungle*, his morality is in keeping his word when he gives it, even to fellow criminals. He's completely professional, he's committed to a "clean" heist through meticulous planning. And he won't tolerate anyone who lies to him, or won't take the job as seriously as he does. These are values that we *ought* to see in society at large, but the noir film understands that we don't. So those values are placed in the antihero, even as his other values (stealing, for example) aren't values a heroic character would recognize.

Getting back to *The Asphalt Jungle*, there's a story about director John Huston that I heard once, I think about shooting *The Treasure of Sierra Madre*. It's an outdoor picture, and on the first day of shooting the cast and crew were ready to go, and it was pouring rain, with no letup in sight. Someone asked him what they were going to do now. "We're going to shoot the most interesting thing in the world," Huston replied. "The human face." It's the closeups, the faces in this film that bring us in. The characters won't crack, and Huston has to bring us inside somehow, so he does it by lingering on faces, especially when no one else seems to be watching. Oh, sure, his camerawork brings us in in other ways, too, but it's the faces - those beautiful black and white faces - that crack these characters open.

The funny thing is, I'd seen this film less than a month before I rewatched it as part of this exercise; my son had come west to visit and pulled it off the shelf. I didn't mind watching it again so soon. It's that rich, that good.

Autumn Sonata

Sweden, 1978. Directed by Ingmar Bergman. 92 minutes, color.

Autumn Sonata is one of the strongest and most gut-wrenching films I've ever seen. People who only know of Ingmar Bergman from *The Seventh Seal* inaccurately think of him locked into enigmatic black-and-white cinema of the unreal, dripping with opaque symbolism. But Bergman was a master of family drama, and when he turned his script over to the astonishing duo of Ingrid Bergman (no relation) and Liv Ullmann, they helped him create an absolute masterpiece. Bergman was a student of music as well as film (in particular he was a Mozart scholar), and the way this film is written, and the way these two superb actors interact with each other is like watching opera, full of crescendos and decrescendos and recitatives. Every anguished memory, every nursed grudge of this mother/daughter relationship is dragged out into the open. By the end of the film our characters are exhausted, and so are we.

The film takes place over 24 hours, almost exclusively in the home of Eva (Ullmann) and her husband Viktor (Halvar Björk), a local pastor. Eva has invited her mother Charlotte

(Bergman) for a visit; she has not seen her mother in over seven years. There's a reason for that; as a world-renowned concert pianist, Charlotte has devoted her life to her art, sacrificing family for both music and her audiences, to which a string of former husbands can probably attest. Charlotte, on the surface, is breezy and happy to be reunited with her daughter, but we soon find that it's a cover for an inability to negotiate human connections. The most relaxed we see Charlotte is when she is guiding Eva (a gifted pianist herself) through Chopin's Prelude No. 2 in A Minor, eventually taking over herself to show Eva how it's supposed to be done.

Eva, for her part, is eager to reconnect with her mother as a daughter, and quietly but firmly inserts domestic issues into the conversation her mother either is unaware of, or has chosen to disremember. Though Eva has dedicated her own life to domesticity, it has not brought her happiness. Her own marriage to Viktor is without warmth or affection, though she respects his mind and the work he does (Viktor's role is relegated to infrequent observer; he does not wish to interfere with his wife's reconnection with her mother, and is dutifully supportive, but silent throughout the film). Eva has also suffered the loss of a child; her son Erik drowned when he was only four years old. And, Eva is mourning the absence of her own mother, not just in the past seven years, but in the distance Charlotte created throughout Eva's life. As Eva quietly but assertively presses her losses, Charlotte becomes visibly more and more uncomfortable; these are exactly the issues that she works hard to avoid. And then Eva drops the bombshell.

Eva is not an only child. She has a younger sister, Helena (Lena Nyman), who is disabled - bedbound and nearly aphasic, with only Eva being able to understand her speech. Charlotte had abandoned this daughter as well, and where Charlotte had safely filed Helena away in a hospital for her care, Eva has brought Helena to her home, and is caring for her there. Charlotte is shocked at the news, and manically tries to mask her guilt with a maternal show of affection for her other lost daughter, but her panic has clearly overcome her. The building guilt, resentment, love, anger, pain, and yearning between the two finally erupt in a series of pleas and arguments, but it's too much for Charlotte. She leaves the next day to the safety of her own life on tour, but in a letter Eva writes, we sense the beginning of a new understanding between the two out of the rubble of the previous night. But we'll never find out how this letter will affect Charlotte, or indeed if it will reach her at all....

I usually avoid films that explore family relationships - it's just not something I enjoy seeing played out - but this one I'm sure to watch every few years, even though it never gets any easier (those of you who have survived family dysfunction probably understand why). I think the reason I keep returning is the performances of these two women are so powerful, so engrossing, that the film feels fresh every time. Both are playing nuanced characters, and will not give in to an easy stereotype of the distant mother or the abandoned daughter. Ingrid Bergman has a particular tightrope to walk. Her character understands why her daughter has called her to her home, and is dutifully reporting, though she is hoping she can control the visit the way she controlled the mother/daughter relationship of their past. That need for control is evident in her career - though an artist, she seems to have turned away from the passion of music to embrace its more technical demands. There's almost something surgical in the way Charlotte approaches her art, though it could be that she truly finds her passion here, away from the messiness of human relationships. But Charlotte knows that her choices have deeply affected her family, and she's terrified of having to face the realities of what those choices have done to Eva, and to Helena.

Ullmann has a tightrope of her own to walk as an actor. From reading my synopsis, you might expect Eva to greet her mother "guns blazing," eager to hold her accountable for her failures as a parent. But Eva anticipates her mother's arrival with cautious yearning. She's hopeful that the two may finally be able to connect as family, as women. Yet Eva is also smart enough to be aware of the power dynamic between the two, and knows that given her mother's dominance, she's going to have to be tenacious. There *is* suppressed anger in Eva, and Ullmann knows when it's time to bring that out, but what she mostly uncovers is that quiet spine of steel Eva has grown throughout her life. Eva needs to release her anger, she knows that, but it's not her endgame, and she'll do it reluctantly. She's tenacious, not to punish her mother, but because after all these years, she still believes she and Charlotte can forge a new relationship. It's an impressive performance, and together with Ingrid Bergman, the two actors play a duet few others can pull off.

So, yes, it's the acting that keeps bringing me back. But I wanted to point out something Ingmar Bergman does (besides writing the script) that helps keep our attention where it should be: on the central characters. There's a technique Bergman uses that once aware of it, you'll begin seeing often in his films, and it demonstrates the way a director can frame a scene to help the audience "see" the underlying tension between two people.

There's a scene where Charlotte and Eva are sitting at Eva's piano, and Charlotte has commandeered the performance of the Chopin away from her daughter. Charlotte is sitting in profile, her attention on the score in front of her. Charlotte is directly in the foreground. Eva is sitting on Charlotte's left, immediately in her background, but Eva is looking directly at her mother; we see Eva facing toward the camera. The two are having a conversation, but they're not face-to-face; there's a disconnect in the line of sight, just as there is in the conversation they're having. Ingmar Bergman will do this often in his films; put two characters' faces in the same frame, but one looking past or away from the other, to show us that they may be talking more "at" than "with" their partner in the scene. I mention this not to give credit due the actors to the director, but to show you that a great director will make careful and deliberate decisions, especially in framing a scene, to allow the full force of the performances to come through.

Yes, *The Seventh Seal* is a brilliant film, and we'll get to that eventually. But I think *Autumn Sonata* shows a human side to Ingmar Bergman most people don't know is there.

A Film Trilogy by Ingmar Bergman

Through a Glass Darkly, Sweden 1961. Directed by Ingmar Bergman. 89 minutes, black and white. *Winter Light*, Sweden 1962. Directed by Ingmar Bergman. 80 minutes, black and white. *The Silence*, Sweden, 1963. Directed by Ingmar Bergman. 95 minutes, black and white.

A Film Trilogy by Ingmar Bergman is packaged as such (along with a bonus DVD, *Ingmar Bergman Makes a Movie*, a 5-part documentary director Vilgot Sjöman (*I Am Curious - Yellow*) made for Swedish television) because the three films were made consecutively, and all deal with a central theme. Bergman at the time (though later recanted in an interview) said that he intended these to be a trilogy exploring the search for God (I'm oversimplifying, but that's a broad starting point). Bergman was the son of a Lutheran pastor and these three stark films are Bergman's most direct commentary on religion - in particular his distant father's Lutheran faith. They're brilliant filmmaking, intense and unrelenting. But they're also intellectually challenging, and I'll admit right now to struggling through these films, as I often do with Bergman's work. So let's run through a synopsis of each film, then try to link them together thematically. Finally, I want to write about exploring symbolism in film in general, and why it seems to be so irresistible to people who write about movies.

Through a Glass Darkly is the first film of the trilogy. The title of the film comes from I Corinthians 13:12: "For now we see through a glass [mirror] darkly, but then face to face: now I know in part; but then shall I know even as I am also known." (KJV) The setting is a small island on the Baltic Sea, a family retreat. The film opens with our four characters laughing following a dip in the ocean: Karin (Harriet Andersson) and her teenage brother, Minus (Lars Passgård), their father David (Gunnar Björnstrand), and Karin's physician husband, Martin (Max von Sydow). Karin is schizophrenic, and when Martin and David find some time to talk privately, Martin reveals that her condition is likely degenerative and incurable. David is a writer and has just returned from Switzerland after finishing a novel. The family will soon learn that despite promises to spend more time with them, David is about to leave again. As the men speak, Minus spends time with his sister, and admits to a growing sexual apprehension that he wishes he could speak to his father about. At dinner, the cracks begin to show. David breaks the news of his upcoming travels to his family, and awkwardly tries to smooth the news over with some gifts; all are inappropriate. Minus has a gift for his father as well; an after-dinner performance of a play he wrote of a prince who chooses fame over love, which goes over with his father about as well as you'd expect. That night Karin wakes and creeps to an abandoned upstairs room, hearing voices, which she believes come from God. On her way back to bed, she sneaks a look into her father's diary, in which his latest entry reads, "Her illness is incurable. I'm horrified by my curiosity, by my urge to record its course, to make an accurate description of her gradual disintegration, to use her." Karin's delusions escalate, until finally, pained at "living in two worlds" Karin agrees to be committed. As a helicopter reaches the island to take her away, Karin equates it with the "spider god" that has been speaking to her. Minus, anxious, is finally able to grab some time alone with his father, and asks him if there is a god. "I do not know if love is proof of God's existence, or if love is God himself," says David, but, "that thought helps me in my emptiness and my dirty despair." Whether that helps Minus or not isn't as important as the final words of the film: "Papa spoke to me."

Winter Light is a lot easier to sum up: It's a film about a rural clergyman's worst day ever. Gunnar Björnstrand (the father in our previous film) returns as Pastor Tomas Ericsson, who has just finished conducting services in a tiny, centuries old chapel to which only seven parishioners show up. Though he is dreadfully sick with a fever, he insists on conducting an afternoon service in a neighboring town, and angrily dismisses the attentions of Märta (Ingrid Thulin), a local schoolteacher and, as it turns out, his mistress. It's clear that Märta loves the widowed pastor, but her attempts to care for Tomas only seem to infuriate him - his rejection of her at the end of the film is direct, bitter, and cruel. Meanwhile, a woman begs for an urgent conversation with

Tomas, her silent husband in tow. The woman (Gunnel Lindblom) is worried for her fisherman husband Jonas (Max von Sydow, back from playing the husband in the last film). He has read an article about the Chinese nuclear threat, and is worried about the futility of life living under the threat of annihilation. Tomas is unable to come up with more than a few platitudes, and the wife suggests Jonas drive her home and return so the men can talk privately. But even given time to prepare, Tomas is unable to connect with his parishioner. At first Tomas attempts to dismiss the fisherman's fears as ungrounded, but can't. Jonas persists in his questions - he really seems to believe this man of God will have something to help him. But after several attempts to explain away the man's fears wither under Jonas's direct gaze, Tomas finally reveals his own doubts to his parishioner. Tomas can only "hope," but he has no reason to be able to find comfort from this. He admits to Jonas that God is as inscrutable to him. He admits that he also is seized with doubt. Jonas, realizing the clergyman cannot provide the words he is seeking, leaves. Later in the day Tomas receives word that Jonas has taken his own life.

The Silence is the trickiest of the three, and for me, the least comfortable. The setting for the film is a kind of limbo. Two sisters, Ester (Ingrid Thulin, back from playing Märta) and Anna (Gunnel Lindblom again, our fisherman's wife) are traveling through an unspecified central European country on the brink of war. With them is Anna's 10-year-old son, Johan (Jörgen Lindström). Ester is the older sister, and is seriously ill, confined through the film to her bed in the once-grand hotel in which the family is staying. Though Ester works as a translator, none of the three are able to communicate with the locals. The two sisters are emotionally estranged from each other and opposite in appearance and temperament. Where Ester is bodily frail and intellectual, Anna is outgoing and sexual. Anna immediately abandons her son and Ester, exploring the town (she's to prove about as capable a mother as Tomas was a pastor). She visits a cafe, where she half-heartedly waves off the advances of a waiter, then goes to a theater; when a couple begin to have sex in the seats near her, she is both repulsed and engrossed, which leads her to return to the cafe and invite the waiter to pick her up later at the hotel. In her absence, Ester has been unsuccessfully trying to connect with her nephew, but Johan finds her illness to be too much. Wandering off, he befriends the hotel's elderly porter, and then a troupe of Spanish dwarfs who are part of a traveling show. Upon Anna's return, Ester begs her sister to stay in, and Anna reveals her "date" with the waiter for that evening. When he arrives, the two retreat to an unoccupied room, but not before Johan has witnessed them kissing. As Ester pounds on the door asking to talk to Anna, Anna turns on the lights so that Ester can see her in bed with the waiter. Anna tells Ester that she once envied her for being "the good sister" but she came to realize that Ester's "goodness" was nothing but jealousy for being unable to enjoy life the way Anna could, and hatred for Anna and her freedom. Ester angrily denies this, and though we later see Anna sobbing in remorse, the rift is complete. Anna and Johan leave by train the next day, Johan carrying a letter from Ester in which she has written down the words of the local language she has managed to pick up, a letter in which Anna seems uninterested. Ester has been left, seemingly to expire in the hotel, her increasing respiratory spasms ministered to by the elderly porter.

So. What connects these three films?

Little, it seems, unless you want to count Bergman's stable of actors who pass through all his films, but unless Bergman himself (and Criterion) had linked these three together, I doubt I would have, and I'm a Bergman fan. Since Bergman himself said these films constituted a search for God - before he took it back - I'm going to take a stab at linking them theologically. The first two have the most direct connection: *Through a Glass Darkly* references a New Testament passage in its title, the character of Karin is openly hallucinating religious themes, and the final exchange of the film is a conversation between father and son about the existence of God. Let's call this first film "The Search for God." In Christianity, God is, after all, a patriarchal figure, and that Minus is given the last line of the film, "Papa spoke to me," indicates that this is what Minus has been searching for all along: a response from his father, standing in for God. That this answer is vague and unsatisfying is secondary; Minus will seize on whatever he can get. Likewise, the schizophrenic Karin has also been searching for God - perhaps her illness allows her to see a less filtered version of God, and perhaps this is what is behind her madness. In any event, she cannot live in both Man's world and God's world, and she chooses the unreality of her schizophrenia. David and Martin are searching, too, but as with Karin and Minus, the search seems to be more meaningful to them than any answers they find.

Winter Light is obvious as well, given that its central character is a clergyman, and that so much of the setting and discussion centers on religion. We'll call this film "The Silence of God." Everyone who turns to God's stand-in - Tomas - comes away with nothing. Märta can find no earthly pleasures, not even warmth or companionship from him, and well, we all know how it turned out for Jonas. Watching the scenes with Jonas and Tomas I'm struck with how often and how directly the fisherman looks to the pastor, and time and again, Tomas is the one who breaks eye contact.

So where does *The Silence* fit in, as God and religion are conspicuously absent from the film? Let's call this one "The Absence of God." If I had to (and again, I'm only doing this because Criterion and Bergman are making me), I would say that this third film gives us a world without God. Notice that the paternal figure (Jonas's father) is absent entirely. The only men in the film are the waiter, there to satisfy his lust, an old and dusty and impotent porter, and the comical troupe of acrobatic dwarfs (though knowing what I do about Bergman and his love of theater, I'm going to put them down as the boy's only joyful companions in a godless existence). Life has become a meaningless way station, in which we can barely communicate with those around us. It is absurd, it is pointless, and it is without meaning.

So how'd I do? Was I reaching, especially with that last

one? This is the aspect of "art" films that appeals to some people the least, and that others seem to revel in. Bergman's films are positively *dripping* with symbolism, and for some people, part of the fun is searching for clues. For other people, it's maddening, and you can fall into either camp and enjoy a rich and fulfilling enjoyment of film. The trick, as in many things in life, is to listen to what as many people have to say as you can. And then make up your own mind.

Listen. Film scholars are people just like you and me. They just have a more specific vocabulary. Like all of us, they want to make sense of the world. So they spend their time at the movies looking for patterns, because it's a lot more satisfying to lump things into categories than it is to take life one messy film at a time. So when a film scholar points to an "obvious" connection in the films of Bergman or Fellini or Renoir, it doesn't mean they're necessarily wrong. But it does mean that they really want to make sense of what they're writing about, and organize it. And it can be easy to think, reading essays like that, that they see something we don't, that they're smart and we're not. But they're just making whatever connections they can, and because other film writers are afraid to say, "Maybe I'm wrong, does anyone else see this?" they're afraid to say it, too. Lots of people in life take their boldest stances on their shakiest ground. So take what you read with a grain of salt. Don't let them make you feel stupid. But don't discard them either.

You're smart. What do *you* think?

The Blob

US, 1958. Directed by Irwin S. Yeaworth, Jr. 82 minutes, color.

Did I mention Criterion likes to throw a curveball now and then?

The Blob is terrific old B movie horror classic. According to an accompanying essay by Bruce Kawin, *The Blob* covers it all, from the "First Victim" trope of horror movies to a critique of American consumerism (notice how the creature hunts for human flesh in an empty market, and finally at a diner) to the growing threat of Communist domination. One of the cool things about *The Blob* (besides Steve McQueen) is that you can take it either as seriously or ridiculously as you want. The middle-aged teenagers kind of push it a little, but if you can de-accustom yourself to CGI special effects, it's kinda-sorta-almost still scary. Well, it was when I was eight, anyway.

The Blob opens in a sleepy, small 1950s American town. The local kids, apart from a little drag racing (I'm trying to revive the slang term of referring to your vehicle as your "container"), confine their mischief to lesser hijinks. They're clean-cut, wholesome, American kids, though the local cops seem to think their youth are a seething cauldron of gang violence. The local police lieutenant (Earl Rowe) is of the "what am I going to do with you kids?" school, while at least one of his officers (an eternally pissed-off Jon Benson) seems to champ at the bit to bust him some heads. Heading the juveniles is Steve (Steve McQueen) and his best girl, Jane (Aneta Corsaut). And for god's sake, whatever you do, *don't call her "Janey Girl"!*

Into our idyllic town falls a meteorite from outer space. Janey Gi- ... sorry, *Jane* has put the kibosh on anything unwholesome going on at the local lover's lookout, so she and Steve decide to check it out. An old man living in a shack in the woods (Olin Howland) beats them to the glowing space rock, which cracks open to reveal goo. The old man considers his options, deciding on a rigorous course of study which begins with Poking At It With a Stick. Big mistake. The goo dashes up the stick onto our old-timer's hand and forearm. It won't come off, and it hurts. Steve and Jane run across the old man and take him to the local doctor (Stephen Chase). Doc Hallen sends the kids to see if they can gather any more specimens, and while they're gone, the goo completely consumes the old man. Steve and Jane return to Doc Hallen's office just in time to see The Blob (for that's what the goo has grown into) consume both the doctor and his nurse.

What follows is a race between The Blob and the local teens. The Blob, after consuming a few victims unwitnessed, heads into the center of town for the main buffet, beginning with a crowd at the local movie theater (conveniently screening a slate of horror films, or "the spook show" as one of the teens calls it). The teens are racing around town trying to convince the adults - any adult - that there is a monster from outer space, the cops in particular ready to lock them up for their stories. Finally, when The Blob's full public appearance causes a stampede out of the movie theater, everyone is on board. But nothing seems to stop this thing, not bullets, not electricity, not fire, and certainly nothing the local militia can throw at it (one of my favorite scenes is old Jasper Deeter jumping out of bed as he hears an air raid siren go off. He grabs a Civil Defense helmet just as the fire siren sounds, then reaches for his fire helmet. Bewildered, he stands in his pajamas and says to his wife, "This has never happened before! I don't know which hat to put on!"). Can anything stop The Blob?

A word about film commentary tracks. When I first got a DVD player, I'd listen to these tracks religiously; I loved the idea of a filmmaker sitting "with" me, guiding me through their work. Either they lost their charm for me, or people began getting lazy on them, and eventually I stopped listening. For my Criterion Tuesdays, however, I'm running each film a second time with the chat track (when available), and I'd strongly recommend running *The Blob* with its Criterion commentary (after watching the film first without, of course).

A good chat track can provide intended and unintended information and entertainment, and this one provides both. One of the stories I loved, told by Yeaworth, concerned a scene where McQueen's character was talking to some other "teens" from his convertible by the side of the road. Yeaworth didn't have the budget to film cutaways, where the scene cuts back and forth between people talking. McQueen - the closest thing to a star the production had - suggested he just arrange the other characters on one side of the car, and not bother with getting his own reaction shots. The scene works beautifully, and Yeaworth credits McQueen with a generosity of spirit toward the production.

Which brings me to the unintended gems we get from this commentary. In addition to Yeaworth's track (which he shares with one of the actors) there's a second commentary track featuring producer Jack H. Harris. The difference is illuminating. Yeaworth takes a team approach to the production, quick to give credit to one of the cast or crew when someone has a good idea, or contributes something on set. Yeaworth's production team was a small one, actually more accustomed to making religious films for a Pennsylvania church. Harris, on the other hand, takes personal credit for anything that looks good, and is quick to pass out blame for anything he doesn't think works well. You don't learn a lot from Harris, but you find out quickly which of them you'd rather make a film with.

I make a lot of fun of this movie in this essay, but I promise you it's out of love. "B" movies (usually genre pictures, often horror or science fiction, made on the cheap by independent filmmakers to fill out a bill at a drive-in) are something I grew up with, and might have been my earliest introduction to films. Way back before streaming services, before cable, we had antenna TV, and the three major networks (ABC, CBS, and NBC) all lived on the lower VHF (Very High Frequency) channels, along with PBS, while the independent stations hung out on the UHF (Ultra High Frequency) channels. The UHF stations were always hungry for content to broadcast, usually showing syndicated shows and reruns. Saturday afternoons seemed to belong to old science fiction and horror films. I still remember Channel 17 out of Philadelphia serving up these kinds of movies, and later Shaw Brothers Kung Fu flicks. I ate this stuff up, and was absolutely delighted that Criterion snatched up the rights to *The Blob* and gave it the full loving treatment. Just as you cannot have a full satisfying diet without a little bit of sweets or junk food, you cannot fully appreciate American cinema without dipping into its glorious B movie past.

And don't be too eager to dismiss their importance. Roger Corman, the legendary director and producer of cheap and tawdry exploitation and genre films, gave a lot of filmmakers work when no one else would. Working for Corman, you learned to shoot fast and cheap; it was guerilla filmmaking, and the repetition of cranking out films for him, learning what would pique the public's interest and what wouldn't was not a bad way to learn to make movies. Just ask Martin Scorsese, who writes fondly of Corman's tutelage.

Finally, if you've never seen this film, do yourself a favor and Google the theme song for *The Blob*. It's half the reason the film is irresistible. It's cheesy and groovy, but groovy in a wholesome 1950s kind of way, not a dangerous 1960s groovy. It's a hoot. And it was written by Mack David and Burt Bacharach, and it was Bacharach's first hit. Not bad for a B movie.

Blood Simple

US, 1984. Directed by Joel Coen. 95 minutes, color.

"Down here, you're on your own."

Tonight, Criterion Tuesday serves up Joel and Ethan Coen's debut, and you can't say they didn't warn us. What starts as film noir takes a hard left into slasher flick and dark, dark comedy. *Blood Simple* defies easy categorization, but isn't that usually the case with the Coen brothers?

Let's take a crack at a plot summary, which is as convoluted as that of any film noir. Ray (John Getz) and Abby (Frances McDormand in her debut screen performance) are driving in the rain. Abby begins to complain about her bad marriage to Julian (Dan Hedaya), who just happens to own the dive where Ray tends bar. The two also discover a mutual attraction, and pull off into a motel for a tryst. What they don't realize is they've been followed by a private detective, Loren Visser (M. Emmet Walsh), who photographs them as proof for Julian. Realizing they've been found out, Abby grabs a few things from home, including a handgun Julian had given her. (Anton Chekhov, the Russian playwright, famously said, "If in the first act you have hung a pistol on the wall, then in the following one it should be fired. Otherwise don't put it there." The Coen brothers have read their Chekhov.[7]) Ray stashes Abby at his place, and Abby warns him to stay away from the bar. Ray, of course, goes there directly to collect his wages. Julian won't give Ray his money, but tells him that Abby will eventually betray him, too. Just listen for the words, "I ain't done anything funny!"

Julian tries to abduct Abby the next morning, but she fends him off. Julian then asks Visser if he'll kill the couple for $10,000. Visser agrees, and breaks into Ray's place and takes Abby's gun. He returns to Julian with photos of the dead couple, and Julian goes to the safe to get Visser's money, slipping one of the photos in the safe on the sly. Visser shoots Julian, takes the money, and leaves the gun. But he's also left behind his distinctive personalized cigarette lighter.

It turns out that Visser faked the photos, and Ray and Abby are alive and unharmed. Ray returns again to the bar that night for another attempt at his pay (Ray doesn't seem to know when to cut his losses) and finds Julian's body and the gun, which, he assumes, is the work of Abby. Ray puts the gun in Julian's pocket and dumps the body in the back seat of his car. But Julian isn't dead after all, and Ray pulls

---

[7] My favorite corollary to the Chekhov Gun Rule is in the wonderful (and non-Criterion) 2018 Russian film directed by Kirill Sokolov, exquisitely titled, *Why Don't You Just Die!* In the opening scene, a young man knocks nervously on an apartment door, answered by a gruff, solid Russian man. The youth is trying to hide a claw hammer behind his back.

over to a field to dig a grave for Julian. Julian finds the gun in his pocket, and aims it at Ray, pulling the trigger three times... but it's empty. Ray finishes burying Julian, alive, as he screams.

Ray returns to Abby, who Ray thinks has killed Julian, but Abby has no idea what has been going on. As Ray tells her he's "cleaned it all up," Abby, bewildered, replies, "I haven't done anything funny." Not what Ray wanted to hear.

From there, it all goes off the rails for our surviving characters (trust me, things are relatively "manageable" at this point compared with what's to come), and if you think the film was dark, you ain't seen nothing yet. Violence in a Coen brothers film isn't tidy, no neat, pinpoint gunshot wounds, or cosmetic knife cuts. But this isn't for shock effect, it's to remind us, no, to *force us* to accept the ugliness in their characters' hearts and souls. The more they try to cover up, kill, and lie their way out of trouble, the worse it gets, the uglier it gets. These characters are fruitlessly trying to tidy up deeds that are brutal and obscene, and the more they try to sweep the mess under the rug the worse the stink gets. The title comes from an old Dashiell Hammett novel, *Red Harvest*, and describes the manic and elemental thinking people do when they spend too much time in violent situations. Ray, Abby, even private dick Visser in the end have gone *Blood Simple*.

There's so much to love here. M. Emmet Walsh at his slimy best. Frances McDormand in a role that her roommate, Holly Hunter expected the Coens to hold open for her (they made it up to her in *Raising Arizona*). The neon. The dialogue, in which none of the characters are talking about *exactly* what they're talking about and don't much care about being understood. Dan Hedaya, who's just... well, he's Dan Hedaya, a great character actor who makes every film he's in memorable just with his eminently filmable face and his 11:00 AM shadow.

I love the Coen brothers. They're one of a handful of filmmakers whose films are "appointment films," I'll be sure to see anything they do as soon as it comes out (Steven Spielberg, Paul Thomas Anderson, Guy Ritchie, Wes Anderson, and Christopher Nolan are others). Nothing they do, whether it's comedy, western, film noir, or tragedy is ever done rote; there's always something (and usually it's in the dialogue) that sets their films apart.

There's a long session in the disc's extras with both Coen brothers and Barry Sonnenfeld, who was the cinematographer for the film, and shot much of it (this was also Sonnenfeld's first major film; a lot of people got terrific careers off the ground with *Blood Simple*). As usual, he's hilarious. In absolute deadpan he talks about how awful a cinematographer he was, while simultaneously telling the Coen brothers how difficult they made his job. In the bargain, you learn a LOT about lighting and shooting a movie.

It's not an easy movie to sit through, as I think I made clear. But with this film, Joel and Ethan Coen announced to the world that they were going to tell stories on their terms, and invited us along for the ride.

Brazil

UK, 1985. Directed by Terry Gilliam. 142 minutes, color.

I've been living in this film for four days.

Brazil is next up for Criterion Tuesday. Way back before you were born, I had a copy of this on VHS, and when I moved to pick it up on DVD, Criterion had the only copy I could find, and was selling it in a three-disc boxed set. Disc One has the 142-minute Director's Cut, in which director Terry Gilliam blended footage from the US and European releases. Disc Two has the supplemental materials, including a 30-minute documentary on the set of the film, and a 60-minute documentary, *The Battle of Brazil*, based on the book by Jack Matthews (more on this later). Disc Three has the 94-minute "Love Conquers All" version sold by the studio to US syndicated television, which includes all the edits the studio wanted, including a happy ending. Both versions of the film have chat tracks, the first by Terry Gilliam, the second by film scholar David Morgan. So, four viewings in total of two versions of this film. It's a lot.

Brazil[8] is a peek into a dystopian society, Orwellian, absurdist, and bureaucratic. Sam Lowry (Jonathan Price) is a low-level government drone. He's bored with his work, but unwilling to move to a more visible position, despite the attempts of his influential mother (Katherine Helmond) to push his career forward. Sam may be unfulfilled in his place as a cog in the hyper surveillant government machine (he dreams at night of soaring above it all, winged like Icarus, and battling fantastical creatures to save a caged damsel), but he believes that the oppressive governmental bureaucracy, while flawed, is intended to better the lives of its citizens. But an encounter with a woman (Kim Griest), a dead ringer for the damsel of Sam's dreams, who has witnessed a neighbor's mistaken arrest by police, and Sam's visit by a rogue HVAC repairman (Robert De Niro) shake Lowry's faith that he works for the good of society. Sam accepts a promotion, hoping that moving higher in the system can help him set things right. Instead, he begins to see more clearly that the government exists only to serve itself.

Brazil is a brilliant film, somehow even more dazzling after

---

[8] Why call the film *Brazil*? That's a slippery one. Gilliam himself talked about being on holiday at the beach, juxtaposing the thought of a paradisiacal getaway from civilization with the realities of urban and corporate life intruding even there; the song that plays through the film stuck in his head as a sort of cheap capitalist jingle commenting on what was supposed to be an exotic land of escape. But I think the title also helps avoid pinning the themes of the film specifically on the UK or the US. It's never clear in the film where in the world we are, suggesting that this homogenized regime might have gone global.

all these years (and viewings). It's both fantasy and science fiction, though I would not call it "futuristic" as its style has a foot solidly planted in the 1940s. Gilliam's artistry and visual flair are all over this picture, and nowhere more than in Lowry's dream sequences. But Gilliam famously had to fight to get the film released at all, to the point where he took out a full-page ad in *Variety* asking the studio head when *Brazil* would be released in the US. And the cut released for television has achieved the status of legend - the entire ending of the film changed to turn a story of bureaucracy consuming everyone and everything in its path, to a feel-good Hollywood ending. It became something of a David vs Goliath tale, the brave filmmaker standing up to the powerful studios. It's this conflict that *The Battle of Brazil* documents, told by the *Variety* columnist who both Gilliam and the Universal executives were talking to at the time.

In listening to Gilliam talk about the film, my first reaction was to credit the studio with more patience and grace than I wanted to. Gilliam is all emotion, takes every perceived slight personally, and is blindly passionate about his work. He is outrageous, bullies, exaggerates, and has no patience for any obstacles to a director's vision. If I were the film's producer, I would let Gilliam nowhere near a studio office. He cannot get out of his own way, and he will stop at nothing until he gets everything he wants. The studio's initial concern - that a 2-hour and 22-minute running time will allow only one evening showing of the film instead of the usual two - seems pretty reasonable.

But Gilliam isn't the only party capable of talking himself

into trouble. The studio execs to a man (they're *all* men, and they've all gotten together on their talking points) insist that they knew from the beginning that the film "wasn't for everyone." They knew they had an arthouse project on their hands, and that the commercial prospects for the film were going to be slim. And then, they began insisting on changes to broaden the film's appeal. Gilliam indeed gave them a cut with a running time they wanted, and the film continued to be held in limbo until Gilliam would agree to the edits they wanted. Only by doing an end-run around the studio, and arranging (probably illegally) for the L.A. critics to see the European cut of the film, was Universal pressured into finally releasing the film, without further edits by Gilliam. They had to - *Brazil* started showing up on "10 Best" lists, and the Los Angeles Film Critics Association awarded it Best Picture, Best Director, and Best Screenplay.

I'd seen *Brazil* probably a half dozen times in my life, but I'd never seen the TV version, figuring it was just cut off before the ending turned dark. I was wrong. The 94-minute "Love Conquers All" version contains all the cuts the Universal executives wanted to make, and it's a textbook example of how editing can ruin a picture. It isn't just that the ending is changed - edits have been made to support the studio's dream of a hero rising from the bureaucracy to challenge his oppressors. That is not Sam Lowry. In Gilliam's version he is not moved to finally act because he is a hero; he has gradually come to see that he is complicit in the crimes of the system, and can bear his guilt no more. In the studio's version terrorists act as freedom fighters to battle for humanity against an evil system and destroy it. In Gilliam's version, terrorism is a much more slippery idea, except that government officials desperately want people to believe it's real. In the studio film, there are a few evil men that can be overcome to make things right. In Gilliam's film, good people are ground by the system to do evil, and that system cannot be conquered. The idea that a citizen accused of a crime will be billed for their prosecution, torture and imprisonment, and must confess before their credit is ruined is entirely absent from Universal's *Brazil*, making the government merely guilty of making an error, not a system dooming innocent people from the start. Michael Palin's character is robbed of both his humanity and his menace. De Niro's Tuttle becomes a mean-spirited malcontent.

The studio version is dumbed-down, witless, and makes no sense to people coming to the film for the first time. A few of the edits are themselves mean-spirited, seemingly done just to punish Gilliam. And the fantastic dream sequences are chopped out, so not only do we lose Giliam's imaginative visuals, but Sam's dreams are where he plays out everything he cannot be in the waking world. It's not simply a lesser film. It's a different film, and it betrays all of the courage of the original. For me, it was the final proof that despite Giliam's tantrums and personal attacks, it was the Universal executives who were guilty of bad faith all along. Worst of all, they think they're experts on art they know nothing about. In their desire to broaden the film's appeal, they end up turning away everyone.

So it was a long time to spend with this film, but it was worth it.

The Breakfast Club

US, 1985. Directed by John Hughes. 97 minutes, color.

"We're all pretty bizarre. Some of us are just better at hiding it, that's all."

First of all, I love that the above quote comes from Andrew (Emilio Estevez), who ought to be the least interesting member of this group. That The Jock can say this (sorry, "The Sporto"), and still be The Sporto, speaks volumes about how deeply empathetically this film is written, and the performance Hughes' actors draw out of his material.

The Breakfast Club, famously, is a film about five high school students, each an archetype ("The Brain, the Athlete, the Basketcase, the Princess, the Criminal," as they self-describe), who are brought together for a nine-hour Saturday detention in their school's library. In a lesser storyteller's hands, this film would be a quick throwaway in how teenagers shouldn't judge each other. But these kids (and Hughes) are smarter than we are. They understand that stereotypes are their shields, something they can hide behind to better manage adult expectations. There is safety in stereotypes, at least safety from having to try to explain themselves to parents and teachers. Only when they are alone can they risk peeking out from behind. Literally from the opening scene, as each child is dropped off by a parent (or absent, as in the case of Bender (Judd Nelson) and even Allison (Ally Sheedy), who looks like she was about to say something before they drove off) we get cinematic haiku in parental expectations. And not one of our teens miss it.

I hadn't seen this film in years, and I had misremembered it as sharing the same exuberance with Hughes' later film, *Ferris Bueller's Day Off.* Instead, *The Breakfast Club* makes me look back on that film with better eyes, looking not just at Ferris, but at his sister Jeanie and his friend Cameron as more serious characters than we generally credit them to be. Because it's astonishing how well Hughes, in his thirties when he wrote and directed this, understands teenagers and the high school crucible. Teens have been exploited in plenty of films before, victimized and criminalized, but I can think of no other film in which teenagers are respected as they are in *The Breakfast Club.* Hughes does not talk down to them, as most of us want to. He lets them speak for themselves, honestly. Even when Allison says, "when you grow up your heart dies," sure, we recognize the words as teen melodrama (well... mostly). But what we forget is how true those words feel at that age, and we forget to meet kids not where *we* are, but where *they* are.

Should I write about the wonderful and virtuosic performances these actors deliver, including Anthony Michael Hall and Molly Ringwald who really *were* sixteen years old at the time (and ironically, had to spend some part of their days on set attending school)? Should I write about how a film grounded so thoroughly in 1980s white suburban culture - how perfectly does Simple Minds' "Don't You (Forget About Me)" work as an anthem for these kids? - still rings with immediacy for us today? In his included essay, "Smells Like Teen Realness," David Kamp writes that a seventeen-year-old John Singleton saw the film in 1985 as his Pasadena high school newspaper's film critic, and immediately identified with the characters in the film: "(Hughes) gave me a template" for his teen characters, he later said. Singleton, of course, went on to write and direct *Boyz N The Hood* as his debut film in 1991. Should I write about how even the adult characters in the film - the principal and the custodian - get their own scenes together, Hughes refusing to reduce *any* of his characters, even the most antagonistic one, to a single dimension?

I had forgotten, misremembered, or flat-out missed so much about this film when I first encountered it. I expected to enjoy it, not to spend the next week mulling it over. I'm grateful Criterion gave me a reason to see it more clearly.

This is as good a place as any to write about what, exactly, the criteria are to make a Criterion film, and here I'd like to emphasize this is all pure conjecture on my part. The Criterion website itself professes to publish "important classic and contemporary films from around the world," and while vague, it's hard to argue with that. But Criterion is a publishing house, not the American Film Institute or the Library of Congress, so it can't claim eminent domain on any film it likes. If a studio isn't going to let go of a film,

Criterion can't give it a Criterion release, which I think explains why we're unlikely to see any Steven Spielberg films in their catalog in the next 70 years (currently in the United States, a film's copyright expires 70 years after the death of the "creator," with "creator" being defined as a film's director, screenwriter, contributor of dialogue, or composer of original film music). So Criterion can't just grab anything they want, though I imagine there's something of a prestige factor for being selected, so that may help a studio agree to let Criterion publish their film (Netflix, for example, has allowed several films to be released in Criterion versions). So if you're wondering why your favorite "great film" isn't published by Criterion, the answer probably lies in reasons of the marketplace.

What I think is a far more interesting question is why Criterion *has* selected some of the films they publish. The perception is that Criterion publishes only the "best" films, even though Criterion itself doesn't claim that. Rather, Criterion seems to cull films that have something to say that may have been overlooked on release. After all, *The Breakfast Club* is no *Citizen Kane*, nor is it *The Blob*, though all three are available as Criterion releases. Lately, Criterion has also begun to expand its search for films (as have I) to countries whose films are underseen in the West. That's what drew me to write about the Criterion Films in my collection; as my list of titles grew, I began to notice the diversity. For every *La dolce vita* there was a *Hollywood Shuffle*. It's not just film snobbery, I think there's an honest love of film behind all this.

Not that they don't come up with some head-scratchers every so often. For a while, Criterion published their own editions of two Michael Bay films: *Armageddon* and *The Rock*. Not that these films don't deliver what they promise, but it's difficult to understand why noisy blockbusters like these made the catalog. My guess is that Criterion was trying to sell itself more commercially and thought these titles would help; for whatever reason they're out of print now for Criterion and back to the studio that produced them. But I kind of like that they offered these films for a while. A good shortstop had better be making a few errors every season; if not it means he's not pushing his limits in his range. To me, a couple missed shots (again, in my opinion) like these means Criterion is willing to consider films from *everywhere*, not just arthouse theaters.

Of course, this leads to the question: Is a film published by Criterion because it's great, or does a Criterion issue bestow greatness on an otherwise ordinary film (assuming, of course, that you respect Criterion's tastes)? It's a fair question. I certainly took a harder look at *The Breakfast Club* because of its Criterion status than I would have otherwise. It's a bias I need to be mindful of as I write about these films.[9]

---

[9] Though it should be kept in mind that I write favorably about most of these films because I'm only going to spend money on a film I've already seen and appreciate, with a few exceptions with mixed results. Remember, I have no relationship with Criterion except as a customer; they don't give me films or suggest titles. I contacted them when I started this project as a blog (mostly to

But I think I'm doing a fair job of keeping my wits and judgment about me, and there has been the occasional film that just didn't resonate with me (I'm looking at you, *Fellini: Satyricon.*) And I'm glad Criterion forced a harder look at this John Hughes film. It certainly holds up to scrutiny.

---

make sure I wasn't going to get sued) and received a brief and supporting email telling me to have fun.

Cat People

US, 1942. Directed by Jacques Tourneur. 73 minutes, black and white.

"What if we never show the monster?"

That was Kirk Douglas's line, playing a movie producer in *The Bad and the Beautiful*, and it was this film he was referencing. *Cat People* is a sadly little-known B movie from RKO (remade in 1982 by Paul Schrader and starring Nastassja Kinski). The film - a low-budget horror movie from a studio still reeling in 1942 from the financial cost of *Citizen Kane* - is mostly known for offering only the smallest glimpse of the panther its heroine turns into, and only at the end of the film. The movie is a study in anticipation and fear of the dark and the unknown, but it's so much more than that. Producer Val Lewton and director Jacques Tourneur are impresarios of building suspense through sound and timing, and DP Nicholas Musuraca uses a noir palette of lights and shadows to keep the audience's fear on the edge of the picture. It's also a story of a European folktale thrown into the suspicious glare of modern American life. Ultimately, it's the story of a woman victimized both by her fears and the men in her life, from her seemingly well-meaning husband to her polished, yet predatory psychiatrist. All that with an undercurrent of sexuality tailor-made for newly-arrived French star Simone Simon. There's a lot packed into the 73-minute running time.

The story involves Irena Dubrovna (Simon), a Serbian immigrant working as a fashion sketch artist. Sketching a panther at the zoo, she encounters the handsome Oliver Reed (Kent Smith). She won't let him see her drawings, and later in the scene we see why; one is a very good likeness of the zoo's panther, but run through with a sword. It seems that Irena isn't just a pretty face after all.

Oliver walks Irena home, and she invites him in for tea. Oliver asks about a statue on a table of a knight on horseback impaling a large cat on his sword (much like in Irena's drawing). Irena tells Oliver of a folk tale from her home village, of a people who strayed from a proper Christian faith into the devil-worship and witchcraft of the past. When these "cat people" become jealous or enraged, they are able to transform into panther-like beasts. Irena believes that the cat persona that lives inside these people will not allow them to feel passion toward anyone; they'll kill a potential mate, or even anyone who arouses feelings of jealousy in them (the knight in the sculpture is a legendary figure who rid the town of cat people - though we suspect he didn't get them all). Because of this, Irena fears falling in love with any man. But Oliver is beginning to charm her, and he himself is smitten with Irena.

Irena is willing to allow Oliver to woo, and then marry

her (things move pretty quickly in 1940s films sometimes), but will not allow Oliver to kiss her, and the marriage remains unconsummated. Oliver is a pretty patient guy, but eventually arranges for Irena to see a psychiatrist for treatment for her neurosis. Under hypnosis in her first session with Dr. Louis Judd (Tom Conway), Irena reveals not only the folk tale from her village, but the fact that she's convinced it's true and fears that she herself is one of the "cat people." After the session, Irena is upset at finding her husband discussing their situation with his BFF from work, Alice Moore (Jane Randolph). Oliver explains that it was Alice who referred him to Dr. Judd, but Irena senses a stronger connection. Indeed, Alice will later confess to Oliver that she is in love with him, and Oliver responds by telling her he is no longer sure he loves Irena. As the two discuss Irena's "condition" through the film, Alice finds herself stalked on two occasions by an unseen creature that growls like a panther. Alice becomes convinced that even if the folk tale isn't literally true, Irena's commitment to it makes her a danger. Talking with Dr. Judd and Alice, Oliver agrees to a plan in which his marriage to Irena will be annulled (leaving him free to marry Alice), and Irena will be involuntarily committed to a psychiatric facility. Toward the end of the film, we finally witness two attacks by a panther (though Irena's "transformation" is never shown); one on Oliver and Alice at night in his drafting office, and a fatal encounter with the psychiatrist, who has revealed himself to also be sexually attracted to Irena. Dr. Judd is mauled to death, but manages to wound the panther with a sword concealed in his cane.[10] In the film's final scene, we see Irena slinking away, clutching her coat to a wound in her shoulder.

Let's talk first about the "Old World vs New World" or "Science vs Folk Wisdom" themes running through this film. Tourneur was a French filmmaker who came to producer Val Lewton's attention when Tourneur worked as a second unit director on *A Tale of Two Cities*. Tourneur moved to Hollywood in 1934, and though he had lived in the United States as a child, brought a European sensibility to his films. *Cat People* is bookended with two quotes which directly address this theme. The first is fictitious, taken from *The Anatomy of Atavism*, written by the film's psychiatrist, and it takes the side of science: "Even as fog continues to lie in the valleys, so does ancient sin cling to the low places, the depressions in the world consciousness." Irena has traveled from the Old World of legends and superstition (the home of most movie monsters: Dracula, Frankenstein's Monster, the Wolf Man) to the urban, science-worshiping America. There is no room here for these old tales, which are easily dismissed, but we dismiss them at our own peril. *Cat People* suggests that the old devils from Europe are not so easily discarded by all of us immigrants who have made America our home. Modern medicine proves useless against Irena's "affliction," as is suggested by an Old-Testament-quoting zookeeper, a common man who warns Irena about the nature of these beasts. And when Oliver and Alice are

---

[10] Yes, the psychiatrist carries a sword-cane. Never trust a mental health professional who routinely carries a sword-cane.

cornered by the panther in his drafting office, Oliver holds a t-square in front of them, immediately suggesting a cross by a cut to its shadow on the wall. When Oliver cries, "In the name of God, leave us in peace!" the panther slinks off into the night. Our closing quote, from the very real *Holy Sonnets* by John Donne, indicates we have come back to the side of folk wisdom and religion: "But black sin hath betrayed to endless night/My world, both parts, and both parts must die."

The decision to not show the creature through most of the film may have been rooted in budget, in technical limitations, maybe even by access to an actual panther, but none of that matters. Once the decision had been made, the horror of *Cat People* is artfully woven in. Most of the film takes place at night, and the choice of a limited palette of blacks, whites, and grays keeps the shadows harsh, and the action hidden once our characters succumb to those shadows. In many of the tensest scenes those shadows are made more menacing in motion. Whether it's the uncertain wavering of shadows cast by firelight, the reaching of tree branches in the wind cast on a blank wall, or - in the film's edgiest sequence - the undulations of an indoor swimming pool's reflections on a wall, we're constantly reminded that unseen danger is alive, crouched in shadows. It's not just that Tourneur leaves the creature to our mind's eye, he actively peppers our imagination using everything at his disposal. Sound is made brilliant use of in *Cat People*, in the distant wailing of creatures from the zoo, in the sounds of footsteps that suddenly vanish - suggesting a transformation from noisy human soles to silent cat's paws. One terrific scene builds suspense through both sound effects and first-rate editing. Alice is walking home alone late at night, and is being followed by Irena. The camera centers each woman from the knees down, as we follow their footsteps. The camera cuts from one woman to the other, the staccato of heels striking pavement growing faster and faster, the cuts between the women growing faster as well. We begin to hear growling, faint at first, then getting louder. We're building to a climax even as Irena's footsteps disappear, culminating in the scream of a wild beast. Only it *isn't* a cat roaring, it's the scream of the air brakes on a bus, suddenly stopping in rescue of Alice. It's a moment of both terror and release, and it's masterful. The result is that the transformed beast is all over this picture; we're just not allowed to lay eyes on it until the very end.

Check out *Cat People*; it's a primer on what a B movie can aspire to if made with wit and attention to detail. I think our horror films are our collective dreams, and dreaming has always served the purpose of processing our deepest waking fears.

This film also carries one of my favorite kinds of chat tracks: One with a film scholar (in this case Gregory Mank) who does his research digging up trivia on sets and actors, and who provided me with my "Aha!" moment when I realized one of the bit characters was Alan Napier - who'd go on to play Alfred Pennyworth twenty years later in the Adam West *Batman* TV series.

Children of Paradise

France, 1945. Directed by Marcel Carné. 190 minutes, black and white.

Tonight's Criterion Tuesday selection is Pathé's epic *Children of Paradise (Les Enfants du paradis)*. It's one of my five favorite films of all time, and I first sought it out because of a beautiful lie.

I'd read about the film in the 1980s, as described in the novel *Still Life with Woodpecker* by Tom Robbins. Robbins described the film as an epic period drama (check) filmed in Paris during the Nazi Occupation (check), with elaborate outdoor sets and a cast of hundreds of extras (also check). Robbins went on to describe the film as being made in secret, "under the very noses" of the occupying German army, and that the filmmakers were risking their lives in the creation of their art. That last bit... not so much, and I apologize to friends I've repeated this to over the years. The script, the cast, and the crew all had to be approved by the Gestapo, and while filmmakers certainly had to be sly about working in their critiques of the Vichy government (in this film, for example, you see it in the way the police or any men of authority are portrayed), a three-hour epic like this simply couldn't have been hidden from view. (Not that director Marcel Carné and screenwriter Jacques Prévert didn't take chances - whenever the Vichy government gave them lists of the extras they wanted cast, each of their suggestions was found to be somehow "not 19th-century-looking" and replaced often with Resistance fighters. Racial laws prevented "Jews and other foreigners" from working in the film industry, but at least two Jews, hiding in Paris in secret, worked on the film under pseudonyms.) But French cinema had been in a shambles with the advent of sound, and depression-era shortages had made it almost impossible for production companies to acquire the technology - or even the film stock - they required. French director Marcel L'Herbier later wrote in his memoirs, "For the most part we film directors had been working in artistic slavery since 1930, even though France was then free. Now that it no longer was, and the Germans had the whip hand, the situation was completely reversed and we regained the right to complete artistic freedom."

Still, the Germans watched carefully for subversive themes set in contemporary times, which is why so much of French cinema turned to the past, to better hide filmmakers' more anarchical ideas (three of the four male leads were actual historical figures, so the film could always claim it was merely biography). And *Children of Paradise* is full of anarchy. It's a film about theater, and the need the poor of the city feel to have art in their lives. It's a celebration of mime - yes, stop rolling your eyes, French mime - and the astonishing beauty and humanity a skilled artist can communicate without words (indeed, part of the reason French cinema had so much trouble moving on from silent films was the reverence toward voiceless acting. And honestly, if you think mime is just a joke, watch Jean-Louis Barrault's Baptiste free a woman from an accusation of pickpocketing with a masterful performance 15 minutes in). It's a celebration, mostly, of love and freedom - freedom of the simple Parisians, and the loss of freedom wealth and power bring. It's the story of a courtesan, and the four men (well... one of them is gay, but still) who love her.

The film is split into two halves, and in the first, we find our characters as "children" of Paris, indeed; each is struggling, unknown, and relatively unencumbered. Baptiste is the son of Anselm Debureau (Étienne Decroux), an actor and director of a theater troupe that produces works of pantomime at the *Théâtres des Funambules*, as the authorities will not permit spoken dialogue there, reserving spoken plays for the official Grand Theater. In his pitch to the crowd outside, calling them to buy tickets, he proudly recounts his family's great acting legacy, but points disdainfully to Baptiste as an embarrassment to a great father, and leaves him outside to perform for the crowd for free (later we learn this is not just a PR stunt; Anselm truly believes Baptiste lacks skill). The woman Baptiste saves from the police is Garance (Arletty), a courtesan currently working in a sort of risqué boulevard peep show. After being rescued by Baptiste, Garance runs into Frédérick Lemaître (Pierre Brasseur), a charming and immodest unemployed actor, who tells her he is destined to play all the great roles, including someday

Othello. Eventually, she stops in on Lacenaire (Marcel Herrand), who makes a living writing letters for illiterate Parisians, fencing stolen goods, and various other acts of skullduggery. While others are taken by Garance's beauty, he admires what he believes to be her cold heart.

Through the first half, we watch Baptiste, Frederick, and Garance all begin to rise in the acting world from their lowly beginnings (all three have rooms in the same Montmartre boarding house). Through happy accidents, Baptiste is given the opportunity to display his sublime pantomime skills onstage, and Frédérick is also able to begin making a name as a silent actor at the Funambules. Baptiste brings in Garance to pose onstage, much to the chagrin of Nathalie (María Casares), who is fervently in love with Baptiste, and from whom Baptiste is unable to disguise his obsession with Garance. But Garance has also been noticed by the Count Édouard de Montray (Louis Salou), who begins to court her with his position and wealth. And at the end of the first half, when a scheme of Lacenaire's has left Garance facing prison, the Count is the only man in a position to save her.

The second half begins after a span of several years. Frédérick, frustrated with being silenced at the Funambules, is now the star of the Grand Theater, and is soon to begin a run as Othello. Baptiste has become a recognized master of mime at the Funambules; both actors find themselves at the height of success, the toast of Paris. But both are still in love with Garance, who has been away from France since her hasty marriage to the Count. Baptiste is now married to Nathalie, with a little boy. Nathalie understands that Baptiste still dreams of Garance, but she is happy, knowing that Garance is now out of reach. Frédérick has not forgotten her, either, but has used his jealousy of the Count to fuel his portrayal of the Moor of Venice. When Garance returns to Paris, and reveals an unhappy marriage to the controlling Count, she brings with her a longing for her carefree days, threatening her own happiness, as well as the stability and the very lives of everyone in her past.

Every time I watch this film, I see a new layer. This time, it's seeing how the actions onstage reflect the personal lives of the protagonists, and how they in turn reflect the lives of Parisians under the Occupation. What makes this even more fascinating is learning that Carné liked to type-cast his actors, so except for Arletty's Garance, each actor had something in common with the character they portrayed. In fact, I learned that the actor originally cast as the ragman Jericho - an odious underground figure ready to spy on and betray his patrons - was known to be a Nazi collaborator. Carné was able to film only one scene with him when the actor was forced to flee for his life from Paris, later tried in absentia and sentenced to death by a post-liberation court.

Watching this epic film twice in two days (the second time with audio commentary by film scholars Brian Stonehill and Charles Affron) was a bit of a commitment, I won't lie. But *Children of Paradise* is well worth it. It is an acquired taste (as you might expect from a 1945 *very* French film), but it gets better every time I see it. And the script is absolute poetry. It gets fresher with every viewing, and says more about love, and how to live, than any other five films put together. I love this film.

Chimes at Midnight

Spain, 1966. Directed by Orson Welles. 116 minutes, black and white.

So... I wasn't terribly thrilled when *Chimes at Midnight* popped up to be my next Criterion Tuesday film. I always thought of this film as a kind of vanity project for Orson Welles. Falstaff - a bloody great drunk, a wit, a glutton, a monster, a lover, a bacchanal, mirror father figure to Prince Hal's distant father King Henry IV - appears in several Shakespeare plays. Not content with the screen time Sir John Falstaff would merit in any one of Shakespeare's plays, Orson Welles cobbled together bits of both *Henry IV* plays, *Richard II*, *Henry V,* and *The Merry Wives of Windsor* to basically make a Falstaff movie. Or so I thought. Honestly, this film has always been hard for me to follow except in the broadest strokes, and I think a lot of that is because I have a better time reading Shakespeare, when I can go back over a line and absorb the unfamiliar language than have lines fired at me in rapid succession by British Actors Smarter Than Me. But critics rate this film a lot higher, and in reading Michael Anderegg's essay, there's a lot more to be found.

I discovered that Welles had worked on this for years, and even directed a stage play, *Five Kings,* which was basically a performance version of the film. By the time Welles shot this film in 1964, his enormous physical presence (he was 6'2" and 300 pounds) was beginning to become something of a joke. Welles apparently didn't shy away from that; he built narrow interior sets to further emphasize his bulk, and the suit of armor designed for Falstaff makes him look practically spherical. He certainly sells the character - Falstaff is who Prince Hal fell in with as a young man in order to sow wild oats, and probably rebel against his father and the destiny that awaited him. At the end, when Hal takes the crown, and pushes Falstaff, his gang, and his wild ways aside (as even Hal knew he would do in an aside at the film's beginning) Falstaff's heartbreak at the betrayal falls more into the tragic than the comic. The way Welles played him, you feel like Falstaff started out working the Prince for the short-term, but then let himself get seduced against his better judgment for the noble life he might finally attain.

Another thing that made *Chimes at Midnight* more interesting to me was reading about Welles' relationship with his own father. Apparently, Orson's father was an alcoholic, and would visit his young son at either university or boarding school drunk and generally embarrass him. One day a professor pulled the young Welles aside and gently advised him that only by setting strict limits on his father's behavior would this ever change. Welles forbade his father from ever visiting again until he was sober. The elder Welles stayed away, and died shortly later from either the effects or consequences of his alcoholism. In interviews, Welles would later say that he still felt responsible for his father's death.

Should we be able to come to a film, a novel, or a painting knowing nothing of the artist and still be able to appreciate it? Shouldn't great art transcend its context? Yes, I think so. Yet I can't pretend that knowing about Welles' relationship with his father doesn't infuse young Hal's dismissal of Falstaff with far more intensity, pathos, and heartbreak than it had on previous viewings. The look on the actor's face of utter despondency - yet also familial pride! - is as compelling as anything else I've seen in film. It's an incredible performance, and beyond that, you feel that you're watching a real human being confront years-old demons of his own.

It's impossible of course for me to now watch the film without "unknowing" this. But there's plenty more to recommend it as well. There's a terrific battle scene that stands up there with anything you've seen on *Game of Thrones*, both cinematic and messy at the same time. And hey, this John Gielgud kid is no slouch, either.

And to be honest, I know that I share a bias most people have against Orson Welles. The line on him is famous: After *Citizen Kane*, he was never able to reclaim that initial greatness. Welles is the Poster Child for Peaking Early. By the time I was aware of him, he was putting his stentorian voice through its paces hawking Paul Masson wine in television ads ("We will sell no wine before its time") and making the rounds of afternoon talk shows as a raconteur-for-hire for Merv Griffin and Mike Douglas. But that's unfair to him, and I think tells us more about our own need to shoot down our geniuses than anything about Welles' actual talent. I think that if you erased *Citizen Kane* and its memory from our collective consciousness, we might have looked a lot more admiringly at the rest of his career, both as actor and director. It's a lesson to me to check my biases before watching any film. And maybe cut a little slack to someone who knows more about performing Shakespeare than I ever will.

Oh, and if I ever find myself with a big stocky dog, like a bulldog or boxer, I'm going to name him (or her) "Falstaff."

City Lights

US, 1931. Directed by Charlie Chaplin. 86 minutes, black and white, silent (mostly).

It's serendipitous that just two weeks after Criterion Tuesday gave me *Children of Paradise* it now offers up Charlie Chaplin's masterpiece, *City Lights*. *Children of Paradise* was a master class in the art of mime, and Chaplin used mime as his primary instrument to speak to the audience. Like Baptiste, Chaplin felt that speaking would detract from the actor's craft, and he stubbornly refused any spoken dialogue in this film, four years into the reign of "talkies" in Hollywood. There is sound and music throughout the film, but in the very opening scene, as politicians and society swells address the public at the unveiling of a statue, their voices are replaced by kazoos and saxophones, much like any adult in a *Peanuts* TV cartoon. From there, it's sound effects and title cards - an act of defiance as so many silent film performers were falling away.

Chaplin himself described *City Lights* as "a comedy romance in pantomime," which may be the best way to sum it up. Chaplin reprises his "Little Tramp" character (more on this in a bit), who falls hard for a blind flower girl he encounters on the street. The film follows our hero through a series of adventures in which he tries to raise money for an operation that will restore her sight.

It's worth a digression to talk a little bit about Chaplin's beginnings. He was born in London on April 16th, 1889; like D.W. Griffith, he was very much a product of the 19th century. His mother, Hannah, was a singer and comedian in British music halls at the time, performing under the name Lily Harley. Chaplin's father (Charles Chaplin, Sr.) was also a performer on the stage, but separated from his wife when Charlie was a year old, and had little to do with his boys from then on. Charles, Sr. suffered from alcoholism, and died when Charlie was twelve years old. Hannah, in the meantime, suffered from ill health (and mental illness), and young Charlie got his stage debut at the age of five when Hannah's voice gave out and he was ushered out on stage to fill her slot. When Hannah was hospitalized four years later, Charlie was thrown out onto the streets, eventually finding himself in one of London's Dickensian workhouses.

It was in 1903 that Charlie was rescued from this life by his older brother, Sydney. Sydney had been away from home since he had turned twelve, working on a training ship, the *Exmouth*. He had begun working as a steward for various shipping lines, but returned to port to find his little brother living on the street. Determined to create a better life for him, Sydney managed to find them employment at which the brothers could both excel: the theater. It was through young Charlie's music hall work that he came to be noticed by an American vaudeville troupe, which led to a contract with the Keystone Film Company.

Those formative years for Charlie turned out to be formative for the Little Tramp character as well. Having been homeless and faced life-threatening poverty, Chaplin developed a lifelong empathy for the poor all over the world. Chaplin also loved his mother dearly. In 1921 he was financially able to bring her stateside to Santa Monica, where he bought her a home and hired caregivers to care for her in the last seven years of her life. Chaplin also credited his mother for his success as an actor, beyond simply introducing him to a life in the theater. According to Chaplin, Hannah taught him to observe people from all walks of life and to mimic them, which led to his brilliance in pantomime.

So Chaplin's Little Tramp persona began to develop as not just a comic character, but one who took the side of the oppressed and the poor. Chaplin was afforded greater and greater control over his work as he jumped from his first film studio (they of the frenetic *Keystone Kops* silent one-reel comedies) to more lucrative offers, ultimately co-founding United Artists in 1919 with Mary Pickford, Douglas Fairbanks, and D.W. Griffith He slowed down the pace without sacrificing the comedy, and lengthened his films from quick one-reel farces (one reel of film translated to roughly 10-12 minutes of screen time, depending on the speed of both the camera and the projector). With the extra reels came more time to allow the Little Tramp to become an observer and silent commentator on poverty in the 20th century. Part of the reason Chaplin held off from joining the talking picture revolution was because he was afraid that if the Little Tramp began speaking English, he would lose his connection to audiences in non-English speaking countries, who had come to identify with his character as well.

City Lights is laugh-out-loud funny, as I rediscovered on a first-pass viewing. But Gary Giddins' essay included with the disc gave me an insight even after a lifetime of watching Chaplin films. Shakespeare showed us how comic relief in a tragedy or history helped an audience vent building tension, giving them a brief respite to process the drama they were witnessing. Chaplin accomplished something even more daring by doing the exact opposite, somehow injecting moments of true suffering and pathos into a comedy. It's like walking a tightrope. One misstep can bring it all down, but Chaplin had a genius for knowing when to make his characters real, heightening both their humanity and the comedy. Giddens also pointed out how rarely Chaplin the filmmaker used close-ups, preferring to use long to medium shots to first set context for a scene, then present a scope of movement. (Also, since Chaplin performed with his entire body, you want his full figure in the shot wherever possible.) At the very end of this film, we get a rare close-up of his Little Tramp. We see the whiteface, we see the greasepaint, but we also see the lines around his eyes, and the weariness of a man trodden on by life. How much more heroic are his antics when we get our most intimate look at this character?

Cries and Whispers

Sweden, 1972. Directed by Ingmar Bergman. 91 minutes, color.

Mo' Bergman! Mo' Bergman!

Should I be surprised that I'm only in the "Cs" of my Criterion films, and Criterion Tuesday has given me *Cries and Whispers*, my fifth Ingmar Bergman picture since I began (with many more to come)? Nah. As you're going to find out as you flip through these pages, it's the films of Ingmar Bergman and Akira Kurosawa that I love the best. I'm just going to give you a brief glance at *Cries and Whispers* - it's a character piece, a family portrait - and then spend the rest of this piece talking about myself and how I came to be fascinated by this particular director.

Not much "happens" in *Cries and Whispers*, which concerns three sisters, one of whom is dying. Agnes (Harriet Andersson) is the dying one, wasting away from cancer in her bed. Her two sisters are there to attend to her, but so involved in their own issues that they're of little use, serving only to echo and amplify Harriet's pain. Maria (Liv Ullmann) is wracked by guilt from a loss of her own. Her husband has left her, and made an unsuccessful attempt on his own life, after uncovering evidence of Maria's long-standing affair - with Agnes's doctor. Karin (Ingrid Thulin) cannot face her sister's cancer; she is self-absorbed and suicidal herself, and cannot look on anyone's suffering but her own (Karin's aversion to human touch of any kind further separates her from both her sisters). Only Anna (Kari Sylwan), the family's maid provides actual comfort to Agnes in her final days, and for her attention that the family cannot provide, she is sent away at the end of the film unrewarded.

We're most familiar with Bergman's stark black and white movies, but he was not afraid to turn to color to add warmth, or in this case emotional heat to a scene. In his book, *Images: My Life in Film*, Bergman writes of the germ of *Cries and Whispers*: "The first image kept coming back, over and over: the room draped all in red with women clad in white. That's the way it is: images obstinately resurface without my knowing what they want with me; then they disappear, only to come back looking exactly the same." He goes on to write, "When I was a child I imagined the soul to be a dragon, a shadow floating in the air like blue smoke.... But inside this dragon, everything was red."

So it is that the action of *Cries and Whispers* is drenched in red interiors. Women working inside of a womb in which family secrets and emotions are straining to emerge. Bergman wrote of this film in musical terms (he was a Mozart scholar), introducing themes that played on each other. Even the film's title, he noted, came from a contemporary's criticism of a Mozart quartet. Like *Autumn*

Sonata, the film crescendos to a fiery conclusion. Swedish reserve and isolation will only dampen reality for so long.

☙ ☙ ☙

So. Why the fascination with Ingmar Bergman? It's personal.

We all have favorite movies, or sports, or songs, or places that bring special meaning to our lives, and I think that these things we hold dear almost never come to us on their merits alone. No one is a Cubs fan because of the way they play. No, the things we hold in our heart get there because they're linked to something else. That doesn't mean they lack merit, but we elevate them because of something else they're connected to. My favorite book, for example, is *Moby Dick* - I've read it six times (and counting). But I'd be lying if I said it was my favorite because it's the apex of literary achievement. It's my favorite because my mother was a New Englander in her heart, bones, and soul, and when I was a kid it was me of the four children she chose to spend a day with at Mystic Seaport in Connecticut. I love *Moby Dick*, and I find something new every time I read it. But I became obsessed with it early in life because it was one of the few points of connection I shared with a parent in a difficult childhood.

So, I can't be objective about *Moby Dick*. I've never recommended it to anyone. I have no idea how the book looks to someone who didn't come to it the way I did. My love for it is all bound up in something uniquely personal. So it is with Ingmar Bergman films. I understand that other filmmakers greatly admire him. But I'll never try to "sell" him to anyone else, because this is why I feel a connection to a foreign filmmaker who's dead and who I never met:

First, we're both Swedish, so that was a natural curiosity. All my grandparents were born in Sweden, and even though neither Bergman nor any other part of Swedish culture that was not connected with Lutheranism was spoken of in my home, I was intrigued by this famous filmmaker my country of origin had produced. Early on in life I was attracted to movies first as an escape, then as almost a source of spiritual nourishment, so although I wasn't to see one of his films until I was an adult, Bergman always seemed to be there in the wings, waiting to make his entrance.

But Bergman was also the son of a Lutheran pastor, as was I - in fact the clergy was something of a family business among the Johanssons, claiming a grandfather, an uncle, cousins, my own brother, and even my brother's wife (though she is - heretically! - a *Methodist* pastor). I, as it turns out, was also headed for a career in the clergy, but something brought me up short at the last minute. That "something" was my atheism.

My atheism wasn't something I chose or desired, or even reasoned my way into (though reason is at the heart of every atheist). No, it was something I discovered about myself, much like my friends in the queer community discover their own natures. Though I'd been trying hard to internalize my family's Christian faith, it just wouldn't take. Finally around the age of thirty, just as my son was about to be born, just when I was looking hard at my own values and ethical system I was about to teach (or at least model) to another human being, I realized - no, I *accepted* - that I had never really believed in a god, and had always drawn my morality from secular places.

Ingmar Bergman, like me, had a distant father. Ingmar Bergman, like me, left the faith of his fathers. And turned first to the stage and then to the movies to search for truth in his life and to make connections with like-minded people; his chosen family.

I understand that when other people watch Ingmar Bergman movies, they're looking for intellectual stimulation. I understand that some people watch him because he's an "actor's director" and can augment and facilitate incredible work from his collaborators. But when I watch one of his films, I'm hungrily sifting for clues. I want to find out how this man negotiated his rift with his family and his church. I want to see how he picked himself up and started over, like I had to, when he abandoned the one thing his family had taught him was the most important. I want to see how he found nourishment in the stories movies tell, and whether there are crumbs he left a brother from another place and another time that *maybe* - and I completely understand how much projection goes on in all of this, I'm not an idiot - *maybe* help him figure out the story of his own life. I'm at peace with my life and relationships and decisions. But I wasn't always, and in those days I looked to Ingmar Bergman as someone who had gone through so much of what I had, and wanted reassurance that things would be OK. After I calmed down, I was left with stories that still touched me, and an appreciation for a director who never stopped challenging himself, never stopped trying to learn.

So, there's a ton of Bergman in *Criterion Tuesdays*. Does

that mean there should be a ton of Bergman in your own film diet? I can't say. But there's someone who speaks to you, too, whether she's a director, a songwriter, a poet, a novelist, an athlete, an actor, a pianist, or a sculptor. Who is she? What does she have to say to you?

The Devil's Backbone

Mexico/Spain, 2001. Directed by Guillermo del Toro. 108 minutes, color.

A rare treat for my horror homies.

It's only been the past three or four years that I've really started delving into the horror genre, so I'm relatively new to Guillermo del Toro's *The Devil's Backbone*. I was surprised to find that like *Pan's Labyrinth* (which del Toro made five years later, but I'd seen first), this was a macabre story told from a child's point of view, and set against the backdrop of the horrors of the Spanish Civil War. In both films - though especially in the later film - I felt that children were turning to a fantasy world, not to escape or dilute the terrors of their wartime lives, but to help them process the violence of the adult world around them.

The Devil's Backbone begins with Carlos (Fernando Tielve), a twelve-year-old boy who has lost his father in the Spanish Civil War. Carlos is dropped off at a remote orphanage by his tutor. Heartbreakingly, Carlos has no idea this is to be his new home until his tutor drives off without him. In a fairly standard trope for the new kid in an orphanage, Carlos is both befriended and bullied by his new brethren. Thankfully, he soon finds his place among the boys, after twice refusing to rat out his chief child antagonist, Jaime (Iñigo Garcés), and once saving his fellow orphan's life.

No, there are worse "bullies" at the orphanage, and only one of flesh and blood. That's Jacinto (Eduardo Noriega), a hired hand and former orphan who is brutally cruel to both boys and staff. Jacinto beats and threatens the boys, is abusive toward his fiancée Conchita (Irene Viusedo), and cheats on her by carrying on a loveless affair with the school's widowed headmistress, Carmen (Marisa Paredes), an amputee with a wooden leg. Jacinto pursues this affair only to discover where Carmen has hidden a stash of gold bars, with which she hopes to some day fund the orphanage. As it is, the bars are useless as revenue in the rural wartime economy, and their very existence has to be kept secret as they would bring unwelcome attention to the orphanage.

And the other two "bullies?" One is in the form of an enormous bomb lodged in the ground of the courtyard of the orphanage, dropped from a plane several months before. The bomb has been deactivated (though several of the boys whisper at night that they can hear it ticking), yet it cannot be safely removed, and serves as a reminder of the violence of the war that threatens not just the boys, but all of Spain. Our third "bully" is said to be a ghost who haunts the orphanage. It is believed to be the spirit of Santi, a boy who disappeared the night the bomb was dropped. On Carlos's first night in the orphanage, he is sent to the kitchen alone on a dare, and hears a voice whispering, "Many of you will die." Carlos, terrified, flees the kitchen, but later works up the courage for another nighttime visit in search of the ghost. His persistence is rewarded when he sees the pale form of a boy, blood slowly floating upward from his head, as if underwater. Later, Carlos finds a drawing of Santi in Jaime's journal, and suspects Jaime knows more about Santi's disappearance than he is letting on.

That's not the only creepy thing at the orphanage. Carlos visits Dr. Caseres (Frederico Lippi) for treatment for a knife slit Jacinto gave him. Jacinto has threatened to kill Carlos if he reveals who cut him, and Carlos believes him, as do we. Caseres talks about the history of the orphanage, and shows Carlos large glass jars containing aborted or stillborn fetuses which are preserved with a treated rum. Caseres sells this rum in the village where it is believed to have powers to cure maladies, including impotence; the proceeds from which are the only reliable income the orphanage has.

In the meantime, the war has come to the nearby village. Dr. Caseres fears the boys are no longer safe at the orphanage and announces they will evacuate. Jacinto, fearing he'll lose his chance at the gold, has already stashed cans of gasoline in the kitchen, which sits above a cistern next to which the orphanage keeps a safe. Conchita discovers the cans before Jacinto can ignite them; she threatens him with a gun and wounds him with a shot to the arm. Furious, Jacinto flicks a cigarette to the floor as he flees, and an explosion rocks the orphanage, killing and wounding children and staff alike, and fulfilling the ghost's prophecy. A mortally wounded Dr.

Caseres vows to protect the boys from Jacinto's certain return, and holds vigil with a shotgun on his lap.

That night, Jaime tells Carlos the truth about what happened the night the bomb fell. He and Santi were collecting slugs in the cistern, when they surprised Jacinto, who had been trying to access the safe. Jaime hid from view, but Jacinto cornered Santi, threatening him if he told anyone what he'd seen. Jacinto pushed Santi against a wall, too forcefully, and Santi's head bounced off a rock in the wall, giving him a head wound and sending him into shock. Panicking, Jacinto tied rocks to Santi's feet and tossed him into the cistern. Jaime tells Carlos he's no longer afraid of Jacinto, and will kill him if he returns. Carlos, no longer afraid of Santi's ghost, seeks him out. He finds the spirit, which tells Carlos to bring Jacinto to him when he returns. Carlos agrees.

You'll have to watch the film yourself to see how it plays out, but you can see this isn't your standard "slasher" type horror flick. In the enclosed essay by Mark Kermode, he writes that del Toro was convinced as a child that monsters in his bedroom were real, and over time made a pact with them, befriending them instead of letting his fear run wild. Later, at the age of eleven, when he heard the voice of a dead uncle sighing in the room in which he used to live, del Toro nurtured the memory rather than let it terrify him.

So watching *The Devil's Backbone*, I'm going to follow Guillermo's advice and listen to the monsters. I want to hear what they have to say.

So let's talk a little about the time-honored tradition of getting scared at the movies. Why do we subject ourselves to horror voluntarily, even seek it out?

I didn't, not for a long time. Blame some of that on me being a particularly sensitive child, but also on a big old house my family where my family lived when I was a kid. It was an old three-story house in a rundown neighborhood in an economically hard-hit Pennsylvania town, which is probably how my parents were able to afford it. My parents, not wanting to have a television in the living room, put our family's first color set in a "finished" corner of the basement; "finished" in the sense that it had some carpet, instead of the cement in the rest of the basement. In order to get to the switch for the TV room lights, you had to walk through the entire unfinished part of the basement, past mazes of storage boxes, past the laundry area, and in each spot you had to walk through some darkness before you reached a pull-chain for a bare light bulb, until you got to a switch for the TV room lights. Which, by the way, was directly next to the furnace room, where only a door with a frosted-glass panel separated me from a coal-eating, belching monster. It's a testament to how much I loved movies that I ventured down there alone at all, and many is the night that I would bolt from the basement to my 3rd-floor bedroom without turning off *any* of the basement lights, preferring a scolding from my parents for my wasteful behavior to turning off a light and *then* walking through a gauntlet of shadows. I would consume an awful lot of Saturday afternoon movies, old B movie horror and sci-fi monster flicks, which seemed like a good idea in the light of day, only to be rerun in my mind as I tried to fall asleep at night....

So I didn't seek out horror films when I started leaving the house, often sneaking out to go to the movies. I remember seeking out comedies in my tween years, then more in the cop or action genres. My first experience being scared in a theater *should* have come in 1974, when some buddies and I saw *The Towering Inferno*, a star-studded Irwin Allen disaster flick (all the rage at the time; these were the days of *Earthquake*, and the original *Poseidon Adventure*). But those films were built for spectacle, not jump-scares, and my twelve-year-old buddies and I ate it up with glee. No, my first experience being terrified in a theater came the following year in the very same theater with Steven Spielberg's *Jaws*. Again, I went with friends, and I have a vivid memory of watching the opening credits over an underwater tracking shot, with *that* music, and thinking, "I should *not* be here." It's not an exaggeration to say it was a traumatizing experience; I remember having difficulty sleeping for weeks after seeing *Jaws*. Put it down to Spielberg's skill as a director, and the fact that none of us had ever seen anything like it before. The funny thing about that is after the film, all my buddies were talking about how *awesome* the movie was, and I joined right in so they wouldn't suspect how scared I really was. It never occurred to me until I was an adult that their bravado was probably as false as mine; I thought they really weren't bothered, and there was something wrong with me. Maybe the fact that none of them made a peep through the whole movie should have tipped me off.

So I avoided horror films for most of my life, a pity, since the 1980s were prime years for them. I do remember seeing *Friday the 13th* with a bunch of friends who dragged me along, but I secretly wasn't happy about it. I took a date to see *The Shining*, but only because I was a devoted Stanley Kubrick fan, disdainful of Steven King (I've since come around to Mr. King as a writer). As I got older, I'd brave other horror movies, but never sought them out. I remember seeing *The Blair Witch Project* because I thought it was a brilliant idea for a film, and a terrific exercise in improvisational acting, and it did not disappoint on either count. *And* it scared the shit out of me, and I was looking away whenever darkness fell in the film.[11]

Why do we voluntarily scare ourselves at the movies? I'm not sure. Part of it is the release - a movie theater gives us a safe place to face fears, process them, and put them to bed. Get scared, get it out of your system. But I think what del Toro does is use horror as a way to get at things in our psyche that really scare us, that are out of our control. Our dreams are where we process our fears, so maybe horror films are where we collectively process the things that frighten us as a society. Before you roll your eyes too much, think about *The Exorcist*.

Sometimes films aren't about who we think they're about. I never really liked the film *Forrest Gump*; I didn't feel I had much of a connection to this figure that fell ass-backward into luck

---

[11] To this day, I maintain that part of the reason I found *The Blair Witch Project* so scary was because it was the first time I'd seen "East Coast" woods in a movie, complete with the brown leaves and twigs of the forest floor. The Maryland woods looked like a hundred places I'd gone hiking and camping.

and fortune, attaining savior status. The reality is, most mentally challenged people find themselves powerless or preyed upon. But if you look at Jenny or Lt. Dan as being the real central characters of the film, I think it becomes much more interesting. So who is it in *The Exorcist* that gets most of the screen time? It's not the little girl, Regan (Linda Blair). It's not a priest, and it's not a devil. The mother (Ellen Burstyn) is in almost every scene of that film. I think she's the central character. I think the reason *The Exorcist* remains so scary today, is that it's really about being unable to protect your child. Chris's daughter is suffering, and no one the mother turns to can help, much less figure out what's going on. As a parent, I can tell you that feeling of powerlessness is more terrifying than any questionable supernatural evil.

These days I must be braver, because I'm catching up on the stuff I missed. I thought the 2017 and 2019 versions of Stephen King's *It* were terrific, and even picked up copies on disc of *Midsommar* and *Hereditary*. I even belong to a Speculative Fiction Book Club in which we read science fiction, fantasy, and horror, and at this writing my buddy Cade has us reading *My Heart is a Chainsaw* by Stephen Graham Jones, which follows a teenager who's addicted to '80s horror flicks, so in the past week I've watched *Halloween*, *I Know What You Did Last Summer*, and the Brian De Palma version of *Carrie* just to keep up with the main character. Went to sleep just fine after each movie, too. Maybe I have conquered my fears.

Or maybe I know I have my Wheaten Terrier, Jonesey (named after the cat in *Alien*) sleeping at my side.

Do the Right Thing

US, 1989. Directed by Spike Lee. 120 minutes, color.

I saw *Do the Right Thing* when it came out in 1989, before, honestly, I was ready to hear all he had to say. Thankfully I'm writing this now, instead of then, because it's an important film in American cinema, as Spike Lee is an important director. It's a message forward type of film, that's powerful and celebratory and angry and bold and fun and beautiful. It's what we've learned to expect from a Spike Lee joint.

It's the hottest day of the summer in the predominantly Black and Latin Bedford-Stuyvesant (Bed-Stuy) neighborhood of Brooklyn. Mookie (Spike Lee) serves as our guide to the neighborhood; his job as a pizza delivery man takes him from one end to the other. Through Mookie, we meet Da Mayor (Ossie Davis) and Mother-Sister (Ruby Dee), the Elders of Bed-Stuy. (The two actors are married in real life and are legends in Black theater.) Da Mayor is an old, well-meaning drunk, constantly verbally scrapping with Mother-Sister, who oversees the goings-on of the neighborhood, and wants for better role models. We meet Mister Señor Love Daddy (Samuel

L. Jackson), DJ at the neighborhood FM station, and voice of Bed-Stuy. There's Buggin' Out (Giancarlo Esposito), Mookie's best friend and a man unafraid to get in anyone's face over the representation of Black Brooklyn. Over here is Radio Raheem (Bill Nunn), sweeping through the neighborhood blasting rap and hip-hop on an enormous boombox; Raheem also sports a four-fingered ring on each hand reading "love" on one and "hate" on the other (a clever nod from Lee to Robert Mitchum's character in *The Night of the Hunter*). There's Mookie's girlfriend, Tina (Rosie Perez, in her first film role. Lee had seen her dance at his birthday party, and was impressed not only by her moves, but her attitude. Perez opens the film with an energetic and combative dance over the opening credits.). Tina has an infant son by Mookie, and is frustrated that he isn't spending more time with his baby, or trying to make more of an income. We meet Mookie's sister, Jade (Joie Lee, Spike's real-life sibling), trying to advance herself in life with quiet dignity and education. Over here is Smiley (Roger Guenveur Smith), a disabled man, hawking pictures of Malcolm X and Martin Luther King, which he hand-accents and sells.

But most of the action centers from and around the pizzeria where Mookie works: Sal's Famous Pizzeria, which Sal (Danny Aiello) has owned and run for 25 years. Sal's two sons work with him, Pino (John Turturro) and Vito (Richard Edson). They don't live in the neighborhood, but they're an uneasy part of it. Pino, of the three, would probably self-describe as racist; he hates the neighborhood, hates its occupants, and wants his father to move the business to their own predominantly white neighborhood. Pino hates that his brother has befriended Mookie, which he sees not only as a betrayal of family, but of whites in general. Sal feels like he's earned a place in Bed-Stuy, but is only willing to reach out to his neighbors on his terms, not theirs. Buggin' Out loudly criticizes Sal's "Wall of Fame," on which Sal has exclusively hung framed photographs of famous Italians and Italian-Americans. Buggin' Out demands that Sal add pictures of Black heroes; Sal refuses, saying it's his restaurant and he can decorate it as he pleases. While Sal does have some affection for some of the neighborhood residents he's fed over the years, he reserves that affection for those who don't challenge him. Sal's racism would likely come as a surprise to him, as "some of his best friends...."

As the temperature rises on that summer day, so do tempers. Sal has already angrily refused to serve Radio Raheem until he silences his boombox, and Sal's earlier argument with Buggin' Out has sent the man around the neighborhood looking for support in either confronting Sal or boycotting his pizzeria. With Radio Raheem (and his boombox), Buggin' Out angrily returns to confront Sal, and with the tension rising, Sal takes a baseball bat to Raheem's music. Raheem goes after Sal, his sons jump in to defend him, and the police eventually arrive. When they do, the cops grab Radio Raheem in a chokehold, and kill him. Stunned, a crowd begins to gather (night has fallen, and Sal's is closed, he and his family having gone home). Some argue for justice, some for revolt, some for a protest, some for a safe return to their homes before giving the police more reason to attack. It's Mookie who finally sets the night in motion.

Grabbing a trash can, he hurls it through the pizzeria window. The crowd riots in anger.

It's a scene that honors the integrity of *Do The Right Thing*; Lee as a filmmaker isn't advocating violence, but he's not afraid to show us where hatred leads. Lee is putting on screen the frustration of the Black community; America won't listen if we speak rationally and respectfully (such as kneeling during the national anthem), but if we show our rage, America responds with violence. But it's better to let Mr. Lee speak for himself. It's worth sharing here in their entirety the two quotes Lee scrolls before our eyes as the film closes:

> "Violence as a way of achieving racial justice is both impractical and immoral. It is impractical because it is a descending spiral ending in destruction for all. The old law of an eye for an eye leaves everybody blind. It is immoral because it seeks to humiliate the opponent rather than win his understanding; it seeks to annihilate rather than convert. Violence is immoral because it thrives on hatred rather than love. It destroys community and makes brotherhood impossible. It leaves society in monologue rather than dialogue. Violence ends by defeating itself. It creates bitterness in the survivors and brutality in the destroyers."

Martin Luther King, Jr.

And,

"I think there are plenty of good people in America, but there are also plenty of bad people in America and the bad ones are the ones who seem to have all the power and be in these positions to block things that you and I need. Because this is the situation, you and I have to preserve the right to do what is necessary to bring an end to that situation, and it doesn't mean that I advocate violence, but at the same time I am not against using violence in self-defense. I don't even call it violence when it's self-defense, I call it intelligence."

Malcolm X

ᕙ ᕙ ᕙ

What struck me in my initial viewing (apart from the vibrant colors and in-your-face style) was the love in the film. Love of a neighborhood, love of community, love of history. The respect of a young man for the older voices in his life. No one can make a film this observant of human beings without love in their heart. I'm sorry I couldn't see it then, but I was heartened to see it now.

The Criterion edition is loaded with extras. Included with the two BluRay discs is a 100-page book, featuring not just an essay by Vinson Cunningham, but a generous excerpt from Spike Lee's director's journal. The journal is a fascinating filmmaker's document, in which Lee records his thoughts as he begins writing *Do the Right Thing* even as he's promoting his previous film, *School Daze*. We get to hear what's going through a filmmaker's mind as the script goes through revisions, as casting, location scouting, and pre-production are all ongoing. Lee felt it was important to get this next film out quickly - he felt pressure as a Black director to prove he could work as productively as anyone else. He also wrote about shopping the script to different studios, not so much worried about getting the best financial deal, but concerned about how the film would be marketed, and overcoming the fears and cowardice of white wealthy studio heads (both Lee's previous two films, *She's Gotta Have It* and *School Daze* were marketed as "Musical Comedies" to avoid audiences paying too close attention to racial issues). He was told more than once that studios were afraid *Do the Right Thing* would incite black Americans to violence. As if Lee were telling Black America something it didn't already feel in its heart and bones.

Other (filmed) extras, in addition to filmmaker/actor commentary, are several documentaries, a Cannes press conference, and the Lee-directed Public Enemy "Fight the Power" video (the song was written for the film itself).

Toward the end of the film, in the chat track, Lee asks a question I needed to consider back in 1989, and need to consider today about the destruction of Sal's Famous Pizzeria following the death-by-cop of Radio Raheem: Do find yourself saying, "Yes, Radio Raheem was killed, *but...*" when maybe you should be saying, "Yes, a pizzeria was burned down, *but...*"? Which loss really hurts us more?

La dolce vita

Italy, 1960. Directed by Frederico Fellini. 174 minutes, black and white.

La dolce vita has been a really hard film for me to get a handle on. It's a world away from the cinema we consume today, one that seems to shut out all but the most serious film scholars. It has a central character (Marcello Mastroianni's quintessentially cool Marcello Rubini), but it's a series of sketches and interludes, cutting through time. It's a film firmly fixed in 1960's Rome, a city torn between ancient and modern visions. It's also impossible to view out of the context of Italian cinema of 1960; a break from the neorealism of films like *Bicycle Thieves* and an Italy still recovering from both WWII and a fascist regime. And it's three hours long. It's a film that demands the attention of the viewer, and we're not used to that. (It also didn't help that this edition has no film scholar chat track to walk me through.) This was always what I called a "vegetables movie:" one I knew was good for me, but not necessarily enjoyable to get down. Honestly, I'd added it to The Collection years ago, mostly because I thought I should, as a student of film.

So, I wasn't looking forward to this. I made my first pass through it Sunday night, when I had three uninterrupted hours to try to get into it. The Gary Giddens essay that accompanied it, splendidly titled "Tuxedos at Dawn" turned out to be even more opaque than the film itself. But Giddens, at the end of his gushing and bewildering essay, gave me something I needed - a road map through the plot itself. And in it, I found one small detail I'd missed in previous viewings that snapped *La dolce vita* into focus, from a film-school monolith to a timeless human story.

The film is about fame, and society's feeding off it. Marcello, our guide, is a writer, but pens a gossip column, and he is as beloved as he is despised wherever he goes, which is wherever the rich and the glamorous are cavorting. (A photographer he collaborates with is named "Paparazzo," which is where the word "paparazzi" comes from.) The film opens with a spectacular image; against the backdrop of the ruins of a Roman aqueduct fly two helicopters. One totes a giant Christ the Laborer statue, and the one behind it contains Marcello and Paparazzo. As they pass over a skyscraper rooftop, bikini-clad women wave and cry, "Jesus, Jesus!" and then "Marcello, Marcello!" as if each are equally deserving of recognition. The scene sets the tone for what we're about to see - a series of scenes and images of satire that mock and castigate celebrity culture, the shallowness of the people at its center, and the price we as consumers pay for glorifying it.

For three hours. As a 21st-century American, you can see where my attention might flag. And why, over two hours in, I'd missed something crucial.

Interspersed with scenes of nighttime revelry with Marcello (dawn always sobers up the film's characters, and cleans their moral slates), we have interludes of his visits with Steiner, a philosopher, husband, and father of two children. Though Marcello claims he only sees Steiner rarely, Steiner is an important friend. Steiner truly seems to have found what matters most in life; meaning and a true human connection to his family. Steiner is the only character Marcello falls silent in the presence of, the only person deserving of Marcello's respect. Marcello's visits with him are outside of his usual life of glamor, and he does not feed off Steiner the way he feeds off others. So, two hours into the film, when Steiner is found to have committed a horrific act - he has shot dead his two children and then put a bullet through his own head - the film drastically changes tone. The scene where Marcello must break the news to Steiner's wife - she is walking home, surrounded by newspaper photographers and doesn't yet understand why - is both heartbreaking and obscene.

And from there, we drastically cut to Marcello at night, racing with his friends in convertibles through the streets of Rome. Previously, this is where the film had lost me. It seemed as if Marcello had shrugged off his friend's death, and we were returning to the sly satire we had been "enjoying" before. When Marcello ends up at the most decadent party in the film, it's just too much.

But here's what I had missed, and was alerted to thanks to Giddin's essay. That party didn't happen later that night, or even the week after Steiner's infanticide/suicide. It takes place years later. And Marcello is no longer writing a gossip column. He is now a press agent. Marcello, once wondering if he might someday move to write about something more important than celebrities, has now slid even further down the food chain. Without the lifeline of his friend Steiner, having been robbed of not just the man but everything Steiner lived for and cherished, Marcello has completely lost his way as a human being. Marcello himself has become a victim of that horrible event.

La dolce vita is a brilliant satire, and a monolith in cinema history. But after all these years, I finally discovered that at heart, it's a tragedy. And *that* is the handle that I finally found to this film after all these years. It took practice and attention, but I finally found the human story that Fellini was telling.

So, eat your vegetables!

Drunken Angel

Japan, 1948. Directed by Akira Kurosawa. 98 minutes, black and white.

Tonight's Criterion Tuesday selection is the first of what will be many from Japanese director Akira Kurosawa: *Drunken Angel.* Though this was Kurosawa's seventh film, he considered it the first film he made where he had full control over the production. It was also his first film with Toshiro Mifune (on my short list, along with Meryl Streep and Daniel Day-Lewis as one of the greatest film actors of all time). Included with the film are two chapters from Kurosawa's 1983 book, *Something Like An Autobiography* in which he writes about encountering Mifune for the first time, a few years earlier. The studio literally didn't know what to do with the young Mifune, who had answered a call for open auditions after working as an assistant cameraman for Toho Studio. Kurosawa writes:

> "On the day of the interviews and screen tests I was in the middle of the shooting of *No Regrets For Our Youth,* so I couldn't participate in the judging. But

during lunch break I stepped off the set and was immediately accosted by actress Hideko Takamine.... 'There's one who's really fantastic. But he's something of a roughneck, so he just barely passed. Won't you come have a look?' I bolted my lunch and went to the studio where the tests were being given. I opened the door and stopped dead in amazement.

"A young man was reeling around the room in a violent frenzy. It was as frightening as watching a wounded or trapped savage beast trying to break loose. I stood transfixed. But it turned out that this young man was not really in a rage, but had drawn "anger" as the emotion he had to express in his screen test. He was acting. When he finished with his performance, he regained his chair with an exhausted demeanor, flopped down, and began to stare menacingly at the judges. Now, I knew very well that this kind of behavior was a cover for shyness, but the jury seemed to be interpreting it as disrespect."

Mifune had more or less stumbled on method acting on his own, oblivious to Lee Strasberg and his disciples in the US. No one at Toho studios had seen anything like it, and the jury was about to dismiss him. But Kurosawa pleaded with the jury to accept Mifune, and the actor entered training and put a few films under his belt in time for Kurosawa to cast him as the volatile gangster Matsunaga in

Drunken Angel. It was to be the first of 17 films the pair made together, in my opinion the greatest director/actor collaboration in film history.

Kurosawa, if known at all to contemporary American audiences, is mostly known for his samurai epics, like *Seven Samurai*, which would place him (and Mifune) on the world stage six years later. But no less a film scholar than my own son pointed out that he feels a director's true talent shines in a medium-budget crime drama, and in watching *Drunken Angel* the viewer is drawn into a noirish post WWII Tokyo. "I wanted to take a scalpel and dissect the yakuza" Kurosawa said of this film, and in the process, the director cuts to the heart of urban Japan under the occupation of American troops (never pictured or mentioned due to rigorous US censorship, but underlying the film - more on this later). Takashi Shimura (another brilliant collaborator with Kurosawa; I'll write about him in a future essay) plays an alcoholic doctor, disgraced, yet continuing to minister to the needs of his community. Mifune is a mid-level crime figure who comes to the doctor for treatment of a gunshot wound, and is discovered to suffer from advanced TB. The yakuza's malaise is endemic in Tokyo - not just tuberculosis itself, but the rot going through Japanese society as symbolized by the sump in the middle of the neighborhood; a bubbling cesspit of refuse and disease. Nothing in the film happens far from this.

As much as Kurosawa was a student of Western literature (many of his later works would be based directly on the works of Shakespeare or Dostoyevsky), it's clear in this film that he places the blame for Japan's moral and cultural decline on the turning away of Japanese culture in favor of Western influences. All of this had to be slipped past not just one, but two US censorship boards. Initial notes on the script for *Drunken Angel* that the studio was required to submit included corrections that went well past political content, including a demand that the title of the film be changed for religious reasons. The only reason Kurosawa was able to skirt some of these demands was that the two US censorship boards famously didn't communicate well with each other, and by 1948 they were having trouble staying on top of the sheer volume of Japanese media. Reading and hearing about the level of censorship, one realizes it's absolutely no different than what Pathé Studios had to endure under Nazi occupation: the galling difference of course, is that in Japan it was being done under the name of furthering US-style "democracy!" It would be years before Japanese filmmakers would be able to truly speak with their own voices. Fortunately, skillful filmmakers like Akira Kurosawa found a way to speak "sotto voce" to their own people, and to the world a few years later.

One last note: The chat track on this version is unique in that the film scholar - Donald Ritchie - was actually on set during the filming of *Drunken Angel*. He was there as a guest of composer Fumio Hayasaka, who was also beginning a longtime creative collaboration with Kurosawa.

Dry Summer

Turkey, 1964. Directed by Metin Erksan. 90 minutes, black and white.

Sometimes you need to be brought up to speed on a film's place in its national cinema to appreciate what you're seeing. Sometimes, as with *Dry Summer*, you get pulled into a taut thriller from the get-go.

That's not going to stop me from sharing what I learned about Turkish cinema from the supplemental materials. Turkish cinema had been limping along for the first half of the twentieth century until the government gave a 50% off tax break to Turkish cinemas screening domestic films. That's all the shot in the arm Turkish filmmakers needed, as suddenly the demand for homemade films skyrocketed.[12]

---

[12] This is a common theme in international cinema, that domestic filmmaking thrives when the government steps in at the distribution level with support. And not just in the Third World. When the UK Parliament passed the Cinematograph Films Act in 1927, requiring British cinemas to screen a quota of British films, demand for domestic films took British cinema out of the

Director Metin Erksan, a film critic at the time, was one of a slew of young Turks[13] who were determined to bring social realism to the national cinema. Erksan, though, was hobbled (as he would be throughout his career) with Turkish censorship boards, both on grounds of prurience and fears that depictions of rural unrest would make the country look like a political backwater. But producer Ulvi Doğan reportedly smuggled the negative of the film into Germany in the trunk of a car, and entered it in the 1964 Berlin Film Festival, where it won the Golden Bear, an unprecedented honor for a Turkish film. The international acclaim made Turkish censors realize that perhaps a broader view needed to be taken to Erksan's film.

Dry Summer is a cinematic and fast-paced story of greed and obsession. Two brothers, Osman (Erol Taş) and Hasan (producer Doğan) farm tobacco in a rural Turkish village. Hasan is the younger of the two, dashing, generous, and warm-hearted, and in love with the beautiful Bahar (Hülya Koçyiğit). Osman, as the older brother, holds a position of authority in the family, but he is a thoroughly loathsome human being; so convincing was Taş in this role that it led to a successful career largely made up of playing gangsters, heavies, and outright villains. The film opens with Osman toting carpentry supplies from the town to his land. There is a spring on his land, and Osman plans to dam up the waters,

---

shadow of Hollywood, as the frantic production of "quota quickies" created jobs in the industry.

[13] See what I did there?

irrigating his entire spread, before allowing what's left to run off to the farmers below him. Hasan, realizing the blowback they'd get from their neighbors, tries to talk him out of this idea - "Water is the earth's blood!" - but Osman overrules him, blinded by the crops he'd be able to grow. Osman also insists that Hasan not follow Bahar's mother's timetable for their marriage and bring her to their home immediately (we find later that Osman is widowed), and though the couple are willing to do this, it creates bad blood with the new mother-in-law.

With Bahar in the house, Osman becomes fixated on her. On the couples' wedding night, Osman drunkenly bursts into the room demanding nephews from the couple, and he is always leering at Bahar, to the point of peeking through a hole in the bedroom wall. He is as coarse as he is bullying. Meanwhile, the neighboring farmers downhill from Osman band together against him, furious that he is hoarding what they consider to be a communal resource in the spring. The farmers convince local officials to order Osman to release the water, but when Osman hires his own attorney to aggressively appeal, these same officials return to oversee Osman's re-damming of the spring (it was this failure of local government that Turkish censors were worried about when they first saw the film). Hasan and Bahar, sympathetic to their neighbors, release water whenever they can, but Osman is quick to shut off the flow again.

The farmers, facing the loss of their crops, desperately take matters into their own hands, including sabotaging the dam. A furious Osman pursues them off his land, Osman firing at them in retreat with a rifle while Hasan merely brandishes the shotgun he carries. Osman kills a farmer with his rifle, and when the brothers are arrested, he bullies Hasan into testifying that Hasan held the murder weapon while Osman carried the shotgun ("You're young, they won't give you a long sentence, the time will fly by!"), and an obedient Bahar goes along with the lie.[14] Hasan is sentenced to eight years in prison, at first in the nearby jail, but soon to be transferred to a distant facility.

All the while Osman holds Bahar at his farm, intercepting and destroying all of Hasan's letters. When he hears that a man by the name of Hasan was killed at the prison, he tells Bahar that her husband is dead, but that she will inherit his half of the land if she stays. Meanwhile, Osman continues to ogle and fondle her, and as he practices a proposal to a scarecrow on his land, realizes she will never agree to marry him. The harassment proceeds to rape.

But Hasan isn't dead, and a new government has instituted a general pardon, which leads to his early release. Hasan has grown embittered with his brother, who never wrote or sent money as promised. The neighboring farmers, meanwhile, know that the wrong brother was sent to prison, and the attacks on the dam have turned into attacks on Osman himself, who is as desperately clinging to the water as he is to the stolen bride, and now patrols his own land

---

[14] Yep, at this time I was so caught up in the film I was screaming at my television, "DON'T DO IT!" Alas, my television never seems to listen, whether it's Criterion films, political ads, or Mariners games.

armed with rifle and pistol. As Hasan reaches home, a shocked Bahar fills him in on Osman's treachery, and he works his way through his brother's irrigation system, dodging Osman's gunfire, finally overpowering and drowning him. In the film's final images, as Hasan releases the waters for good, Osman's body rises to the surface and floats down the sluices to the farmers below.

Part of what makes this film so good is Erksan's attention to technique, particularly in the way he shoots the dominant Osman from below, and the farmers from above to reinforce their position. He's also clever at using visual cinematic techniques to tell his story; early on as Bahar playfully flirts with her lover, she uses a mirror to signal him from across a field, and we see the reflection play across Hasan's face. The two then search for each other in the dappled shade of a forest, light playing across their bodies as they seek each other out. But it's in the editing that Erksan shows his genius, as the film is unrelenting in its movement toward a showdown we know is inevitable from the start. Osmon covets. That's the center of his entire being, and as his coveting turns him into a monster, it also poisons those around him, seemingly, even the water. Erksan's editing pushes us ferociously to the final scene, as Osman's greed consumes him. It's easy to forget you're watching a film from another continent, another time.

Dry Summer, for all its recognition, was little seen in Turkey, and soon forgotten, and there's a story of "brotherly" betrayal there, too. The original negative never made it out of Germany, and Turkish audiences were denied the cut that won the

Golden Bear in Berlin. Instead, producer Doğan recut the film as soft-core porn, using a Hülya Koçyiğit look-alike to shoot sex scenes, and sold the film to the West titled, *My Brother's Wife*. Gradually, Erksan became disillusioned with filmmaking, and turned to writing and teaching. He died in 2012, but not before *Dry Summer* had come to the attention of Martin Scorsese's World Cinema Project through board member Fatih Akin, a German-Turkish filmmaker who recognized the importance of the work. In 2008, the film was restored (minus the opening and closing credits, which were never recovered) by the Cineteca di Bologna and The World Cinema Project, and Turks were able to see for the first time this groundbreaking film in its entirety.

Fanny and Alexander

Sweden, 1982. Directed by Ingmar Bergman. 188 minutes, color.

Fanny and Alexander was Bergman's last film (though he continued to work in the theater and for Swedish television for the next 20 years), and it's possibly his most personal. Bergman was emerging from a dark period in his life, a period of psychological depression. He had been in Munich in exile for four years, having been charged with tax fraud by the Swedish government. Eventually, Bergman was cleared of these charges, the Swedish tax office issuing a public apology for its overzealousness in the investigation. Bergman was able to return to Sweden, and began planning an epic film (a five-hour version was broadcast on Swedish television) in which he would once again work with the actors and crew who were a second family to him; Bergman even cast two of his own children in key roles. (One of Bergman's star actors, Max Von Sydow, was offered the role of Bishop Vergérus, but miscommunication between Von Sydow's agent and the Swedish studio prevented him taking the part.) Bergman intended *Fanny and Alexander* to be his cinematic swan song, and in it, seemed to work out his demons with his strict upbringing, as well as proclaim to the world his deep love of both film and theater. "The theater is like a faithful wife," goes the famous Bergman quote. "The film is the great adventure - the costly, exacting mistress.[15]"

Set in the transition from the 19th century to the 20th we meet the boy Alexander (Bertil Guve) in the opening seconds of the film setting up a toy theater stage. Fanny (Pernilla Allwin) and Alexander Ekdahl are brother and sister in a sprawling theater family. The film opens at the matriarch's opulent home, servants preparing the table and living quarters for a multigenerational Christmas Eve celebration, even as the theater's company is being lavishly and lovingly feted by the family. When the entire family gathers to celebrate, servants included, it's a formal dinner full of old-world tradition and customs, yet even so, the family members are joyful and full of familial warmth (even the theater-owner uncle's dalliances with the domestics are shrugged off by the women of the family). It's a home of generosity of food, ideas, and affection, and for Fanny and Alexander it's all about to change.

Their father, Oscar (Allan Edwall) suffers a stroke while rehearsing (a bit pointedly) a scene where he's playing the ghost of King Hamlet, and dies a few days later. Their mother, Emilie (Ewa Fröling), after a few months, marries

---

[15] According to Peter Cowie, when he asked Bergman years later if this was still true, Bergman replied, "No. Now I live in bigamy."

the clergyman who presided over their father's funeral, Bishop Edvard Vergerus (Jan Malmsjö). Hint: Anyone named "Vergérus" in a Bergman film, like the interrogator in *The Magician*, is going to be devilish in both temperament and function. He's a harsh, severe man, who requires his new bride and her children to come to his stark 15th-century home with none of their worldly possessions. Once there, he begins a brutal battle of wills with Alexander, who may have stumbled onto an old family secret. A central scene is a sadistic and formal "trial" of Alexander for the sin of lying, prosecuted by the Bishop while Emilie is away. It becomes clear to us - and to Alexander - that this is really all about humiliation and control. For the former Ekdahls, life is now a prison to be endured.

It's here that the film begins to lean into the fantastical. There is talk of ghosts haunting the childrens' new home, and both Alexander and his grandmother have interactions with what appears to be the spirit of Alexander's father. The children are spirited off to a puppet-maker's home (magically?); their savior is a friend of the Ekdahls and a Jew (not coincidentally revealing the Bishop to be a raging antisemite), a man apart from "normal" Christian society. Lost in its hallways at night, Alexander has encounters with its strange occupants, and perhaps God himself, eventually finding himself with the androgynous, secluded, and possibly dangerous Ismael (Stina Ekblad). Ismael seem's to assume Alexander has a connection to spectral forces, and through him seems to facilitate Alexander's wish for the death of his tormentor. Is this an admission by Bergman of spiritual forces beyond our world? Is this the intrusion of the modernism of a new century? Is this simply a child seeking an escape from a brutal reality (I can't help but think of Guillermo del Toro's *Pan's Labyrinth* as I watch this)? Or are we witnessing Bergman's coming of age and birth as a filmmaker, himself the victim of an oppressive father? Bergman seems to be spanning his career in the telling of this story: we open with the warm interiors of *Cries and Whispers*, segue to the starkness of *Winter Light*, and delve into the allegory of *The Seventh Seal*.

My second pass of the film is with commentary by Peter Cowrie, who seems to be Criterion's in-house Bergman scholar; I feel like I know him by now. Cowrie suggests that Alexander himself may have some sort of sensitivity to a more spiritual plane, as his father's appearances seem to be witnessed by Alexander with increasing frequency, and Alexander seeming to will the Bishop's death from afar. It's a fascinating notion, and one I think I'll take farther than Cowrie himself has. There's a scene in which Alexander tells his sister and one of the Bishop's servants a story about the Bishop's previous wife and daughter, who we found out drowned on the property. Alexander claims that the ghost of the Bishop's former wife told him that the Bishop killed them after they tried to escape after being locked up. Cowrie puts this down as Alexander's fertile gift for storytelling, but I think he may be telling the truth. Witness the Bishop's reaction as he's told the news; the second his servant leaves the room, a reaction of absolute horror crosses his face. I think he's been found out.

The film ends where it began, with Emilie and her children safely ensconced in the grandmother's home, at another feast in which two new babies are welcomed. An uncle gives a loving (and lachrymose) toast to the family he loves, and it's easy to hear Bergman's voice addressing his film and theater families in this scene. But in the final scene, Alexander is tripped up by another vision - this time that of the Bishop. Perhaps Bergman is telling us that old demons aren't so easily exorcized after all.

It'll be a while until we visit with Ingmar Bergman again. But I'm thinking of two weeks ago, when I watched Fellini's *La dolce vita*. In an interview, Fellini was asked which contemporary filmmakers he admired. Fellini was coy, saying he didn't have time to watch a lot of films. But after a few minutes, he mentioned two directors that he found to be "astonishing." One was Akira Kurosawa, director of last week's *Drunken Angel*. The other was Ingmar Bergman.

Fantastic Planet

France/Czechoslovakia, 1973. Directed by René Laloux. 72 minutes, color, animated.

This Criterion feature is... well, it's pretty trippy. It's also (at this writing) my lone Criterion entry in animated films, though I was surprised to see that Disney/Pixar offered up one from their vaults to Criterion, which is now publishing the underrated *WALL-E* in a Criterion edition (which I sadly won't be writing about, since I already have a copy on disc from its first release).

Anyway.

The 1973 animated film *Fantastic Planet* is psychedelic, radical, and - since the project took four years to develop - as much a product of the late sixties as it is the early seventies. It's an allegorical sci-fi tale; on the planet Ygam, a human-like race called the Oms are enslaved by blue giants called the Draags. The Oms are treated like pets (though without the dedication many of us treat our own), made to fight each other, and exterminated when their numbers get too high in the wild. When a little girl experiments with educating her Om the way Draags are educated, revolution is afoot.

Whatever counter-culture themes you're looking for, you can find in this film - the struggle against fascism, a plea for animal rights, an expose of genocide, technology vs nature - it's all in the pot. Or none of it is. Maybe it's just a children's story. Maybe it's a call to revolution. Maybe it's a hallucination. Help yourself, you'll find it here.

I read something really interesting in Michael Brooke's enclosed essay that I hadn't known. While the film is the product of French animators (René Laloux is the director), the French film industry had practically no funding for feature-length animation. Pre-1970 only a handful of French animated films had been produced, and they were exclusively children's fairy tales, or franchises like Asterix or Tintin. So, *Fantastic Planet* became a French-Czechoslovak coproduction, since Czechoslovakia had far more funding and infrastructure (mostly Ministry of Culture subsidized), and took animation a lot more seriously. This is not a film one would have expected to be co produced from behind the Iron Curtain at the time, so it seems especially radical knowing its pedigree. My guess is that like much of 1950s-era low budget science fiction, and most likely the whole of the animated genre, the film wouldn't have been considered worthy of attention by official Czech censors.

Let's talk animated films, and their print cousins, comic books. I facilitate a monthly online book club with some friends. The founding idea was not to have everyone be assigned the same book, but find their own books in a shared genre. I'd been frustrated by book clubs where we seemed to be reading the same types of novels month after month, usually assigned by the extroverts in the group. It felt too much like school work sometimes, too much like a chore. And inevitably, a book that had "changed someone's life" would read tedious to others, and you'd be in the awkward position of having to admit that someone else's soul-defining read was to you, a ream of shite. And I didn't relish the idea of bullying my friends into reading my biases any more than I especially wanted to read theirs (some of my friends I love best I know from experience I cannot trust with film or book recommendations, and I hold dear those rare friends - like my son and my buddy Cade - who seem to never steer you wrong). So the conceit behind this book club was that we would meet monthly, and each member could talk about a book they had chosen themselves from a common genre (say, "History" or "Romance" or "True Crime"), and give a little oral book report. That way everyone chooses their own book, no hard feelings if a title rubbed you the wrong way. We'd all get the benefit of finding out how broad these genres really are. And - and this was the best part - by choosing a random genre out of all the genres we could think of (any member is free at any time to suggest a genre I'll throw into the "Bucket O' Genres, a tin *The Force Awakens* popcorn tub I picked up at my local suburban Bijou), sooner or later each of us is reading a book outside their comfort zone.[16] That became the

---

[16] For me it was "Romance" and I'm proud of myself that I did it right. Instead of downloading a title onto my e-reader, or even consulting the staff at my local independent bookstore (shoutout to Browsers Bookshop in Olympia, WA!), I went straight to the source: the paperbacks aisle of my local chain supermarket, and grabbed one with a hunk on the cover. I was dying of curiosity;

name of our group: the Discomfort Zone Book Club.

Wouldn't you know it (bear with me, there's a point coming), our maiden genre turned out to be "Graphic Novels." I'd been a casual consumer of the genre, but for several of our members, this was their first experience with comics, and a lot of them were amazed at the wide range they represented. Basically any genre you can find in a bookstore - Science Fiction, Fantasy, History, Biography, Queer Studies, etc. - you can find in a graphic novel. A ton of stuff for children, tweens, young adults, and full-fledged, ripened grownups. It's far more than superheroes; in fact none of our members chose a book in the superhero oeuvre. Do yourself a favor, walk into your local comic book store and do what I do. Ask the first employee that greets you, "What do *you* want me to read?" Leave with two purchases: the first one that the employee thinks of, and something you're drawn to yourself.

Animated films are the same way. Because they're thought of as entertainments for children, most of what's out there - apart from the over scrutinized Disney behemoths - is ignored by mainstream culture, and that is a breeding ground for *sotto voce* themes, characters, and discussions. So much of the things we really find interesting, the characters,

---

were these books PG-rated stories of chaste-ish reveries, or is Meemaw's dirty little secret off-the-rails hardcore porn? I had no idea, and this was my chance to find out. I chose *A Thorn in the Saddle* by Rebekah Weatherspoon (part of the Cowboys of California series, apparently). Even made myself read it in public. It was an education; actually kind of enlightening. And, no, I won't tell. You'll have to read one yourself.

the social commentary, the dreams, the yearnings, the personal stories fly straight under the radar in animated films. They're not just for kids, sometimes they're not even for kids at all. And above all, they're *beautiful.* They're art, after all. Don't believe me? Check out *Kubo and the Two Strings* from 2016. Or the 2003 *Triplets of Belleville.* Or even the classic Japanese manga *Akira* from 1988.

No chat track for *Fantastic Planet*, and the film is only 72 minutes (in contrast to the three hours of last week's *Fanny and Alexander*), so this is more of a confection. And it's a beautiful confection; I enjoy the low-budget, pre-computer, un-Disney artwork. A cool coda: The success of this film allowed Laloux to open up his own animation studio. While he never made another film this long or elaborate again, he enjoyed success, and spent his final years teaching and championing the work of a little-known Japanese animator: Hayao Miyazaki of Studio Ghibli.

The Furies

US, 1950. Directed by Anthony Mann. 109 minutes, black and white.

The Furies is a western directed by Anthony Mann, and stars Barbara Stanwyck and Walter Huston in what I believe is his last film role. Like the better-known director John Ford, Mann makes full use of location, but to a different end. In the essay that accompanies the film, Robin Wood writes that Mann was fascinated with Shakespeare's *King Lear*, and harbored an unfulfilled lifelong ambition to bring the story to screen. Mann doesn't bring the play to the screen, but he does seem to bring Lear himself, in the person of Huston's Temple Caddy "T.C." Jeffords, a vain and ultimately foolish ranch owner who cannot hold onto the kingdom he has built. Barbara Stanwyck plays Vance, T.C.'s equally strong-willed daughter. What makes this western unusual is it brings a woman's life and prospects front and center, in a genre that nearly always relegates women to virginal prizes, whores, or silent housekeepers. Vance has work of her own she wishes to do in her life, and is unwilling to let chance - or men - dictate it.

T.C. owns a sprawling New Mexico ranch in the 1870s that he has named "The Furies." T.C. is narcissistic, autocratic, and combative, but he does have a worthy opponent in his daughter, whom he loves dearly, partly because she's one of the only people in his life who's willing or capable of standing up to him. Together they run the spread, although they butt heads over the Herrera family, who are squatting on their land. Vance has a close bond with Juan Herrera (Gilbert Roland), whom she has known since childhood, and resists evicting the family. There's also tension between father and daughter over inheritance of the land. Vance knows that she's expected to marry, but seeks a suitor that will run the ranch as an equal partner after T.C. passes, if not leave her to manage the family spread entirely. T.C. isn't about to cede control of the ranch, and ties ownership after his death to his approval of Vance's spouse. You can imagine how this goes over.

Vance falls in love with Rip Darrow (Wendell Corey), himself no pushover, and a man who bears a grudge against T.C. over some land on The Furies he believes is rightfully his. When Vance presents Rip to T.C. as the man she intends to marry, T.C. offers Rip $50,000 to walk away from his daughter, and to Vance's shock, he accepts. Rip owns a saloon ("The Legal Tender") and uses T.C.'s bribe to open a bank next door.

Meanwhile, an interloper appears, in the person of Flo Burnett (Judith Anderson), whom T.C. announces he plans to marry (T.C. is a widower, and his former wife's room has been kept intact as a sort of shrine to her). Flo is a woman of some wealth from the East - a true outsider to The Furies who T.C. met on a business trip - and is straightforward about marrying T.C. for financial stability, even if she is fond of him. But she has seriously underestimated Vance, and when the couple break the news to her that not only are they to be married soon in San Francisco, but that they have planned an extended tour of Europe for Vance, that alone would be too much for her to take. But Flo also tells Vance that she has hired an outsider to manage the ranch in Vance's absence, and that this manager has been instructed to once and for all evict the Herreras. Vance, infuriated, hurls a pair of scissors at Flo, permanently disfiguring her face.

Vance races on horseback to the Herreras to warn them; in the meantime, T.C. is assembling a posse to confront the family. When the posse arrives, the Herreras hurl boulders down a cliff at them, and return the posse's gunfire; Vance fights on the side of the Herreras. Eventually, they are forced to surrender. But instead of being content to oust the family, T.C. - out of either feelings of revenge or the need to punish his daughter for opposing him (probably both) - orders his men to hang Juan. It's the last straw for Vance, and in one of the greatest scenes of familial rage and betrayal ever filmed - seriously, it's that good - Vance swears that she and her father are now enemies, and she will loathe him for the rest of her life.

But T.C. does have an Achilles heel, one his arrogance has provided. Though rich in land, throughout his life he's been at times cash poor, and during those times has printed up "T.C. notes" with which he has often paid employees and used to settle bills. Essentially, they're IOUs, and whether they've sufficiently substituted for legal tender in the ranch environs, or (more likely) T.C.'s employees and creditors simply had no choice but to accept them, there are a *lot* of T.C. notes in circulation. Enlisting the help of Rip and his new bank, Vance begins traveling the West, buying up all the outstanding T.C. notes she can find (probably for less than face value). This begins to seriously devalue T.C.'s wealth, and faced with losing The Furies, T.C. turns to Flo for a loan. Calmly and rationally, Flo turns him down, telling T.C. that since her disfigurement has made her unpresentable, she has only her own modest wealth to fall back on. The marriage is off. It's a scene that earns her not only T.C.'s grudging respect, but the audience's. T.C. can't argue with her logic, but soon hears of an "Angel investor," a wealthy Californian who is willing to loan T.C. the funds to save his ranch. Returning to The Furies to collect his loan at the bank, he finds that the mysterious investor is actually Vance, who pays him $140,000 in now-worthless T.C. notes. T.C., financially at least, is finally broken.

Where Ford used the western to play out American mythological archetypes, Mann goes Freudian, and this is one of the things I love about genre pictures, how different filmmakers paint such different colors using the same palette. Father and daughter fiercely love each other, respect each other, and ultimately go to war with each other, and they relish in bitterly salting the battleground between them. In obsessively loving/destroying each other, each of them causes real damage (emotional, physical, and lethal) to those close to them. Both actors are up to the task, and it's a joy to see their performances.

This is one of three Criterion films I own that includes the source novel along with the film (the other two are *The Man Who Fell to Earth* and *Ugetsu*), and I made time to read Niven Busch's book over the weekend. (He also wrote the novel *Duel in the Sun*, which King Vidor made into a garish melodrama that Martin Scorsese remembers seeing as a young child, his first real exposure to sex, violence, and Technicolor Gone Bad. You could accurately call it the *Gone With the Wind* of westerns, in equal parts admiration and disgust. But I digress.) I wish I hadn't read it before this viewing; I think I would have enjoyed the film more. It isn't just that the novel had more time to play out the battle between the two, or that the prohibitive Hayes code had defanged much of the violence and scandal in the book, weakening both principals. But I think some poor choices were made in the adaptation of the screenplay; one the twist at the end of Vance's financial retribution that in the book, comes as much as a surprise to the reader as it does to T.C. The other is a reconciliation in the final scene of the film that belies all the passion the father and daughter held for each other, as well as Vance's independence. I suspect the studio had something to do with the latter.

P.S. It's the cinephile's curse/delight the rabbit holes a film can send you down; the chat track on this film introduced me to the wonderful *Westward the Women*, directed by William Wellman. It's another rare Western featuring strong women, and is welcome to those of us who enjoy more honest representation in genre films.

Gate of Hell

Japan, 1953. Directed by Teinosuke Kinugasa. 89 minutes, color.

This week's Criterion Tuesday selection is the sadly neglected *Gate of Hell*.

Gate of Hell enjoyed critical acclaim on its release; it won the Grand Prix at the Cannes Film Festival in 1954, and Oscars for Best Foreign Language Film and Best Costume Design. This was also one of Japan's first color films, and director Teinosuke Kinugasa was eager to experiment with the new technology to bring to life a famous episode from Japan's medieval past: the Heiji Rebellion of 1159-1160. It's also possible (though I can't pin this down) that you could consider *Gate of Hell* to be an adaptation of one of the earliest graphic novels ever published. Perhaps I should explain.

A bit of Japanese history, first. Though Japan was still technically under the rule of an emperor, each emperor relied on powerful families to carry out his rule; this was to be a time of the rise of the Samurai or warrior class. In 1156, Emperor Go-Shirakawa had emerged victorious from a previous rebellion, and immediately decreed all Japanese lands to be his property; his right-hand man Shinzei would enforce the decree. What kept other families from immediately rebelling was an understanding that though "ownership" of their lands may technically fall to the new emperor, de facto ownership - the right to control their land and occupants with their own samurai - would be retained by each clan. But it was also a time of shifting political winds, the emperor's reign was fairly new, and factions began to form. So even if individual clans pledged loyalty to the throne, they might find themselves in opposition in claiming themselves as the true stewards of the emperor and his lands.

One of these factions, led by Fujiwara Nobuyori in alliance with the warrior Minamoto Yoshitomo, attacked Sanjo Palace, stronghold of Shinzei forces and the now retired Emperor Go-Shirakawa and the current Emperor Nijo (Go-Shirakawa's previous first prince). Shinzei escaped, but the palace was laid waste to, the emperors captured (or "rescued," depending on who you sided with), and the residents massacred. This attack was depicted in a 23-foot scroll painted a century after the Rebellion. Reading right to left, the scroll is intended to be unfurled in sections, and contains text and artwork describing the battle. Among the events depicted were women of the palace jumping into a well as a hiding place; so many sought refuge there that those at the bottom were drowned, those in the middle suffocated, and those on top burned to death. The scroll depicts the conquering army mowing down fleeing palace occupants with a fusillade of arrows. Even today the artwork is impressive, combining the sweep of battle with smaller portraits of combat (the scroll itself currently resides at the Museum of Fine Arts in Boston).

You can see the intent during the opening credits; images from the scroll depicting warfare in fiery reds and yellows dissolves into full-color live action. The entire look of the film is built around the art direction, and it works masterfully - the color palette is bold without being garish, and the green of the Japanese mountains set against a clear blue sky brings the past to life. It works both as an homage, and a contemporizing of the artistry of the scroll.

Ironically, that became the reason the film was forgotten for so long. Kinugasa used a new Eastman Kodak single-strip negative, designed in 1950 to be an inexpensive and convenient alternative to Technicolor. The film delivered on what it promised, but was found to have a much shorter shelf life. Before the decade was out, prints of *Gate of Hell* began to fade, and audiences were left with a pale version of what they might have seen in the film's first release. Though *Gate of Hell* would be a superior production even had it been filmed in black and white, it was known for bringing color to Japanese cinema, and was forgotten quickly. Fortunately, one of the things Criterion is serious about (and why their editions tend to be a little pricey) is restoring film. They took a new digital master created in 2K in 2011 by the National Film Center of the National Museum of Modern Art in Tokyo, and supervised a new 4K master under cameraman Fujio Morita from 35mm duplicate negatives and prints. The result is breathtaking, and I'm sure the equal of what 1953 audiences would have enjoyed.

The story is loosely based on the pandemonium of that day, and includes people and events not recorded on the scroll (but since the scroll itself isn't considered a historical document, the license is permitted). The film follows a warrior, Morito (Kazuo Hasegawa) who volunteers to guard Kesa (Machiko Kyô), a lady-in-waiting for the empress, who will flee the palace in a royal carriage in an attempt to draw the invading army after a decoy.[17] The strategy is successful, and during it, Morito proves to be a valiant warrior, fearless in defending Kesa, even to the point of attacking his own brother, who has sided with the invading army. He is the pinnacle of military virtue, but we begin to see a much darker side. Morito becomes obsessed with Kesa, and demands his general to intercede to allow Morito to take her as his wife, in recognition of his bravery. Problem is, Kesa is already happily married to Wataru (Isao Yamagata), a palace guard, and is horrified by Morito's increasingly aggressive advances and threats. Eventually, she sacrifices herself to save her husband. As Stephen Prince points out in the accompanying essay, it's an interesting theme for a post-WWII Japanese film: the honor of military service usurped to an ugly end. Art direction aside, the drama is compelling, and I'm glad this film has been restored so that audiences may enjoy it again.

---

[17] This may be based on a bit of historical fact. Emperor Nijo was said to have had feminine features, and the invading army disguised him as a woman being "rescued" from Sanjo Palace in a carriage. It's said that the disguise fooled at least one opposing samurai, searching for the retired and reigning emperors.

Gilda

US, 1946. Directed by Charles Vidor. 110 minutes, black and white.

"This is the part I really like. This is when she does that shit with her hair." - Red (Morgan Freeman)

Gilda, starring Rita Hayworth, Glenn Ford, and George Macready is an amazing film, with one foot in the 1940's big-studio musicals, and the other firmly in new and unknown territory: Film Noir. According to Sheila O'Malley's essay "The Long Shadow of 'Gilda'," American film reviewers were lukewarm about it (honestly, I don't see how) but French filmgoers, starved of most American films during the war years, were astonished at the darkness, cynicism, and sexuality the post-WWII years brought them. According to Raymond Borde and Etienne Chaumeton in their 1955 book, *A Panorama of American Film Noir (1941-1953)*, "With little news of Hollywood production during the war, living on the memory of Wyler, or Ford and Capra... French critics could not absorb this sudden revelation." But they knew they were seeing something remarkable and ground-changing, even if we hadn't noticed.

But it's hard for this film not to leave an impact, even today, even looking back through the lens of classic noir. The film is brazen with sexuality and passion - a film whose characters don't find their passions kindled with love, but with hatred. You could call it a love triangle (or "passion triangle"), but as smoldering and coyly aggressive as Hayworth's Gilda appears (and this film deservedly rocketed her to stardom), sometimes it's the two male leads whose hatred for each other consumes all the oxygen in a scene. "Hate can be a very exciting emotion. Very exciting. Haven't you noticed that?" These lines appear twice in the film, just in case we weren't paying enough attention.

Let's have a bash at a plot synopsis, shall we? Johnny Farrell (Ford) is an American expatriate, seemingly on the drift in Buenos Aires. Johnny is cleaning up in an alley craps game; never a good idea when you're alone in a foreign city. For his pains he's ambushed as he's leaving the alley, but due to the kindness of a passing stranger (and a dagger Johnny's rescuer keeps in his cane), Johnny is able to retain both his winnings and his life. The stranger is Ballin Mundson (Macready), who tells Johnny about a casino in the city, and that Johnny should check it out some time, though Ballin warns him against trying to cheat there. Johnny seems to accept this as a personal challenge, and enjoys a run at blackjack, after insisting on cutting the deck before each deal. It's not long before Johnny is flanked by a couple of the casino's torpedoes, who whisk him to a visit with the owner, who turns out to be the cane-wielding Ballin. Ballin (like Lyndon Johnson) seems to think it's better to have Johnny inside the tent pissing out than outside the tent pissing in, and besides, he kinda respects the guy, so Ballin offers Johnny a job managing the place.

Ballin leaves Johnny in charge of the casino, and when he returns, enter The Dame. Ballin has not only met a woman, Gilda (Hayworth), on his trip but married her. It's clear when Johnny meets her that there is history between the two, but both keep this quiet from Ballin. Gilda clearly enjoys the high life of Buenos Aires, and takes a sadistic pleasure in aggressively chasing after the men in the casino. Johnny knows that part of his job is to protect his boss's reputation, so whether Gilda does this to torture Ballin or Johnny isn't clear; most likely she gets her kicks from giving both men fits.

But life is about to get even more complicated for Ballin. He's been working with some German mobsters who have had to stay in the background while the Allies are still at war with Germany, so they financed a tungsten cartel (yeah, I don't know, either) putting everything in Ballin's name. Now that the war is over, the Germans are ready to have ownership transferred to them, but Ballin isn't having it. In a confrontation with the Germans, Ballin kills one of them, and Johnny spirits Gilda back to her place to keep her safe.

Johnny and Gilda have it out; whatever history the two have, it didn't end well. After declaring their mutual hatred of each other, the two clench and kiss. Passion - of any kind - begets passion. But Ballin has observed all of this. Johnny, feeling guilty, escorts Ballin to a waiting airplane to make his escape. But shortly after takeoff, the plane explodes.

Gilda inherits everything, and Johnny marries her. But unbeknownst to Gilda, Johnny hasn't married her out of love, but to punish her for her infidelities to Ballin. Johnny will have nothing to do with his new bride, but when she inevitably seeks entertainment away from Johnny, she discovers he's having her tailed by a private detective to break up every rendezvous she attempts. She tries to get out of the marriage, but Johnny won't let her off the hook.

Re-enter Ballin. Turns out he faked his own death by parachuting out of his plane before it exploded as a neat way of avoiding the German mob. But he's come back to exact his revenge on both Johnny and Gilda. Ballin is about to shoot the pair when he is fatally stabbed by the bartender, Uncle Pio (Steven Geray), who has befriended Johnny during his time at the casino. When the police arrive, Johnny tries to take the fall, but the cynical Detective Obregon (Joseph Calleia) points out that Ballin was already "dead" and makes no arrest. Gilda and Johnny reconcile, though for how long is anybody's guess.

Gilda is equal parts *Casablanca*, *Public Enemy*, and *Chinatown*. From the opening scene (a dice roll tumbling straight toward us, from a greasy-looking Glenn Ford on his knees in a faceless hostile crowd) to the last (a farewell that might suggest a happy ending, but only if you're a sucker), this film breaks molds. You can absolutely see why the prisoners in *The Shawshank Redemption* couldn't get enough of *Gilda*.

Richard Schickel did the commentary track, and I was curious to hear his voice after growing up reading him in

Time magazine. For the first time, however, I bailed on the commentary track after 45 minutes. Schickel was awful. He was sleepy, lazy, and came across as unprepared and disinterested. He can't even seem to work up any enthusiasm for the film, much less his listeners. Dry I can handle, but this was borderline insulting, especially compared to the great chat tracks I've heard. But there's a short interview with Martin Scorsese and Baz Luhrmann talking about the film. Terrific!

Gimme Shelter

US, 1970. Directed by Albert Maysles, David Maysles, and Charlotte Zwerin. 91 minutes, color.

Today's Criterion Tuesday selection is *Gimme Shelter*, the first documentary in my Criterion pilgrimage. The film set out to chronicle the Rolling Stones on their 1969 US tour, but fate - along with brilliant directorial and editorial decisions and attentive camerawork - conspired to make *Gimme Shelter* a definitive documentary of the 1960s. We begin at Madison Square Garden in New York, Mick and The Stones amped, energetic, and the undisputed Greatest Rock and Roll Band on the planet. We end up at the Altamont Speedway in San Francisco, horrified along with the band as the Hell's Angels they invited as security stab and beat to death Meredith Hunter, an 18-year-old Black man (who had pulled a gun - whether out of aggression or self-defense, we'll never know). If I had to choose between the two most influential rock and roll documentaries to come out of the '60s - this and Michael Wadleigh's *Woodstock* - I think *Gimme Shelter* better captures the violence and disillusionment that overtook the Hippie optimism that began the era.[18]

The filmmakers start us off with the Stones performing "Jumping Jack Flash" at MSG, and if all you wanted was a concert film they could have done no worse than keep the cameras there. But after that number, the crowd noise still in our ears, we cut to Mick Jagger in an editing bay, wincing and wordless as he views footage of the Altamont concert that we as viewers haven't seen yet. In an instant, we're in a "making of" documentary, and the reflection of the violence in Jagger's and Bill Wyman's faces lets us know that this will not end well. The concert at Altamont was free; the Rolling Stones had been criticized in the press for high ticket prices ($15!), and whether in answer to that or a desire to give something back, a San Francisco free concert was hastily arranged. There's footage of Melvin Belli (yes, the same attorney who defended Jack Ruby and built a career out of Hollywood clients), scrambling to find a venue that would hold the 300,000 eventual attendees. It was all put together on the fly, and how the California Hell's Angels came to provide "security" is in dispute. Sonny Barger, in an essay included with the disc, bitterly castigates the Rolling Stones for indifference to their fans, and insists "I ain't never been nobody's cop!" He protests that all the violence wreaked by his gang was in defense of people sitting/standing on their motorcycles. But this is belied by footage that shows a

---

[18] Want a fun fact connecting these two documentaries to East Coast/West Coast filmmakers? Martin Scorsese was an assistant editor on "Woodstock." George Lucas did some camerawork on "Gimme Shelter."

procession of Hell's Angels riding their bikes to the stage, parting the crowd like the Red Sea, and then joining the band onstage, clearly in close consultation with Jagger and stage personnel. The Stones, for their part, were certainly naive about who they were working with, though other supplemental materials suggest that British Hell's Angels were of an entirely different character; more about counterculture than violence. Even without the benefit of hindsight, it was an extraordinarily bad decision. Members of the infamous motorcycle gang are seen drugging just as hard as the concertgoers. And as the violence unfolds, the viewer can see the realization hitting the faces of the band while onstage, as well as watching footage: "We're complicit in this.[19]"

---

[19] Listening to the chat track, a lot of the "arrangement" with the Hell's Angels becomes clear. The Rolling Stones had used British Hell's Angels (as I mentioned above, an entirely different culture) as a sort of "Honor Guard" escorting the band to the stage in Hyde Park in London. Stanley Goldstein (who worked with the directors and appears on the commentary track) believes this is what the Stones were expecting, not having had experience with the California Angels. In California, there was kind of a loose association between the Hell's Angels and concert promoters. The Angels liked to stake out territory at concerts near the stage where technical equipment was often kept. This territory they reserved for themselves, and other concertgoers entered at their own risk, often for their ignorance. People organizing concerts were well aware of this, and would often unofficially toss the Angels a case or two of beer. Nothing was said, but the unspoken agreement was the Angels wouldn't mess with the equipment (or technicians), and the concert organizers would let the Angels do

Besides Barger's piece, there are three more essays included, and in one by Stanley Booth I found something I might have missed underneath the weight of the Altamont story. The film does follow the band through other stops, including recording studios in Memphis and throughout the South, without detracting from the main narrative. Whatever else this documentary has become, it is also, and maybe primarily about rock and roll, and the music of the Rolling Stones. I'll let Mr. Booth close out this post:

"The Rolling Stones... worshiped at the altar of the blues. The Rolling Stones' audiences in 1969 did not, necessarily, worship at that altar. But by stopping in mid-show and turning off the electricity - as they did on that tour - to sing a song by Fred McDowell and another by Robert Johnson,

---

whatever they wanted there. The Rolling Stones hadn't toured in three years, and were probably unaware of both this informal arrangement and the nature of the stateside gang. So it's easier to see (without excusing this) how the Hell's Angels might have gained access to the stage if someone with the Rolling Stones had approached them before the concert. In addition, the main chapter of Hell's Angels (including their leader, Sonny Barger) wasn't due to arrive until closer to the time the Stones were due to take the stage. Hell's Angels "pledges," on the other hand, got there early to establish a presence. These "pledges," eager to show the gang that they were tough enough to make the gang, probably were even more eager to jump on the crowd than established Angels. It wasn't just Hunter who was beaten - there's plenty of footage of Hell's Angels members and/or pledges swinging around weighted pool cues they had brought with them. None of this excuses the violence, or the Rolling Stones' role in it. But it does make it easier to see how it happened.

the Stones showed where their hearts were: 'You may be high/You may be low/You may be rich/You may be po'/But when the Lord gets ready/You got to move.'"

Godzilla: The Showa-Era Films, 1954-1975

Godzilla, Japan, 1954. Directed by Ishiro Honda. 96 minutes, black and white. *Godzilla Raids Again*, Japan, 1955. Directed by Motoyoshi Oda. 81 minutes, black and white. *King Kong vs. Godzilla*, Japan, 1963. Directed by Ishiro Honda. 91 minutes, color. *Mothra vs. Godzilla*, Japan, 1964. Directed by Ishiro Honda. 89 minutes, color. *Ghidorah, the Three-Headed Monster*, Japan, 1964. Directed by Ishiro Honda. 93 minutes, color. *Invasion of Astro-Monster*, Japan, 1965. Directed by Ishiro Honda. 94 minutes, color. *Ebirah, Horror of the Deep*, Japan, 1966. Directed by Jun Fukuda. 86 minutes, color. *Son of Godzilla*, Japan, 1967. Directed by Jun Fukuda. 85 minutes, color. *Destroy All Monsters*, Japan, 1968. Directed by Ishiro Honda. 89 minutes, color. *All Monsters Attack*, Japan, 1969. Directed by Ishiro Honda. 69 minutes, color. *Godzilla vs. Hedorah*, Japan, 1971. Directed by Yoshimitsu Banno. 85 minutes, color. *Godzilla vs. Gigan*, Japan, 1972. Directed by Jun Fukuda. 89 minutes, color. *Godzilla vs. Megalon*, Japan, 1973. Directed by Jun Fukuda. 81 minutes, color. *Godzilla vs. Mechagodzilla*, Japan, 1974. Directed by Jun Fukuda. 84 minutes, color. *Terror of Mechagodzilla*, Japan, 1975. Directed by Ishiro Honda. 83 minutes, color.

Today's Criterion Tuesday selection started a few weeks ago. Yes, I am a Kaijuphile, and apparently so are the good people at Criterion, because this is a collection of the fifteen (!) Toho *Godzilla* films of the Showa Era (Godzilla films have spanned the reigns of three Japanese Emperors (so far), and these 15 films were released under Hirohito's reign, known as the Showa Era). My workday doesn't start until 11:30 AM, so it's been breakfast with Godzilla[20] for the past three weeks. Before I watched each film, I also read the corresponding chapter in David Kalat's *A Critical History and Filmography of Toho's Godzilla Series*. Blessedly, only the first film had a chat track (though both the Japanese and US versions are presented), which cut down on the March Monster Madness considerably.

Yes, the Godzilla films turned silly pretty much after the first sequel, as they became mostly aimed at children. My love

---

[20] And yes, it's fine to write and say "Godzilla" as the translation. It's true that the original film has been translated as "Gojira" in English, but translating Japanese characters into a Latin-script alphabet is more of an art than a science, and open to several methods. The "j" in "Gojira" is pronounced by the Japanese as a "dz" sound, and the Japanese language doesn't differentiate between the western "L" and "R" sounds anyway. So if you actually listen to the way Japanese actors pronounce the creature's name (as I have more times in three weeks than any human should have to), you will discover that "Godzilla" is a perfectly acceptable rendition into English.

for Godzilla came out of fond memories of the Saturday afternoon monster flicks broadcast on Channel 17 out of Philadelphia. But the first Godzilla movie was a dead-serious horror movie, and I'll get into the source material for that in a bit. But first you need to understand that almost no American has seen the same Godzilla films Japanese audiences have. To understand how different the American and Japanese versions are, you need to understand what happened to these films after they arrived in the United States, before they were sent to theaters or broadcast on television. To really appreciate that, let's look at a hypothetical example of how a foreign distributor might trash a beloved Western film:

Imagine you're an Iranian film distributor, and you've just acquired the rights to *The Fellowship of the Ring*. It's not a great print, it's got some scratches, and you certainly don't have access to the original negatives. You don't really know much about US or New Zealand films, and you don't much care; you just want Saturday afternoon filler for the local VHF station, or a second bill for the drive-in to attract teenage audiences (who you also couldn't care less about). Basically, you're looking for content. The first thing you do is start hacking the film down to a manageable running time. Now you're thinking that the film doesn't "flow" the way you want it to, so you begin rearranging the scenes. For example, you think the film would be better if it ended with Gandalf's battle with the Balrog, so you clap that scene at the end. But you still like the scenes where the Fellowship (or what remains of them) visit Galadriel, so those scenes are pushed earlier. You understand it won't make sense for

Galadriel to ask "What happened to Gandalf?" so you edit out those references, leaving your audience to wonder why Frodo and company feel such despair. Still, you don't think your audience will be able to relate to the story, so you add an Iranian narrator - someone Iranian moviegoers will recognize - and shoot a bunch of scenes with this narrator in the role of a scribe or whatnot, and splice these scenes in. These scenes, by the way, will be shot with entirely different film stock, lit differently, and generally stick out from the rest of the film. Oh, and now that you've added these scenes the running time is creeping up, so more original footage is cut, more shuffling of scenes.

You're happy that you've got an 85-minute product that will fit your time constraints, but the film you've got is in a foreign language: English (and Elvish, but you've probably cut all those scenes, anyway). You don't want to add subtitles, because even if you had respected your own audiences in the first place, you understand that they're not going to want to read through the trash you're subjecting them to. So you decide to dub it into Farsi. Forget the fact that "all dubbing is bad dubbing" - as David Kalat writes in his book above (and yes, I reread as I watched each film). You don't have the budget to hire A-list voice actors, and you don't much care anyway. So you replace Viggo Mortensen's, Ian McKellen's, Christopher Lee's, and the rest of the cast's voices with barely trained actors, some of whom sound nasally, or speak in monotone, or overact. Their lines in Farsi are poorly translated anyway; English phrases might be translated literally, out of cultural context of the Iranian viewer, or they may be mistranslated entirely. Oh, and since you've chopped the film up so much, Howard Shore's Oscar-winning score is no longer intact, and the continuity of his themes for different characters and places has long gone by the wayside. So you keep the title theme, but replace most of the other music with whatever music lies in the public domain.

This is exactly what happened to *Godzilla*. Ishiro Honda directed the original, and he was an established director with Toho Studios. He had learned his craft under the guidance of Akira Kurosawa, who was about to cement his status as Japan's greatest filmmaker with *Seven Samurai*, also released in 1954. This was a big-budget, major production, attracting acting and industry talent from among the best. Professor Kyohei Yamane, the lead scientist in *Godzilla*? He was played by Takashi Shimura, who had the lead in *Seven Samurai*. (Fun fact: The New York Times acclaimed Shimura as one of the greatest film actors of all time in its review of *Seven Samurai*. In their review of *Godzilla* they said, "no one in this film can act." Whether that's racism, the effects of the film's American mistreatment, or both remains a question.) Akira Ifukube, who wrote the music for the film was one of Japan's leading composers; for the rest of his life he considered the score to *Godzilla* one of his proudest achievements. The original film attracted the best of Japan's special effects artists. And before you laugh at the Guy in the Suit (Suitmation, as we Kaiju-heads like to refer to it), consider that you're probably remembering the old, reused suits sadly used in the sequels, when budgets were slashed.

The actor in a suit was deliberately chosen because filming a human-sized creature meant that the models of Tokyo could be larger and have more detail (and the model making is one of the highlights of the series).

So, Japanese audiences saw a different and better film than US audiences. So what? What did it matter?

To answer that, consider what had happened in Japan on March 1 of 1954, just months before *Godzilla* hit theaters, and less than ten years out from being the only people on Earth to suffer an attack of nuclear weapons. On that day, a Japanese tuna boat named "Lucky Dragon No. 5" was fishing outside of Bikini Atoll with its crew of 23 souls. That was the day that the US conducted a massive H-bomb test, just over 500 miles from Japan itself. The US had warned Japanese boats not to come near Bikini, but had never explained why, wanting to keep the nuclear tests a secret. (The Japanese later insisted the boat was well outside the limits; the US government disagreed - but fallout from the bomb spread far further than the US scientists predicted, due to the explosion measuring fifteen megatons instead of the expected six megatons. To me, that lends credence to the Japanese telling, along with the US insisting the fishing boat was a "spy vessel.") Sailors on the boat reported seeing a "second sun" in the sky before the wave of fallout hit them. All of the crew were burned brown with radiation, unable to open their eyes. The radio operator, Aikichi Kuboyama, became the first person to die from the blast.

Godzilla opens with the crew of a small fishing boat witnessing (though they do not know it) the "birth" of

Godzilla. They also witness "a second sun" in the sky. The first of their crew to die from exposure is the radio operator.

The original Japanese *Godzilla* is both a horror story and a morality tale. In the 1970s, Godzilla would come to be a protector of the Earth, but in this film he is a vengeful god. He is not only the product of nuclear weapons, but the Earth come calling to exact a terrible revenge for what we have wrought on the planet. He is also a metaphor for what the United States had done to the land and people of Japan. The original film is full of scenes of the human damage Godzilla has wrought, including a heartbreaking shot of a little girl, apparently unscathed, setting off a Geiger counter pointed at her as her mother holds her close. It's not silly, and it's not a children's film. It's why so many established Japanese film professionals were eager to work on the production.

And, yes, it all goes downhill fast in the 1960s. But even as the films get sillier and sillier (Baby Godzilla, for example, becomes the JarJar Binks of the franchise), there's something US distributors add to the films that is missing from every Japanese production. In most Godzilla films shown in the US, there is at least a discussion or a line of dialogue in which nuclear weapons are considered against Godzilla or one of his opponents. For the Japanese, it's a settled question. The only people to suffer a nuclear attack will never consider the use of nukes on their own soil, even if that decision amounts to destruction by other means.

I'm embarrassed to admit that I have many other Toho Godzilla films in The Collection, as well as several of the later US original productions, but since they're not Criterion versions, we're both spared from a further marathon.

One last note. There was something I appreciated in an interview on a bonus disc with Ishiro Honda, who directed eight of these films (besides the fact that the Japanese director interviewing him called Honda "sensei"). The Japanese film industry went through some tough times in the 1990s, and many Japanese filmmakers were criticized for leaving Japan for America or India at a time when they were seemingly needed in Japan. Honda was asked about this, and his response to these filmmakers is that they should always go where the work is. He told them that being Japanese, no matter where they were working, they would always bring their culture with them. They couldn't help but make "Japanese" films no matter where they were working. I thought that showed an extraordinary generosity of spirit.

Grand Illusion

France, 1937. Directed by Jean Renoir. 114 minutes, black and white.

Grand Illusion is the original prison camp escape film, but that's only a small part of what it is. It's an anti war film, but one that shows none of the horrors of combat - in fact the film was criticized by some at its release for not depicting the hardships of POW camps, but there's a reason for that which we'll get to in a bit.

Both the film and the filmmaking are set at specific times. The setting of the film is World War I, but at a time before America had become involved, when it was still a European conflict (as far as the actual fighting). This was not a war of demagoguery, but of class. The filmmaking was done in 1937, while war was brewing in Europe, but had not yet erupted, nor had Hitler solidified his grip on Germany. "Nor had the Nazis," said Renoir, "who almost succeeded in making people forget that the Germans are also human beings." It's important to keep these specific points of history in mind, because in them is what I believe to be the key to *Grand Illusion*.

During the first World War, two French aviators are shot down behind enemy lines; one is the aristocratic Captain de Boeldieu (Pierre Fresnay), the other the working-class Lieutenant Maréchal (Jean Gabin). They've been shot down by a German captain, von Rauffenstein (Erich von Stroheim, the great German filmmaker and actor). The German captain, upon return to his airfield, sends a soldier to find out if the enemy pilots are officers, and if so, to invite them to lunch. Over an elegant table, the two captains discover they know many of the same people, and von Rauffenstein expresses his regret that circumstances do not allow him to be a more gracious host.

The two Frenchmen are sent to a prisoner of war camp, where they meet a variety of countrymen. To pass the time, the prisoners stage a vaudeville - this shortly after learning the Germans have taken Fort Douaumont in the Battle of Verdun. But during the show, the prisoners learn that the French have retaken the fort, and Maréchal interrupts the festivities to lead the men in "La Marseillaise," for which he is thrown into solitary confinement (to add insult to injury, the Germans retake Douaumont during Maréchal's punishment). Upon his release from solitary, Maréchal and de Boeldieu assist their fellow prisoners in digging an escape tunnel, but before it can be completed, the prisoners are all relocated to other camps. Maréchal tries to alert an incoming British prisoner to the tunnel in progress, but the language barrier prevents word from getting through.

Maréchal and de Boeldieu are transferred through a series of camps before finally reaching Wintersborn, a mountain fortress at which they are reunited with two old friends. One is Rosenthal (Marcel Dalio), a fellow French prisoner from their first POW camp. Rosenthal, a wealthy naturalized French Jew, eagerly shares the food parcels he receives with his fellow prisoners. The other is von Rauffenstein, who is the camp's commandant. Having been wounded in combat, he has been promoted to this administrative post, and the German officer is despondent at being so far from battle. But he is cheered at being reunited with de Boeldieu; at last he will have a peer he can converse with. Still, he reminds de Boeldieu that escape from the Alpine fortress is impossible.

But de Boeldieu has noticed a flaw in the guards' training. Whenever there's a disturbance, all the guards run to the action, leaving the rest of the facility unsupervised. Selflessly, de Boeldieu makes an "escape" of his own, distracting the guards while Maréchal and Rosenthal climb out a window, down a homemade rope, and flee. Meanwhile, von Rauffenstein pleads with de Boeldieu to give himself up, as the French officer is leading the guards in a merry chase over the rooftops. de Boeldieu will not, and the German commandant shoots at the Frenchman's legs, before his men can fatally open fire. But his aim is off, and de Boeldieu takes a bullet in the abdomen. Heartbroken, von Rauffenstein moves the prisoner into his own quarters to nurse him. In his final moments, de Boeldieu laments that the upper classes have outlived their usefulness to society, and that dying in battle is the only remaining service the bourgeoisie can provide.

Maréchal and Rosenthal, having successfully broken out

of Wintersborn, now have a long and perilous journey ahead of them, and Rosenthal injures his foot, slowing them down. They'll set out on foot for Switzerland, but will need to evade German patrols in their flight. And when they arrive, exhausted and starving at a German farmhouse, they'll need to decide whether they can trust the sole occupant to keep them hidden....

Peter Cowie (who I've "met" before on Criterion's Bergman films) wrote the essay and provided the commentary on this disc. He writes that Renoir believed that the world was divided socially in horizontal, not vertical terms. Renoir once wrote "If a French farmer found himself dining with a French financier those two Frenchman would have nothing to say to each other. But if a French farmer meets a Chinese farmer, they will find any amount to talk about." This idea is at the center of the film; we see the French officers in the POW camp aligning with those who shared occupations and class; even a discussion about Paris restaurants quickly assigns the men into sub-camps ("Maxim's" is mentioned as a favorite of the aristocratic de Boeldieu, too pricey for others). But more than that, through meals placed near the beginning and end of the film, we see how class unites people across national lines. When von Rauffenstein hosts his French "guests" at his luncheon early in the film, the German and French officers are all bonded to each other by their military service, and von Rauffenstein immediately warms to de Boeldieu as a fellow aristocrat (later we find out that von Rauffenstein has also patronized Maxim's pre-war). Later in the film, when we find the two escaped soldiers welcomed to the table of a German widow and her toddler daughter, nationality becomes irrelevant as they repay her kindness by helping with chores around the farm. In the film, Renoir takes pains to portray the German guards as human as their prisoners, and given to acts of generosity, warmth, and respect toward their fellow soldiers. Civility still dominates a pre-Hitler Germany.

The film is also about art, and the power of the arts - how could it not be, as director Jean Renoir was the son of French impressionist Pierre-Auguste Renoir? The younger Renoir started his working life making pottery, but gave it up when he realized people were only buying his ceramics because of his famous father. In this case, it's music and theater that fill the lives of the men and help unite them. Two scenes in particular will be echoed by later filmmakers: the rousing rendition of "La Marseillaise" that must have still been ringing in Michael Curtiz's ears when he filmed *Casablanca*, and even a rambunctious "It's a Long Way to Tipperary" that I'm willing to bet Wolfgang Petersen was fondly referencing when he had his U-boat crew singing it in *Das Boot*.

But mostly, this is a film about love. Love between soldiers, and the sacrifices they make for each other, and love that cuts across lines of nationalism and even race. I recommend this one.

La haine

France, 1995. Directed by Mathieu Kassovitz. 97 minutes, black and white.

Mathieu Kassovitz's gritty 1995 drama, *La haine* (*Hate*) stands in sharp contrast to the other French films I've written about. Set in a contemporary urban environment, it's a story that will be all too recognizable to North American audiences.

La haine follows three marginalized young men (Vincent Cassel, Hubert Koundé, and Saïd Taghmaoui) negotiating life in the housing projects outside Paris. Over the opening credits runs real-life news footage of the death of Malik Oussekine, an immigrant from Zaire killed while in police custody, and the subsequent protests turned to riots as French police met protesters in the projects. What follows is twenty-four hours in the life of three young men, a white Jew, a Muslim, and a Black man, filled with rage, empty of hope, and in possession of a handgun lost by a cop during the protests. In the land of "*liberté, égalité, fraternité*" they find that they are not just unwelcome, but even closed off from Paris proper, and that the police prowl their own neighborhoods like an occupying army. It's a story that's instantly recognizable to 21st century Americans, and proof that while each nation has its own flavor of xenophobia, the suffering and rage that come out of trying to repress "the other" into substandard lives and housing is universal.

Like most people that have seen this film - even French audiences and international audiences in 1995 - I'd heard a lot about *La haine* before I saw it. On my first viewing a few years ago, I had trouble getting past the film's visual style and into the story itself - it doesn't help that all three of the male leads have unlikeable qualities, and won't settle into a "victim" mentality that might help white American audiences find a human connection (but certainly, that's part of the point, isn't it?). On this viewing, however, ready to look past the angry facade and anti-French New Wave filmmaking, I saw a lot more of the substance in the film, and found the camera movement and even the black-and-white cinematography used to further the message of the film.

Like Spike Lee with *Do the Right Thing*, Kassovitz's film premiered to accusations that he was stirring up trouble in the *banlieue* - the poor and majority non-white neighborhoods - as if those citizens didn't know full well what it was like to live there. That's not where the similarity ends; though Kassovitz in his commentary frequently cites (and the film references) Martin Scorsese, it's Spike Lee who is really evoked, through the film's stylish camerawork and hip-hop soundtrack. But references to many American gangster films run throughout *La haine*, even two sightings of a billboard featuring a view of the planet and the words, "The World Is Yours" à la *Scarface*. In his commentary,

Kassovitz explains that all young people in the *banlieue* have grown up watching American crime dramas, which inform them not only how to talk and act, but how to behave toward police. It's instructive, because with all their posturing and bravado about what Vinz, Hubert, and Saïd would do if they came across a gun (Kassovitz said in his commentary he kept the first names of his actors as characters so as not to confuse the crew), it turns out the three lack the malevolence of the French police in fighting back.

This wasn't the first French film that took the poverty and oppression of Parisian neighborhoods as its subject, but it opened a conversation in French cinema that other filmmakers eagerly joined; some similar in style, though even eventually leading to the superlative action franchise of the *District 13* films. Some have accused Kassovitz of exploiting the ghettos in *La haine*, but I think his pedigree says otherwise, as he told the British newspaper *The Guardian* in an interview on the film's 25th anniversary in 2020:

> "'I just wanted to make it easy for my father to understand what was going on in the projects,' he says. 'He didn't get why I was hanging out with black guys: "You're a little Jewish guy, what are you doing?"' Dad was the Hungary-born director Peter Kassovitz, his mum the film editor Chantal Rémy; Kassovitz grew up in central Paris, but gravitated towards the *banlieue* as a teen thanks to his involvement in the city's nascent B-boy scene. A small network of record shops and parties were

a mixing ground for all social classes, including middle-class kids such as Kassovitz and Cassel, whose younger brother Mathias was a founder member of NTM's rivals, Assassin.[21]"

Even though little seems to have changed in the *banlieue*, Kassovitz believes (as do I) that his film has made a difference, including in how the neighborhoods are policed. "If we didn't do what we did, it would be duck-hunting season. We created cop-watch. We got people on their toes, so that when they see a cop in the street [mistreating people], they say: 'You cannot do that.'" Reform is as agonizingly slow in Europe as it is in America; it's impossible to change generational and deeply entrenched attitudes with just one book, one film, one movement. But change can *begin* with a film, especially one that screams as loudly as *La haine*.

If this all sounds like a hard film to watch, it is. It may be reassuring to watch this film as an American and say, "See, these problems are everywhere," but I think that's dishonest and lets our own culture off the hook too easily. Instead, I think this film shows that herding your "lesser" citizens into lesser lives is a recipe for violence no matter what country you're in. It's also a lesson in rage, in listening to artists even as - *especially* as - they are making us uncomfortable. If we don't like to hear the kettle whistling, we'll like it less when it boils over.

---

[21] From "'It Was Our Life, But Larger Than Life;' How La Haine [sic] Lit a Fire Under French Society," *The Guardian*, May 23, 2020.

Hamlet (1948)

UK, 1948. Directed by Laurence Olivier. 153 minutes, black and white.

The DVD edition I have of Laurence Olivier's 1948 *Hamlet* is surprisingly light on extras: no chat track, no documentaries, only a brief essay by Terrence Rafferty.[22] So, even though I'm no Shakespeare scientist, I'm left to my own devices on this viewing, and since I'm a recovering English major from my life before nursing school, I know just enough to get myself into trouble. Still, I've gotta say, after living with this play for over 40 years, here's what strikes me on this viewing: Hamlet is kind of a dick.

Though the film was praised immediately on its release (it picked up five Oscars as well), critics have come to approach Olivier's *Hamlet* (as with all other screen versions) with knives out. Even at the time, it was noted that Olivier at 40 was a little long in the tooth to be playing the role

---

[22] It's also out of print at this writing on the Criterion website. I'm hoping this means a new version on Blu-Ray is in the works; Criterion does this from time to time. So keep checking their website!

(Eileen Herlie, who played Hamlet's mother, Queen Gertrude, was 13 years Olivier's junior, and Jean Simmons (Ophelia) was 18), and critics in subsequent years have compared this production unfavorably with Olivier's other Shakespeare films, *Henry V* and *Richard III*. But it's an incredibly tricky role to play, whether because of its complexity or - dare I say it? - flawed character construction by Shakespeare, and any actor taking it on is burdened by soliloquies that by now are familiar to the point of mockery. I challenge any actor to say the words "To be or not to be" as if they were fresh (which perhaps explains why so many film versions of this play - from Akira Kurosawa's *The Bad Sleep Well* to Michael Almereyda's 2000 *Hamlet* - are transposed into other times and places). As a director, Olivier makes a fascinating choice that does no favors to Olivier the actor: In several soliloquies, lines are presented in voice-over with the camera still on the character, as if thought instead of uttered aloud, and the challenge of reacting silently to an internal monologue is daunting, even for an actor - a Shakespearean actor! - as accomplished as Olivier.

And the character is fundamentally unlikeable. Though he's famously indecisive in how or if to avenge his father's death, he's quick to judgment in the way young adults tend to be (anyone who knew me at Hamlet's age can attest to my own arrogance). He's disdainful of advice coming from any quarter, seeking none, and is quick to mansplain to his elders - to the point of instructing a troupe of professional actors how they should ply their craft (one can imagine them thinking, "What *is* it with these court people?!" while they smile and nod). And there is no getting around Hamlet's brutal cruelty toward women - his treatment of Ophelia runs to sadism (or would if he considered her to be a human being, which he appears not to). His venom toward his mother similarly shows no thought to her own trauma; if Hamlet had thought that she had been in on this with Claudius from the beginning, his hatred might be understandable, but Hamlet never shows any indication he thinks this is the case. In fact, writing this now makes me wonder why Gertrude endured any of this from her brat. Guilt? Elizabethan propriety? Or *was* Gertrude in on the plot after all? Shakespeare himself won't say, and one might argue that our attention to the men in the play has pushed to the side the one woman who might shed better light on the whole plot. (Check out Tamara Tubb's insightful character analysis of Gertrude on the British Library website.[23]) Hamlet is both indecisive and arrogant, and balancing the two may be past all but the most brilliant of actors.

Olivier plays the character with distance, and Olivier the director often gives us distance from the action as well, throwing in God's-eye views of some scenes that take us out of human frame of reference. Olivier's performance and pacing seem to accelerate as the film goes on - only when Hamlet is given a clear plan of action does he snap out of his brooding. Hamlet's sword fight with Laertes in the last act,

---

[23] "Character Analysis: Gertrude in *Hamlet*" by Tamara Tubb. https://www.bl.uk/shakespeare/articles/character-analysis-gertrude-in-hamlet

I believe, remains one of the top movie sword fights of all time. And Olivier stages it with some wonderful scenes in deep focus that bring several characters into the frame at once. There's a brilliance in keeping the camera on Gertrude, poisoned chalice at hand, as we hear rather than see Hamlet and Laertes battling - the tension, even when we know the outcome, is palpable.

I didn't enjoy this as much as I thought I would, and I'm not sure why. Maybe it's coming to the play after a long absence - or at least this version of it; Branagh's sumptuous unabridged version is a feast in itself - or maybe I'm less intimidated by "classics" the older I get. Or maybe I'm a fool. What I would have loved from this film is a chat track by Kenneth Branagh; I'd love to hear his thoughts on Olivier as both actor and director, not to mention from one Shakespeare scholar on another.

Final thought: I remain convinced that the poisoned goblet was not intended as a backup in case Hamlet won the duel. The chalice was for whoever won. If it were Laertes, Claudius knew he was a loose end who would figure out how he'd been played sooner or later. Mrs. Claudius didn't raise no dummy.

Häxan

Sweden, 1922. Directed by Benjamin Christiansen. 105 minutes, black and white, silent.

I love silent films. I love watching filmmakers experiment with new technology, watching the ground rules of film grammar being shaped in real time, seeing directors loose themselves on material before genre boundaries have been clearly established. *Häxan*, a 1922 silent Danish film directed by Benjamin Christensen, occupies a space somewhere between Horror and Documentary, before either genre had been fully established with filmgoers.

Häxan (*The Witch*) begins as an exploration of the history of witchcraft in Europe. We start with still photographs, centuries-old illustrations and etchings of witches and demons, a kind of prototype PowerPoint presentation. But during the second chapter of the film (which is divided into seven sections), Christensen uses sets and actors to present recreations of what witches were accused of doing, their persecution by the Church, and even dream-like fantasies of their supposed supernatural effects and influences (the director himself revels in playing Satan). It's all going somewhere - by the end

Christensen purports to demonstrate that women accused of witchcraft were actually suffering from "hysteria" - but in getting there the film leans as heavily on lurid and sensationalist images as it does on investigative research. But what I found astonishing was how sophisticated not just the special effects were (especially the makeup effects), but how well Christensen had a handle on using the framing and editing of his images to tell his story. In one sequence we see an old woman accused of witchcraft tortured for a confession. The camera lingers on the instruments used, then holds only her face in close-up; something familiar to us today, but filmmakers at the time could only guess that early audiences were able to fill in the missing images on their own (they did). There's a clever "good inquisitor/bad inquisitor" scene in which this poor old woman is literally pulled from one frame to another by interrogators alternately cajoling and threatening her. It's terrific editing.

The film is credible in asserting that women (poor women, exclusively) were being preyed on by both a patriarchal church and state. Once an accusation was made, the entire system was rigged toward a guilty verdict, but not before it had "proved" its necessity by creating further accusations through torture (if you thought trial by dunking, where if a woman floated she was guilty and drowned if she was innocent was something just out of *Monty Python*, there's a text printed in 1486, *Malleus Maleficarum*, that proscribes this exact procedure). What's fascinating is that in the final section of the film, Christensen presents women suffering from "hysteria," a fairly new diagnosis in the infant days of psychology. What Christensen demonstrates (and

I'm not sure this is intentional) is that psychiatry has taken over the work of the Inquisitor. Once a woman is suspected of mental illness, nothing can shake either the medical community nor the courts of stepping in and taking away her freedom and autonomy. It's just the patriarchy spiffed up.[24]

Though *Häxan* is presented as an almost scientific document, the film certainly doesn't shy away from shock value. It was banned or severely edited by countries in both Europe and North America, intact copies disappearing almost as quickly as they were being distributed (which couldn't have been good news to its producers, as it was reported to have the highest budget of any Swedish film of the silent era). Here's Stephen Volk speaking to a BBC writer about the film in 2022:

> "'It is a visceral experience disguised as an erudite thesis,' adds Stephen Volk, noted horror screenwriter of the BBC's infamously scary Ghostwatch (1992), another horror masquerading as a documentary. 'I don't believe for a moment that the director's real motive was anything other

---

[24] I'd like to tell you that attitudes have changed, but there is still a long way to go. I started my nursing career as a psychiatric RN in the mid-1990s, and I can tell you that many health care providers (including myself as a new RN) tended to see the fact that they'd been admitted to our facility as evidence of mental illness. Thankfully, I've grown wiser over the years. Or more cynical.

than to shock, if not to rock the audience from complacency, as good horror does. A lot of guff is written about "cursed films" being "imbued with evil" – but with this one, you can almost believe that. There is something about the format that does that to you – the authenticity of an earlier era, I suppose.[25]""

In 1968 the film - or a version of it, anyway - was re-released in the United States under the title, *Witchcraft Through the Ages* by Metro Pictures Corporation. It was heavily re-edited, and added a jazz soundtrack and narration by William S. Burroughs. That version is included on the Criterion disc, and while it's a fascinating declaration on the state of cult films in the 1960s, it really does the original no favors, at least looking back from a 21st-century point of view. Scratch that: it at least brought *Häxan* itself back to the attention of the film world, and the Swedish Film Institute set about restoring the film no less than three times, in 1976, 2007, and 2016.

The print is absolutely gorgeous - actors really come to life in this edition, and it's worth seeing crisp and clean images when what most of us have seen of pre-1930 cinema is scratchy and herky-jerky. *Häxan*, whatever else it is (and this is seriously one weird effing movie), is the product of

---

[25] From "Why Documentary Horror Häxan Still Terrifies, a Century On" by Adam Scovell for BBC.com, September 28th, 2022.

artists. There's a beautiful score with it that reflects pieces chosen for the film's premiere by the director, for which Christensen hired a 55-piece orchestra (Criterion settled for 13, but it still sounds good).

Two fun facts: 1. The production company that made *The Blair Witch Project*? Haxan Films. 2. Knowing I'd be busy today, I watched this on my portable Blu-Ray player on a flight from Seattle to Philadelphia (with headphones), which is a great way to keep your seatmate from engaging with you.

High and Low

Japan, 1963. Directed by Akira Kurosawa. 143 minutes, black and white (with pink smoke).

Here's how *High and Low* begins:

A wealthy industrialist, Kingo Gondo (Toshiro Mifune), is hosting a tense business meeting in his spacious home, perched high in the hills above Yokohama. Gondo runs a factory for Japan's largest shoe manufacturer, and his fellow executives are demanding he switch from manufacturing quality footwear to a shoddier product with higher profit margins, or face expulsion from the company where he has worked all his life. Gondo angrily refuses and throws them out. The executives, furious, vow to expel Gondo from the company, and ruin him. But Gondo has a plan: He has accumulated more shares in the company than they realize, and has borrowed against every asset he has (including, as we find later, from organized crime) to raise enough money to buy a controlling interest in the company. His assistant is about to be dispatched with a check for 50 million yen to complete the deal.

The phone rings. Gondo's only child, Jun, has been

kidnapped. The kidnappers are demanding 30 million yen in cash within 24 hours for Jun's safe return. Gondo has nothing left to raise cash against. If he is going to pay the ransom on Jun, he will be ruined financially, thrown out of his livelihood, unable to pay back his debt (including to the Yakuza). But even if he pays, how does he know his son won't be killed anyway? Or if he pays, will police detectives be able to apprehend the kidnapper (and the money) in time to save Gondo's career? And if he refuses, how will the buying public react to a man who sacrificed his son to save his business?

As we begin to consider these questions, Gondo's son runs into the living room. He has not been kidnapped after all; his playmate, Gondo's chauffeur's son has been mistakenly snatched in Jun's stead. The phone rings again; the kidnapper has realized his error, but the deal is still on - 30 million yen or young Shinichi dies. Now we begin the ethical calculus all over again. Is the value of a loyal employee's family the same as Gondo's own flesh and blood? If Gondo was willing to face financial ruin for his family, does he owe that to a servant's family as well?

The source material for this film was a novel from Ed McBain's "87th Precinct" series, *King's Ransom* (1959), but Kurosawa departed from the novel almost immediately after the premise. *High and Low* (released internationally as *Heaven and Hell*) is nothing more and nothing less than a police procedural, but working within that genre framework, Kurosawa gives us a brilliant treatise on classism, the Americanization of Japanese culture, and filmed storytelling itself. Let's start with that last bit first.

Kurosawa shot *High and Low* in Tohoscope, Toho studio's anamorphic widescreen answer to Hollywood's Cinemascope. This would seem an odd choice for a film set for a full hour in a domestic living room, and the claustrophobic interior of a high-speed train; after all, we're used to seeing western vistas and Biblical spectacles on a screen this size. But Kurosawa, like a stage director using his performance area, fills each section of every frame with information. In one scene, Kurosawa goes in tight and claustrophobic in order to bring our focus on the faces of three people receiving information. Gondo's chauffeur, Aoki (Yutaka Sada) is almost always in frame, whether foreground, midground, or back; we can't escape him any more than Gondo can. And to capture all this, Kurosawa used two cameras. The first was set low on a dolly (the actual set was raised, as if a stage), to sweep across and capture the action at low angles. The second camera was on a crane dolly, designed to move vertically as well as horizontally. In one of two essays included with the disc[26] Donald Richie, present at filming, writes about the camera rehearsals Kurosawa conducted, after the actors had rehearsed and blocked their scenes. Most directors do most of their scene-building in the editing room, using footage from whatever cameras were shooting. Kurosawa wanted to be sure each frame carried as much information as possible, so when a character moves, he wanted the camera to move with them, while keeping the

---

[26] The other essay, by Geoffrey O'Brien, is full of smart-sounding criticspeak, and (I think) mostly opaque.

other characters in shot. The results pay off. You have scenes of Gondo meeting with family, or with creditors, with police included in frame at a respectful distance. There's a scene with Gondo in the background, mulling his choices, while in mid- and foreground, five different activities are taking place from five different characters. The effect is to make this spacious room cramped and claustrophobic, and Kurosawa could not have done that with a smaller aspect ratio. Or without scrupulous planning and rehearsal. And then to follow up the challenge of a relatively static stage piece with nine (!) Tohoscope camera operators chasing actors around the inside of a high-speed train - no stage sets, Kurosawa shot this in a real moving train - results in one of the most kinetic scenes in cinema. (Kurosawa said that he liked to use just two cameras because it was difficult to keep the spatial relationships between actors and cameras straight with more than that. One can imagine nine cameras on a moving train was a feat closer to a Bach fugue than a movie shoot.)

Again, *High and Low* is a police procedural, and a tense one at that, and without shortchanging the genre, Kurosawa speaks volumes about contemporary Japan. The title refers concretely to the physical positioning of the main characters. The industrialist, Gondo, lives high, in a "heavenly" space above the city, isolated from the lower classes. In the city it is sweltering; not so for Gondo, who keeps his windows closed because his home is air-conditioned, a luxury as yet unavailable to the middle and lower classes. The kidnapper needs only lift his eyes to see Gondo's palatial home - as the rest of Yokohama - and as Kurosawa drops his Tohoscope cameras into the city slums and even into the police station, the screen is filled with desperate, sweating crowds. Even one of the cops remarks that it's easy to feel contempt for the industrialist's house viewed from 100-degree hell.

But even Gondo's social strata have layers within it. After all, he's fighting the other executives of the National Shoe company over old-fashioned craftsmanship. He despises their willingness to put out a disposable product for a greater profit margin. Gondo, though a wealthy man, comes to stand for the traditional values of the craftsman. When the police need to rig a pair of valises with a chemical pellet that will release pink smoke when burned, Gondo has his old tool kit brought to him, dumps it on the floor, and sits down to get to work. He began life as an apprentice shoemaker, after all, and tells the police that shoemakers used to make cases, too. It's no wonder that this industrialist begins to earn the respect of the working-class cops over the other executives in the company.

It's also in these scenes that Kurosawa points to what may be the real culprit - the overtaking of Japanese culture not just by Western values, but specifically by American values. Nearly everything in Gondo's home is Western - from the lace doilies on the couches to the Westminster chiming clock. Only Gondo's wife's traditional kimono tells us we're in Japan. Jun and Shinichi are playing at sheriff and outlaw, complete with cowboy boots, six-shooters, and cowboy hat; it's because the two have swapped costumes to change roles that the wrong kid was grabbed in the first place. And as we follow the kidnapper (Tsutomu Yamazaki) through the hellscape of the lower heroin district, it's American rock and roll we hear in American cafes full of American faces (Kurosawa used actual US GIs as extras throughout these scenes). That the National Shoe executives have embraced an American brand of capitalism over traditional Japanese craftsmanship is clear, just as the Yokohamans in the streets have turned to American consumerism to try to fill their lives. Kurosawa was a student of Western literature and music his entire life (his films are frequently based on Shakespeare and Dostoyevsky works - not to mention Ed McBain - the directors he admired were John Ford, Ingmar Bergman, and Frederico Fellini, and the man loved Beethoven). But with *High and Low*, as with all of his films, Akira Kurosawa stands for Japanese culture, and with his fellow Japanese citizens.

As you can tell by now, I love this film. I believe it belongs with *Seven Samurai* as Kurosawa's finest work. Watch this, and as I do, come back to it often.

The Housemaid

South Korea, 1960. Directed by Kim Ki-young. 108 minutes, black and white.

The Housemaid is *so* many things, stylish and riveting for openers. It's a melodrama, a horror film, a noir, a tale of obsession. It becomes a haunted house story as the characters find themselves locked in together. It's *Cape Fear* and it's *Fatal Attraction*. It's the darkest of satires, skewering Korean middle class aspirations and marital values. It's creepy AF. It never should have been released in the first place, and we shouldn't be able to watch it now.

Simply put, *The Housemaid* is a story of a family torn apart by marital infidelity. The only names we're offered of the central characters is the surname, Kim (apart from the two children, daughter Ae-soon (Lee Yu-ri) and her little brother Chang-soon (Ahn Seong-gi)). The father (Kim Jin-kyu) is a piano teacher, who also leads a singing club at the women's dormitory at a local factory. The mother (Ju Jeung-nyeo) works from home as a seamstress, and we'll soon find out that she's pregnant. The couple are trying to claw their way to the upper middle class, and are on the verge of

179

moving into their new two-story home. But Mrs. Kim, suffering from exhaustion, cannot cope with the increased housekeeping demands of the larger home. So, Mr. Kim seeks out, and hires, a housemaid (Lee Eun-shim).

(It's worth mentioning here that in an interview with Bong Joon-ho - acclaimed director of *Snowpiercer*, *Parasite*, and *Okja* - he points out that few middle class families at the time were able to afford a house with more than one level, so Korean audiences would have recognized the Kims as a family on the make, socio-economically. While it wasn't as rare to hire domestic help, these were often rural girls fresh to the cities or suburbs, their backgrounds a mystery. Most were working to send money home. A few were running from something....)

When Mrs. Kim takes the children to her mother's home for a few days, the housemaid, in a show of sexual aggression probably unprecedented in Korean cinema at the time, pulls the husband to her bed. That's not to take responsibility away from Mr. Kim; Kim (and later, his wife) correctly assign him blame for the affair. But the scene establishes early on the housemaid's single mindedness in pursuing what she wants at all costs. And of course, she becomes pregnant. Later in the film, as she throws herself down the flight of stairs to terminate her pregnancy, she becomes insistent that the loss of her child shouldn't be the only loss the Kim family suffers.

It's pure melodrama, or would be if director Kim left it at that; earlier in the film when the piano teacher receives a love letter from a student at the dormitory, he turns her into her employers, resulting in the girl's suicide over her dismissal. But the film becomes *so much* more than that. The film's opening credits are played over an image of the Kim children passing back and forth the strings of a cat's cradle over sinister music, presaging the web of entrapment about to ensnare the family. Kim Ki-young isn't afraid to push the melodrama to seemingly ridiculous lengths, even challenging the audience's suspension of disbelief as the housemaid runs rampant over the family. It works because of the dark social satire in the film. *The Housemaid* isn't really about marital infidelity, it's about a couple's greed in trying to become the wealthiest family in the neighborhood, or at least achieve that appearance. The Kims are trapped in their home with a madwoman only because the housemaid so skillfully recognizes their fear of the husband's infidelity coming out - not because it will risk their marriage, but because it will risk their economic standing. Even as the housemaid takes from the family everything they hold dear, at times lethally, their ambition has made it impossible for them to exorcize this demon from their lives.

Stylistically, Kim Ki-young has developed a bag of tricks that ratchet up the suspense. It feels like all the action happens in the home, because the scenes shot there are so claustrophobic. Kim moves the camera around his characters, circling them. When the housemaid enters a scene, the camera zooms in on her; likewise when one of the family members steps back in retreat, the camera follows them, reminding us that they can't get away. In a few scenes where husband and wife are able to talk alone - usually in the middle of the night - their refuge is broken up by an auditory intrusion by their maid. She had been instructed early on never to touch the family's piano, but when she discordantly hammers on the keys, she's signaling both her need for attention and her refusal to play by their rules. And then there's *that* bottle of rat poison which keeps appearing and disappearing in the film, kept in *that* spot, in *that* cupboard, waiting, waiting, waiting. (Why keep it around? Why not toss it? Another way the family has trapped itself in their untenable existence.)

And those stairs! Kim makes the stairs a character of its own in the film. *So much* happens on that staircase, the horror of the vengeful maid played out there more than in any other setting. It's the central image of the family's aspirations, and it is the scene of not just the family's calamities, but of their refusal to be content with a simpler lifestyle. Did I mention that daughter Ae-soon is in leg braces? Her parents keep challenging her to strengthen her legs through exercise, but it's clear that they have chosen their own "upward mobility" over the child's.

How can this film even be? In the Boon interview I mentioned above, he tells us that all of Korean life, especially the arts, were fastidiously examined by government censors; you could be stopped in the street if your hair was too long or your skirt too short. Boon suspects that the film's framing of a story within a story - two brief bookending scenes of a husband and wife (suspiciously with two small children and a piano in the home) - discussing the film as a newspaper story, the husband even addressing the audience directly at the end, let some of the steam out. Perhaps that was enough to shape the film as a cautionary tale. But Kyung Hyun Kim's essay, "Crossing Borders" also suggests that during the 1960s there was an explosion of production in Korean cinema, and censors were so busy with the output that some otherwise objectionable material may have slipped through.

Given the artistic and commercial success of contemporary South Korean filmmakers like Bong Joon-ho and Park Chan-wook, one might think that now is the one and only "golden age" of South Korean cinema. But the 1960s and 1970s saw another boom in national cinema, yet even today's Koreans may not be aware of it. The reason for that is a strange tale of the erasure of Korean films, oddly at the hands of milliners and chemists.

Post-war Koreans in the 1960s, a waste-averse people in the first place, were faced with shortages of all kinds. Manufacturers of straw hats, popular among farmers, found that film celluloid lent sturdiness to a hat's brim, adding a spot of fashion at the same time. They began buying up 16mm and 35mm film prints in bulk, and chopping them up for use in farmers' headwear. Later, chemists found a way to extract silver from the celluloid film stock, and began buying up whatever the hat manufacturers hadn't picked over. The result of South Korean consumers cannibalizing their own film heritage is that 70% of films made before 1960 are now gone forever. Director Kim liked *The Housemaid* so much that he remade his own film twice in 1971 and 1982. But not even a VHS print of the original remained, and when Boon saw the remakes, he was *dying* to see the original.

Fortunately, Kim had self-financed *The Housemaid*, or at least his wife had, from her dental practice, so he had a 35mm copy. Unfortunately two reels were missing, and not until the early 1990s was another print found, a print made for foreign film festivals, at the Korean Film Commission. The missing reels had been recovered, but the English subtitles had been burned into the film, hand-painted by calligraphers in huge script, sometimes three lines high, obscuring the lower third of the film. Even with financial support from the World Film Project, it proved impossible to scrub the subtitles from the film, and as they seemed to jump from right to left over already kinetic camerawork, made those reels unwatchable. Salvation finally appeared from computer scientists at Seoul National University's Intelligent Signal Processing Laboratory, along with other film technicians, who were able to remove the offending subtitles frame by frame (you can still spot these reels, however, by the watery appearance of the bottom third of the picture).

It's a miracle this film is available, and not, say, in pieces on farmers' straw hats. Catch it if you can; you'll find an example of a thoroughly developed national cinema long before most of us were even aware it existed. And hang on! *The Housemaid* is a tense psychological ride.

Insiang

Philippines, 1976. Directed by Lino Brocka. 94 minutes, color.

There's a problem artists face when living in countries in the shadow of the United States; it takes longer for writers or musicians or filmmakers to develop a national voice. Any art takes money and infrastructure to develop, filmmaking most of all, and when your culture is awash with the imports of a nation that has both, native voices can be lost in the cacophony. *Insiang*, the first Filipino film to be shown at Cannes, is a clear voice from the Islands that national cinema was stepping out of the shadow of Western culture.

Director Lino Brocka was an insanely productive filmmaker, cutting his teeth, like most Filipino directors, on the genre films and melodramas that made up the bulk of Filipino film. He worked quickly and incessantly, often filming a theatrical release, a television drama, and rehearsing a staged play all at the same time. He did not like to keep his cast or crew idle; most scenes were printed after one take, shoots limited to a week or less; it was not uncommon for one of his films to appear in theaters as little as 17 days after shooting. There's a downside to working this quickly, and in *Insiang* we find Brocka often turning to rote television soap opera conventions, like ending scenes with characters caught in a faraway look, while the same melodramatic chords play over the soundtrack. But practice also makes perfect, and having committed the rhythms of melodrama to muscle memory, Brocka is also free to improvise and play with the genre expectations, giving us a character study of a woman trapped by poverty in urban life.

The very first shot of the film is a shocking one; blood pouring out of a pig at a slaughterhouse. From there we move to the crowded city markets, then to scenes from the poverty of the shantytown neighborhoods. Those opening scenes, shot documentary style, do more than just establish the setting of urban cruelty; they reveal a director with the courage to show real life in The Philippines, even as dictators Ferdinand and Imelda Marcos worked hard to scrub the image of both their nation and their reign.

Insiang (Hilda Koronel) is a beautiful young woman, living with her aggrieved mother, Tonya (Mona Lisa), who works at the market. At the beginning of the film, their small home is filled with extended family from the country, family members whom Tonya angrily tosses out. They, like Insiang, remind Tonya of the husband who deserted her for another woman, a hatred for whom Tonya holds deep in her heart. Tonya is bitterly cruel to her daughter, blaming her for all her ills. "I feel no affection from her anymore," Insiang quietly confesses to a friend.

But there's another reason Tonya wants the house cleared

out; she's about to take in a much younger lover, Dado (Ruel Vernal). Dado works at the slaughterhouse (it's Dado we see slaughtering the pig in the film's first shot), but he spends his free time bullying the locals in the neighborhood, especially Bebot (Rez Cortez), Insiang's boyfriend. But even as Dado is sharing Tonya's bed, it's Insiang he has his eye on. Trapped alone with him while Tonya is at the market (Insiang must do all the cooking and cleaning in the home), Dado becomes more and more aggressive in pursuing Insiang. Inevitably, he rapes her. But when Insiang tells her mother about the rape, Tonya sides with Dado, convinced by him that Insiang led him on. Tonya furiously turns all the blame for the rape on the victim, and demands that Insiang join her at work so she won't "seduce" Dado any more. Dado responds by getting Tonya drunk at night, then slipping into Insiang's bed when the mother is passed out.

Life is a living hell for Insiang. She turns to Bebot, begging him to elope with her, but Bebot is terrified of Dado, who has threatened Bebot if he continues to see Insiang. Bebot reluctantly takes her in for a night, promising to elope. But in the morning, he abandons her.

Throughout the first hour of the film, Insiang has convincingly played the part of the victim of a melodrama. But melodrama, as film historian Pierre Rissient tells us in an interview, is "the facade behind which tragedy lies." At some point, she internally begins to plan not just a way out, but revenge on Dado, on Bebot, and on her mother. I'm looking forward to watching the film again to try to spot the moment when Insiang makes that turn, so closely does she guard her thoughts. Is it when she confesses to a friend about Tonya, "I feel a kind of hatred for her. A deep hatred."? Could it have been as early as when Dado moved in? That's unlikely, but at some point, Insiang takes control, without drawing suspicion, and maneuvers all three characters to their fates.

That's why it's so fascinating to me that Brocka bends the tropes of melodrama to unexpectedly give us the story of a woman fighting back. Melodrama is generally a paternalistic genre, as it's almost always the torment of women that's used to get at our heartstrings; melodrama relies on women as victims. Yet, twice, Insiang is told by the men in her life, "I'm just a man," as if they're animals themselves, unable to control their behavior. In the context of the story, it is Insiang who alone is able to subjugate her emotions to do what must be done. If that's "civilization," then she's the most evolved character in the film.

The final scene is a kind of denouement that Rissent feels was tacked on against Brocka's wishes, urged to provide some kind of "happy" ending, or at least some kind of absolution. Insiang visits her mother in prison (I won't say why Tonya is in prison, but you can probably guess), we imagine seeking some kind of closure. It plays like a scene of forgiveness from the two for each other, and a promise to heal. But the scene is so smartly and subtly written (and acted) that I don't think it's that at all. Given how shrewd Insiang has proved herself, I think it could be read as a final twist of the knife. Certainly Tonya, finally defeated, falls short of reclaiming her daughter, at least if you pay attention to her words. I might be completely wrong, but that's what I found so engaging about *Insiang*; you can't be sure. Since Brocka so effectively pulled the bait-and-switch with the melodrama genre, we're looking deeper into this film and its characters than we might otherwise.

The Irishman

US, 2019. Directed by Martin Scorsese. 209 minutes, color.

As a Scorsese fan and amateur scholar, something surprised me when watching *Gangster's Requiem*, a video essay by film critic Farran Smith Nehme included on the bonus disc of my Criterion copy of *The Irishman*. In a career spanning more than thirty films, Martin Scorsese has made only four - *Mean Streets*, *Goodfellas*, *Casino*, and *The Irishman* - that center on the Italian-American Mafia. Even if you throw in *The Departed*, or even *Gangs of New York* to push the organized crime genres, most of Scorsese's filmography doesn't involve organized crime. The reason we think of Scorsese as a master of the gangster film, according to Nehme, is because he does them so well.[27]

This viewing of *The Irishman* was my third, and I felt even more engaged with this film the third time around than

---

[27] I agree with Nehme, and I would add that mob movies tend to appeal more to men, who usually have the loudest voices in film criticism and fandom. How many men would also remember *Alice Doesn't Live Here Anymore*, *Hugo*, and *Silence* are Martin Scorsese films?

I did in my first two viewings. I think the reason for this - apart from the daunting 3-hour, 29-minute running time - is when watching a Scorsese gangster movie, I'm tensed in anticipation for the moments of action or violence, and since I was going over familiar ground, I paid much more attention to the character development and the storytelling than the plotline. In the characters, I found a much richer story, and one that hasn't really been told before on film; the story of the gangster at the end of his life, looking back.

Scorsese and all three of the principal actors in this film (Robert De Niro, Joe Pesci, and Al Pacino) are all well into their seventies, and much has been made of the CGI techniques created to de-age the actors in order to play younger versions of their characters. I'll get into this in a bit myself, but here you have four men who are contemplating their own careers as they near the end of their working lives, and this sentiment drives the entire film, told in flashback by an old mobster from his wheelchair, alone in a nursing home. We've seen young mobsters, like Henry Hill, filled with the invincibility of youth and addicted to the glamor of power. These are men long past that, men who have seen contemporaries die in prison. Within that framework, and through powerful, powerful performances, each scene becomes colored with its repercussions through time.

The film is edited by Scorsese's longtime collaborator Thelma Schoonmaker at what one critic (approvingly) called a "metronomic pace;" the conversations especially allow time for the characters to absorb and breathe. There's as much negative space in this film as there is action, and it gives the actors time to show us through their faces what's going on in the characters' minds. Joe Pesci is astonishing - he's the measured center of the three of them, the antithesis of his character Tommy in *Goodfellas*. It's his character who holds the most power of the three, and yet he never raises his voice, and in fact is rarely seen standing in the film. As in most mob films, euphemisms are used when the most direct action is required (the source material for *The Irishman* is Charles Brandt's book *I Heard You Paint Houses*, itself a euphemism for assassination). When Russel Bufalino (Pesci) says "It is what it is," he pauses to allow Frank Sheeran (De Niro) to absorb that the decision to kill Jimmy Hoffa (Pacino) has all but been made. In all other gangster films we understand these euphemisms allow mobsters protection from prosecutors if their conversations are being taped, overheard, or reported. But in *The Irishman*, we come to realize these verbal substitutions allow characters to essentially lie to themselves. By speaking in coded language, these mobsters are coating their own consciences with a layer of protection from the horrors their work brings them to do. At the time, they think they're insulated (I'm a *soldier* not a *murderer*) but as *The Irishman* shows us, over a lifetime the self-deception erodes away. Where the more measured pacing works most brilliantly is in Frank's relationship with his daughters, particularly Peggy (Lucy Gallina and Anna Paquin). Peggy never verbally confronts Frank on what he does, but through a series of illuminating observations and facial expressions as both a child and an adult, Frank (and we) understand that she has seen through all of the obfuscation.

One of the reasons we root for the gangsters in films like *The Godfather* and *Goodfellas* is because our view of mobsters is so insular. We almost never see the harm they do outside their own world. The people who are "whacked" are players in the same game, and we don't have to look at the vast collateral damage outside their own world. *The Irishman* is the first mob movie I've seen where the characters' actions are set against a long-term backdrop of historical events. This isn't just their world - their actions have impact outside their community, and the greater community impacts them much more than we've seen. Add that to Frank's looming and inescapable betrayal (merely a choosing of sides to Russell, in *his* attempt at self-protection), along with his failure to his daughters, and Frank is faced with a lifetime to atone for. The priest in the final scene has no idea what Frank is alluding to ("What kind of a man makes that call?"), but we know exactly the burden he carries.

Scorsese risked the film on this CGI de-aging process, and it was a bigger risk than one might imagine. He just couldn't see using De Niro, Pesci, and Pacino for only a third of the film, and refused to burden his actors with motion capture technology ("How can they act with golf balls on their faces?"). A fascinating extra with the film, *The Evolution of Digital De-aging*, shows us a further obstacle to be overcome. You can't just "swap faces" digitally with "The Young De Niro" because there is no single "Young De Niro" (or Pacino, for that matter). These actors look different in every film they're in: the De Niro of *Taxi Driver* doesn't look the same as the De Niro of *Raging Bull*, and even with a shave and a haircut, Frank Serpico doesn't look much like Michael Corleone. One of the ILM artists explained that they found that actors playing different characters with different emotions actually alter the blood flow to different parts of their faces, essentially changing their appearance. So without the use of both their motion capture and animation departments, their solution was to come up with a camera rig that had two infrared cameras on either side of the main camera, capturing performances without shadows on the faces. If it hadn't worked convincingly, the entire film would have become a joke. Instead, it's the most human look at gangsters I think we've ever seen.

Kagemusha

Japan, 1980. Directed by Akira Kurosawa. 180 minutes, color.

Before he got into films, Akira Kurosawa was an artist, a painter.

The 1970s was a difficult decade in Akira Kurosawa's life. He had acquired a reputation among Japanese film studios of being difficult to work with, too demanding, his projects going overtime and over budget. He was hired, then quit as director of the Japanese scenes in *Tora! Tora! Tora!* There was a film in the Soviet Union, *Derso Uzala*, which despite its critical success led to physical collapse from filming in a Siberian winter. His own production company had failed. There was a suicide attempt.

This film, *Kagemusha*, was what Kurosawa clung to in his creative desert. *Kagemusha* was a grand vision, not just of the story he wanted to tell, but of the images he wanted to share with the world; indeed, in many cases the images preceded the story. Kurosawa couldn't film, so he painted. He spent years sitting in his office painting the scenes he wanted to shoot. An assistant eventually shopped the paintings around

Japanese studios, but that wasn't the point at the time. Kurosawa simply needed to get his visions out of his head and to the world. In the end, there were more than 200 paintings, 22 of them included in a booklet with my DVD copy of the film, and they're arresting, phantasmagoric. Think Edvard Munch. Think Van Gogh. At times the slashes and swirls of color seem more like screams or sobs from the paintbrush (or the artist). I don't know art, so I'm out on a limb here, but you get the idea.

Toho - Kurosawa's home studio - balked at the budget Kurosawa needed for this historical epic, the difference being about $1.2 million in American dollars. Help came from two Americans who had cut their teeth on Kurosawa films while in film school: George Lucas and Francis Ford Coppola. Neither had seen the paintings at the time, or seen a script. They just knew the world would be a better place if Akira Kurosawa was making films, and Lucas convinced 20th Century Fox to give Toho $1.2 million in return for international distribution rights. "I told them I needed a favor," Lucas laughed, "*Godfather* style." Given the financial success of *Star Wars*, it was an offer the studio couldn't refuse.

Kagemusha is a historical film, set in the 16th century near the end of the reign of samurai warlords, Japan at the cusp of unification. But Kurosawa uses history much in the same way Shakespeare did: Not to teach literal fact, but as a fascinating backdrop against which to explore human character and moral themes. Certainly the people of *Kagemusha* - Shingen Takeda, Nobunaga Oda, Ieyasu Tokugawa - were central to historical events in which rival clans fought for territory and power. But while Kurosawa draws from historical texts, he'll rearrange storylines and fill in gaps in the record to flesh out real figures into more compelling human beings. Shakespeare couldn't have known how the principals in *Richard III*, for example, spoke and acted, but found a compelling story to tell about loyalty and ambition. So here Kurosawa.

Kagemusha (meaning "Shadow Warrior") concerns Shingen Takeda (Tatsuya Nakadai), head of the Takeda clan, who will sometimes employ doubles on the battlefield, most frequently his brother, Nobukado (Tsutomu Yamazaki). When Nobukado comes upon an unnamed thief (also Nakadai) about to be executed, Nobukado is struck by the thief's uncanny resemblance to his brother, hidden from others underneath his grime, poverty, and sneering resentment. The thief is cleaned up and dressed like Shingen, and the result is a perfect double. The thief will be trained in the people and places at court, and in Shingen's speech and mannerisms. But shortly after, Shingen is mortally wounded by an assassin's matchlock shot (there's a fascinating sequence, eliminated from the US version, in which a sniper demonstrates to his generals how he was able to use a plumb line in daylight to aim his firearm at a spot he will return to after nightfall; a literal "shot in the dark"). Since this happens when the clan is at a precarious point in its warfare with two other clans, news of Shingen's eventual death will be catastrophic to the morale of the Takeda clan, and an admission of weakness to its enemies. Our thief is now forced into the role of Shingen indefinitely.

What follows is an exploration of the nature of

leadership, and the nature of men. The most basic question is this: Can a person from the dregs of society pass himself off as a man at society's apex? It doesn't seem likely, but as the thief puts on the clothing, speech, and mannerisms of the dead lord, he seems to assume Shingen's spirit. And this isn't so far-fetched when one considers (as Kurosawa scholar Stephen Prince points out in the commentary track) that these samurai clans were Buddhists, and mindful that the eternal nature of a great man might inhabit those who followed him. Indeed, we find our thief initially trying to flee his new (if luxurious) "prison," only to later beg for the opportunity to serve his deceased lord.

But what I found to be most fascinating is this question: Who knows a man best? Since word of Shingen's death is a closely-guarded secret among only the generals he commanded, Shingen's double must also fool those who knew him most intimately. The thief's first test is a child, Shingen's five-year-old grandson, who immediately points at him and shouts "No! That is not my grandfather!" Only an inspired adlib by the double convinces the boy he's who he claims to be (which again makes us wonder if the thief isn't "channeling" Shingen after all). Others the thief needs to convince are the horse that only the lord could ride, the lord's concubines, and the lord's servants and pages.

(In Prince's commentary, he reveals a historical fact that would have likely escaped most of *Kagemusha*'s audiences, both foreign and Japanese. In samurai culture at the time, the samurai's male pages would have certainly been expected to have a sexual relationship with the samurai, just as the samurai's female concubines. This wasn't something hidden or shameful, and there are historical records of some samurai having great affection for their male pages. This isn't directly referred to in *Kagemusha*, but Prince believes Kurosawa could not have been unaware of this, as he studiously researched samurai culture. Prince points to the pages in the film often weeping and displaying subtle "effeminate" behavior, while Kurosawa cast as his pages young men who had soft features.)

But it's Shingen's enemies who most need to be convinced, and Kurosawa hints that this may be the hardest of all. As military leaders and martial artists throughout time will attest, to successfully battle one's enemies, one must understand them best of all (think George C. Scott in *Patton*: "Rommel, you magnificent bastard, I read your book!"). This idea was most likely first expressed by 5th-century Chinese general Sun Tzu in his *Art of War*, and it is passages from this text that we find on the Takeda clan's banners.[28] Who knows us best? The people we work with? The people who love us? Or the people who want something from us?

All this historical drama, all this exploration of the human psyche is played out in absolutely gorgeous colors. This was only Kurosawa's third film in color, and after seeing samples of his paintings while in creative exile, one can see the film developing in his mind's eye in fevered splashes. I think that if he had made this film in better times he may

---

[28] As well as American MBA textbooks, which would likely have Sun Tzu rolling in his grave.

have tried to stick with his beloved black and white shadows and contrasts, but this film is a vision bursting onto the screen. There's a dream sequence in *Kagemusha* that's particularly vivid in which our thief is first pursued by, and then searches for his dead lord. The backdrops of those sets were literally painted by Kurosawa himself, and they scream the visions that haunt both subject and artist. Light and color become characters themselves, as infantry marches along a ridge at sunset, or in the uniforms and banners of the battling armies. It's miraculous coming from a director who had established himself as a master of black and white cinema, until you remember one thing:

Before he was a director, Akira Kurosawa was an artist, a painter.

The Killing

US, 1956. Directed by Stanley Kubrick. 84 minutes, black and white.

So, let's talk about Stanley Kubrick.

Talking (and writing) about certain films and directors is a lot like talking (and writing) about wine. There's a whole vocabulary (*symphonic, oaky, mise en scene, extracted*) that people use as sort of code to communicate with peers, and if you're not in on these code words, you're lost. Is this language sometimes deliberately used to obfuscate and keep people out? Sure. So I'm going to try and fumble around in plain language to give those of us who didn't take film classes at NYU a handle on what makes Stanley Kubrick's films so distinctive. And in the *two* films included in this edition, *The Killing* and Kubrick's first film, *Killer's Kiss* (US, 1955, 67 minutes, black and white) we catch an early glimpse of a great filmmaker finding his vision.

But before we do that, I'm going to throw one ten-dollar word at you that you may already know: *determinism*. Determinism is a philosophical idea that much of what happens to us in life - including, to an extent, our reactions to people and events - are more or less controlled (or *determined*) by forces outside of us. It's the yin to free will's yang, and it's one of the things Kubrick is known for. We'll get back to this in a bit. But first, I want to talk about *Killer's Kiss*, and why it's not considered by critics to be Stanley Kubrick's first "Kubrick" film.

Stanley Kubrick grew up in New York City, and by the time he turned his attention to movies, he was already established as a gifted (and published) photographer, particularly of the city itself. This is all over *Killer's Kiss*. Scenes are beautifully framed and photographed, and inserts of street life and shop windows of New York City firmly establish the story as an urban tale. Kubrick is clearly beginning on familiar ground - his work as a photographer.

The story concerns a washed-up boxer (Jamie Smith) and a dance hall girl (Irene Kane) trying to flee her controlling and abusive boss/lover (Frank Silvera). Our boxer and dancer fall in love and are trying to flee to his home of Seattle, and a presumably more wholesome and nurturing life as far from New York City as they can get. It's almost a melodrama, at least in story, and it's capped off with a happy ending, a reunion of our two at the train station, having overcome all obstacles to a hopeful future together.

It's the first and last time Kubrick will allow characters of his to shape their own destiny.

Now to *The Killing*, our feature film. In Haden Guest's essay, "Kubrick's Clockwork," he talks about determinism. He compares the plot of the film - a meticulously planned hold-up of a racetrack - to a machine set in motion. Once it's put into motion, there's little anyone can do to change the outcome. What Guest points out is how Kubrick uses the images of his film to support his idea that his characters are not in control. In the case of *The Killing*, Guest writes, look at how many scenes in the film begin or end by the opening or closing of a door. Look at the prominence of boxes in the film, how many props are pulled out of a box, just at the moment they're needed to move the caper along. It's all a Rube Goldberg contraption, and when our mastermind, Johnny Clay (mesmerizingly played by Sterling Hayden) finds himself the ultimate victim of his plan's machinations, we understand that he was never in control to begin with.

The film plays with time, pieced together by showing different characters preparing for the heist, during, and after, so instead of a smooth flow, we feel like a jigsaw puzzle is being assembled. A disembodied narrator tracks the times and places, his voice joining the racetrack announcer in chronicling events no one can control. There's a fatalism in the relationships as well; as Elisha Cook's George Peatty seems to believe a financial windfall will win him back the affections of his faithless wife (Marie Windsor), but we can see from the start her plans to rob and ditch her husband won't end the way she intends, either.

There are certainly these kinds of images in *Killer's Kiss*, especially as Kubrick shoots the cheap rooms our lovers inhabit in the same flophouse - scenes shot viewing each other, caged by window panes across a courtyard, sometimes further boxed in a mirror's reflection. But these images don't serve the film's fairy-tale ending, merely emphasize what they want to escape from. *The Killing* is the first film in which Kubrick fully commits his imagery to a deterministic story.

In subsequent films, hallways and corridors will play a major part. In a corridor you have two choices - move forward or move back. This is Kubrick's view of the world, that our choices are limited to the binary of letting the machine run its course or standing still. Think of the trenches in *Paths of Glory*. The tracking shots of Alex in *A Clockwork Orange*. The hallways of the Overlook Hotel in *The Shining*, including those wonderful dolly shots following Danny in his Big Wheel. The hedge maze of the Overlook. And Kubrick's ultimate corridor, the Stargate of *2001: A Space Odyssey*. To Kubrick, we are set in motion by forces beyond us. It's no wonder he's often criticized for not spending more time fleshing out the characters of his films. He's not interested in them. He's interested in the clockworks.

I'm glad I had the opportunity to see both these films together (along with a terrific set of interviews with Sterling Hayden for French television; trust me when I tell you he's someone I'd love to go back in time and have a drink with). The compare/contrast of Kubrick's early work is tremendously helpful in understanding the appeal of his later films. If you haven't seen much of Kubrick, or have been left cold or disinterested by his movies, I hope this helps you understand what a fan of his films sees in them.

Kwaidan

Japan, 1965. Directed by Masaki Kobayashi. 161 minutes, color.

I have so much I want to say about *Kwaidan*, and I scarcely know where to begin. It's long and stately and lush and scary, and I think anyone who loves horror should see this film. It doesn't help that I own an old DVD copy that has none of the extras the subsequent BluRay edition contains; I have no commentary track, no documentaries, only a brief essay by David Ehrenstein to guide me. It's mostly me this week. But *Kwaidan* has been in my life for a long time - I even once owned a two-tape VHS copy. So let's see what I can tell you.

Let's start with what it is: the word *kwaidan* comes from two root Japanese words (or *kanji*): *kai*, meaning "strange, mysterious, rare, or bewitching apparition" and *dan*, meaning "talk or narrative." So, basically, "ghost story." *Kwaidan* gives us four of them, all set in feudal Japan. They are:

- "The Black Hair:" A young rural samurai, falling into poverty after his lord dies, leaves his devoted wife for an opportunity at court. He meets and marries a rich man's daughter, but as the years pass he longs for his first wife. Eventually he flees, and returns to her. His old house has begun to fall into ruin, but his wife, grateful for his return, seems to have not aged a day. He vows to remain with her forever, and falls asleep in her arms. In the morning, he discovers what he has sworn to....

- "The Woman of the Snow:" An old woodcutter and his apprentice are caught in a snowstorm in the forest, and take refuge in a shack. The apprentice wakes in the morning to find the woodcutter dead, and a ghostlike woman leaning over him. The spirit (for that's what she is) tells the apprentice that she had planned on killing him, too, but because of his youth and beauty she will spare him. Before she leaves, she warns that he can never tell a soul about what he has seen here. Ten years later, we find him married to a beautiful and devoted wife, who - though having borne him three children - has never appeared to have aged since the day they met. One night he glances at her and sees a fleeting shadow of the spirit who killed the woodcutter. He begins to tell his bride about a strange experience he had ten years ago....

- "Hoichi the Earless:" We begin by witnessing an ancient battle at sea between the Heike and Genji clans. When a royal guardian of the infant Heike emperor sees the battle is lost, she takes him in her arms and plunges into the sea, rather than leave his fate to the Genji. Seven hundred years later, at a monastery sitting near the site of the battle, we encounter Hoichi, a blind and gifted *biwa* musician, who is skilled in singing ceremonial songs of the battle (a *biwa* is a four-stringed Japanese instrument, sort of like a banjo). One night the servant of "a great lord" speaks to him about performing his songs nearby, and escorts Hoichi to his audience, with the request that he tell no one about his lord. After a few nights of this, the monks take notice that Hoichi is disappearing after sunset, and have him followed. The monks find Hoichi playing at the cemetery near the ancient sea battle, and while the monks can see no one, we see the images of a royal court, with a baby sitting in the central position. The head monk (wonderfully played by Takashi Shimura, an Akira Kurosawa regular) explains to Hoichi that he is in grave danger, as he has been playing for the ghosts of the Heike clan, who will tear him apart when he is finished, to bring his music to them eternally. To protect him before the next sundown, the priests paint the surface of Hoichi's body with sacred texts, thus rendering him invisible to the spirits. But they forget to paint Hoichi's ears....

- "In a Cup of Tea:" Our story begins with a storyteller writing a tale, and a narrator explaining that there are some texts that end abruptly, wondering whether a writer has been called away never to finish, has died mid-transcript, or has had something else interrupt the process. As we go into the story our scribe is relating, we meet a warrior who is startled to find a stranger's face in a cup of tea. Looking up, there is no one there, but he keeps seeing the same face reflected in liquid surfaces wherever he looks. Eventually, he is confronted by a man bearing the reflected face, who challenges him to a duel. The warrior attacks, but his opponent is supernaturally elusive, as are three others who join in the fight. The story is interrupted by a scream, as the writer's household staff discover a horror of their own reflected in a barrel of rainwater....

These are all tales of horror, but if you're used to the gore and "jump-scare" tactics of American slasher films, you'll need to adjust to an entirely different mood and pace. It helps to keep in mind how much the Japanese value negative space in their art: negative space being the "empty" unpainted areas between the lines of a drawing, or the sparseness of a haiku, or the rests or spare instrumentation of traditional Japanese music. Think of the slow dance of *noh* theater. For that matter, it's my belief that the reason the Japanese so thoroughly appreciate my other passion - baseball - is because it's a sport filled with negative space;

think of the nine players covering a large field, or the pregnant moments of inaction between pitches.[29] You'll see an appreciation for the contemplation of negative space throughout the history of Japanese film, and it's present throughout *Kwaidan* as well. These are stories of horror, not terror, and they are stories of the presence of a spirit world, and its intrusion upon our own corporeal existence. "Negative space" is never empty; depending on who is considering it, it is filled with dark matter, memory, or spirits. The pace of *Kwaidan* allows us to consider this.

Kwaidan is also a film about painting. Our first clue to this (apart from the rare commitment to shoot the film in color in 1965 Japan) is in the opening credits: drops of colored ink swirl through clear water as the title credits appear (The spirit world invading our own? Or the other way around?). Painting is key in the stories the film tells. Only one scene is shot outdoors in the entire film, a brief scene far from anything supernatural in the first "The Black Hair" episode. All the rest - including the flashback to the sea battle - are conspicuously shot indoors. There is realism in the sets themselves (apart from the aforementioned sea battle, in which red fog is prominent), but the skies are beautiful, swirling, unworldly colors. In fact, in "The Woman of the Snow" episode, an eye, or the outline of lips will appear over the treetops. *Kwaidan* is moving us into a space in which the borders between our world and the spirit world are porous.

---

[29] Pregnant moments to fans, anyway, probably tedious moments to others.

It's using painting to permeate and disturb the realism of the film world; our patience with this is assumed, and if we offer it, rewarded.

I read something interesting in David Ehrenstein's essay regarding the source material for the film that I'd like to close with, and I'll quote him directly:

> "...*Kwaidan* is based on the writings of Lafcadio Hearn, a folklorist of Greek-Irish ancestry who came to the United States in 1869 and later moved to Japan. Hearn became a naturalized Japanese citizen in 1895, and changed his name to Yakumo Koizumi. If total assimilation of his adopted culture was Hearn's goal, then he clearly achieved it, for it's impossible to tell that *Kwaidan*'s source material is in any way western. As directed by Kobayashi, Hearn's four tales unfurl across the screen like versions of the classic Japanese paintings of the historical periods in which the film was set."

That surprised me, but also encouraged me. It tells me that the art at the heart of any culture can be powerful enough to speak to people no matter where they are from. Consider that as you approach this unusual, dream-like film. Perhaps it won't be as "foreign" as you think.

The Complete Lady Snowblood

Lady Snowblood, Japan, 1973. Directed by Toshiya Fujita. 97 minutes, color. *Lady Snowblood: Love Song of Vengeance*, Japan, 1974. Directed by Toshiya Fujita. 89 minutes, color.

Lady Snowblood is one of the greatest revenge pictures ever made, hands down. Most famously, it serves as the inspiration for Quentin Tarantino's *Kill Bill* movies, though with Tarantino (and I say this as a fan) the line between inspiration and outright thievery is blurry at best. The narrative structure, the blending of *manga* (Japanese comics), camera shots and imagery, even the title song, "Shura no hana" ("The Flower of Carnage") are all lifted wholesale from *Lady Snowblood* into Tarantino's opus. But *Lady Snowblood*'s bloody fingerprints find themselves on many other films as well, including Korean director Park Chan-wook's brilliant *Sympathy For Lady Vengeance*. It's that revolutionary. It's that unforgettable.

We begin in a women's prison in 1874 - "Meiji 7" we're told, the seventh year of a particularly turbulent era in Japanese history (more on this later) - during an excruciating childbirth. A prisoner is in labor, and as she suffers she threatens her attending midwives with death if they allow the infant to die to save the mother. We later discover the circumstances of the baby's fatherhood; the mother has been having sex with a series of guards, disregarding the contempt of her fellow inmates, solely to become pregnant with a child who will carry out the mother's revenge outside the prison walls. "Yuki," she tells her newborn daughter, moments before she dies, "you will live your life carrying out my vendetta. You are an *asura* demon." Yuki (Meiko Kaji) is placed with an accomplice of the mother's outside the prison, and the young girl's brutal training soon begins.

It's not until later in the film that we learn the mother's story. Sayo (Miyoko Akaza) is out for a stroll in the country with her husband and young son when they are attacked by four criminals (all because her husband is dressed in a white western suit, leading the attackers to believe he's a government spy). Sayo's husband and son are slaughtered by the quartet (one a woman), and she is raped by the three men and abducted by one of them. She is able to kill and escape from her abductor, but that leads to her eventual arrest and incarceration, a life sentence. Hence, the child (which she was hoping to be a boy) to exact the vengeance she cannot.

Is it bloody? It's *arterially* bloody! It's a revenge flick, so the bloodlust is half the point. Yuki tracks down her mother's tormentors with a samurai sword concealed in an umbrella, so, yeah, the vengeance is painted across the screen. Fujita's canvas in the scene when we meet the adult Yuki is virgin white snow. And that's not just for visual effect. In Howard Hampton's essay, "Flowers of Carnage" he reveals the Japanese translation of "Lady Snowblood," Yuki's *nom de guerre* - "*Shurayuki-hime*" - is only one letter apart form "*Shirayuki-hime*," which is the Japanese name of Snow White. Lest you begin to think the violence is gratuitous, it's all in the service of making the crimes committed against Sayo and her family that much worse. What was done to Yuki's mother was so devastating (to her) it warranted the abandonment of maternal nurturing to a far darker and more ruthless purpose. The violence against Sayo has not merely robbed her of her liberty, but of her motherhood, and her daughter's freedom.

The story is based on the *manga* by Kazuo Kamimura (fans may recognize him as the creator of the *Lone Wolf and Cub* series), and Fujita goes so far as to intersperse panels from the comic into the film. Other influences include American (and Italian) westerns; certainly a genre rich in the theme of revenge. And as a life-long student of Hong Kong martial arts movies, I couldn't help but notice their contributions, particularly to the combat scenes.

Lady Snowblood is set against the backdrop of the Westernization of Japan, and it's sequel, *Lady Snowblood: Love Song of Vengeance* explores the era even deeper (it has to do *something*; what's left when a character's literal reason for existence has been fulfilled in the first movie?). Where the backdrop of the first film is Japan's struggle to retain its identity while being thrust on the world stage, in the second, fighting against a militaristic and corrupt government becomes Yuki's motivation to keep fighting. As in period Hong Kong films I mentioned earlier, we begin to see the old ways of the sword may have met their match in the equalization of firearms: where the power to kill has traditionally been earned after years of study and training in martial arts, now it is cheaply available to anyone who can pull a trigger. *Love Song of Vengeance* fails to crystallize the narrative with the laser focus of the first film, but it does begin to expand the social commentary past a personal revenge story. Though, don't worry, a love interest will guarantee Yuki has plenty of personal reasons to keep her sword sharp.

Who are these films for? Fans of martial arts movies, for one. Students of Japanese cinema who want to explore the more exploitative, less artful side of that nation's cinema. And fans of Quentin Tarantino's *Kill Bill* movies as well, to see where his inspiration came from (and to be fair to Tarantino, both his fight scenes and dialogue are brilliantly original). But it's also worth keeping in mind how American films were portraying fighting women during the 1970s. You had to look hard to find them, usually in low budget B movies and blaxploitation films, and they always needed to get the drop on their male counterparts to best them in a fight. It was acceptable to see a woman fell a man with a kick, but the idea of being able to deliver or take a punch was inconceivable. In Asia, women martial artists (even while battling other forms of sexism in their industry) were portrayed as being as skillful, as committed, and as strong as their male opponents. It would take almost 30 years for American audiences to catch up.

The Last Temptation of Christ

US, 1988. Directed by Martin Scorsese. 163 minutes, color.

It's confounding to write about *The Last Temptation of Christ*. All the oxygen around this film is taken up by the controversy surrounding it; indeed that's the entirety of David Ehrenstein's essay included with the film. No one I personally know has seen it, nor had the fundamentalist Christian protesters who limited its release (who even persuaded Blockbuster Video to ban the film from their stores), nor the Catholic patriarchy that forbade their parishioners from seeing it. The entire controversy around the film was fabricated from the preconceptions of people who had no access to the film while they were decrying it. No one ever objected to the film itself. Only to the idea of it.

And yet, this is a film that's deeply important to me, that the years have allowed me to appreciate apart from its undeserved reputation. When I wrote about *The Irishman*, I wrote that I was surprised to discover that it was only Scorsese's fourth film about the Mafia. If you include *Mean Streets* - and I do - to be a film about religion, Martin

Scorsese has matched that total with *The Last Temptation of Christ*, *Kundun*, and *Silence*. He is a Roman Catholic who has always taken his faith seriously: In the film's commentary track Scorsese admits that when asked by a studio executive why he wanted to make this film, he found himself blurting out, "I want to know Jesus better!" This film is not a mockery. This film is not a condemnation. It is a serious attempt by a believer to understand the duality of Christ.

The film is based on the novel by Nikos Kazantzakis (who also wrote *Zorba the Greek*), and knowing this film was on my horizon, I took the trouble to reread the book over the last two weeks. It's a sprawling, allegorical, and fictional account of the last three years of Jesus' life, and I have to credit Paul Schrader with distilling it into a workable (and filmable) script. Forgive me, but I'm going to share a long excerpt from the prologue of the novel, which Scorsese also quotes the moment we enter the film. It's worth reading:

> "The dual substance of Christ - the yearning, so human, so superhuman, of man to attain to God or, more exactly, to return to God and identify himself with him - has always been a deep inscrutable mystery to me. This nostalgia for God, at once so mysterious and so real, has opened in me large wounds and also large flowing springs.

> "My principal anguish and the source of all my joys and sorrows from my youth onward has been the incessant, merciless battle between the spirit

and the flesh... and my soul is the arena where these two armies have clashed and met.

"The anguish has been intense. I loved my body and did not want it to perish. I loved my soul and did not want it to decay. I have fought to reconcile these two primordial forces which are so contrary to each other, to make them realize that they are not enemies but, rather, fellow workers, so that they might rejoice in their harmony - and so that I might rejoice with them.[30]"

Does this sound like a man who is unserious about Christianity, or his own spiritual life? Would a filmmaker driven to put this work on the screen, do so out of contempt?

At the core of Christian theology - at the core of Roman Catholicism in particular - is the insistence that Jesus was both fully God and fully Man. This is the idea that both book and film wrestle with. Most of the time, religion focuses on the divine aspect of Jesus, and that's certainly what Hollywood has exclusively focused on in their Biblical epics. Kazantzakis and Scorsese want to explore the other half of what their theology was insisting was at the heart of The Christ - a human heart, a human spirit. This is not blasphemy. This is Church doctrine.

The "last temptation of Christ" is Jesus' most powerful

---

[30] Nikos Kazantzakis, *The Last Temptation of Christ*, page 1, Simon & Schuster, Inc.

one, even more than the temptations of wealth and political power and divine power Satan offers him in the desert. Knowing that Jesus has a human body - complete with a human heart and soul, as Christianity insists - Satan knew that the strongest pull away from Jesus' divinity would be living a completely human life. Of course this means the draw of bread, of wine, and yes, of the flesh. But more importantly, Satan shows Jesus what half of him must have longed for: The simple joys of human existence. To work hard all day, and come home to a meal with his family. To be a neighbor, a friend, a spouse, a father. To experience the hardships and sorrows of life, making the moments of honest human contact that much sweeter. To worship God not as His Son, but as any other grateful man. The temptation comes to Jesus not in the desert, but in the form of a hallucination while he is being crucified. Of course he is tested when he is most vulnerable. Of course he must consider what he is giving up. How could his sacrifice mean anything otherwise?

None of the fundamentalist Christians who picketed the film, and successfully limited its release, had seen it or read the book. They didn't care about a serious exploration of the Duality of Christ. They allowed their minds to go to the most vulgar depiction possible - an imagined pornographic image of Jesus fucking Mary Magdalene - and use this distortion as an opportunity to flex their political muscles. That's it. They didn't know about the message of the film and they didn't care. This was always all about telling the rest of us what to do.

(There *is* a lovemaking scene between Jesus and Magdalene (Barbara Hershey) as part of Jesus' hallucinated human life. It's after they've been married, it's seconds long, and their bodies are not exposed to the camera. It's tasteful.)

The reaction of the Roman Catholic Church, to me, was even worse. Why? Because the Nikos Kazantzakis novel was required reading for seminary students, for the men they were training to become priests. The Church knew the novel Scorsese was adapting. They weren't afraid of sensationalism. They just didn't trust their laity discussing the themes of the book. At least not without telling them what to think.

The odd thing is, there actually are some portrayals Christians clinging to a literal Gospel account might find blasphemous if they were to see the film. The first is that Jesus (Willem Dafoe, who Scorsese cast after seeing him in *Platoon*), when we meet him, is already in terrible pain. He has no idea what God wants from him, only that he is suffering from painful attacks because his human life is at odds with what God has planned for him. He has no idea what is wanted from him; as he explains later in the film, "God only tells me a little at a time." In fact, he's not even sure it's God who's tormenting him, as he discusses with his mother, Mary:

Mary: "You're sure it's God? You're sure it's not the devil?"

Jesus: "I'm not sure. I'm not sure of anything."

Mary: "If it's the devil, the devil can be cast out."

Jesus: "But what if it's God? You can't cast out God, can you?"

But Jesus does suspect it's God behind these attacks, and that it's God who wants something from him. So what is Jesus doing when we meet him? He's making crosses for the Romans, the only one willing to do so, and he is despised for it. "You're worse than the Romans!" Judas (Harvey Keitel) spits at him. "You're a Jew killing Jews!" Jesus is doing this out of fear that he's been selected by God for something - he can think of no better way to amass such a weight of sin, to prove himself so unworthy, that God will be forced to saddle someone else with holy purpose. We suspect Jesus knows this won't turn God's attention from him but it's the only way he can think of to rebel. It's difficult to think of anything more "blasphemous" than this, and proof to me that those criticizing the film have never seen it.

Or Judas, for that matter. The Gospels say little about Judas Iscariot as a man, and are contradictory when it comes to his death and his fate. They agree only that he's a thief - but if that's the case, why would Jesus and the other disciples ever make him treasurer of their group, entrusting him with the communal purse? (And if so, why the need to sell Jesus out for silver; why not just run off with the corporate funds?) Shouldn't he be portrayed as weak and untrustworthy? Conniving? Serpentine?

That Judas is portrayed as Jesus' strongest disciple is

further proof to me that those who cry "blasphemy!" haven't seen the film. Judas argues with Jesus constantly, head-on, challenging him to throw off the Romans. Judas is the only fighter among the disciples, the strongest believer, the most radicalized. Judas is the one Jesus turns to for strength. As Paul Schrader puts it, Judas is "Jesus' spine." Judas is the only one who struggles for freedom as fervently as Jesus, and when Jesus finally realizes God's plan for him is to be the sacrificial lamb, he turns to Judas to betray him. Judas won't hear it. "Could you do this if you were me?" he asks. "No," Jesus replies, "that's why God gave me the easier job. To be crucified."

(But is this portrayal really so heretical? Biblical scholars have long been dissatisfied with the common understanding of Judas Iscariot in the public mind. Catholic theologian Uta Ranke-Heinemann devotes an entire chapter of her eye-opening volume *Putting Away Childish Things* - "The Fairy Tale of Judas the Traitor" - arguing that Judas is a fictional character created to act as a foil to Jesus' sacrifice. (My opinion is that Judas has a useful role to play as the Gospel writers carefully shift blame for Jesus' crucifixion off the Romans and onto the Jews.) Kazantzakis, in creating the character of Judas, was most likely aware of scholarship that points to Judas' "last name" as a corruption of *Sicarii*, a group of radicalized Jews who committed acts of terrorism against the Romans. Indeed in the film, Judas (shown killing Roman soldiers with his bare hands) has initially been sent by his sect to assassinate Jesus for being a false prophet, and a distraction from revolution. What neither Kazantzakis nor

Scorsese could have known was that in 2006 a discovery and translation of a 150 AD text (copied from ancient Greek to the Coptic language around 300 AD), soon to be known as "The Gospel of Judas Iscariot" would confirm the *Last Temptation* portrayal of Judas.)

If you're a Christian, and you've never had a thought to get past the Bible stories you heard as a child, this film isn't for you. But I think it's the responsibility of every Christian who really wants to try to understand how Jesus can be called *both* fully human and fully divine to use this film as a springboard for contemplation, and hopefully, discussion. This is an idea at the heart of Christian theology, and to just shrug your shoulders and say, "It's a mystery" does a disservice to both your religion and yourself. For nonChristians, this film is also a rich exploration of the spiritual vs the physical, and how difficult it is to embrace one at the expense of the other. For me, an atheist with a childhood grounded in Lutheran theology, a man who doesn't think Kazantzakis is exaggerating when he speaks of his anguish, and his soul being a "battleground," I am unable to stay away from this film for more than a year or two at a time. There are maybe five films that I return to like a parched soul to a well, and *The Last Temptation of Christ* is one of them. Joseph Campbell used to say that no culture would create myths except about the inexpressible truths most dear to them. I don't come to this film for blasphemy. I come to it for truth.

Perhaps anticlimactically, I need to now write about the "movie" end of things, what I would be writing about with almost any other film. How does Martin Scorsese do it? In listening to his commentary, particularly in hearing Scorsese talk about the Biblical epics he loved growing up, I realized that the dialogue and the voices relied on the casting choices he made. Scorsese wanted to bring audiences into the film, and he felt that if he incorporated "British accents" or even the lofty poetry of the New Testament, viewers would immediately go back to the films they grew up with. He wanted to make the characters sound as if they were talking in real life, and since he felt subtitling Aramaic would distance audiences even further, he gave his characters the vernacular of contemporary prose. Nothing anachronistic, but he dropped the "thees" and "thous" of what we were used to hearing, and changed the language to what we audiences are familiar with. When Jesus is delivering his Sermon on the Mount, for example, he is not standing, orating while backlit to a multitude of thousands. The world was smaller then, Scorsese maintains, and since people mostly traveled by foot, Jesus would have spoken to a smaller crowd that could walk to where he was, relying on his audience to talk to others about what they'd heard. So our Jesus is crouched on a hillside, level with the few dozen who have gathered to hear him. He avoids the term "parable," instead, Jesus tells a "story." Individuals in the crowd argue back with him, as they would today. It's amazing how well it works, how much it brings us into stories we know by heart. The first time I saw it, Harvey Keitel's New York accent was jarring at first, but not by the end of the film. It's actually more authentic. He verbally wrestles with Jesus the way we would. And Keitel is a brilliant actor; there's a terrific scene in which he and Jesus are arguing about whether you first heal the body or the soul to liberate people. Keitel's Judas is forcefully arguing his side, but in the actor's reactions, you see the character struggling to understand and weigh what Jesus is telling him. It's remarkable.

There are a few "British accents," as you might hear in the old epics, but Scorsese carefully casts them as voices outside the apostles; most notably the voice of Satan, and a character who later appears as an angel. And I can't let pass David Bowie's small but beautifully understated performance as a weary Pontius Pilate. But the rest of the cast aren't speaking and acting as people from a long-distant time or a long-distant land. You could set almost any of these conversations in a New York deli, or at a family table, and they wouldn't seem out of place.

Scorsese's style is instantly recognizable here, but it's all in service of bringing you into the picture, not making you more aware of it. His camerawork is as deft and balletic as ever, but in *Last Temptation* the swooping movements with their elevated POVs recall the angels that Jesus believes are attacking him early on, "digging their claws into my scalp." Scorsese has also set up certain shots to recall scenes of The Passion through Western art, including works by Hieronymous Bosch, though he takes pains to correct historical misinterpretations of the posture of a victim of crucifixion. (In one of the disc's extras, we can see a forensic examination of the bones of a crucified Jew discovered in contemporary Jerusalem, and I now know more than I want to know about the physiology of the act. I also never want to hear another actor complain about what they went through for a role. Willem Dafoe matter-of-factly revealed that he could go for about, oh, sixty to ninety seconds in a scene, then would have to come down to catch his breath. I think without realizing it, Dafoe was literally suffering crucifixion, which kills by asphyxiation.)

Finally, Scorsese is never careless with the music he puts in a film, and the score by Peter Gabriel (yes, that's right, "Sledge Hammer" Peter Gabriel) is wonderful. It's Middle Eastern in feel, reliant on instruments and voices of the region, but with contemporary rhythms, and even the insertion of an angelic British choirboy to great effect.

Please watch this film. Watch it, talk about it, argue about it. Don't let the people who never watched it have the last say.

Law of the Border

Turkey, 1966. Directed by Lütfi Ö. Akad. 76 minutes, black and white.

The story of how *Law of the Border* came to be made, as told in Bilge Ebiri's essay, "Breaking Boundaries and Building Bridges," is worth getting into.

By 1964, director Lütfi Ö. Akad was tired. He had been making films since 1949, genre pictures mostly, though films that showed care and conscience. By the mid-sixties he had established a reputation as one of Turkey's premier directors. But like other Turkish filmmakers he was frustrated by trying to placate censorship boards and stay in the good graces of those in power, while also trying to please domestic intellectuals, quick to scoff at national cinema when compared to what was coming out of the West. Akad was burned out, and hadn't directed a film in years. It was at this time that a young Yılmaz Güney walked into his office.

Güney was an up and coming action star, already building a fan base of his violent low-budget films. He had come to pay his respects to Akad. "I fed myself on your movies," Güney told him. "I slept on top of the boxes holding your reels." This was literally true; Güney, before he started acting, had a job transporting films from village to village in rural Turkey. Güney told Akad that he had dreamed of the day when he could work with the director he idolized. Akad was moved by the young man, and apologized to him that the director had given up on the industry. "No, brother," Güney told him. "You're going to make many more movies, right here. We'll make them together."

A few years later, Güney, a sort of Turkish version of Bruce Willis, with a dose of Clint Eastwood stoicism thrown in, had become a certifiable star with a string of populist action movies. He then sent Akad a script for *Law of the Border* that featured a smuggler and ladies man shooting down opponents left and right. It was rubbish. But Akad was intrigued by the setting; the harsh borderlands of Turkey, beset by poverty and non-arable land, in which smuggling was often the only way for Turks to survive. Against that backdrop of barbed wire fences and mine fields, Akad saw far more dramatic possibilities beyond a mere shoot-em-up. Even though it meant a less popular film, Güney agreed to Akad's rewrite.

The film plays out like a western. Güney plays Hıdır, a man trying to get by any way he can on the border while raising his young son, Yusuf (Hikmet Olgun). Smuggling (in this case, 3,000 head of sheep) is a dangerous means of making a living, but there is little else to subsist on. The government is cracking down on smuggling, but Akad here tiptoes past the censors by making government officials aware of the poverty of the border Turks, and willing to do something about it in the form of establishing a school there. Hıdır is eager for his boy to attend school; he sees it as a way out of poverty that he himself never had. But other smugglers don't see the need for education in this harsh land, and see the school as only an excuse for more of a government presence.

Thus, Hıdır finds himself caught between government officials - some sympathetic, some not, but all cracking down on contraband - smugglers themselves, and the wealthy landowners profiteering off the whole mess. Güney of course brings his "tough guy" persona to the role, and Hıdır has the respect of friends and enemies alike. But Hıdır is fighting for something other than himself in this film - both his boy and the future of the village - which added depth to his character. And the climactic shootout in a mine field is more than the action star could have hoped for.

Akad brought a realism to this film that he felt was important; he wanted the land to stand out as a character as much as the people, and this is reflected in his sparing use of closeups throughout the film. To prepare for the script rewrite, Akad traveled to the village of Urfa to talk with both military personnel and smugglers. According to Ebiri, when he asked to be introduced to older smugglers who had more experience, he was told that there were none. Smugglers never had the chance to grow old.

The collaboration with Güney recharged Akad, who picked up his work as a filmmaker again after *Law of the Border*, elegant and eloquent realistic films which would help put Turkish cinema back on the map. Sadly, *Law of the Border* would later suffer for its association with the increasingly radical Güney (more on him in a bit), and in the Turkish coup d'état of 1980, prints of the film were confiscated by the government and destroyed, along with many other films. Only one very badly damaged copy remained, which was cleaned up by the World Cinema Project in 2010, making *Law of the Border* presentable, but a shadow of the film it once must have been.

Güney's career following *Law of the Border* might be made into a film itself, as he seems to have established himself as the most badass actor/director in world cinema history. Güney continued to star in crowd-pleasing, predominantly action films, and his star grew ever brighter, even as his politics took a hard turn left. Güney spent a good deal of the 1970s in prison for harboring and aiding left-wing guerrillas, and later speaking out for Kurdish issues in his film work.[31] Far from impeding his film work (and writing a few novels), Güney somehow was able to continue to direct films *from prison*, as apparently the prison guards were also huge fans. 1982 was a banner year for Güney, as he wrote and produced the film *Yol* from behind bars, then *busted out of prison*, editing the film on the lam. Despite having to work *with INTERPOL on his tail* (you cannot make this shit up!) *Yol* was presented at Cannes, where it shared the Palme d'Or with Costa-Gavras's *Missing*.

---

[31] Lest you think it was all social-consciousness related, Güney also spent a night in the slammer while on the shoot of *Law of the Border* for firing a handgun in a bar brawl, and years later for murder (though whether this conviction was cover for a political transgression I don't know).

Letter Never Sent

USSR, 1959. Directed by Mikhail Kalatozov. 96 minutes, black and white.

This week's film, *Letter Never Sent*, is the first Criterion film I'll be writing about from the old Soviet Union. It may surprise some to learn that the USSR had a robust and influential film industry going back to the days of silent pictures. In fact, Soviet film pioneer Sergei Eisenstein (whose films *Battleship Potemkin* and *Alexander Nevsky* I have on non-Criterion editions, so I won't be writing about them here) taught the world lessons it's still absorbing on film editing, bringing Cubism to motion pictures. But it helps to take a moment before watching a Soviet-era film to understand what filmmaking in the USSR - all art, for that matter - was in service of.

Films from the Soviet Union were always, *always* in service of The State, at least outwardly. Soviet films were by government mandate meant to educate, to enrich, and to hammer home patriotic themes. They were always about the collective over the individual - characters in any Soviet film were always seen as driven to serve their comrades, not themselves. Where an American film might shine the spotlight on an exceptional individual, that bright light was always to be deflected in a Soviet film to the cause of building society. You'd see it in small ways, as when every individual who worked on a film, whether cameraman, star, or director would be listed simply by first initial and last name, ostensibly so no individual would stand out (even when the great composer Sergei Prokofiev provided the score for Eisenstein's *Alexander Nevsky*, he's listed along with the rest simply as "S. Prokofiev"). But you also see it in central themes, and even the personal dialogue between characters.

What this does is create a lot of melodrama that most of us are unused to. There's a love triangle in the middle of *Letter Never Sent*, and when the two male characters, Andrei and Sergei (Vasili Livanov and Yevgeny Urbansky) confront each other over Tanya (Tatyana Samoilova), their conversation necessarily segues into a philosophical discussion on the nature of love in society, all so the two individuals don't make their personal problems the heart of the picture. Add to that nationalistic and patriotic motivations for all action in a film, and it can be easy to get bogged down in the earnestness of the film's message. So it helps as a movie watcher to try to put yourself in the place of Soviet audiences when you watch this. You need to prepare yourself for a different movie experience.

And if you can do that, you're going to enjoy one of the most exciting adventure films ever made, and not necessarily *despite* the propagandistic melodrama, but *because* of it.

This is a film about a team of geologists searching for diamonds in Siberia - diamonds which have never been found, but which the geologic strata in the area, similar to South Africa, suggests must be there. If this were an American film, you might end up with something like *Treasure of the Sierra Madre*, in which greed propels human drama against a wild landscape. Dreams of individual wealth would motivate characters to persevere against the elements. In *Letter Never Sent*, the quartet of geologists search for riches not for themselves, but for the economic advancement of their fellow Soviet citizens Think of the development, the jobs this could bring to Siberia (the lead geologist, Sabinin (Innokenti Smoktunovsky) even *hallucinates* a scene of industry, for God's sake), the exports to other nations, the advancement to the space program! And even if it does sometimes seem a little hokey to capitalist viewers, you can't help but let their selflessness win you over. When the geologists battle nature, it's in service of something greater than themselves, and you can get caught up in the appeal.

And the battle they face? A raging forest fire that engulfs the team and blocks their way home - one of the last messages they receive from their base on their failing radio is that the front is a thousand kilometers long. Grueling labor has unearthed some hard-won diamonds, but unless they're able to get the maps and samples home, no one will ever know their expedition has been a success. Whether they find themselves in a fully engulfed forest (I watched this scene in awe, having no idea how this was safely filmed at the time), plodding through a frozen desert, or navigating an ice-clogged river in the most primitive of makeshift rafts, injury and death whittling them down, they are always, always,

always driven by two obsessions. Get the diamonds home. Pull the fallen along to their last breaths.

It's in the camerawork and cinematography that *Letter Never Sent* graduates from "interesting" to "first-rate adventure picture." As our geologists are racing through the forest, the hand-held camera is racing not just alongside them, but in and out of their path in convoluted and intricate choreography, turning the viewer into a character running with them. Remember the Indian attack at the beginning of *The Revenant*, when we found ourselves in the middle of an ambush, arrows whistling and striking from every direction the camera turned? Well, Alejandro Iñárritu remembered *this* film, I'm sure of it, because that's the only other movie in which I've seen camerawork as deft as this, and Kalatozov did his job without nearly the technical equipment contemporary directors have at their disposal. And the cinematography is just gorgeous, even - maybe especially - in black and white. It would be enough if Kalatozov (with his cinematographer Sergei Urusevsky) simply rested his camera's eye on the magnificent Siberian wilderness. But that, too, is part of the story, right from the first breathtaking shot, as the geologists wave to the camera in the helicopter that dropped them off, pulling back seemingly endlessly to reveal the unpeopled wilderness they are about to lose themselves in.

Despite the propaganda, despite the melodrama, I found myself riveted by the drama unfolding before me. This was a spare disc; no extras, no commentary track, just an essay by film scholar Dina Iordanova. But *Letter Never Sent* didn't seem to need the extras. Just a high-definition restoration, and the art of a film industry most of us never knew was there.

The Life Aquatic with Steve Zissou

US, 2004. Directed by Wes Anderson. 118 minutes, color.

"Well, if you'll excuse me, I'm going to go on an overnight drunk and in ten days I'm going to set out to find the shark that ate my friend and destroy it. Anyone who would care to join me is more than welcome."

I thought a lot about *The Life Aquatic with Steve Zissou* when I saw this film was next in line, and about Wes Anderson and why I like his films so much. I came to a conclusion that surprised me. Wes Anderson does not make films about the esoteric problems of quirky people. The characters in his films are deeply human, and radiate honest, relatable emotions. *The Life Aquatic*, after all, is simply a film about a midlife crisis, a man unsure of his future, his legacy, his place in the world. Anderson simply takes these characters and cloaks them in lives and situations so wholly unlike our own that we're fooled just long enough to pay attention. Anderson seems to know that this will make their troubles - and ours - a little easier going down.

In this case Steve Zissou (Bill Murray) is a Jacques Cousteau-type figure; he travels the seas in the *Belafonte* ("it's an old WWII sub hunter we bought from the Navy for $900,000") with a crew of filmmakers, scientists, and unpaid interns, making underwater documentaries on badly outdated film equipment. Interest (particularly the financial kind) is fading in his films, when he suffers the loss of his lifelong friend and colleague, Esteban (Seymour Cassel). On a dive, Esteban is fatally attacked by a "jaguar shark," or at least something that looked like a shark with feline markings ("I don't know what it was, it just popped out of my mouth."). As he begins the search for the creature that killed his friend, Zissou has to contend with an ex-wife (Angelica Houston), her current love and his professional rival (Jeff Goldblum), his financier (Michael Gambon), a "bond company stooge" (Bud Cort, who I can't remember seeing in anything since *Harold and Maude*), an investigative reporter (Cate Blanchett), and Ned (Owen Wilson), a young commercial pilot from Kentucky who may or may not be Zissou's biological son. Oh, and pirates, and a possible mutiny.

You can see where Zissou might not come off as... *relatable.* On top of all of that, there's a Peter Pan quality to Zissou's existence, or as Anderson says in the commentary track, "He's more of what a young boy might think an oceanographer is like[32]." His (mostly male) crew dress in

---

[32] I have to admit to abandoning the commentary track featuring Anderson and co-writer Noah Baumbach after fifteen minutes or so. They recorded it in the same restaurant where they went to write the film, which sounds like a cute idea, but the noise of the restaurant actually overtakes the conversation, which quickly

matching outfits, including speedos and red caps. Along with film labs and scientific workstations on the *Belafonte* there's a full time masseuse, a sauna, a recording studio, and a guy (Seu Jorge) whose job seems to be covering David Bowie songs on an acoustic guitar in Portuguese (this is actually quite wonderful). They've rigged diving helmets so that techno music can be piped in, played on old Casio keyboards while they're working. If this all seems like a run from adult life, Zissou's problem is he's running out of track.

What further removes us from realism is Anderson's filmmaking style. Anderson is an artist, and loves spending time on the details in the sets and props he films. If you've seen any of his other films, you know how much he delights in setting up a room almost like a diorama, each item neatly (and often symmetrically) placed. As a director, Anderson gets to order the lives of his characters in a way we never get to order ours in real life. And in *The Life Aquatic* Anderson finds the ultimate container for his human drama in the *Belafonte*. Not content with simply filming on the actual ship, Anderson has constructed an enormous cross section of the vessel so we can follow characters from room to room, level to level. There's little realistic about it; you feel like you're on the set of a play. Or perhaps in a cel of a Sunday comic.

---

became frustrating. Besides, Anderson and Baumbach seemed to forget about the audience after a while and just slip into insular chitchat. When you listen to as many commentary tracks as I do, you grow to appreciate the people who really want to reach out to the person listening.

Finally, Anderson has abandoned all realism when it comes to sea creatures, spectacularly highlighted at the end, when we join Zissou and friends in a submersible. There is no actual aquatic life filmed, nor is there computer-generated imagery. Instead, Anderson has playfully, perversely perhaps, showcased stop-action animation to depict the creatures of his imagination. Yup, the same kind of special effects we saw in the 1933 *King Kong* and the 1981 *Clash of the Titans*. It's as if Anderson is daring us to take his characters seriously.

And yet....

And yet, we do. Against our better judgment, behind our backs, even, Anderson and his cast have made us recognize ourselves in these outlandish people in their ridiculous situations. Amid all the surrealism, when Zissou meets Ned, we instantly recognize Steve's need to cling to the hope of redemption. It doesn't seem to matter whether his paternity is legitimate or not (it probably isn't), Ned represents Zissou's chance to reach back into his past and make everything alright. The outrageous Klaus (Willem Dafoe) melts us for a moment when we realize Zissou has been *his* father figure all these years. We've been fooled by Anderson into believing this confection of a film is far away from the cares of our own lives. And so, with our guard down, these important human moments actually permeate the artiness and silliness of what we think we've settled into. Maybe that's why I keep coming back to Anderson's films (and I've seen them all). At heart, he tells human stories.

And as with all Anderson films, the soundtrack is brilliant

and unexpected. I defy you to find a cooler closing credit sequence than the one Anderson has given us - unless *maybe* the one from *The Adventures of Buckaroo Banzai Across the Eighth Dimension* (also starring Jeff Goldblum) which, c'mon, just *had* to serve as inspiration to Anderson.

Limite

Brazil, 1931. Directed by Mário Peixoto. 120 minutes, black and white, silent.

The story goes that *Limite* director Mário Peixoto got the idea for his film when he saw a magazine cover in Paris in 1929. Just 21 years old at the time, Peixoto was arrested by an image on the cover of *Vu* magazine; a woman staring at the camera, a man's fists handcuffed together around her neck. The image stayed with Peixoto, and when he returned home, he approached two of Brazil's leading filmmakers, Humberto Mauro and Adhemar Gonzaga to ask them to film a scenario he came up with based on the image. Both directors recognized the personal nature of the project and urged Peixoto to direct it himself. Peixoto was only 22 when he shot the film, and it was the only film he would ever make. It would soon pass into legend.

Literally.

The avant garde non-narrative silent film was barely seen by the public on its release in 1931. But artists and cineastes were intrigued, and the lone print started to get passed around the Brazilian arts community. A screening was arranged for Orson Welles when he visited the country. *Limite* was screened annually at the Faculdade Nacional de Filosofia, the National School of Philosophy. By 1959, the film was too damaged to screen any further, having been improperly stored and exposed to the high salinity of the air in Rio. It was kept at the school and then confiscated by police in 1966. Pereira de Mello, who had seen the film as a student at the Faculdade, managed to recover the print later that same year, and set about restoring it. The project occupied him for the next twelve years, and another ten years would pass until a VHS copy of the film would be released. For over fifty years, *Limite* was unseen by all but a few privileged individuals, and legends built up around the film, as if it were a lost Picasso masterpiece. The film was written about, whispered about so much that it was impossible for it to live up to the hype when it was finally seen. And yet, it did.

What Peixoto did was to recreate his emotional response to that image on the magazine cover (which he reproduced at the beginning and end of the film), and imagine the bare bones of a story that works around the theme of "limits." The film opens with three people in a rowboat lost at sea. He doesn't even bother to name his characters; they're listed in the credits as Woman 1 (Olga Breno), Woman 2 (Taciana Rei), and Man 1 (Raul Schnoor). The three are adrift, and though they speak to each other, there are no intertitles to translate for us (this is a silent film, after all). In a series of stylized flashbacks, we are given clues to their backgrounds. Woman 1 has escaped from prison, Woman 2 from a bad marriage. Man 1 is in love with a married woman. Peixoto intercuts these flashbacks with images that establish not literal fact, but that evoke emotions, so it'll be a frustrating experience if you're looking for a straightforward story (which probably was the reason behind the film's poor audience response on its original release). But he did so with a remarkable array of visual techniques that would not be seen again in Brazilian cinema for decades. Flash pans, zooms, images in negative, the camera swirling or turned sideways. Cinematographer Edgar Brasil even took the camera in his hands, circling one of his actors, an image we're all familiar with, but one I've never seen in a silent film.

It's worth a detour to visit a couple terms in film theory, montage and découpage. We're all familiar with "training montages" in sports and superhero movies, and decoupage in the craft world as gluing paper cutouts or objects to a flat surface. But in film, montage ("assembly") and découpage ("cutting up") have very specific meanings. Montage, of which Soviet director Sergei Eisenstein launched an entire international school of film theory, is the idea of taking two different images and juxtaposing them in a way that a third idea is created, all through visuals alone. For example, let's say that you show an image of a man giving a speech in an auditorium from behind a podium. The next image is of a rifle barrel poking out from behind some curtains. That's montage. Taken together, these two images create a third idea, that the speaker is about to be assassinated. All through visual images, no narration needed. Seems obvious today, but in the early days of film, studios weren't even sure that audiences would catch on to what was meant.

Découpage is what happens before montage. In découpage, a director, writer, or cinematographer goes through a script, and translates dialogue or meaning into visual images. You take a scene of a couple arguing, for example, and translate that into images that represent anger, conflict, or confusion - whatever you're trying to get across in the scene. These images may not necessarily link to plot, but to emotional triggers to what the filmmaker wants the audience to *feel*. This is what's going on in *Limite*. We may not understand what the characters are saying or doing on a literal level, but we absolutely connect with their emotions, their frustrations and disillusion. It doesn't make literal sense to cut to, for example, stone crosses on churches when Woman 2 is confronted by her drunk husband, but if you understand that symbol as an unyielding expression of marital and patriarchal confines, you get it. Peixoto was simply experimenting with these techniques at the time, and that he had such a clear idea of what he was trying to do with them - again, all as a 22-year-old freshman filmmaker - is astonishing. I've written elsewhere that "silent" films were never really viewed in silence, and Peixoto curated a soundtrack of pieces to accompany the film from Satie, Debussy, Stravinsky, Ravel, and Prokofiev that beautifully add to the melancholy of the film (I'm listening to the opening Satie piece as I write this).

I'll be honest, after reading about this film, I wasn't looking forward to watching two hours of something so experimental, and *Limite* isn't for everyone. But going in prepared for something out of my comfort zone helped me to reset my expectations and meet the film somewhere near its level. It never hurts to check out avant garde art, whether it's in theaters, music halls, or museums. Even if you don't have a taste for it, it helps to create understanding so you can recognize it when it's incorporated into more mainstream art. I'm willing to bet that something from this film will show up in the next Spielberg, Malick, Scorsese, or other director's work who wants to nod to the past. More than just deepening your understanding, you feel like you're in on a secret message from a great filmmaker.

M

Germany, 1931. Directed by Fritz Lang. 110 minutes, black and white.

If I had to choose a favorite decade for movies, it might be the early 1930s. In the US, most genres - the horror film, the gangster film, the musical, the western - were still not yet fully formed, still subject to experimentation and surprise. But mostly, I love watching filmmakers grapple with a new technology, and there was no bigger technological challenge to moving pictures than the development of sound in the late 1920s and early 1930s.

M (the "M" is for *mörder*, German for "murderer") is a bold film straddling both silent and sound eras. M concerns a neighborhood of Berlin terrorized by a serial killer of children, with both the press and the populace desperate for the killer to be found and arrested. When we meet the killer (Peter Lorre) we're certain from the beginning of his guilt, even though his crimes are never depicted on screen. We open with a bird's eye view of children playing, and we're certain at once that they're being staked out by a predator. The police are not incompetent, but have little to go on, as the killer's victims appear to be chosen at random. Without much in the way of clues, they begin a dragnet, harassing the "honest" criminals - the prostitutes, thieves, gamblers, and panhandlers that make up the lower strata of Berlin society. With so many police around, the underground can't function, and they decide to employ a network of beggars to canvas the city, and burglars to search the buildings. In an ironic echo of the city's official judicial system, they form their own bureaucracy, and manage to catch and try the killer a step ahead of the police.

What makes *M* so commanding a film is the way Lang approaches his first sound picture with such advanced technique. It's not enough to present a simple soundtrack to one of his old films, Lang wants to really put the new technology - and the audience - through its paces. We *hear* the killer before we ever see him. Lorre's character - Hans Beckert - eerily whistles a snatch of Grieg's "Peer Gynt Suite" (you'd know it if you heard it) as he prowls the streets, and it's this sound that gives him away to a blind balloon vendor to start the manhunt. Beckert ends up hiding in the attic of an industrial building, unseen by the mob searching for him, but again exposed by sound, this time the scratching of his pocket knife against a lock. And in several brilliant scenes, Lang demonstrates to the audience that the ears can sometimes "see" what the eyes cannot. In one of these scenes, the camera looks down on an alley filled with the visual activity of running figures, but eerily silent. Only when all the actors have run out of frame do we begin to hear the whistles of the police, and the panicked shouts of the nocturnal mob. This happens against a visually still, empty alley. Lang is a gifted director at play; here is what I can show your eyes, now here is the story I speak in your ear. It's remarkable - I lost count of how often Lang uses sound to tell an off-screen story. All this from a man who had never made a "talkie" before.

And even as I decided to pay attention to sound in *M*, Lang reminded me of his mastery of visual imagery. What's been lost to us in the 21st century is the art of filmmakers (and actors) who had nothing but visuals to tell their stories (tragically, less than 10% of films made in the silent era survive today, mostly because of the perishable filmstock on which they were photographed). Remember, if you wanted dialogue in a silent picture, you had to present it on title cards, along with any narration or exposition you wanted to provide. Well, a smart filmmaker knew that people didn't come to the pictures to spend half their time reading, so they were visual poets in the way they used images to replace intertitles. When we meet the first victim of the film (seven children, I believe, have already been murdered by this point), she is cheerily bouncing a ball down a street, and begins dribbling it against a police bulletin on a wall, an announcement describing the latest children gone missing, and begging the public's help in solving the crime. A shadow falls over this bulletin, a silhouette, along with a whistled tune and an exclamation, "What a pretty ball!" Later, this same ball rolling out of a park, along with a shot of the child's balloon trapped in tension wires, are all we need to confirm the child is dead. Lang learned from years making silent films how our minds will use images he gives us to fill in the blanks for actions he will not show. In *M*, Lang is confident he can do this with sound as well.

And why title the film "*M*," and not the full, "*Mörder*"? Because Beckert runs through the streets at one point with the letter M surreptitiously chalked on the back of his overcoat, as easy for the criminal mob (and the audience) to follow as the child's red coat in Spielberg's *Schindler's List*. Another arresting (pun intended) image from this film.

What also makes this work so expertly is using actors trained in silent film, who had to learn to make their facial expressions, their postures speak the way their voices could not. Lorre is especially skilled in this - caught by a vigilante mob, he is finally free to express his terror in his voice, but it's in his eyes, and body language that he briefly wrests our pity from us, against our will. Police, mothers, criminals, so many characters - so many actors! - play out for us what Lang will not allow us to see in their reflected faces. So much of the action of this film happens offscreen, but we'd swear we were witness to so much more, so expressive are the actors Lang has cast in reflecting the action through their reactions.

We get so involved in Beckert's pursuit, and in the racing emotion *M* roils up that we forget there's a whole other story being told here; one that feels familiar to us today, a century later, of what a free society is willing to give up for security, how rumor and innuendo can fire us up well past the point of reason. When I first saw this film, I thought it was an interesting commentary about a society about to be taken over by the Nazi Party. Now, it feels like there's nothing historic about it. It feels like current events.

Sadly, my copy of this film is an early Criterion DVD release (they've even changed their logo since this one came out), so I got none of the extras the Blu-Ray edition now contains, just an enclosed essay by New Republic film critic Stanley Kauffman. So there's little scholarly insight I can offer you, just my own observations. But I may have to remedy that with their more recent edition. This film is worth the upgrade.

The Magic Flute

Sweden, 1975. Directed by Ingmar Bergman. 138 minutes, color.

The idea began simply enough. Magnus Enhörning, head of the Sveriges Radio music department ran into Ingmar Bergman at a concert, and they chatted during the intermission. The fiftieth anniversary of Swedish Radio was approaching, and Bergman suggested staging a performance of Mozart's *Magic Flute* (charmingly in Swedish, *Trollflötjen*) to air on Swedish television. The film to eventually come out of this, *The Magic Flute*, would come to be recognized as one of the finest opera productions brought to celluloid.

And no wonder. It's difficult to imagine a better person to bring this work to the screen. Ingmar Bergman was something of a Mozart scholar; his parents had brought him up on the classics, and it was Mozart's music that Bergman loved best. Before he began working in film (and after, as often as he could) Bergman worked on stage, first as an assistant, learning the ropes, then later as a director and producer. But Bergman's connection to the opera goes back even further than that. It was the first opera he attended, as a twelve-year-old boy, and he was enchanted. Bergman ran home to a puppet theater he shared with his siblings, in which he was already staging plays of increasing complexity. He dearly wanted to stage a production of *The Magic Flute*, but suffered his first brush as an artist with budgetary constraints: He couldn't afford the complete set of 78 RPM records the "soundtrack" would require. It's safe to say Bergman never got the idea of staging the opera completely out of his mind.[33]

More serendipity: As a youth, Bergman roamed Stockholm and its environs by himself, letting his feet and his thoughts guide him. One day Bergman came upon a replica of a restored baroque 18th-century theater in nearby Drottningholm. In his autobiography, *Images: My Life in Film*, Bergman wrote of that day,

> "For some reason the stage door was unlocked. I walked inside and saw for the first time the carefully restored baroque theater. I remember distinctly what a bewitching experience it was: the effect of chiaroscuro, the silence, the stage.

> "In my imagination I have always seen *The Magic Flute* living inside that old theater, in that keenly acoustical wooden box, with its slanted stage floor, its backdrop and wings. Here lies the noble,

---

[33] When later opportunities arose, he always deferred to older, more established stage directors.

magical illusion of theater. Nothing *is*: everything *represents*. The moment the curtain is raised, an agreement between stage and audiences manifests itself. And now, together, we'll create![34]"

"And now, together, we'll create!" Remember that line; we'll get back to it later.

Of course, years later, Bergman returned to the theater in Drottningholm, determined to stage and film the performance there. In an interview with Peter Cowie on the disc, Cowie mentions the importance to Bergman of getting the right stage - since the opera was premiered in 1791, Mozart would have had the dimensions of a baroque stage in mind. Cowie mentions that Bergman knew the size of the stage he needed from Mozart's score. In one scene, a character (Papageno) quickly checks on three doors on stage, and Bergman measured the steps the score would have allowed the actor to take between lines at each door. The Drottningholm stage was of course the right size, but Bergman was denied filming interiors there because of the fragility of the curtains and set dressings. So Bergman had the stage itself recreated in a film studio.

Opera is notoriously difficult to translate to film, and having attended a handful of Metropolitan Opera simulcasts at movie theaters, as well as owning a couple DVD versions in my own library, I can tell you that you feel even further

---

[34] *Images: My Life in Film* by Ingmar Bergman. Arcade Publishing, page 353

removed from what's going on than the audience does. Bergman addressed this difficulty in a number of ways. To begin with, he scrapped the idea of filming a "live" staged performance; there are some "audience" members present, but they are only there for a few scenes. Instead, while confining the action to the stage, Bergman brings the cameras onstage, giving us the close-ups and points of view a live audience wouldn't have access to. The performers are all professional opera singers who sang their own roles, but not live - they're lip-synching to themselves on playback. Because of this, Bergman was able to cast performers who had warmer voices that might not need to reach the far corners of a packed opera house. They were also young, cast not just for voices, but for youthful looks and energy (Håkan Hagegård's Papageno practically steals the show). And in this production, an aside to the audience is an aside to the camera, directly to the viewer. Bergman also often films behind the scenes; in a delightful introduction to the puckish Papageno, we see the actor napping, waking just in time to hear his musical cue, and scramble past stage hands in the wings to ready himself for his entrance. It's a brilliant bit of theater, because it beautifully melds performer and character. And at intermission, the camera wanders backstage, catching our cast on smoke breaks, reading comic books, or in the case of our young heroes Prince Tamino and Princess Pamina, playing chess. (In a delicious role reversal, Pamina sweetly and condescendingly pats Tamino on the cheek when she takes his king.) In his companion essay, Alexander Chee writes that these moments put him in mind of backstage scenes on *The Muppet Show*. I think Bergman would be unoffended at the comparison.

The opera *The Magic Flute* can stand up to this kind of fourth wall breaking, and I think it's about time we discussed the actual story. The story... is a mess. It's a fairy tale involving a prince (valiant and honest, but not the sharpest tool in the shed, the way Josef Köstlinger plays him) and the adventures he gets into when the Queen of the Night (a sort of woodland faerie queen) enlists his help in rescuing her daughter, imprisoned by the evil Sarastro. This is after Tamino has been chased by a dragon, and the birdcatcher Papageno falls into being Tamino's sort-of-squire. From there it gets complicated. Suffice it to say that not all is as it seems, that Tamino finds that he's wandered into a family squabble, and that appearances all around are deceiving. Bergman wisely decides not to get bogged down with plot details, and instead draws out themes of love and beauty, fantastical creatures and magic as the true "heroes" of this delightful opera. He even goes so far as to make a few clarifying changes in the libretto. Chee grants Bergman this, reasoning that since Mozart wrote *The Magic Flute* near the end of his life, Bergman lived with the story longer than the composer did.

The resulting film was a success far beyond Swedish television, spreading across European television and beyond. Eventually, Bergman printed a 35-mm cut for theatrical release, and it's been charming audiences ever since.

Now let's get back to that line from Bergman's autobiography. During the overture, Bergman turns the camera to the audience, showing us the faces of the people gathered for this production. They're not just bland white Swedish faces, either; Bergman has drawn in a multinational audience, children and elderly, European, Asian, African, and others. But during the opera, he keeps coming back to a young girl, as if gauging her reaction to the experience. For Bergman, both as a filmmaker, but most important as one brought up in the theater, there is no art without an audience. A play, an opera, a film, is always to Bergman a conversation, a collaboration. I believe Bergman is declaring his affection and respect for his audience here, for all his audiences he has ever played to. To Bergman, we are his peers. When you watch this (and you should, if you've never seen an opera), or when you watch any of Bergman's films, listen. He says to us:

"And now, together, we'll create!"

The Magician

Sweden, 1958. Directed by Ingmar Bergman. 101 minutes, black and white.

Last essay, when I wrote about *The Magic Flute*, I wrote about how Ingmar Bergman came to see his art as a collaboration between himself, his actors and crew, and his audience. That still stands, but in this week's *The Magician* we're going to encounter a darker Bergman, an artist at odds with himself, his work, and the movie audiences and critics who judge his output. Where the former film is joyous, opening out, the latter turns morose, looking inward.

The film concerns Dr. Albert Emanuel Vogler (Max von Sydow) an itinerant 19th-century magician/mesmerist, and the troupe that assists him with his act. They are his stage assistant, Mr. Aman (Ingrid Thulin, later to be revealed as Vogler's wife), Simson (Lars Ekborg), a bawdy and jovial manager, and Vogel's grandmother (Naima Wifstrand), who claims to be nearly 200 years old, and may or may not be an actual witch. Vogler himself is impressive; he travels in costume, false beard and sinister make-up, and is mute, but he is seen through immediately when the company stops to assist an old, dying (and drunk) actor. "Are you a swindler who must conceal his true face?" he asks Vogler. It's no wonder that the actor (Bengt Ekerot) sees through Vogler so quickly; besides being a fellow performer, his name - "Spegel" - translates from Swedish as "mirror." From the beginning we know that even if Dr. Vogler and company are legitimate, much depends on theatricality as well.

Already trying to stay ahead of charges of fraud, the troupe find themselves summoned to the home of Consul Egerman (Erland Josephson). There, they are commanded to perform for the Consul and his wife, the chief of police, and his guest Dr. Vergérus (Gunnar Björnstrand), a physician eager to expose Vogler as a charlatan. The group is treated with contempt and condescension, at least by the "better" members of the household. By the servants, they are sometimes greeted with fear, sometimes welcomed as a diversion.

The first piece of equipment we see as Vogler sets the stage for the following night's performance is a "magic lantern," a candle-powered contraption for projecting images. From this moment, we understand that Bergman has placed himself on trial as an artist. After all, what Bergman does, either as a stage or a film director, is to deal in illusion, exactly as our magician does. The trial isn't over whether either of these artists "cheats" our emotional response, it's whether their art is worth pursuing at all. Bergman had begun receiving criticism for his films being too obsessed with death, or too cerebral. He wrote that he was beginning to feel himself drying up creatively, and was wondering if his skill in storytelling was enough to pull him through, or whether he himself was being "exposed" by critics and audiences as a fraud.

It's here that many film fans will throw their hands up at the artist wasting our time with this kind of self-obsession and navel gazing, and they may be right. Honestly, it's difficult for me to recommend this film to anyone who isn't already a fan of Bergman. There are some interesting plot twists (a few, like "Aman's" exposure as a woman you can't believe anyone could have missed), some scenes of ribald humor, and one of terror. But these are all notable only in relief of the Bergman oeuvre; you're in little danger of busting a gut laughing or spilling your popcorn from fright. It's film-school stuff for the most part, maybe interesting, but not much to humanly connect with.

Unless, like me, you've seen a lot of Bergman and understand that the man isn't going to give us anything without substance. Filled with doubt? Wondering if you're an imposter? Fine, then Bergman will make a film about *that*. It's not that he thinks his troubles are worthy of our attention, far from it. Bergman simply has to use film to explore truth, and if the only truth he has at hand is that he's feeling insecure and besieged, then that's the truth he'll explore until something better comes along. There's an honesty to that I admire. We may not be able to relate to his problems, but at least we see an honest struggle. Bergman is a carpenter who finds himself with a pallet of inferior wood. He can't *not* make something, he's going to make the best he can with the materials he has available. And the craftsmanship won't suffer in the process.

The Swedish title of this film - *Ansiktet* - literally translates into Swedish as *The Face*; it was retitled for

American release. According to one of the essays with this edition ("Through a Glass Drolly" by Geoff Andrew), Vogler's face was literally his façade, and why he stayed mute and in costume even while traveling. His face is the story, the lie he presents to the rest of the world (the façade Spegel saw through immediately). The lie is necessary, though whether to suspend belief to tell a greater truth or to swindle is the issue. After all, would we pay attention in the first place if the man didn't look the part? Everything Bergman has learned about framing closeups goes into this film, especially in scenes with Von Sydow, who spends most of the film communicating only with his face and hands. But the faces of others reveal their own façades as well, in particular the odious police chief who is revealed by his wife to be even more duplicitous than Vogler.

So skip this one if you like; there are far more accessible Bergman films. But after sitting with this for a few days, I think I'm going to pop it in again. I value people struggling honestly with their doubts and insecurities. Some patience on my part might be rewarded.

A Man Escaped

France, 1956. Directed by Robert Bresson. 101 minutes, black and white.

The first thing we see in *A Man Escaped* is handwritten text signed by the film's director, Robert Bresson. It reads, "The following is a true story. I present it as it happened without adornment." This is more or less accurate. "Less" accurate because while the film is based on the story of André Devigny, a French lieutenant who escaped from a German prison in 1943, Bresson has changed the name of his character to Fontaine (François Leterrier), and made some changes to the account of the escape published by Devigny himself. Not to mention the fact that *any* recreation of a historical event by any filmmaker will of course be subject to "adornment," no matter how faithfully the story is told. But it's where we find this statement as "more" accurate that we learn volumes about Bresson as a filmmaker, and how he strived to remain true to the story he told.

In Tony Pipolo's essay for the disc, "Quintessential Bresson," he writes that Bresson felt that actors had no place in the world of film; he believed that the unblinking camera would pick up on the actor's artifice. He didn't want what he felt was insincere emotional communication from his actors' faces or voices, and so cast nonactors for their physical attributes, and most importantly for their "virginal" presence before the camera. Leterrier, for example, was a philosophy student when he was cast as Fontaine, having never acted or sought to act in his life; in an interview on the disc recorded decades later, Leterrier remarked that Bresson called his cast "models" instead of "actors."

So how does one elicit character development out of untrained "models"? Bresson believed that the true nature of human beings comes out of not what we say, not whether we scream or cry or laugh, but out of what we *do.* So at the beginning of the film, as Fontaine is driven to prison, Bresson turns the camera not to Leterrier's face, but to his hands. Fontaine is trying to decide when to make a break from the car, and as the noise of the traffic tells us what's going on outside, Fontaine's hand inches toward, and then away from the door handle on his left. It works brilliantly. His hand tells us what he's considering, and the tension builds. Even when he finally makes a (failed) break from the car, we never see the action, just Fontaine being thrown back in the car and handcuffed. No elaboration is required, and we've learned a great deal about the character without conventional acting.

Where Bresson's decision to limit the "acting" in his film really becomes inspired is in the way the story is told once Fontaine reaches prison grounds, and where we will spend most of the rest of the film. Fontaine rarely speaks, but narrates over his performance, as if recalling for a court the events of his time in the German prison (we don't find out until later in the film what he's been arrested for). The narration is flatly recited, and Fontaine is careful to keep his face free of emotion. It sounds tedious, but what it does is focus all our attention on what he *does*, the routine of making a chisel from a purloined spoon, of making ropes and grappling hooks from blankets and bedsprings. We discover that it *is* Fontaine's activity that best describes him, the meticulous and unrelenting small gestures and routines of a man who has faith that freedom will be earned through his plodding attention to detail. Fontaine's face never changes; his narration at times tells us, "my heart was pounding" or "I felt relief" because we realize his face cannot betray any of these emotions to his guards. Fontaine has to rigorously keep himself small and unnoticeable, and the "model's" performance, focused solely on his activity, speaks volumes to us.

One of the marvelous extras on this disc was a visual essay "Functions of Film Sound" in which selections of a text by David Bordwell and Kristin Thompson were read to scenes from the film. The prison setting is of course stark and austere, and everything is shot either in closeup or medium shots. So, just as for the prisoners, there isn't a lot of visual information, and Bresson artfully uses sound to fill in the rest. We hear Fontaine sharpening his chisel against the cement floor, or scratching away at the wood panels in his cell door, and we hear these more acutely because there's little else going on. We understand that in the quiet of the prison these small sounds grow to a point where they may attract attention. We have no idea what's going on outside prison walls, but we can hear train whistles and engines, and fall into the same rhythms the inmates do when they use these sounds to cover up conversations. We begin to locate guards by the rhythm and volume of their footsteps, or of keys clanging against bars. Even as Fontaine begins his escape, we can't see any farther than he can, but sound lets us know what's around a corner, or on the other side of a wall. And in case we ever forget where we are or what the stakes are, at random and unexpected times we hear the rifle reports of a firing squad, executing another prisoner.

There's so much more I could say about this film - about Bresson's spare use of sacred music, or about his spiritual and religious themes. But I'll leave you with one of the most arresting scenes in this film.

Toward the end of *A Man Escaped*, Fontaine is brought before the prison's commandant and informed of the charges against him (sabotage) and his sentence (execution). He realizes that his escape attempt must happen in the next few nights, or not at all. Shortly after returning to his cell, he is surprised with a cellmate - he's never had one before, all his time apart from the prison washroom and yard has been in isolation. His cellmate is a boy, can't be older than seventeen. The timing is more than suspicious, surely this must be a spy planted by the Germans. If so, the boy will need to be killed before Fontaine escapes. But what if he isn't a spy? Fontaine can't murder an innocent youth, and would have to let the boy escape with him. Does he help him? Or kill him? All this deliberated through calm narration, none of it revealed in the "model's" face. The more Fontaine works to quiet his impossible predicament, the louder it becomes.

If there's an argument to be made for Bresson using nonactors to tell the stories in his films, this would be one of the most powerful.

The Man Who Fell to Earth

UK, 1976. Directed by Nicolas Roeg. 139 minutes, color.

In an interview included on the disc with Walter Tevis, who wrote the source novel for *The Man Who Fell to Earth* (actually included with my DVD copy of the film), he mentions at one point that the science fiction novel was really a metaphor for the author's descent into alcoholism. When I heard that I said, "I knew it!" but the fact is this film has a different allegorical interpretation for director Nicolas Roeg, for screenwriter Paul Mayersberg, and for everyone else who talked about this film, and all their claims are valid. That's partially due to an auteur director filming a hallucinogenic take in a hallucinogenic era, but it's also due to smart filmmakers recognizing that great science fiction is anthropology in masquerade.

The story concerns Thomas Jerome Newton (David Bowie, in his first film role), an extraterrestrial who comes to Earth from a dying planet. His civilization has all but destroyed itself through nuclear war, turning the face of the planet into a waterless wasteland. Newton's dwindling people have only the resources to send a single one-manned craft on a one-way flight to Earth, which they have "explored" through television and radio broadcasts. Newton, passing for human, plans to patent his advanced technology, grow a multinational corporation through the sale and exploitation of these patents, eventually having the resources to build a larger spacecraft that can travel back to his home planet to collect the last of his people and bring them to Earth. Newton is aware this will take years, but will push ahead; among the people he left behind are his wife and children, and he has no guarantee they'll still be alive to rescue if this all comes together.

The film spells none of this out, and if I hadn't read the book first, I think Newton's backstory might have been much more vague - we learn of it mostly through wordless flashbacks. The film is much more concerned with the alien's "otherness" and his observations of human society and interactions. Newton is injured early in his visit (in the book we learn that the gravity on his planet is much less oppressive than Earth's), and so must rely on live-in help (Candy Clark) where he'd hoped to keep his privacy. From her, he learns volumes about life as a human on Earth. He also learns alcoholism, and soon enough, romantic entanglement; Roeg decided to make their relationship sexual (a change from the book's platonic relationship) because he felt it would further pull Newton down to Earth - "You can only go so far with looking but not touching. But once you touch, you're in trouble." It's not long before this human society has infected Newton, and once he's fallen, he's vulnerable to betrayal by his friends and apprehension by a suspicious US government.

This is where all manner of allegory comes in. The myth of Icarus, falling after flying too close to the sun, is prominent in both book and film, and in the end, Newton is brought down by our own government, not because he's an alien, but because his company has grown too big for Washington's comfort. But Newton's story might apply to anyone who simply appears alien to the rest of society, and is unable to find the security and community that those of us who are more easily accepted can enjoy. It's also an allegory of how alienating true genius is (Isaac Newton, anyone?) to those who are jealous of it. Or maybe, Newton is just like us, after all. His planet, despite advanced technology (or maybe because of it) has been wrecked by its occupants, just as ours is in the process of. Perhaps Newton is really just one of us after all, visiting from a future we're headed toward. No wonder he can be brought down so easily.

There's a 1970's lack of inhibition to the film (especially in the sex scenes) that threatens to push contemporary viewers away, but there's also a solid cast that pull us back in, including Rip Torn and Buck Henry (in the commentary track, Henry said that one of the reasons he took the part was because of the director and cast. "David Bowie? Nic Roeg? Rip Torn, Candy Clark? That's not a film crew, that's a dinner party!"). And everyone involved with the film talks about how the androgynous, the elegant David Bowie was perfectly cast as the alien, and that's certainly true. But having the benefit of hindsight (foresight?), I watch this now marveling at David Bowie's acting talent. Some in interviews on the disc attribute this to Bowie's stage presence from being a superstar musician, but I think there's much more to it than that. Bowie carefully chose film roles here and there, including work with Martin Scorsese and Christopher Nolan (not to mention Jim Henson), and his attention to those different roles shows, as does his calm and measured performance here. Cinema from that era is littered with male rock stars - Bob Dylan, John Lennon, Paul Simon, James Taylor, Mick Jagger - who made a film, maybe two, and that was it.[35] David Bowie's resume is the exception.

It's a pity that the Criterion edition of *The Man Who Fell to Earth* is no longer in print (though it can be found online through other distributors, albeit without the Criterion extras). I'm glad I was able to grab my copy while they still sold it. The Tevis novel is worth the read (interestingly, his other two novels made into films were *The Hustler* and *The Color of Money*), and at 160 pages, not that much of a commitment. It did help give me a bit of a road map to a nonlinear film, and the interviews gave me some perspectives I might not have considered. I can't recommend it to everyone. Like most auteur films, you're not going to have your hand held throughout. But if you're a fan of Bowie, or of films of the 1970s, you'll be rewarded.

Final note: Criterion lists this as a US film, and maybe that's who did most of the financing. But I'm listing it as a film from the United Kingdom. Though filmed in the US,

[35] Women - here I'm thinking Bette Middler, Cher (and today, Lady Gaga) - seem to do better.

all the crew were British, and the film premiered first there intact. Two months later it made its US premiere, but apparently in a cut so butchered and bowdlerized as to be a vastly inferior version. The UK version is the one that appears on my disc. If you decide to watch *The Man Who Fell to Earth*, check the run time first (139 minutes) to be sure you're watching the truest version.

Modern Times

US, 1936. Directed by Charlie Chaplin. 87 minutes, black and white.

There are two main things I want to write about *Modern Times*, but one of them puts me on some thin ice, so I'm going to save that one for the end.

The thing that isn't *as* precarious is the cojones on Mr. Chaplin to release an all-but-silent picture in 1936.

Charlie Chaplin came to film at a remarkable time. He is a product of the nineteenth century (his brutal London childhood is almost literally Dickensian) who broke ground in a fledgling twentieth century art form (and technology). Along with contemporaries Buster Keaton and Harold Lloyd, Chaplin defined not just the one- and two-reel comedies that made him an international star, but pioneered how the nascent film industry itself would be shaped. Unlike Keaton and Lloyd, Chaplin's star would continue to burn bright into the 1930s and the era of sound pictures. But Chaplin did not go gently into that good night.

Getting his start as an entertainer in London music halls, Chaplin became a master of pantomime, relying on the kind of physical comedy that wouldn't need to cut through the raucous crowds of the theater. He was a natural for silent film, and believed that speech could only dumb down great film stories. When I wrote about Chaplin's 1931 film *City Lights*, I wrote that his decision to make a silent film four years after the advent of sound pictures seemed almost defiant. In 1936 it must have made Chaplin look irrelevant; a staid vaudevillian, refusing to change with the times. *Modern Times* is by no means a silent film - there's a score that Chaplin himself wrote, and a careful and sparse application of sound effects that holds up even today. And there is speech scattered throughout the film, though never from a live character, always first filtered through some bit of technology; a phonograph, a radio, a futuristic video screen. Still, Chaplin gives us most of our information through action and a few economic intertitles. He won't dilute the power of pantomime. He won't give in.

And then in the last reel... Chaplin sings! He does it on his terms, he's a singing waiter who has lost the song lyrics he'd written on his sleeve. So he sings a gibberish song (it sounds like a mishmash of French and Italian syllables), but pairs it with a wonderful pantomime that tells the full story to the audience. And you know what? Watching it, I thought, "The man was right." Not right in that you can't have spoken dialogue in a motion picture. But absolutely right about the power of great mime, and the ability to charm and delight and communicate wordlessly. This was the last film Chaplin would make without talking, and his last performance as The Little Tramp (films like *The Great*

Dictator and *Limelight* were to come later). And he goes out absolutely on top of his form.

Now comes the "thin ice" portion of the essay. I'm going to disagree with David Robinson, the Chaplin biographer who recorded the commentary track for the Criterion edition of *Modern Times*, and who certainly knows more about Chaplin than I ever will. But first, you should know what the film is about.

It's an episodic plot for the most part, some arguing that Chaplin put together four two-reelers. Chaplin, simply billed in the credits as "a factory worker" is trying to get by in the big city during the Great Depression. Throughout the film he finds employment on a factory assembly line, as a department store night watchman, and an engineer's assistant, until we finally get to his singing waiter gig. Along the way he runs afoul of the law, twice by accident, once on purpose. And he meets "the gamin," (Paulette Goddard, who was romantically involved with Chaplin and would go on to become his common-law wife). "The gamin" is a romantic interest, but more than that, she's an equal partner to Chaplin's character, and the two of them struggle mightily simply to avoid poverty.

The title of the film is *Modern Times*, I think because it's a direct commentary on what urban life has become in the 1930s. You're probably familiar with images of Chaplin from the first two reels of this film, comically struggling to keep up with an assembly line, and eventually being threaded bodily through the clockworks of the factory itself (much like film through the sprockets of a projector!). Laborers throughout are depicted as enduring dehumanizing, repetitive, and exhausting work - in contrast the president of the Electro Steel Corporation (Chaplin regular Allan Garcia) is seen in his office toying with a jigsaw puzzle and reading the funny pages. The police are on the side of management, mercilessly breaking up strikes (and a pro-union march) with their billy clubs. Hunger is rampant in most of the city, and it's our couple's driving force in their life together, just to get to the next meal, anything grander just a dream.

This is where I differ with Mr. Robinson, who throughout the film insists that Chaplin is not making political or social commentary, but simply bringing to light the human condition. Chaplin, Robinson argues, wants us to empathize with the humanity of all people, and is not looking to point fingers of blame or to critique political systems. And I get why Robinson says that. When Chaplin left the US with his family in 1952 to attend the London premiere of *Limelight*, as he sailed off, the US government revoked his reentry permit, advising that he would have to submit to interrogation before returning, the latest victim of McCarthyism. Chaplin would end up settling in Switzerland, not to return to the US for decades, and then only to accept a special Academy Award for his achievements. In glossing over the political elements of *Modern Times*, I think Robinson was trying not to add fuel to the accusation that Chaplin was a communist. And I think Robinson was right about Chaplin always trying to bring to light the human face of the working class.

But I can't look at Chaplin's life and not find a powerful political message in all his work. As his fame and finances allowed him to travel, Chaplin embarked on what would turn out to be a world tour in 1931, just after the release of *City Lights*. This 16-month tour took him to England, France, Germany, Austria, Spain, Switzerland, Algeria, Italy, Japan, Sri Lanka, China, and Bali. On that tour, he met British prime minister Ramsay MacDonald, Winston Churchill, Mohandas Gandhi, Albert Einstein, and Japan's president Tsuyoshi Inukai, but he also spent a great deal of time observing how the rest of the world's working class was faring under a global Depression. In the included essay, "Chaplin Sees the World," Lisa Stein writes:

> "There can be no doubt that the social consciousness of this world tour helped Chaplin to develop affected his subsequent creative work. This new emphasis is evident in his next three films: in the rise of the machines and the fall of the worker as portrayed in *Modern Times*, the palpable and destructive nationalism of Hynkel's followers in *The Great Dictator*, and the tacit desperation of the lowly bank clerk forced to kill the weak and trusting in order to feed his own family in *Monsieur Verdoux*... Chaplin's awakening to the plight of the common worker became clearer to me the more I trundled through his papers over the course of several years' research in the Charlie Chaplin archives, housed first in Paris and later (and currently) as digital scans, at the Cineteca di Bologna in Italy."

Chaplin wrote about his trip for the *Woman's Home Companion* and thereafter his activism - which has eluded any simple labeling - became more a part of his stardom. While he never linked himself to a politician or political movement or party, he spent the rest of his career campaigning against authoritarianism, whether it took on the guise of Communism, Fascism, or Capitalism. I can't see the scene in *Modern Times* where our gamin finds her father's body in the street after a riot between unionists and police and think that Chaplin merely wants us to feel pity for her. I think social criticism is at the heart of *Modern Times*, and I think that's what elevates it to a classic that speaks to us today.

My Man Godfrey

US, 1936. Directed by Gregory La Cava. 93 minutes, black and white.

So... what *is* a "screwball comedy," anyway?

Well, *My Man Godfrey* is, practically definitively. It's not the first screwball comedy - that honor generally goes to Frank Capra's 1934 film *It Happened One Night* - but this one is pretty much at the genre's zenith. What's required is a certain amount of mayhem and zaniness, certainly. But what separates a screwball comedy from a Marx Brothers comedy like *Duck Soup* is the love story at its heart, and specifically a love story between two people that crosses class boundaries. A screwball comedy is an "opposites attract" love story only in that the lovers find themselves basically two sides of the same coin, but from vastly different strata of society. And *My Man Godfrey* hits all these notes and is an absolute treat to boot.

My Man Godfrey - following a clever and neon-lit opening credits sequence - settles on Godfrey (*The Thin Man*'s elegant and consummately witty William Powell), gathered with some fellow down-and-out Depression-era drifters in their Hooverville on the city dump. A brace of limousines pull up and deposit the Bullock sisters, Cornelia (Gail Patrick) and Irene (Carole Lombard). Cornelia offers Godfrey five bucks to come back with her to a party, where she can win a scavenger hunt by producing a "forgotten man" to her society pals. Godfrey firmly passes, but when the ditzy and unfocused Irene sits with him, in pleading for his assistance (while Godfrey silently absorbs the fire hose of Irene's stream of consciousness logorrhea), she unexpectedly identifies the problem:

> Irene: [A scavenger hunt] is like a treasure hunt, except in a treasure hunt you try to find something you want, and in a scavenger hunt you try to find something that *nobody* wants.
>
> Godfrey: Hmm. Like a forgotten man?
>
> Irene: That's right, and the one that wins gets a prize. Only there really isn't a prize. It's just the honor of winning, because all the money goes to charity, that is, if there's any money left over, but then... there never is.
>
> [Pause]
>
> Irene: You know, I've decided I don't want to play any more games with human beings as objects.

With that, Godfrey decides to let Irene take him back to the party, if only so she can defeat the snooty Cornelia. But when displayed to the crowd alongside a monkey and a goat, Godfrey takes advantage of the opportunity to let the gathering of society elites know exactly what he thinks of them, and how grateful he'll be to return the decent people of his shantytown. Smitten, Irene offers Godfrey a job on the spot. "Can you buttle?" she asks him, and the next morning an inexplicably spiffed-up Godfrey reports for duty as the new Bullock butler.

The wealthy Bullock family is quite a handful. In addition to the flighty Irene (who after the party apparently found time to steal a horse, ride it home, and stable it in the family library) and the supremely bitchy Cornelia (also busy after the party vandalizing windows), there's the hysterical matriarch Angelica (Alice Brady), who gets so drunk she sees pixies in her morning DTs. Angelica is sponsoring a live-in "protégé," Carlo (Mischa Auer, whose character the studio censors were desperate to avoid being interpreted as a gigolo). Carlo's main talents seem to be eating, swooning, and doing a cracking gorilla impression upon command. Overseeing it all is Alexander (Eugene Pallette), who understands his family is privileged, wasteful, and dysfunctional, but seems unable to bring order. Godfrey - who has his own secrets as we're about to learn - is the latest in a revolving door of butlers. From the first day, Godfrey steps into the role of a sort of hobo Mary Poppins to the Bullocks household.

During the Depression years of the 1930s, Hollywood

was competing with racetracks, ballparks, and dance halls for America's not-so-disposable income. In order to win the begrudging entertainment nickel from the public, film studios turned often to musicals and comedies - something to get audiences' minds off their troubles, perhaps give them an exciting glimpse into the carefree lives of the glamorously rich. But there was a tightrope to be walked. On the one hand, you wanted to reveal the "common man" as the true hero in the world. But on the other hand, if you blamed the wealthy for the country's ills, you'd risk inciting revolution. The solution - as in *My Man Godfrey* - was to make them buffoons. The screwball comedy allows us to laugh, lets us fantasize about spending our evenings in gowns and tuxedos in the most glittering venues, yet still celebrates the common sense of the Little Guy as the backbone of society. Godfrey, as it will turn out, becomes the savior not just of the Bullock clan, but of the "forgotten men" whom he champions.

The marvelous cast helps set this film above the rest. Director Gregory La Cava assembled a team that made this film the first to receive Academy Award nominations in all four acting categories. There's a fascinating interview on the disc with critic Nick Pinkerton, in which he credits La Cava with casting not comedians for the film, but solid actors who knew how to do comedy. Pinkerton feels that a roomful of comedians would be competing with each other for laughs, but that actors knew how to work as an ensemble, building a scene together. You see this in the way Powell - certainly an actor who knows comedy - becomes the calm center around which the whirlwind blows. There was another actor in consideration for the part of Irene, but Powell (whom everyone knew would make the perfect Godfrey) would not agree to the film unless Carole Lombard was instead given the role. Lombard and Powell had been married from 1931 to 1933, but after the divorce retained a sincere friendship and a mutual respect. In his essay for the disc, "The Right Kind of People," Farran Smith Nehme writes:

> "Lombard was and remains one of the most beloved stars of the thirties, and *My Man Godfrey* is her most famous role, though her character is 180 degrees from the actress's own lightning intelligence and common sense. 'She told me *My Man Godfrey* was her toughest picture,' recalled her friend the director Mitchell Leisen, 'because she had to be nutty, slaphappy, goofy, and her lines lacked continuity, were unrelated and without thought. They were hard to grasp.' "

Credit also La Cava, a director Pinkerton believes would be better known and admired today if his career hadn't been derailed by alcoholism. La Cava encouraged his actors to improvise and add to the script, but preceded the shoot with an unusually long rehearsal period in order to give the ensemble room to experiment and feel comfortable together. By the time La Cava was ready to film, both cast and director had a feel of the flow of each scene, each had contributed, and the result is something that looks on the screen to be freewheeling and spontaneous. If the film comes off as souffle-light, it's because of the hard work put into it.

Sometimes viewing one of my Criterion films feels like an obligation (I'm looking at you, *Fellini Satyricon*) but this one was an absolute delight. And the cherry on top was a bonus reel of outtakes on the disc. This is standard for contemporary films - and honestly, seeing famous people flub their lines always strikes me as "you had to be there" humor. But it's *very* rare in older films, probably because the studios were so fiercely protective of the images of their stars. So I don't know where or how Criterion managed to unearth the outtakes from *My Man Godfrey*. But five minutes of Carol Lombard swearing like a sailor when tripping over lines is a gift from the movie gods.

My Own Private Idaho

US, 1991. Directed by Gus Van Sant. 104 minutes, color.

It's tempting to describe *My Own Private Idaho* (as it has been described) as a tapestry, or even a mash-up of styles and genres. It's a road movie for sure, a western, an ode to Shakespeare, and a coming-of-age film that never settles on itself, and never seems to need to. Instead, it seems to move in and out of focus in both its story and on its characters. Except the stuff that is *out* of focus is dreamlike, but also important, as if we're on a passenger train in winter, and our windows keep icing and deicing throughout our journey. What we don't see clearly is as real as what comes through sharply.

Idaho follows a time in the lives of two young men, street hustlers turning tricks in Portland, Oregon. One of them, Mike Waters (River Phoenix) is narcoleptic and homeless. He was abandoned by his mother as a young boy, and one of the narrative frameworks of the film is his search for her through the Pacific Northwest (and briefly in Italy). So it's a road movie, but not for him. Road movies, according to an interview with film scholar Paul Arthur on the disc, are attractive to filmmakers because of their built-in structure. Road movies by definition have a beginning, a middle, and an end. Not so for Mike, whose origin is elusive and whose end is past the horizon of our time with him. Mike's narcolepsy, attacking him when he's stressed or confronted with maternal figures, is like a reset button on his journey; he's continually waking up in strange places, unaware of how he got there. The road for Mike isn't a means to get from one place to another, it's the closest thing to a home he has. The film opens and closes with Mike on a deserted highway. "I'm a connoisseur of roads," he says. "I've been tasting roads my whole life."

But this *is* a road picture for his companion and guardian Scott Favor (Keanu Reeves). Scott's story decidedly has a beginning, middle, and an end; he's the son of the wealthy mayor of Portland, fleeing the expectations of his father by immersing himself in the street life of Portland grifters. His father figure in that life is Bob Pigeon (William Richert), an oversized ringleader around whom the street youths of Portland gravitate. And if this all begins to sound Shakespearean, this is where the film's focus gradually narrows to a retelling of the Henriad and Orson Welles' *Chimes at Midnight*. Scott is very much Prince Hal and Bob, Falstaff, and as soon as we begin to suspect the connection, Van Sant drops in episodes straight from Shakespeare. The background music begins to change, the language becoming more and more formal, until we understand we've fallen into a Shakespeare adaptation. Consider this speech from Prince Hal, when he wakes Falstaff, who asks him what time it is:

"Unless hours were cups of sack, and minutes capons, and clocks the tongues of bawds, and dials the signs of leaping houses, and the blessed sun himself a fair hot wench in flame-coloured taffeta, I see no reason why thou shouldst be so superfluous to demand the time of day.[36]"

Now here's Scott's reply to Bob when he asks the same question:

"Why, you wouldn't even look at a clock unless hours were lines of coke, dials looked like the signs of gay bars, or time itself was a fair hustler in black leather. Isn't that right, Bob?"

And as soon as the camera moves away from Bob, we're out of the Shakespeare adaptation and back to Mike. We're privy to the landscapes of his dreams (through some gorgeous time-lapse photography), until we unexpectedly find ourselves in the fields of... documentary.

Van Sant originally wanted to cast the entire film with adolescents and young men he knew from the streets of Portland, but realized that wouldn't fly with anyone financing the film. He was surprised that his first choices for the roles of Mike and Scott immediately signed on, and so on the strength of two bankable stars, used actual Portland street kids (and, well, Red Hot Chili Peppers' bassist, Flea)

---

[36] Henry IV Part 1, Act I, Scene II

to fill out the rest of the Portland cast. At one point our characters are gathered in a Chinese restaurant, and Van Sant himself sat across from them (off camera) and asked them to tell stories about living on the streets as sex workers. And they do, and it's intimate and amazing. Even if you don't know this is the case, it feels real.

This confidence in letting his actors stray from his script leads us into coverage of another genre of American cinema, the western. Many a western has a nighttime scene around a campfire, cowboys or a posse staring into a fire as the events of the day quiet down. This is the time we often hear a character's backstory, or his goals, or the woman he pines for. It's the closest men get to intimacy in the genre. The genre tropes are definitely there; where we might see a horse tied up we instead see Scott and Mike's motorcycle parked. Van Sant added into the background the faint nighttime noises of the West; a lonesome train whistle, the howl of a coyote, even nearly inaudible Native chanting. The scene is unforgettable to those who have seen *Idaho*, and it was rewritten entirely by River Phoenix. He wanted to do it in as few takes as possible, and Van Sant agreed, filming it only as few times as were needed for camera coverage. And in that scene, Mike haltingly, nervously, almost inaudibly tells Scott he loves him.

It's time to talk about the acting in this film, and Phoenix and Reeves serve as far more than just the stock that makes this ratatouille of a film come together above its disparate themes, styles, and ingredients. I didn't realize at the time what we lost when we lost River Phoenix, but I have an inkling of it from this. Phoenix strips away the entire veneer of the teen idol he was becoming at the time, and throws his whole body into his performance. As an actor, I've rarely seen anyone become more vulnerable for a part (few male actors, anyway), and use that vulnerability to breathe life into a character. He's a revelation. In discarding grace, he becomes graceful. And Reeves is more dynamic than I've ever seen him, shed of the constricting woodenness of his previous and future masculine roles (Reeves had just come off of filming *Point Break* before this). I've never seen him so free. Not to detract from the man's body of work, but seeing him play Scott makes me wonder what other performances his acting choices locked inside him.

This has been a difficult essay for me to write, and if *My Own Private Idaho* comes across as a directionless film, blame me for fumbling this essay. Well, it *is* directionless, in a sense. But it's beautiful, and it works. It makes me want to see it again, and I will.

One last thing I feel I want to mention, and that's the way sexuality is presented in the film. I don't know to what extent *Idaho* counts as a "gay" film; I suppose that's up to the queer community. It's difficult to label any of the characters in this film, particularly because as homeless sex workers, these characters don't really have the luxury of following their own sexuality when survival is on the line. On the one hand, the filmmakers, in interviews on the disc, talk about the people they've met who told them watching this film gave them the courage to come out, and I believe them. Young gay men are certainly portrayed as resourceful, courageous, and protective of each other. But I also know that this film was released at a time when homosexuality itself was still being portrayed in films as something unnatural, and even predatory (see the excellent documentary *The Celluloid Closet* for more on this). Certainly homosexuality is something Scott needs to shed before he can assume his father's mantle, and a quick sex scene with an Italian farmer's daughter allows him to attend his father's funeral heterosexually wedded. So whether the film gives visibility to gay men (at times joyfully so, as when a rack of gay porn magazines begin to speak to us, and with each other, *Brady Bunch*-style), or locks them out of the American Dream - that conversation I'll leave to a broader audience. For me, *My Own Private Idaho* is a square on the patchwork of LGBTQ+ cinema, as it is a square on the quilts of so many other cinema forms.

Mysterious Object at Noon

Thailand, 2000. Directed by Apichatpong Weerasethakul. 89 minutes, black and white.

"Once upon a time...."

These words flash on the screen at the beginning of Apichatpong Weerasethakul's remarkable debut film, *Mysterious Object at Noon*. Mr. Weerasethakul[37] - who graciously goes professionally by "Joe," at least to his Western colleagues, and I will gratefully take him up on that for the remainder of this essay - studied at the Art Institute of Chicago before turning to film. Whether Joe picked up an interest in art theory there (he majored in architecture before picking up an MFA in film) or brought it to Chicago with him, *Mysterious Object at Noon* invites the viewer into a conversation about how we tell our stories, in films and beyond.

The film is based on the "Exquisite Corpse" game, sometimes done in writing, but usually drawn. One person

---

[37] And, yes, in Thailand the family name comes second, like in the West, and unlike most other Asian names. I checked.

draws the head of a person or animal on a piece of paper, then folds it over to hide what they've drawn, and passes the paper to the next person, who adds to the drawing (arms, wings, torso, whatever). The paper is then passed along, and when finished, the entire figure - usually fantastical - is revealed. It's very much like a group of people sitting around tossing the narration of a story back and forth, only in this case, the storyteller doesn't have more than a few lines from which to go, so what came before is unknown to each new narrator.

This is what Joe does with his film, except that he adds the framework of a cross-country road trip to find his narrators. After the "once upon a time" intertitle, we find ourselves looking out the windshield of a car or van winding through city streets (I believe it's Bangkok, but I might be wrong). There is no narration, but the sound of the vehicle's radio, sometimes playing music, but for the most part tuned to a radio soap opera. This serves to introduce two themes we'll follow through the film, that of travel, but also an exploration of the various media through which we tell and receive stories. The film also bounces between documentary and fiction, as parts of the developing story are acted out in film, and in one instance, performed by a group of folk music performers.

We begin with a young woman talking in the back of a moving van. She's recounting a heartbreaking memory of coming to the city as a child with her father, and visiting an uncle and his wife. Her father has been trying to find work in the city, but has run out of money, and needs to return to the country. The father sells his daughter to his brother for bus fare home. It's shocking, but the part I'll never forget is when the woman talks about overhearing her aunt and uncle talking as she's trying to fall asleep that night. Up until then, her story has been told matter-of-factly in a flat tone of voice. But when she tells us she overhears her aunt say, "She's a nice girl. What kind of a father abandons her like that?" the tears begin to flow. It's as if up until that point, she could deny her father's abandonment, telling herself it couldn't really have happened that way. But hearing confirmation come from someone else put an end to that denial, bringing the full weight of the betrayal down on her. It's one of the most moving and relatable things I've seen in a movie. How often have you or I told ourselves something *couldn't* have happened the way we experienced it, only to hear a friend say, "They did *what*?!" to breach the dam. It's actually outside the main story in the film, but I have the feeling Joe couldn't leave it out, just as I'm including it here.

Our young woman takes a breath, and someone off camera asks her if there's another story she'd like to tell, real or imagined. She begins a story about a disabled boy, shut off from the rest of the world, except for the visits from a teacher who comes every day, often sharing pictures with him. The teacher also cares for her own father, and brings him to the doctor for hearing aids. While there, she asks the doctor about a rash that's appeared on her neck. The doctor isn't too concerned, and sends her to the drugstore for a topical cream. But the next day, when visiting her student, she suddenly collapses on the floor, and the boy sees a mysterious object rolling across the floor from under her dress.

That's the beginning of our story, and as Joe travels into the country, an older woman picks it up from there. The "mysterious object" (from whence we get the film's title - the "at noon" was added later when someone else wanted to put a timestamp on events) turns out to be a star, and from this star is born a young boy. From there the story is passed on to a group of men working near the jungle, with elephants. It's tossed to a pair of girls at a school, who give us the next section in sign language, then to that troupe of actors, who sing and dance their contribution to the tale. The story gets more and more convoluted as it grows, circling back in time to add backstory to the characters. It's decided that the crippled boy was originally wounded in a plane crash during the Vietnam War; during this passage, Joe gives us newsreel footage of the war while the story is being told. Honestly, it got too convoluted for me to follow, but I didn't care; the joy was in seeing all these people, an entire country, connected through storytelling. At the end a group of schoolchildren, mostly boys, ruthlessly kill off our characters, like pulling wings off flies. But even that doesn't matter, because they've got a new story for us, featuring a Witch Tiger. A story may end. Storytelling goes on forever.

It's the kind of experimental avant garde cinema you'd expect from an art student; the unexpected part was how engaging and relatable it all was once you settled into Joe's mixed-media presentation. I especially enjoyed the kind of universal reaction; people started out slow at first - "Is this alright?" - then as they found they were holding Joe's attention, began to relax and enjoy the creative workout. Even better if the storyteller had a friend next to them, adding a detail or character as they got stuck; storytelling as collaboration happening right before our eyes.

The World Cinema Project certainly wants to promote the films of artists the Western world doesn't usually get to see, but their main job is film restoration. So what need of restoration is there from a film less than ten years old when they worked on it? Plenty, Martin Scorsese tells us in his introduction. The film has a grainy look to it; usually this happens when the print is enlarged, in this case shot in 16mm black and white and blown up to 35mm for exhibition. Film stock, as opposed to digital images, remains perishable, and every step away from the negative - including enlargement - takes a little bit away. In this case, cleaning up the picture (while retaining some of that grainy image the filmmaker was going for) was secondary to getting the work committed to a digital format where it would never decay, something a lot of filmmakers may not have the resources for.

I'm glad we'll have *Mysterious Object at Noon* for the generations to come, because I have a feeling this will age beautifully. There was never a time in human history when we didn't tell stories, and it's impossible to imagine a time when we no longer need to. Watch these people as they talk, it doesn't matter that they're a world away, it doesn't matter that they bring in aliens and demons and gods to the story. The flash in their eyes as they create something to be shared is universal. The joy of connection - even with other storytellers they'll never meet - beats at the heart of this film.

Nanook of the North

US, 1922. Directed by Robert Flaherty. 79 minutes, black and white, silent.

Admit it. You thought *Nanook of the North* was a cartoon character, like Dudley Do-right, or a kind of generalized epithet for an Eskimo. Nope. Nanook was a real-live "Itivimuit" Indian (now known as Inuk), and the subject of one of the earliest documentaries we have on record.

Robert Flaherty was an explorer and a prospector - not, as his widow and co-editor Frances maintains in a video interview on the disc, primarily a filmmaker. He was hired originally in 1910 by Sir William MacKenzie to scout out the Hudson Bay area in Northeast Canada, and somewhere in the years following, picked up a film camera and began shooting the land and its people. Flaherty is often credited with creating the documentary, but he didn't bring it into being out of nothing. In the early years of cinema (1895 through the mid-aughts) film was being used to record travelogues and portraits of industrial life; how factories churned out widgets, and so on, as Dean Duncan writes in the disc's essay. Flaherty simply combined the two types of "actualities." What might have made the difference, as Frances tells us, is that Flaherty always had in mind a broader, more commercial audience for this film.

To reach this broader audience, Flaherty saw himself as a storyteller, and as acting so commits a number of ethical breaches that would end a film documentarian's career today. Flaherty wanted to present the Native family thriving and triumphant over a hostile environment, so he refused to allow Nanook access to guns on his hunt, or motorized watercraft, even though these were quickly becoming the preferred tools of the Inuk's trade. There's a scene in which Nanook is engaged in a tug of war with a harpooned seal, Nanook nearly pulled into Hopewell Sound a few times as it pulls back; the seal in reality is already dead, and Flaherty had some men pulling on the other end of the rope to simulate the contest. And Nanook's "family" who travel with him on his hunting expedition? Other Inuk, cast from the most photogenic of Nanook's clan. Even the man's name is a lie; our hero really goes by Allakariallak.

Do these ethical lapses matter? After all, *Nanook of the North* seemed to pass muster well enough with audiences in 1922. Maybe we can give Flaherty a bit of a pass; since the film documentary genre didn't really exist a hundred years ago, neither did its ethical standards. After all, the reason legitimate news organizations today recruit journalists with university degrees is so their employers can be assured that their reporters have studied not just the tools of their profession but its ethical code. But it does mean that the honest student of film needs to do some extra fact-checking before relying on the source material. And if Flaherty really felt this was all on the up-and-up, why not trust the audience with that information? Why lie?

What clearly isn't a lie is the stuff that can't be faked; Nanook's easygoing affection and familiarity with his fellow Inuk, and theirs with him. The skill and speed with which Nanook carves blocks out of the snow to fashion an overnight igloo for his family, right down to carving out a six-inch thick block of ice to serve as a window.[38] Whatever white lies or exaggerations cloud Flaherty's story, the truth can be found in Nanook's hands, in the way he skins a seal, or spears a salmon brought to the surface to investigate Nanook's dangling polished walrus tusk. We may not be getting an accurate picture of how the Inuk lived in 1922, but we are getting a remarkable first-hand look of the craftsmanship and lore that kept generations of indigenous North Americans alive and thriving in the desert of the Arctic. All in all, I'm grateful to Flaherty for seeing these resourceful people in their vanishing environment and recognizing that they were worthy subjects for his camera. In fairness to Flaherty, he had spent more than ten years among the Inuk before releasing *Nanook of the North*. There's affection and respect in this film. Flaherty even went to the considerable effort and expense of dragging along with him

---

[38] Maddeningly, even *here* Flaherty almost ruins the film with a lie. I was suspicious that the interior shots of the family bedding down for the night seemed so spacious and well-lit; sure enough, Flaherty asked Nanook to fashion a second, three-sided "igloo" specifically so he could get these shots.

developing and projection equipment. He wanted to run the film he'd shot past Nanook and the Inuk at the end of each day, for their approval before incorporating footage into the finished product.

Was Flaherty an explorer? An exploiter? An anthropologist? A colonialist? There's no easy answer to that. He was a filmmaker, and his film is worth studying on those terms. Watch *Nanook of the North* with your eyes open to both its faults and its clarity. Appreciate that neither the exploitation of Allakariallak nor the respect paid to them can completely obfuscate the other.

Nanook died some two years after the film's release. Robert Flaherty claimed it was from starvation on a last hunting trip into the Arctic wilds, probably to punch up the threat of constant danger in his life. Local records suggest Allakariallak died in his bed of tuberculosis. Frances Flaherty smiled fondly when she noted that because of the international success of the documentary, Nanook's obituary was published in newspapers all over the world.

Nights of Cabiria

Italy, 1957. Directed by Frederico Fellini. 118 minutes, black and white.

Nights of Cabiria was my first Fellini film, seen years ago. I hated it.

More specifically, I hated the title character. Cabiria (Giulietta Masina) is a streetwalker in Rome, and at first pass she is the stereotypical screeching, claws-out Italian diva. Cabiria is a hot mess, a handful. Nothing is ever her fault, and the world and everyone in it is out to get her. She'd rather shout than talk, she'd rather take offense than get along, and if you see her walking toward you, avoid eye contact. The film begins and ends with men literally trying to kill her, and while that's, you know, awful and everything, in Chris Rock's words, I *understand* it. Cabiria is all sharp edges, even to her friends, of which she has none. She is the Godzilla of Italian streetwalkers.

But I couldn't get either the film or the character out of my head, and a few days later I watched it again. And what I began to see - and still see today - is a remarkable collaboration between actor and director to tell a human story.

Of course as a sex worker, and as a woman in a world of men, Cabiria simply will not survive without cultivating a tough exterior. In her world, offense is the best defense, and what better defense than to come at life swinging, spitting, and belligerent. Let your guard down just for a moment, and life is guaranteed to make you pay. And on my second viewing, I noticed that there are in fact plenty of times Cabiria lets her guard down. She risks being vulnerable, risks hope, and is punished for it every single time. And it isn't that as an actor Masina didn't make these moments memorable. She did, she absolutely did, or I never would have returned to this film for a second viewing. It's just that her defensiveness and anger are so spectacular and so convincing (to the outside world) that it's the tough shell we walk away remembering. But the vulnerability Masina allows us to see penetrates her shell without cracking it. After the noise of the film dies down, the quieter, more human scenes rise to the surface.

Nights of Cabiria is more or less divided into two main sections. In the first half, following a brawl with a sister streetwalker (Cabiria simply cannot let anything slide), she flees to a ritzier section of Rome, a place she is even less welcome than in her usual neighborhood. Improbably, Cabiria finds herself in a movie star's convertible after he and his girlfriend have split up in an argument outside a nightclub. The actor (Amedeo Nazzari) takes Cabiria to another nightclub, and then back to his home for a late supper, never really paying much attention to her, but giving her a close look at society life. But a chance to playact the high class woman is denied Cabiria as the actor's girlfriend storms back into the house. Cabiria, already in her date's bedroom, is forced to spend the night in the bathroom, locked away from even a prostitute's version of *la dolce vita*. In the second half, unwittingly voicing her dreams under the spell of a music hall hypnotist, she is swept away by a man she believes will take her to a new life, only to have that dream turn against her as well.

I mentioned this was a collaboration between actor and director, and in this viewing, I began to see how Fellini used his camera to document Masina's performance. In every scene, the camera sweeps, taking in everything it can, but it always, *always* settles back on Cabiria. "What do *you* see?" Fellini seems to be asking her, "How does the action in this scene affect *you*?" We see what Cabiria sees, but she is our anchor and reference for the entire picture. This may not be her world - Cabiria is not really welcome anywhere - yet we are going to see it through her eyes, and reflected in her face. It's also telling that Fellini - fairly early in his career - chooses to make Cabiria both the subject and the lens of a film.[39] The "essay" included with this disc is actually an excerpt from Fellini's autobiography, *I, Fellini*, and in it, the director talks about the actor herself, appearing in smaller roles prior to

---

[39] Fellini tells a great story - that even he admits isn't true - about when he supposedly offered the script of *Nights of Cabiria* to a film producer. "You've made pictures about homosexuals, you had a script about an insane asylum, and now prostitutes! Whatever will your next film be about?!" Fellini is said to have angrily replied, "My next film will be about producers!"

this, convincing him that an entire picture could be made based on her characters. "The brief appearance of the Cabiria character near the end of *The White Sheik* revealed Giulietta's acting abilities," Fellini wrote. "As well as being an excellent dramatic actress... she revealed herself capable of being a tragicomic mime in the tradition of Chaplin, Keaton, and Toto. In *La Strada* she emphatically reinforced this impression.... I sensed that Cabiria had the potential for an entire picture based on her character, starring, of course, Giulietta."

Chaplin? Indeed. More from *I, Fellini*:

> "If there was any influence on me, it was Chaplin's *City Lights*, one of my favorite films. Giulietta's portrayal of Cabiria reminds me, as it has many people, of Chaplin's tramp.... Her exaggerated dance in the nightclub is reminiscent of Chaplin, and her encounter with the movie star is similar to the tramp's encounter with the millionaire, who recognizes Charlie only when he's drunk. I leave Cabiria looking at the camera with a glimmer of new hope at the end, just as Chaplin does with his tramp in *City Lights*. It is possible for Cabiria to yet again have hope because she is so basically optimistic, and her expectations are so low. The French critics referred to her as the feminine Charlot, their affectionate name for Chaplin. That made her very happy when she heard it. I was happy, too."

I'll admit, "Chaplinesque" might have been the word farthest from my mind when I first saw this film. But so help me, on this viewing, I saw it. I saw it in the way Masina threw her entire body into every scene, using her hands, a leg, a hip, to accentuate her words and expressions. You don't notice it right away, but she's petite, like Chaplin, her ferocity making her seem larger in memory, but almost waiflike next to even other women. And I even saw the hope in Masina's eyes, hope I never would have found under Cabiria's circumstances, not just at the end, but whenever she allowed herself to think this time it was going to be different.

That's what made this film different, and better for me on this viewing. I would not have looked for optimism from Cabiria, not from this streetwise porcupine of a character. I could not have found optimism in her life, her circumstances. But Cabiria can, because she's stronger than I am. She won't accept my pity or anyone else's. But she'll teach me, if I'm tough enough to listen.

Okja

US/South Korea, 2017. Directed by Bong Joon Ho. 121 minutes, color.

Okja is some pig. *Okja* is some film.

Korean director Bong Joon Ho is known for making films that cross, bend, and erase genre boundaries, and *Okja* is no exception. Bong's previous films include *The Host*, *Snowpiercer*, and Academy Award and Palme d'Or winner, *Parasite*, so his work is familiar to American audiences even if his name isn't. Where Bong has previously blended action, horror, science fiction, and social commentary, *Okja* similarly slips from fantasy to adventure to political statement. You can't pin this film down, nor would you want to. It's charming, funny, and horrifying. It's *Babe*. It's *Charlotte's Web*. It's Spielberg *and* it's Tarantino.

The film is about a GMO food conglomerate (think Monsanto or Perdue on steroids) that has created "superpigs" in a lab in New Jersey. In a publicity stunt, twenty-six of these animals are shipped out as babes to twenty-six small, local farmers around the globe. These will be raised for ten years, the most impressive specimen to be crowned in a media spectacle in New York City. After a media announcement by the company's CEO (Tilda Swinton), we settle into a gorgeous mountainside in South Korea, where our titular pig is being raised by a young girl, Mija (An Seo Hyun) and her grandfather, Hee Bong (Byun Heebong).

For the next thirty minutes, give or take, we are allowed to witness the Edenic life led by our human and porcine heroines, and it's here that Bong shamelessly - and successfully - ensnares our hearts. Have Kleenex handy, because I defy the toughest of you to complete this section of the film with their eyes dry. It's a team effort. Part of the credit goes to Bong and his director of photography Darius Khondji, who slow down the camera movement to a country pace and give us time to take in the beautiful natural setting. Part of the credit goes to a crack team of animators - even children these days can spot CGI characters, and as adults we're sophisticated enough to understand when we're being played, but even Baby Yoda has nothing on Okja when it comes to charm. In an interview on the disc, Bong tells us the giant pig was actually based on manatees, hippopotami, and pigs, but the eyes and demeanor were all puppy dog. He even hired a voice actor to lay down the fundamentals for Okja's grunts and squeals (he gives the actor a cameo as a woman in a wheelchair in an underground mall scene). Finally, credit the performance of An Seo Hyun, who goes for naturalistic; her character is a fearless and adventurous girl. In her own interview on the disc, the actor credits her relationship with the lead "puppeteer" who inhabited a huge Okja head on set for reference, and her astonishment that when Bong asked her what changes she might make to the creature's design, actually incorporated her ideas so that she might better bond with the character.

The result is that we firmly establish that our little family of three are happy in their rural life. And that Okja is capable of giving and receiving loyalty and affection, is highly intelligent, and by all accounts, sentient. When Mija whispers into Okja's ear (and even Okja to Mija at the end), we buy it, and even respect Bong's decision never to let us in on their confidential conversation.

And then the fairy tale ends. Okja has been chosen as the prizewinning superpig, to be whisked (as far as a giant pig can be "whisked," that is) to the faraway isle of Manhattan. And so our film's pace picks up, Bong's camera begins to swoop, jump, and zoom to an urban tempo, and Mija takes off to try to rescue her pig.

This is where the film becomes something else entirely, something far less charming, even sprinkled as it is with moments of humor. The corporation - Mirando - has bred these animals for sale and human consumption after all. The company has a dark past it's trying hard to put a better face on, and with the help of a vain and amoral celebrity zoologist (Jake Gyllenhaal in an appropriately manic performance), tries to make us all forget where our pork chops come from. The film is now racing toward an excruciatingly cruel and graphic finale in a New Jersey slaughterhouse in juxtaposition with Okja's paradisiacal Korean piglethood. Racing with Mija is the Animal Liberation Front, a nonviolent animal rights organization led by Jay (Paul Dano, whose guileless face punctuates every earnest word he speaks). Are they Mija's allies? It's hard to say, because the film refuses to take the morally easy route with anyone, and the ALF certainly have their own agenda and prove themselves capable of breaking their own ethical ideals. It's also where Bong as a filmmaker will not simplify any subject. From Karen Han's essay, "big love" included with the disc:

> "There's no easy way to sum it up: it's not a kid's movie, yet it shies away from the so-called grimdark tendencies of similar films that have courted adult audiences, and even Bong's own generally more sober palette; it's not an action film, despite reaching Spielbergian heights when its characters are set loose; and it's not even a call to vegetarianism or veganism, despite the bleak picture it paints of the meat industry. In other words, it's much, much more complex than the fairy tale its premise may initially suggest."

It might be easier to suggest that the horrifying slaughterhouse scenes actually do warn us away from eating meat, except that Mija and her grandfather eat chicken and fish in their "idyllic" pastoral life (and one of the ALF members is so adamant about leaving a light footprint that he's continually passing out from malnutrition). *Okja* must be an attack on capitalism, then, and the corporate carelessness toward living things; witness our first view of urban Seoul after leaving Mija's country farm - commuters herding themselves into subway tunnels like, well, pigs to the slaughter. Except even Bong tells us in his interview, "Filmmaking requires more capital than any other art form." He admits that he is a part of the culture he wants to criticize - we all are - and that our problems require far more complex solutions than "live this way, or that."

I think this is why the different styles of *Okja*, even the discordant ones, help to glue the film together into a satisfying whole. In the end, Mija can't change the system (though Okja certainly makes all the difference in one piglet's life). None of Bong's films are really about individuals successfully toppling unjust systems; that's just not the way life works. But by morphing from fairy tale to action film to comedy to political manifesto, I think this film hints at all of those genres in our own lives. Our lives, and this story, and the world can't be held by just one convention, one way of looking, one line of attack. We can choose a way to live, a way to look at the world. Life can be a carnival, or a box of chocolates, or nasty, brutish, and short. But we'd best be able to take another point of view from time to time, to see life a little more clearly.

Once Upon a Time in China: The Complete Films

Once Upon a Time in China: Hong Kong, 1991. Directed by Tsui Hark. 134 minutes, color. *Once Upon a Time in China II*: Hong Kong, 1992. Directed by Tsui Hark. 112 minutes, color. *Once Upon a Time in China III*: Hong Kong, 1993. Directed by Tsui Hark. 111 minutes, color. *Once Upon a Time in China IV:* Hong Kong, 1993. Directed by Yuen Bun. 101 minutes, color. *Once Upon a Time in China V*: Hong Kong, 1994. Directed by Tsui Hark. 101 minutes, color. *Once Upon a Time in China and America*: Hong Kong, 1997. Directed by Sammo Hung. 102 minutes, color.

The *Once Upon a Time in China* film series (hereafter abbreviated to *OUATIC*) is first and foremost a celebration of kung fu action, but it's also much, much more than that. Westerners may be surprised to learn, for example, that Wong Fei-hung, the character at the heart of these historical epics, has been portrayed on film more often than any other human being. Don't get me wrong - you can enjoy any or all of these films for the kung fu fireworks alone (and in many ways I cut my cinematic teeth on Hong Kong martial arts flicks). But to understand what makes them so exceptional, it's necessary to take a look at a bit of Chinese history and a bit of Hong Kong film history as well.

Wong Fei-hung was a physician and martial artist born during China's Qing Dynasty, the last orthodox dynasty in Chinese history. He has no counterpart in American history; he is celebrated as a hero of the people, a champion of Chinese independence, and a master of martial arts. Like all our heroes, his story and his traits are altered and embellished when society has need of them. Here is what we know of the real-life Wong Fei-hung, according to the essay "Life of a Legend" by Grady Hendrix:

> "In 1847, in the southern-Chinese city of Foshan, the owner of a medical clinic had a son. As the boy grew older, his father taught him a martial art called Hung Gar, and the two traveled from village to village demonstrating it and selling medicine. Occasionally, a local martial artist would challenge them, and the son became famous for never losing a fight. He grew up to inherit the clinic as well as his father's position as a martial-arts coach for the local militia, and eventually opened a second clinic in another city. He married four times and had four children, but after one of his clinics burned down during antigovernment riots in 1924, he became despondent, and, following a slow decline, he died the following year."

It is said there is a Chinese curse, "May you live in interesting times,[40]"and that was certainly true for Wong Fei-hung. The Qing dynasty - indeed China's entire dynastic system - was in disrepair, with local gangs and sects challenging the Emperor's authority: Both the Boxer Rebellion and the Wuchang Uprising happened during Wong's adult years. China was in upheaval, and at the worst possible time: American, British, and other European imperialists saw what they considered to be a backward and technologically inferior nation as ripe for exploitation. Western culture, Western dress, Western politics, and Western religion were all sweeping aside centuries of Chinese society. Worst of all, cheap and plentiful Western firearms were threatening to make China's proud martial arts heritage obsolete. Why dedicate a lifetime to perfecting your techniques when seemingly greater power could be instantly bestowed on anyone by a gun?

Cut to 1949. China (and I'm completely oversimplifying for the sake of this essay; please don't seek out my "expertise" on Chinese or any other kind of history) is undergoing another era of turmoil. A brutal eight-year occupation by Japanese forces, ending with World War II, has given way to four years of civil war, fought between nationalist and Communist forces, with both American and Soviet governments poised to intervene for their own interests. China needed a unifying hero to turn to, so they reached back into the past for a likely candidate to turn into the

---

[40] There's not. It's actually a Western expression, and a fairly recent one at that.

PETER JOHANSSON

symbol they needed for their times. Mythologizing our past is often how we fulfill our needs in our present: The Soviet Union did it with Alexander Nevsky, America has done it with George Washington and Davy Crockett (and even baseball did it with Abner Doubleday). And so Kwan Tak-hing, a 44-year-old actor facing the end of his acting career, was cast to play Wong Fei-hung by Chinese director Wu Pang.

Kwan's Wong Fei-hung became a figure preaching the unity of China. Wong remained a kung fu master, but his battles were frequently against gangs or individuals trying to tear China apart, or separate Chinese people from their culture. The series became enormously successful; between 1949's *The Story of Wong Fei-hung* and 1961's *How Wong Fei-hung Smashed the Five Tigers*, Kwan starred as Wong in 75 films. Numerous TV series, novels, and museums pushed the patriotic legend. As actor Kwan aged (Kwan last played the role in 1970, at age 65), understandably his Hung Gar style began to slow, and the character was given to stop in the middle of a fight to deliver Confucian-style monologues. But the 81 films Kwan starred in were massively successful, and while the series dropped off in the 1970s, Wong's cultural importance never did. He would continue to pop up in Chinese culture, even to be played by Jackie Chan twice in *Drunken Master* and its sequel, released in the US as *The Legend of the Drunken Master*.

Which brings us to the 1990's and our present *OUATIC* films. Once again, China faces troubled times. The country is still reeling from the 1989 Tiananmen Square protest and massacre, and ahead looms the uncertainty of Hong Kong's independence - and the independence of Hong Kong's prolific (and massively profitable) film industry - as Great Britain prepares to turn control of Hong Kong over to China. Two people would bring Wong Fei-hung and his cultural message to a new generation.

The first is director and producer Tsui (pronounced "Choy") Hark. Tsui remains a giant in Hong Kong cinema; it doesn't take long to come across his influence in films from the '90s and beyond. As Maggie Lee writes in her essay, "Past Master,"

> "The creative force behind the series, Tsui went on to direct four of the five [*OUATIC*] films, while presiding over all of them, in addition to the stand-alone *Once Upon a Time in China and America* (1997), as producer. One cannot imagine Hong Kong cinema without Tsui - its golden age would lose its luster. He has been called the Asian Steven Spielberg, for his childlike wonder, trendsetting genius, and box-office wizardry. But he earned this comparison while working with far fewer financial and technical resources, under pressure-cooker conditions. He has summed up his Hong Kong career as 'fighting in a narrow lane.' "

What Tsui also brought to his Wong Fei-hung reinvention is evident in a 1976 documentary film Tsui worked on while studying film in New York, *From Spikes to*

Spindles. Tsui (acting as cinematographer on the Christine Choy-directed film) shows early on his social consciousness as he joins other young filmmakers in giving voice to the residents of New York's Chinatown, after the brutal beating and death of protestor Peter Yew at the hands of the NYPD. That outlook is clear in all the *OUATIC* films, especially the last, when Wong travels to America to champion not only his fellow Chinese, but American Indigenous people as well.[41]

The other person to reinvent Wong Fei-hung was the new actor to portray him: an up-and-coming star named Jet Li. Where performers like Jackie Chan and Sammo Hung learned their craft as apprentices at the Beijing Opera (think part circus acrobat, part martial artist), Li was a five-time wushu national champion from Beijing. Even the legendary Bruce Lee had only ever competed once, as a teen (he won), so Li was something of a rarity, having established his bona fides outside the film world. His Wong (Li wasn't even out of his twenties at the time) was ideal for the more extended and frenetic fight scenes the world had come to expect from Hong Kong kung fu. Where Jackie Chan used speed and power in a more staccato fighting style (my opinion), Jet Li is fluid and graceful, sacrificing none of the speed. This is Li at his finest, and these are the films that launched his international career.

So, beyond the fighting scenes, are the films any good?

---

[41] A journey that the real-life Wong Fei-hung almost certainly never took.

The surprising answer is yes, they are.

Not to sound crass, but once you get past "II" in any film franchise, we're used to quality falling off drastically. I'd known that *OUATICII* was one of those rare films considered to equal if not surpass the original, but until my son gifted me with this boxed set, I had no idea the series had so many films. The warning signs are there: after *OUATICIII*, a new director (Yuen Bun) and a new Wong (Vincent Zhao) take over. But Tsui continued to produce all the films, even returning as a director for *OUATICV*, and Li as Wong in *OUATICAA*. And while the quality may dip a little (budget constraints for *OUATICIV* become visible, as do some wires in the actors' rigs), it doesn't suffer much. And the character of Wong Fei-hung gradually develops over the course of six films.

In the hands of both director/producer Tsui and actors Li and Zhao, Wong Fei-hung comes to mirror China itself. In the first film Wong simply defends his people from the threat of foreign imperialists, struggling to defend attacks on both Chinese lives and Chinese culture. As a human being, Li plays him as bewildered by Western ways and technology, socially naive and awkward around foreigners (he is also remarkably stubborn, a thoroughly human trait that endears him to us even more). But as the films go on, Wong begins to see that his country is under attack partially because there are so many factions of Chinese fighting for control of their own land. As some extremist groups develop in response, looking to demonize and dehumanize foreigners prior to eliminating them, Wong recognizes this reaction as a lethal poison to the Chinese spirit. He also begins to see that some of the "progress" offered by the West is harmful to his people, some of it is beneficial, but *all* of it is inevitable in some way. As Wong wrestles with adapting to outside influences, so does China. Wong even eventually is forced to use a pistol, but it becomes a necessary tool of the martial artist, never a replacement for his discipline. In these days of franchise films it's easy to say Hong Kong film studio Golden Harvest was milking every last drop out of their cash cow, and maybe that's not wrong. But even if it were the case, Tsui Hark took the opportunity in each film to expand his story just a little. By the end of the series, Wong Fei-hung has realized that China's only choices are to halt its progress, surrender, or adapt. He has completed his journey from citizen to statesman.

So, over the course of six films, we see a contemporary filmmaker take a figure from the past and use him to carry on a conversation with modern audiences about where their society is heading. Voltaire said "If God did not exist, it would be necessary to invent him," and China has it both ways with Wong Fei-hung. A man from China's troubled past is conferred with in popular culture whenever the people have need of him, and they will inflate him if that is necessary. Tsui is a filmmaker who cares deeply about his people at home and across the globe, and when it became his turn to tell Wong's story, it was to provide hope and guidance to his fellow Chinese. "Remember your past," Tsui seems to be telling his audience, "remember who you are." Rooted in that, adjust and adapt as the Chinese people have always done. A more profound message than we generally expect from our action flicks.

Especially the ones that righteously deliver kick-ass kung fu!

Paris is Burning

US, 1990. Directed by Jennie Livingston. 76 minutes, color.

Paris is Burning is a documentary about a twice-marginalized community: the LGBTQI+ Black and Latinx people of 1980s Harlem. It's a statement of pride and desire. It's a film about a community that is happy to share its stories, but refuses to explain itself. Much, much more than just a documentary about drag balls (as if that's not enough), *Paris is Burning* is a film about the American Dream.

A primer: The New York Ball scene started out as competitive drag shows among different "Houses," modeled (pun intended) after the fashion houses of Europe; *Paris is Burning* features the House of Corey, the House of LaBeija, the House of Xtravaganza, the House of Ninja, the House of Saint Laurent, the House of Pendavis, and the House of Dupree. Some Houses have Fathers, but each House is headed by a Mother (in every instance in this film a drag queen), whose job it is to guide and counsel her Children, support them, even offer them loans or a place to stay when times get desperate. This is no mere rhetorical device. Many of a House's Children have been tossed out by their own biological families. Unlike the houses of Europe, the Mothers of the Houses of Harlem are reclaiming human beings. They're saving lives. Members of a House, no matter what age or circumstance, proudly call themselves Children, as if to remember their relationships and responsibilities to their House, their Mothers, and each other. (A possible alternate title, as I learned from one of the interviews on the disc, was *You Know How the Children Can Be*, which I think may have been the perfect blend of affection and sass.)

The people featured in this film didn't create the drag balls of Harlem; Pepper LaBeija, Mother of her House, talks about going to balls as a child in 1950s Harlem, watching her own neighbors perform (in this essay I'm using the preferred pronouns - where available - of each performer). But they go back much further than that, as Michelle Parkerson writes in her essay, "The Fire This Time:"

> "The ballroom culture documented in *Paris is Burning* was a contemporary expression of a ritual that had been nurtured by Black and Latino gay men since the late nineteenth century. According to researcher Oliver Stabbe, 'In 1869, within Harlem's Hamilton Lodge, drag balls began... The balls were crucial in the creation and maintenance of LGBTQ culture.' By the 1920s, the Harlem balls had metamorphosed from clandestine community gatherings into lavish spectacles. These were annual, eagerly awaited events throughout the thirties, sponsored by civic groups such as the Grand Lodge

of Odd Fellows, or extravagant costume masquerades held at large social halls - the Rockland Palace or the Savoy Ballroom. The soirees were often benefit galas attended by well-to-do Harlem strivers, the general public, and white 'swells' slumming it uptown. The sensational details of these balls were highlighted in the society entertainment columns of mainstream Black newspapers (the *New York Age*, the *Amsterdam News*) and weeklies of the time."

If the film stopped at being a celebration of queer culture, and a story of how a besieged community cares for its own, that alone would make for a powerful documentary. But the drag balls morph into something much more interesting in the 1980s, and much more inclusive (though the film was released in 1990, director Jennie Livingston spent seven years collecting footage and seeking financing). The contestants at the drag balls compete in categories, and in addition to categories for crossdressing and nonbinary performers, categories arose for straight, cisgendered participants. Categories like Sportswear, Eveningwear, Schoolboy/Schoolgirl Realness, Executive Realness. What is "Realness"? It's Black and Latinx people dressing for their version of the American Dream. It's showing the rest of the country that the people of Harlem - queer and straight - have the same aspirations we all have. And more than that. These categories suggest that the only difference between the business executive and the working stiff, the college student and the drop out or never-went is *the look*. The Children of

Harlem are telling the world, "We can look the part. Therefore, we can *be* the part." And at that point, Livingston brings her cameras outside into bright midtown Manhattan, and we see the white wealthy and upper-middle-class preening and posing in their own attire, and we can't help but wonder whether success isn't really based more on looking the part than it is on talent. It's a fascinating moment in the film. Where you might expect a satire of American consumerism, instead you find acceptance of it. "We embrace this, just as you do. We want this, too. Our dreams are the same as yours."

Voguing grew out of the drag balls. Its master practitioner is Willi Ninja, Mother of his own House, an athletic and expressive dance of hands, arms, legs, staccato stylized poses (*Vogue* magazine is where the name of the dance came from), a sprinkling of Egyptian hieroglyphics, and more attitude than you can handle. It was *not* created by Madonna for her "Vogue" video, but appropriated. Voguing itself led directly to this documentary, when L.A. resident Jennie Livingstone discovered a group of men performing in Washington Square Park. She had come east to study photography and maybe film, but had no money for school. She asked the performers for permission to photograph them and asked, "What are you doing?" They sent her to a drag ball directly, and in her the Children found someone to tell their stories (Livingston didn't know it at the time, but she was soon to awaken to her own queer nature).

Oh, their stories. Two teens - two (small "c") children, 13 and 15! - seemingly happily hustling on the streets, a gift life has given them away from the families that rejected them. Mother Dorian Corey, telling her stories as an elder, putting on her face for the thousandth time as she tells us, "When I grew up you wanted to look like Marlene Dietrich or Betty Grable. Unfortunately, I didn't know that I really wanted to look like Lena Horne. When I grew up, Black stars were stigmatized. No one wanted to look like Lena Horne. Everyone wanted to look like Marilyn Monroe." And Venus Xtravaganza, a soft-spoken delicate-looking slip of a young thing (but tougher than nails), who wants only to have a sex change and get out of the city and to a place where no one knows her ("The Peekskills, or Florida, maybe"), and get married in white. She never got there, found murdered later, strangled, her body found after four days under a bed in a sleazy hotel. Her Mother, Angie Extravaganza, who had to identify the body can only tell us, "That's part of life, that's part of being a transsexual in New York...."

My only criticism of the film is that there aren't more of these stories. In an interview on the disc, Livingston talks about the difficulty of editing a documentary; when there's no script, a story has to be written in the editing room, not before filming. She had hours of material that needed to be whittled down, but I think she overshot her mark, with the film barely passing the hour-and-a-quarter mark. Then again, maybe she feared begging the indulgence of mainstream film audiences past that. But there are almost two hours of outtakes on the disc, and these are people well worth spending more time with. Watch the outtakes, if you happen to see the Criterion disc, as well as the entire episode of *The Joan Rivers Show* director and cast appeared on - it may make television history as the first time a chat show host asked a guest their pronouns (though I'll leave it to someone else's research skills to confirm that).

One last story. You'll find Sol Pendavis, Father of his House in *Paris is Burning*, but not this story, which he told in the extras. Sol was in the army at the time of filming (he retired in 2012 as a Captain, according to his IMDB biography). Remember, this was prior even to the "don't ask don't tell" years, though at the time of this story Sol hadn't yet awakened to his own sexual identity. Sol had to run dinner over to someone at a ball, and happened to be in uniform at the time. As he crossed the floor, the emcee yelled to him, "Walk over here." Sol did so. "Salute!" Sol did. "Walk back!" Sol complied, and was handed a trophy for the first-ever "Military Realness" category; Sol maintains that he is the only person he knows to have personally originated a category. Later, Sol decided to join House Pendavis (Sol was born with the surname Williams), and while each House has its own requirements, they all share this one: You must compete in the Butch Queen First Time in Drag at a Ball category. Sol obliged, but a picture of him in drag got back to his commanding officer. Facing a court martial, Sol told his C.O. it was actually a picture of his mother, and when Sol produced an actual photograph of his mother, his superior, noting the resemblance, dismissed the case.

Paris, Texas

France/Germany/US, 1984. Directed by Wim Wenders. 145 minutes, color.

Paris, Texas opens with a beautiful shot of a terrible place: the Mojave Desert. Through it walks a man in a suit, a red baseball cap, and taped-up shoes. He has just run out of water. He looks, as a character tells him later, "like forty miles of rough road." He cannot, or will not speak. He is a walking catatonic, seemingly produced by the desert itself. He makes it to an all-but deserted bar (scrawled on a chalkboard: "The dust has come to stay. You may stay or pass on through or whatever."). He chews on some ice from a cooler, and collapses. The only other individual in the place, a Good Samaritan pulling at a bottle of beer, walks over and pokes at the fallen man with his boot.

Paris, Texas is a film about the aftermath of a family blown apart. It is a love story, culminating in an act of astonishing sacrifice. It's a road movie, no, two road movies... it's easy to lose count. It's a story of the American West, of the desert. It's a story of brothers, and family, and healing. It's a picture postcard, and a cinematographer's showcase.

That the film gets the American Southwest, and Reagan-Era America so *right*, so poetically *and* realistically at the same time might seem miraculous coming from not just a foreign filmmaker, but from Wim Wenders, a pioneer of the New German Cinema born of the 1970s. But I've learned that sometimes it takes an outsider's eye to see things we Americans overlook. Listen to Sam Shepard, the film's screenwriter, speaking in an interview with film historian Bernard Eisenschitz in 1984, reprinted in the disc's booklet:

> "Wim has this fascination with America that I have, in a way. But I feel that, because of his... Europeanness, there are certain qualities about American culture that... ordinarily, certain American directors would totally overlook. They wouldn't find a neon sign of a stagecoach going like this that fascinating. But because of his European background, I guess, this thing suddenly strikes him as having an obsessive quality about it."[42]

Of course, it didn't hurt when Sam Shepard, rodeo aficionado and prolific American playwright agreed to pen Wender's script. Or that Wenders turned to American music icon Ry Cooder to score an unforgettable soundtrack for the film, Cooder sometimes just improvising on his slide guitar

---

[42] I wrote something similar when I wrote about *The Apu Trilogy*, and how director Satyajit Ray, having grown up in the city, so beautifully portrayed a boy's life in rural India.

an old Blind Willie Johnson tune as he watched footage on a screen. But consider this, something I read years ago in a fascinating book, *Watching Movies*, a collection of interviews from a *New York Times* column of the same name. Rick Lyman sat down with actors and filmmakers and watched a film with each of them (of their subject's choosing), and foreign filmmakers talking about American films was particularly eye-opening. If you'll indulge a digression, I think we Americans can learn volumes from how outsiders experience our culture. Here's Janusz Kaminski, Steven Spielberg's go-to cinematographer, describing watching the great 1971 American film *Vanishing Point* from behind the Iron Curtain on Polish television:

> "Perhaps in the mind of the Communist government, the reason it was allowed to be shown was that it was seen as a decadent American movie. Under the circumstances it was viewed as negative and a criticism of America. But the people who were responsible for putting on the television programs in the system at that time were not the dumbest. I think they were able to slip this through because it appeared to be criticizing capitalism. But it really wasn't, and I think they knew that.

> "I am so curious to see this movie again. You know, I have not seen it in more than twenty years, not at all. But I have this great recollection of thinking as I

was watching it, 'Wow, this is what America is all about; this is what freedom of expression is all about.' Here is an individual who is willing to sacrifice, even to sacrifice his own life, for the sake of his idea of freedom and independence.

"These are the movies that influenced me and, I think, millions of other young people all across Eastern Europe.... This is the way we learned about the world, we Eastern Europeans - from the movies.... For me, I saw America not as this country of plenty, this country of wealth, where everyone has a car and everyone has a house, but as a country of freedom where the individual is free, the ideology is free. That is why I so much wanted to come here.[43]"

In an interview on the disc, director Wenders said he felt the reason the film was given a lukewarm reception in the US (it won the Palme d'Or at Cannes when it was released and was acclaimed internationally) was precisely because he felt American audiences didn't appreciate foreign filmmakers commenting on America. He said that in Europe audiences were used to filmmakers from other countries crossing borders all the time. And as a German born in 1945, he said he felt he was born into a nation of silence, where his fellow Germans looked down and avoided talking about their own

---

[43] *Watching Movies*, by Rick Lyman, Times Books, pp 12-14.

society. Had it not been for French, British, Italian, and other foreign filmmakers, Wenders felt *no one* would have been looking at Germany in those years.

But it's a beautiful, soulful film, and no matter how often I see it I get engrossed in it. Harry Dean Stanton is Travis, the man wandering out of the desert, and Dean Stockwell is his brother Walt, who having feared Travis dead after vanishing four years earlier, flies from L.A. to bring him back to life. Let me say that again: Harry Dean Stanton and Dean Stockwell play *brothers*. That's a two-man A-Team of '70s and '80s character actors right there, and it's a pleasure to watch these men work. Travis went missing after he and his young wife, Jane (Nastassja Kinski) split up and vanished; their 3-year-old son, Hunter (Hunter Carson) appears at Walt and his wife Annes's (Aurore Clément) front door a few weeks later, and they take him in. With loving patience, Walt coaxes Travis back to human existence, and the two drive back to L.A. (Travis refuses to fly) so that he can be reunited with his son. Eventually, Travis and Hunter drive back to Texas to search for Jane. The last scene of the film is one of the finest in cinema. It takes place in a Texas peep-show, our two characters reaching out through a telephone and one-way glass. It was a masterpiece of lighting, editing, and cinematography to make it actually work, but you don't need to know any of that because the effort never shows on screen. And it's shot, acted, and written (by one of America's finest playwrights) as a one-act play. It's remarkable. And I know this piece is already quote-heavy, but it's worth reading what Stanton told Eisenschitz in *his* interview about acting that last scene:

"The painful part, with Sam's writing, was to understand how to do it. Because you don't have to act his writing. Finally, Wim said, 'Don't act these lines. You just say them, like poetry, say it with a meter.' and that's what Nastassja and I tried to do at the end, just say the lines. That's the problem, I think, with people who do Sam's plays. They try to act it, and his writing you don't act. You don't even have to motivate it if you can just be simple, because all that needs to be said is in the writing."

Paris, Texas is beautiful in practically every way a film can be beautiful. The music and images are as natural as they are unforgettable. The human relationships, the heartbreak along with the joy, all told gently and earnestly with intelligent performances, and brilliant writing and direction. The film doesn't speak to us today as it would have back in 1984, only because it's so specific to an America of that time and place. But the beauty of this film will never fade.

The Passion of Joan of Arc

France, 1928. Directed by Carl Theodor Dreyer. Silent, black and white, 81 minutes.

What stands out for me the most in *The Passion of Joan of Arc* isn't the story of the film's restoration, isn't the controversial use of closeups by director Carl Theodor Dreyer, not is it the oratorio *Voices of Light* composed by Richard Einhorn in 1994 for this film. No, what stands out for me is the choice found in the title of the film. This is not a story of the life of Joan of Arc, nor her role in French history (she was canonized just eight years before this film was released). *The Passion of Joan of Arc* documents only her trial and execution, and if the title echoes the passion of Christ, that's entirely intentional.

Any woman watching this today will immediately understand what's going on. Even though Joan is being tried by the English church, this is not about heresy, this is not about nations or politics. This is about power and dominance. This is about old men isolating and bullying a nineteen-year-old girl because she dared to claim that God spoke directly to her and not through the Church. These men are so threatened, so offended by the idea that they are, however briefly, unnecessary, that they are willing to forge evidence against her and torture her to death.

In a title card at the beginning of the picture, Dreyer is anxious to provide his documentation for his film: it is taken from trial documents found at the Bibliothèque de la Chambre des Députés in Paris. Dreyer is going back to the records of the 15th-century trial itself to let us know he is not elaborating (at least not in the script) on what was said at Joan's trial. Dreyer himself saw the film as something of a documentary, to the extent that he added no credit sequences to his film whatsoever (these were added later in restoring the film). He felt that even acknowledging that he used actors and technicians would detract from an audience's feeling of authenticity of the film.

That we even have this *Passion* is remarkable. Film from this era was both perishable and highly flammable; as a result we have lost roughly 90% of all silent films ever made. (To put this into perspective, when George Lucas sought to refurbish and re-release the original *Star Wars* trilogy after twenty years, he found that original prints and negatives from 1977 had begun to deteriorate already.) The original film premiered in April of 1928, and French authorities immediately demanded changes to the Danish director's film, made without Dreyer's consent. So for a while there were two versions in circulation, until in December of 1928 a fire destroyed the labs of the UFA studio in Berlin, and Dreyer's original negative was lost, with only a few prints in circulation. But Dreyer was famous for putting actors through multiple takes, and was able to cobble together a second "original" version from alternate takes, which had been stored elsewhere. This second negative was lost to a second fire in 1929, and this time Dreyer feared his film was gone for good. Twice through the years, in 1933 and again in 1951, prints of *Passion* were discovered and released, but were so corrupted by added scenes and soundtracks to court mass appeal that the film was unrecognizable.

Then in 1981, while cleaning out a closet in the Kikemark Sykehus, a mental institution outside of Oslo, a workman found a set of film canisters. These were sent to the Norwegian Film Institute - which promptly stored them without review. When they were finally opened, not only did the containers reveal an intact print of *The Passion of Joan of Arc*, but the original wrapping bearing the Danish censor's stamp of approval from 1928 - an especially exciting find as it was well known that the Danish censors had required no changes to the original film. The film was carefully restored, perhaps ironically, by the Cinémathèque Française, which made sure to restore Dreyer's original version, and not the edited version French officials had previously insisted on. Had it not been for this discovery, we would not have this powerful film today.

Earlier I mentioned Dreyer's use of closeups throughout the film. *The Passion of Joan of Arc* is a story told in faces; I believe I counted two establishing shots in the whole film to let us know where we were. Dreyer's choice was unpopular even in his time; it was thought that a closeup shot of a character's face should serve as the emotional climax of a scene, to be used sparingly for greater effect. Dreyer felt that keeping the camera always on the characters' faces would bring the viewer closer to the subjects themselves; we would be able to *feel* Joan's persecution more vividly. For a while, Dreyer is right, I think. Renée Falconetti, who plays Joan, is heartbreakingly expressive, her innocence, her tears both bringing us in. But after a while it's disorienting, especially when we have no idea where in the room her interrogators are standing. It becomes unclear whether Joan is looking at them directly as she answers, or gazing elsewhere, perhaps at an image none of the judges can see.

Finally, this disc allows the viewer to watch the film with the *Voices of Light* oratorio, and I highly recommend you do so. The music is haunting, glorious, and beautifully accentuates what is going on onscreen. And it's not cheating; "silent" films were almost never really "silent;" they would be accompanied by piano, soloists, even orchestras at times for major productions or large venues. (When I was talking about this film to my son, he reminded me that Harpo Marx wrote in his autobiography that he got started playing the piano for silent film screenings. He said he only knew two songs, and would simply play them fast or slow, depending on what was happening on screen.) It's not a stretch at all to imagine Dreyer himself approving Einhorn's reverent score.

The Phantom Carriage

Sweden, 1921. Directed by Victor Sjöström. Silent, black and white (tinted), 106 minutes.

There's an old Swedish folk tale that tells of a ghostly horse-drawn coach, invisible to the living, that travels the land collecting the souls of the deceased at the moment of death. The horse and the carriage never change, but the driver does. Whoever dies at the stroke of midnight on New Year's Eve is condemned to spend the next year driving the coach, reaping Death's harvest, until the next unlucky soul passes at midnight a year hence. This folk tale, given brief new life in the post-WWI spiritualism revival even as it was about to succumb to 20th-century intellectual realism, is at the heart of *The Phantom Carriage*.

The Phantom Carriage earned a reputation as a masterpiece of early cinema. Charlie Chaplin called it the best film he'd ever seen. Ingmar Bergman saw it as a child and as an adult cited the film as an influence on his own work, and his decision to become a film director. It's a folk tale, a melodrama, a ghost story, and a social commentary. And while *The Phantom Carriage* didn't pioneer the use of multiple exposures as a special effect (that honor probably goes to the fantastical late-19th-century works of Georges Méliès), it was the first to use this technique so artfully, so eerily in service of its story, that even today the effect is haunting.

The story is told in flashbacks (another relatively untested technique). We begin at the bedside of Sister Edit (Astrid Holm), a Salvation Army Sister who is dying of tuberculosis. Attended by her mother and another Sister, she is distraught, pleading that "David Holm" be brought to her, a request that causes nothing but consternation from those comforting her. But she is insistent, and eventually David Holm (director Victor Sjöström himself) is discovered drinking in a nearby graveyard with some mates. It is New Year's Eve, and Holm has just spooked his chums with the story of the ghostly coach told by his friend Georges, an otherwise cheery fellow, who insists that Holm take extra care not to put himself at risk the last night of the year. Holm refuses to go to the dying Sister Edit. His drinking companions, aghast, try to force him to go. They fight, and Holm is felled by a bottle to the head. As he lies still in the graveyard, a clock chimes midnight....

The coach arrives to collect Holm's soul and turn the reins over to him. But the driver is none other than Georges, who had in fact died at midnight the previous year, just as he feared. He tells Holm that he feels responsible for his fate because it was Georges that turned Holm away from his wholesome family life toward alcohol. Like Dickens' ghosts of *A Christmas Carol*, the coachman takes Holm on a tour of his previous life, in the hope that he may reform him, and give him a second chance at life.

It's worth noting that in 1921, the Temperance Movement was alive in Europe. The United States was just one year into Prohibition, and according to film historian Casper Tybjerg, who provides commentary on the disc, Swedish voters had narrowly defeated a prohibition referendum of their own, 51% to 49%. In one scene we see Holm picnicking with his wife and young children in a meadow, the ideal family man. In the next, he and his brother have been lured to a saloon, and alcohol turns both men vicious. Holm wakes up the next day in a prison cell, arrested for drunkenness, but before he is released, prison officials take him to see his brother, who is to begin a long sentence for killing a man while intoxicated. Holm swears to reform, but upon returning home finds his wife has vanished with his children. His remorse immediately turns to rage against the woman who "betrayed" him.

Eventually (we're still in flashback mode) Holm's search for his wife takes him to a newly-opened Salvation Army, where he meets Sister Edit. By this point Holm has contracted tuberculosis himself, and is reckless and uncaring in who he exposes to his disease. He's become a monster, delighting in cruelty, even to the Sisters who are trying to help him. Before he leaves the next morning, Sister Edit begs him to return on New Year's Eve; she tells him she has prayed that their first guest will have a wonderful year, and wants to see if God has blessed him.

What follows is pure melodrama, a genre popular at the time and one US audiences knew well thanks to D.W. Griffith.

Holm tracks down his wife and promises to make her life hell; he even breathes heavily on his young children, explaining that if he infects them, his wife will suffer even more when they die. When Holm passes out, his wife locks herself and the children in the next room; in a scene that hearkens forward to Jack Torrence in *The Shining*, Holm goes after the door with an axe, intercut with his family cowering under the assault. But though we are in melodrama, Sjöström avoids acting melodramatically; as ferocious and hate-driven as he is, when his wife passes out, he cradles her to revive her with a glass of water. We are meant to see the battle within the man between his two sides (or between drink and sobriety).

Thus, when Georges finally brings Holm's soul to the dying Sister Edit, we see him wracked with tears for the brutality he has caused. Because Sister Edit is dying, she is able to see both Holm and Georges, and is heartbroken that she didn't do enough to bring the family back together. Holm is determined to put her at peace, and Georges agrees to return Holm's soul to his body, reviving him, to give him a second chance at being a good man.

That's a lot of ground to cover, and the story takes more than one viewing to get straight (I've left out a few stray points). But it's so artfully told, that the audience is rooted throughout, and we care about which side of Holm wins out. The effects of the ghostly carriage are so seamlessly and carefully shot, that they truly end up calling more attention to the story than to themselves - something filmmakers even today struggle with. One choice Sjöström made that I think worked beautifully was to leave the indoor scenes a sepia tone, but use blue tinting for all the outdoor nighttime scenes, as if to bathe the film in moonlight.

You have a choice of soundtracks on this disc. I watched the film once through with each of them, and you can't go wrong with either. The first is a chamber music-type score written by Swedish composer Matti Bye, and is rich and poignant without being saccharine. The other is a more dissonant electronic (mostly) score by the experimental duo KTL (Stephen O'Malley and Peter Rehberg), and even though it seems like it may be at odds with a century-old film, the mood perfectly accentuates the visuals.

But before I close, I need to nitpick, from my 21st-century vantage point, so this is less a criticism of the film itself than it is perhaps a societal change in outlook. *Why* give Holm this second chance at all? Is it worth it to gamble with the lives of his wife and children, much less the other people he has hurt (it's strongly implied that Sister Edit contracted tuberculosis from breathing in the germs from a coat of Holms she stayed up all night mending)? Does Georges have the right to make that call? After all, Holm has already reneged on one promise to reform in the time it took him to walk home from jail to find his family fled. Maybe driving the coach might be a penance of sorts for Holm, a sentence he would carry out for a year. Finally, who's to say who will be tasked with driving the carriage if Holm doesn't? An innocent child? A tired old woman? Perhaps Sister Edit herself, who also dies on New Year's Eve! Enough damage has been done by well-meaning people trying to reform this man. Maybe a year on the coach would be the best thing for him, and his family.

Police Story/Police Story 2

Police Story: Hong Kong, 1985. Directed by Jackie Chan. 100 minutes, color. *Police Story 2*: Hong Kong, 1988. Directed by Jackie Chan. 120 minutes, color.

A few essays ago we talked about Jet Li. Now we're going to talk about Jackie Chan.

Police Story and *Police Story 2* represent the world's greatest action star coming into his own during the golden age of Hong Kong cinema, and completely changing how action movies are made, not just in Asia, but worldwide. To understand this requires a digression into the history of Chinese and Hong Kong martial arts movies, and a little background on Chan himself.

We've all seen vintage martial arts movies with hoary old bewhiskered kung fu masters announcing their techniques ("Eagle Claw!") to their mortal enemies before attacking. This was more or less the state of martial arts movies by the time Bruce Lee came around in the 1970s. They came from a place of action filmmakers wanting to be true to the various fighting styles that had evolved in China over the centuries. They celebrated the past, and they celebrated the old masters who fought for justice and fought for China. They were about showcasing the strength of China's people and her culture. If they weren't propaganda films, they were at least morality tales. The actors and crews who made these films cared less about making good movies than they did about being true to the heroes of the past, and their fighting techniques.

Jackie Chan was born in Hong Kong in 1954. When he was six, his family emigrated to Australia, but Jackie struggled with academics, so his family sent him back to Hong Kong to attend the China Drama Academy, one of the Peking Opera schools. If you're not familiar with Chinese Opera, it's a highly stylized form of theater, similar to Japanese kabuki theater in that actors subsume their appearances and personalities under elaborate costumes and makeup, rigorously adhering to ancient scripts, songs, and acting styles. *Unlike* kabuki theater, there's plenty of action and acrobatics, as duels and battles are fought out onstage. Think of it as an almost circus-like blend of gymnastics, martial arts, and musical theater. This is the kind of training Jackie Chan grew up with. It was... well, it was probably child abuse by today's Western standards; training was long and rigorous, discipline was swift, and when Chan finally left the Academy at age 17, no one had gotten around to teaching him to read or write. But Chan excelled at the physical arts, and earned expertise in something no other martial artist had studied: entertaining an audience.

And somewhere along the way, Chan learned to love movies, especially the comedic masters of the silent era, like Buster Keaton and Harold Lloyd, to the extent where he lifted gags straight from their films into his own. Chan became an avid consumer of cinema, not just action films, but all of it. When his time arrived, Chan was determined to put the kind of production values into martial arts films he'd seen in Hollywood movies. Chan watched movies to learn his craft not as a fight choreographer, but as a film director.

The death in 1973 of Bruce Lee, the face of Hong Kong martial arts cinema, threw the industry into turmoil. Chan (who had done stunt work in one of Lee's films), along with dozens of other hopefuls was called upon to take his mantle, but Jackie wasn't comfortable in the traditional role. He didn't have Lee's need to prove his martial arts mastery. Chan wanted to entertain audiences.

The 1978 film *Drunken Master* gives us an early look at the direction in which Chan wanted to go. In this film, he takes on the role of Wong Fei-hung, the legendary physician and martial artist Jet Li portrayed in the *Once Upon a Time in China* films. But Chan's Fei-hung isn't the stoic old master, he's a young man. Fei-hung is cocky, unmotivated, constantly trying to get out of his strict master's training, or hustle a free meal. But he's a likable, relatable guy, as often the victim of hijinks in the film as the perpetrator. He just needs to find purpose, and that's what *Drunken Master* is about. The film has more training sequences than fight sequences, and more Fei-hung getting his ass kicked than prevailing. And it's *funny*, full of coarse humor, fart jokes included. The fight scenes lean on comedy as much as they do athleticism. It's Jackie Chan announcing to the world, "I'm not Bruce Lee. I can't do what he does. I'm Jackie Chan. This is what I do."

So when Chan finally got the chance to do movies his way, here's what he brought to *Police Story* that hadn't been done before: He brought the martial arts film into the present day, into a contemporary setting audiences lived in. No longer did fights take place in rural villages or Shaolin temples, but on streets, playgrounds, and in shopping malls. He replaced the wise, unflappable master from the kung fu epics (as well as the tough, brutal "Dirty Harry"-type cop) with Ka-kui ("Kevin" in the US dubbed versions), a young police inspector who works hard, has a sense of fair play, and a girlfriend (Maggie Cheung) he loves and who drives him crazy. Chan's background at The China Drama Academy made him care much less about strict martial arts technique than about what looks good on camera - in an interview on the disc, Chan says, "I don't want 'pretty.' I don't want fighting. I want dance." Chan had a film student's desire to tell human stories using established techniques. And Chan had one more asset that no other filmmaker in the world shared: The Jackie Chan Stunt Team.

There's a long and worthwhile documentary included with this version where Chan takes us on a tour of his team's facility, and it's eye-opening even to someone like me who's followed Jackie's career for years. He actually calls it a lab, and Chan is forthright and gracious about how much of his success relies on the stunt team he works with. Chan trains with them, works out with them, listens to their ideas, and plans new stunts with them. Along the way they develop a level of trust that would be impossible with performers unfamiliar with each other. Jackie knows who excels at falling stunts, who has the best kicking stance, who the best drivers are. When Benny Lai comes in with a kick, Chan knows how long his leg is, and how hard he may connect. All those little shouts you hear in a fight? In a Jackie Chan fight, a "Hah!" may signal a kick coming in, and from which direction. "Hoo!" might signal a punch, so Chan is reminded who is doing what and from where. All this is necessary because of the complexity of Chan's action sequences. Chan *hated* watching Bruce Lee fight multiple opponents on film, because they all danced around him waiting for their turn to come after him individually, which Lee did so you could get a clear view of his technique. Jackie knows you don't care about his technique, so he wants all his opponents to come at him at once. And that fundamentally changes the fight scene in a couple of ways.

First, every move has to be planned out and rehearsed, that's a given. *So much* of Chan's action scenes depend on critical timing. But when a performer comes in and delivers a kick, sending you into the next performer advancing with a punch, or a knife attack, you've got a lot of moving parts, especially if that move sends you into an office chair you're going to slide across the set in. So it's not enough just for the performers to know the "dance," they have to do multiple takes to make sure each punch lands where it should, that the actor's face isn't obscured, and that everything is in frame. And Jackie is a perfectionist when it comes to how scenes look on screen. So lots of takes, more chances for performers (including Chan) to get tired, more chances to make mistakes. Especially as most of the kicks are actually connecting. Chan prefers real effects, and Hong Kong studios never had the budgets for added effects anyway. So Chan and his team designed special padded shoes that look like the real thing, that they can add chalk to for that little extra visual "oomph" in the shot. Which means performers can't miss, but don't want to connect too hard either. Add to all *that* split-second automotive stunts, where Jackie's life depends on a car stopping *after* he begins a jump, that you begin to understand how much trust is required to make movies the way Jackie Chan does. It would be impossible to choreograph this with strangers, as Chan found out the few times he needed to.

But the other thing this fight style did was realistically change the nature of the fight and the *character* of the protagonist. Unless the hero under attack has superhuman abilities, they are not going to escape an attack in a contemporary setting unharmed. Jackie Chan's entire style of fighting revolves around blocking and defense, enduring what blows you must, escaping if you can. When Bruce Lee fought on screen, no one laid a hand on him, at least not until he worked his way to the final villain, who'd usually leave a scratch with an edged weapon to show how tough Lee was (and to give him the chance to rip off his shirt). Jackie Chan gets the shit kicked out of him in *all* of his fights. Ka-kui would much rather run than fight, or not fight at all. It's a last resort. There's a scene in *Police Story 2* where Ka-kui doesn't even land a single blow on an opponent, just blocks, deflects, and endures until he can take him down by other means. When he's outnumbered by bad guys on the street in *Police*

Story, he runs to a playground, where he can find more cover. He fights to give himself distance so he can run away. He's not fighting to prove his skills, but to defend and protect. Bruce Lee's signature move, copied in *The Matrix*, was the "come here" hand gesture, an invitation to combat. Jackie Chan's signature move is sitting down. After fighting off opponents, he'll plop down on a chair, or a ladder and shrug, as if to say, "Are we done now? Can we talk?" It was for this reason that when my son began taking Tae Kwon Do at the age of six, it was Jackie Chan I introduced him to so that he could see his sport at its highest level of proficiency.

Police Story and *Police Story 2* are where all this first comes together. The modern setting, the fight team, the working-class cop, the love of film, the humor, the athleticism, the need to *entertain his audience*. It's not just that Jackie Chan works harder than anyone else, takes more risks, though he does. It's that in these films he's ready as a filmmaker to show what he and his team can do. All those years as a child training for the Peking Opera? They show up in the cadence of the fight scenes, building, crescendoing, and then relaxing to give us a chance to catch up. One can almost hear a metronomic rhythm to the action, as young Jackie would have heard as he trained to music.

Chan will take no easy road. Why simply cross a street on foot, when you can instead get there by jumping on two moving buses, leap Mario-style under and over oncoming street signs, and crash through a glass walkway? *Police Story* begins with an arrest gone wrong on a hillside shantytown, culminating in its destruction by an avalanche of a car chase.

It ends with an epic extended scene of mayhem in a shopping mall involving escalators, motorcycles, and *lots* of broken glass. The final stunt in the sequence is Chan leaping onto a pole of Christmas lights and sliding three floors down, bulbs popping, and falling through a wooden gazebo. Jackie repeats the shot three times from different cameras - he only did the stunt once - so his fans can be sure it was really him and nothing was faked. The electrician on the film set (the gaffer) was supposed to hook the lights up to a car battery, but instead had to plug them into mall current, resulting in 2nd-degree burns on Jackie's hands, followed by what was later diagnosed as two cracked vertebrae on the landing. Nevertheless, when Chan completes the stunt, he immediately pops up running to pursue the escaping villain.

Much has been made of Jackie Chan doing his own stunts, and ending his films with outtakes of he and his stunt team enduring pain and injury for the sake of the fans. I was surprised to learn where Chan originally got the idea. In the early 1980s he came to the United States to take a small part in a major American film. He couldn't bring his stunt team, no one really knew what to do with him, and he was even cast as a Japanese character. He returned to Hong Kong, worried he'd blown his one shot at working in the US, but determined to get back to work and perfect his style of filmmaking. That film was the Hal Needham-directed Burt Reynolds vehicle, *The Cannonball Run*. Needham ended that film with a reel of stunt outtakes, mostly to show off the camaraderie of his stunt crew, and the stars they worked with (well... Burt Reynolds, at least). Jackie took that idea as a way of proving to his fans his dedication and the dedication of his stunt team to *them*. It became his way of telling his fans "I won't lie to you, and I won't cheat. I'm one of you, and I'll risk my body to prove it."

It's also a great way of showing a six-year-old what happens when you try movie stunts in real life. Thank you, Jackie, for keeping my boy safe.

Portrait of a Lady on Fire

France, 2019. Directed by Céline Sciamma. 121 minutes, color.

Portrait of a Lady on Fire is a film about looks, and looking. It's a mesmerizing love story, a collaborative dance between artist and subject. As we watch the film, director Céline Sciamma teaches us how to observe. It's beautiful and political. "All art is political," Sciamma tells us in an interview on the disc. "If you're not being political, you're saying that everything is fine the way it is."

An artist, Marianne (Noémie Meriant), is called to a seaside, cliffside home in 18th-century France. She has been commissioned for a wedding portrait of Héloïse (Adèle Haenel), but since Héloïse has already refused to sit for one artist, Marianne must work in secret, observing her subject while she can, painting at night (Héloïse has been told Marianne is there to escort her on walks). Héloïse has been summoned out of a convent to marry the man who was betrothed to her older sister; the sister died a suicide rather than face her fate with her husband-to-be. Marianne steals looks and sketches as she can, and finishes the portrait, finally telling Héloïse her true purpose there. Héloïse demands to see the portrait, and asks Marianne, "Is this how you see me?" If Marianne will begin again, Héloïse will sit for her, but Marianne has to look at her subject more closely, more openly. Héloïse looks back. And in those looks, the two fall in love.

Men are physically all but absent in *Portrait of a Lady on Fire* - Héloïse's mother is directing the portraiture - but the weight of men can be felt throughout the film. Neither of these women are free; Héloïse must marry, and Marianne herself would not find work unless sponsored by her better-known painter father, whose studio she hopes to one day take over. These women, along with the servant Sophie (Luàna Bajrami), have perhaps a week to make a home for themselves before the men of the world reclaim them. Everything is different for these women. The male gaze, even - especially! - when seducing demands submission. Our lovers look upon each other openly, with warmth, interest, desire, and collaboration. The artist/subject hierarchy is smashed as Héloïse joins Marianne shoulder to shoulder behind the canvas, the women equals in assessing the art they are *both* creating. In the middle of the film - in another upsetting of hierarchies in the absence of men - both women take Sophie to a woman abortionist to end her pregnancy. Marianne averts her eyes, but Héloïse tells her "Look." (How many times will we hear that word?) They'll be fully present for Sophie for the procedure, and when they return home, Héloïse has Sophie lie down, recreating her pose, while Héloïse assumes the pose of the abortionist. "Paint this," she tells Marianne, and we begin to understand what types of scenes we might find in museums if women had been free to document their own lives, themselves, through art.

The film - as it must be considering its subject - is beautifully shot, and several decisions Sciamma made early on bore remarkable fruit. Together with director of photography Claire Mathon, she shot some test footage of the setting and of assistants' faces in both digital and 35mm film. The two were convinced from the beginning that digital cameras would be their choice, as they yielded much richer and more subtle skin tones. In addition, this would allow the filmmakers to shoot under natural or minimal light, including candlelight at night. It's astonishing what they were able to photograph; it makes you think of what *Barry Lyndon* might have been if infused with more human passion. But the drawback was a narrower field of focus; with digital cameras, if one actor takes a step or two away from the other, one of the two of them would fall out of focus. So the action moves with the grace of a dance, as Sciamma carefully choreographed the movement of the camera with the natural movement of her actors walking and talking.

And those scenes of movement became necessary because Sciamma knew the painting and sketching scenes would mostly be taken up by shots of the canvas with reverses to the actor, and needed to break those scenes up. But here is where Sciamma made another inspired decision. All the paintings and drawings in the film, each portrait in its various stages, would be done by an artist on set. Sciamma found Hélène Delmaire on Instagram, a contemporary painter able to paint in an 18th-century portrait style. Delmaire had never worked on a film before Sciamma approached her, and it is her hands we see whenever art is made in the film. Delmaire talked about her work in an interview on the disc, and pointed out that there were many women artists in the 1700s, their names and art erased as men took over the art world in the 19th century. Delmaire spoke with respect of Merlant's performance in *Portrait* - the artist said that in observing her work, Merlant never tried to imitate her hand gestures or brushwork. Instead, Delmaire tells us, Merlant learned the painter's "dance" of when to step back, or to the side while painting to gauge her progress, when to study her subject, and when to study her canvas. It may seem like a small detail, but when two professionals whose work depends on observation are in such sync, the results are bound to show up on the screen.

There are so many beautiful visual moments in this film, including an image of Marianne, having jumped into the sea to rescue her supplies, now sitting by a fireplace nude smoking a pipe as her clothes and her canvases dry - both artist and materials bare before painting. But I also need to mention the arresting use of sound in this film. There is no soundtrack, no incidental music. The only music we hear is within the film itself - a bit of Vivaldi heard first on harpsichord played by Marianne, then at the end of the film in a concert hall, and a haunting *a capella* work sung by women around a bonfire. All the rest is natural sound, and it adds to the verisimilitude of what you see on screen. The women occupy a sparsely-decorated, mostly empty house

(Héloïse must marry to improve the family's fortunes), and every time a character approaches from offscreen, you hear her solid footsteps lending gravity to the surroundings. Outside we hear the wind and the sea, inside we hear the crackling of a fire, the weight of crockery on wood tables, and always, those wonderful footsteps. It's hard to remember a film in which the interior feels so real, our ears and eyes almost beguiling the rest of our senses that we are in the house with our characters.

You can't watch this film about an artist and model breaking down barriers without imagining a conversation with filmmaker Sciamma herself. She's inviting us to stop looking at art objectively, and to converse with the artist about what we are *both* observing. We can't watch this film passively, not after we've received such eloquent education in paying attention. And because of two arresting scenes - you'll know them when you see them - I will never look at a human being in another painting again, no matter from which age or era, without wondering, "What is she thinking? What is happening in her life at this very moment?" *Portrait of a Lady on Fire* is that powerful a film as to remind you that life is the source of all art.

The Qatsi Trilogy

Koyaanisqatsi: US, 1983. Directed by Godfrey Reggio. 86 minutes, color. *Powaqqatsi*: US, 1988. Directed by Godfrey Reggio. 99 minutes, color. *Naqoyqatsi*: US, 2002. Directed by Godfrey Reggio. 89 minutes, color.

Ugh.

I've been putting off writing about *The Qatsi Trilogy*. Not because the films aren't good - they're remarkable - but because they're unclassifiable. *The Qatsi Trilogy* is three films - *Koyaanisqatsi* (coy-YAN-us-kaht-see), *Powaqqatsi* (POW-uh-kaht-see), and *Naqoyqatsi* (NAH-koi-khat-see). All three are wordless films, without characters or conventional narrative structure (which means no plot). They're quasi documentaries, sorta/kinda nature films, or arthouse-esque cinema, without really being any of those. They're political statements to which the viewer must bring their own ideology. They sound unwatchable, right? They're not. They're engrossing. Did I mention they're scored by Philip Glass? You can get lost in these films.

Let's start with Godfrey Reggio, the director and creative force behind the trilogy, whose path to filmmaking is unique in itself. Reggio spent fourteen years - from age 14 to 28 - as a Christian Brother, essentially a monk in a strict Roman Catholic community in New Mexico, a life dedicated to silence, fasting, and prayer. Gradually, Reggio became disillusioned about his work; from an interview with Scott MacDonald:

> "One of the vows you take as a Christian Brother is to teach the poor gratuitously... There were all sorts of rational and 'correct' reasons why the brothers were not able to teach the poor; it wasn't practical; if they *did* teach the poor, they couldn't sustain their lifestyles. In fact, almost all the children in the schools where I taught were middle-class kids, and yet I lived in *this* community [Santa Fe], where about 40 percent of the people had no access to primary medical care and where the barrio was being eroded out from under the poor. There was great social disintegration... So there was a huge community of poverty, and I felt drawn to give some kind of assistance if I *could*."

Reggio left his religious brotherhood to work directly with the disenfranchised of Santa Fe; cofounding organizations to provide medical care to the poor and one to aid children in Santa Fe street gangs. Eventually his drive to reach out further to the community led him to cofound the Institute for Regional Education, a media collective that began working with the ACLU to produce television spots, wordless ads that fought government invasions of privacy and the use of technology to alter behavior (fairly prescient for 1977!). It was there that Reggio began his first work as a filmmaker, with the idea that movies, while thoroughly embracing the technological, were themselves ideal vehicles for raising social consciousness.

Still with me? Good. We're about two paragraphs away from getting into what these films *are*.

Reggio wanted us to really *look* at the world we created, see it from the point of view of someone standing outside society. He wanted to do that through the two main senses through which we experience films: sight and sound, images and music. Reggio felt that we as human beings, especially through technology, had grown disconnected with the world we share. Reggio wanted to take the background of film, the part we take for granted, the part we don't even see any more because we're so immersed in it, and move it to the foreground, make it the subject of his film. How to do that? Take everything most films are about: plot, characters, dialogue, "talking heads" (in the case of documentaries), and excise it. What remains? The world we live in. Background becomes foreground.

Feeling that language wasn't up to the task of describing our world, Reggio turned to one of the unwritten languages of the world, that of the local Hopi (Reggio initially wanted to "title" his films with images, before admitting that *everyone* on his creative team told him this was impossible). The Hopi word *qatsi*, meaning "life" is at the root of all three films. *Koyaanisqatsi* (according to the end title of each film) translates as "1. crazy life. 2. life in turmoil. 3. life out of balance. 4. life disintegrating. 5. a state of life that calls for another way of living." This film focuses on man and nature in the Northern hemisphere, images of both landscapes and animals, cityscapes and technology. For we in industrialized nations, it's what we're doing to ourselves. *Powaqqatsi* is "(*powaq* sorcerer + *qatsi* life) an entity, a way of life, that consumes the life forces of other beings in order to further its own life." This film is set in the Southern hemisphere, and it's largely about the impact of industrialization on those citizens (i.e., what we industrialized nations inflict on others). Finally, *Naqoyqatsi*, we are told is, "1. a life of killing each other. 2. war as a way of life. 3. (*interpretation*) civilized violence." This is global.

So. *The Qatsi Trilogy* is images - astonishing images - in which director, editors, and photographers passed their work back and forth with composer Philip Glass to provide a beautiful, emphatic, and reflective accompaniment (Glass's score has gone onto a life of its own; you may be familiar with it without realizing where it came from). Directors of photography Ron Fricke (*Koyaanisqatsi*) and Graham Berry and Leonidas Zourdoumis (*Powaqqatsi*) shot images so beautiful and intense that they hold up as fresh even going on forty years later (*Naqoyqatsi* not so much. Despite being the only film of the trilogy released in the 21st century, this entry, predominantly stock footage with computer-generated animation and effects, is the weakest entry of the three and suffers - ironically - from looking the most dated.). Reggio uses in-camera effects to alter some of what we're seeing to give us a new look at the familiar - the first film predominantly features time-lapse photography, the second, predominantly slow motion. Clouds look like oceans, or living beings. Cities pulse with automobile lights through their veins. Industrial sites become living entities of their own, whose purpose seems to be to consume the land. Human beings are reduced to cogs in these great machines, until the camera stops: and slowly, lovingly, Reggio pans across the human faces looking back at us, forcing us to recognize the beauty of these "background people" the film has suddenly thrust into the foreground.

What makes all of this work - besides the fact that the beauty of the photography in these films must be seen to be believed - is that Reggio treats all subjects, whether human, animal, or technological, as worthy of our attention. There is beauty in technology, even as it threatens to separate us from ourselves, just as there is ugliness and destruction in nature. Reggio refuses to simplify and won't pontificate. He relies on his audience to interrogate our world as we watch. For this he's been criticized for glorifying technology, but I think that criticism misses the mark (more worrying to me was a comment he made in an interview implying that the lack of education and health care in underdeveloped countries reflected a "valid culture," but I think *Powaqqatsi* sufficiently demonstrates that industrialized civilization has made it impossible for the working poor to enjoy the benefits of either culture).

What *The Qatsi Trilogy* really is is a testament to the power of film. I think in removing all the "foreground" from these movies, with the intent to better show us our world,

Reggio has also stripped cinema down to its very essence: moving images and (today) music. In laying bare the environment around us, he has also laid bare the bones of filmmaking, and why this particular (and, yes, technological) art form is so different from literature, music, theater, graphic arts, photography, and all other ways we have of telling our stories. *The Qatsi Trilogy* (and I fear I've "killed the frog" in this essay in the course of dissecting it) on one level is a confection to behold, on another level a challenge to our ways of living. And to me, it's a joyous exploration of the moving image, and Lesson One to every student of film.

Quadrophenia

UK, 1979. Directed by Franc Roddam. 120 minutes, color.

It's not a rock opera.

The Who had done one of those, *Tommy*, in 1975, and were looking to do something different with *Quadrophenia*. Based on the concept album of the same name - an album that told no linear story, but was filled with songs of frustrated and disaffected youth - they turned the project over to young filmmaker Franc Roddam, then stepped back to see what he'd do with it, consulting only on the music for the soundtrack. The Who do not otherwise appear in this film, except in the background, on posters, and briefly on a television broadcast. A brave decision by a rock band, but one that resulted in a seminal film about Britain's youth in the 1960s, and a moving commentary on the pain of facing an adult life you don't want and can't escape.

The film's hero/antihero is Jimmy (Phil Daniels), a London working class youth. Jimmy is probably nineteen or so, living with his parents and sister, working a menial job as a messenger, hitting the clubs with his mates at night. Jimmy is a Mod; if you were a young person in the UK at that time, you were most likely either a Mod ("Mod," incidentally, being short not for "Modern," but for "Mode of dress") or a Rocker, and the two groups hated each other. The Rockers patterned themselves after the motorcycle gangs of the 1950s; tough, hypermasculine, head-to-toe leathers, motorcycle-bound. The Mods rode Italian scooters - cheaper, and with encased engines, so your girl wouldn't get her outfit greasy perched on the back. For the rest of it, here's Roddam, speaking on the disc's commentary track:

> "The Mods became very fashion conscious and even wore makeup. They were tough guys, but they wore eyeliner, they dressed well, they cut their hair short and very very neat. Even the drugs they took - speed - it was very efficient, not the lazy dope like hippies, this is like, fast.

> "For me, this is a very political era when I made this film, but the Mods in fact were not political, they didn't want revolution, they just wanted rebellion. There's a big difference there. They didn't want to escape from prison, the tyranny of work, they just wanted the top bunk. They'd work hard, they'd play hard, they'd dress well, and they had their own style."

There was precious little class mobility in Britain in the 1960s, so when young people looked around them, looked at their parents and neighbors, they saw their own future, and that future wasn't bright. Working hard at a dull job for little money, maybe eventually reaching a mid level position of authority. Evenings at the pub or in front of the telly. In television interviews with Mods on the disc, most of them imagine turning into their parents in the next few years, starting the cycle all over again with their own children. It's no wonder that they rebel at this age, look for a style, for music, for a lifestyle that they can claim as their own, more for the better if that identity is an affront to adult society. The television interviews I mentioned come from a French news program of the time; they're fairly snotty in tone, referring to English life as bleak and drab, but harsh as they are, they have a point. These kids realize they have a small window for acting out, and want to take advantage of it before it's too late.

One of the ways they'd rebel was in open warfare between Mods and Rockers. Honestly, the biggest difference between the two groups was what they spent their hard-earned money on; Rockers their bikes, Mods their suits. But tribalism is built on such seemingly insignificant details as these, and part of the identity of each group was animosity toward the other. Roddam recreates an actual event in the seaside resort town of Brighton as thousands of both groups converged on a weekend and rioted in the streets (press coverage at the time was certainly sensationalized, but the fights added to the notoriety of both Mods and Rockers in the public eye - and by extension youth in general). We even see Jimmy struggle with this as he early on runs into a childhood friend (an almost unrecognizably young Ray Winstone in an early role), now a Rocker. The two reconnect when they're alone, but the friendship can't survive peer expectations when their gangs clash in the streets.

Daniels' performance as Jimmy - moments of bravado giving way to intense vulnerability - along with Roddam's unblinking camera combine to almost immediately bring us on the side of a confused and clueless young man, still trying to cling to adolescence and delinquency. By the time Jimmy's crush breaks his heart, we feel it, too, because Roddam knows how lovesick young men can get, even if we men fear acknowledging it. (It's a thoroughly male world in *Quadrophenia*, something the Mods and Rockers probably wouldn't recognize as having in common with the older generation, so ingrained as it is. There really was no style template for Mod or Rocker women except as ornaments. Roddam makes an attempt at rectifying this reality with a couple strong women roles, but this is really about the boys.) By the end of the film, Jimmy has been rejected by family, peers, love interest, and even his role model, and Daniels and Roddam make us feel it, too, and fear for the character in the film's closing scene.

Other casting decisions brought a pulse to *Quadrophenia*. Because The Who were more or less bankrolling the film themselves, Roddam didn't have to answer to a studio, and so had the kind of freedom he'd never enjoy again. He didn't want to use recognizable faces, and certainly didn't want more experienced actors playing down in age, so he cast 18- 19- and 20-year-old actors in what was generally their first film, if not professional acting gig. Roddam talked about giving them weeks of rehearsal before shooting, and assigning them to come up with their own backstories for their characters, and then getting together with the other actors to work out the characters' relationships. Who's jealous of who, which characters grew up as neighbors, who's clinging to the Mod identity, who's just playing along to have a social group? The energy the young actors bring infuses the film, and on second viewing as I watched how background characters reacted to someone speaking, I saw the integrity it brought to the film. It struck me that this was a particularly insightful decision on Roddam's part, not just in working with actors, but in giving young actors investment in the film itself. You can ask more from people, you *get* more from people, when they feel their contributions are respected. Even the one small role I thought was stunt casting - the part of überMod Ace Face played by Sting - turned out to be serendipitous. The Police hadn't even released their first album when Sting was cast; Roddam just liked his look and cast him in his first film role.

Quadrophenia could have easily turned into a forgotten vanity project for a pop band. Instead we get an engrossing film that still plays fresh today. It's not just a snapshot of a specific time and place, but uses that setting as a platform to tell a relatable human story that spans eras and cultures. It's a fascinating and moving work of cinema. And I'm going to make a recommendation I've never made to casual movie fans: If you happen to run across the Criterion disc of *Quadrophenia*, watch it twice, the second time with the commentary track. The chat track, featuring Franc Roddam and cinematographer Brian Tufano is one of the most entertaining I've ever had the pleasure to listen to. You learn a lot about practical details of shooting a film, along with bits of trivia, like "Quadrophenia" is meant to rhyme with "schizophrenia," as in Pete Townsend had the idea that his central character in the album would be accused of being twice as crazy (2 x schizophrenic = quadrophenic) as anyone else in his family. But Roddam and Tufano are also true raconteurs, and there are terrific stories on the chat track. I'll close with one of them:

In auditioning to direct the film, Roddam was required to meet individually with each of the four band members of The Who separately, and gain their approval. The last person Roddam met with was drummer Keith Moon, whom Roddam met at Moon's house along with Moon's ever-present bodyguard, rumored to have killed at least one man. Roddam said Moon enthusiastically greeted him with, "I have an idea! *We should direct this film together!*" Now, if you know anything about Keith Moon, you'll know how terrifying that idea is. Roddam thought for a minute and replied, "It's a deal. But I get to play drums on the next Who album." Roddam said Moon burst into laughter, and the co-director idea was never brought up again.

A Raisin in the Sun

US, 1961. Directed by Daniel Petrie. 128 minutes, black and white.

A Raisin in the Sun is the film version of the Broadway play staged just two years earlier, in 1959. All of the principal cast of the stage production, including Sidney Poitier, Ruby Dee, Claudia McNeil, and Diana Sands reprised their Broadway roles. Lorraine Hansberry, the playwright, adapted her play for the screen after she became the first Black playwright to have a play produced on Broadway,[44] and at 29, became the youngest person and only the fifth woman to receive the New York Drama Critics Circle Award. Thanks to the work of these professionals it remains a powerful human drama, despite the attempts of Columbia Pictures executives to water down the film in order not to risk offending white audiences.

---

[44] That alone is a story in itself. *A Raisin in the Sun* had difficulty finding a home on Broadway before it premiered at the Ethel Barrymore Theatre. It first had to prove itself in Philadelphia and Chicago, as well as the customary run in New Haven, Connecticut.

A Raisin in the Sun[45] is set in Chicago's South Side, with almost all the action taking place in the small ghetto apartment housing the Younger family. Walter (Poitier) is a chauffeur and his wife Ruth (Dee) works as a domestic. Walter's mother Lena (McNeil) and Walter's sister Beneatha (Sands) share the apartment's only other bedroom. Walter and Ruth have a young son, Travis (Stephen Perry), who sleeps on the sofa in the living room. Their apartment has no bathroom of its own; there is one down the hall which they must share with an unknown number of other families. Walter is bitterly dissatisfied with the lack of choice for a Black man in Chicago, and each member of the family dreams of something better. Especially, as they are soon to learn, that a new baby is on the way.

We meet the Younger family the night before Lena is to receive a $10,000 check following her husband's death, a life-changing sum for people forced to live paycheck to paycheck. Beneatha wants to use the money to become a doctor; Walter wants to go in on a liquor store with two friends, to finally have a business of his own. Lena wants to better the entire family's standing, and places a downpayment on a house, which happens to be in an all-white neighborhood. Just before the family is to move they receive a visit from a nervous little man representing their new neighbors (a splendidly cast John Fiedler). It takes him an eternity to say what he is desperately trying *not* to say directly: The white neighborhood does not

---

[45] The title is taken from a line from the Langston Hughes poem, "Harlem."

want a Black family to move in, and they are willing to purchase the home from the Youngers for more than they paid. No trouble is threatened, but trouble always comes from these things, doesn't it?

The acting, as you'd expect, is magnificent, and not just from Poitier. Each of the cast just ran with what Hansberry gave them, and their work together on Broadway pays off in a familiarity not just with the material but with each other. But I think it's playwright/screenwriter Hansberry's contribution that makes *Raisin* far more than just an actor's showcase. Each of the characters occupies a stock role of the Black family, but then moves far beyond it. Lena is the family's matriarch, and has done her job for the family by moving them north, out of the rural south, but recognizes that the family cannot rest where it is, and must rely on a new generation to take it forward. When Lena does look back to the past, it's to find guidance in looking ahead. Beneatha is young, feminist, and searching for cultural touchstones in her African heritage, but at the same time recognizes the work and the contributions of the less radical women in her household even as she seeks to avoid their fates. And Walter is young, angry, and ambitious beyond what white Chicago will allow him, and while he does tend toward bitterness (and patriarchy, especially to our 21st-century sensibilities), he still loves his family and wants success for them. These complex characters, beginning from stereotypes but refusing to be shackled to them make them more real to us. It's easy to miss, but as much as *Raisin* centers on racial issues, it's as much about gender roles and expectations, generational divides, and the barriers of class apart from race.

The film has been criticized for its lack of a cinematic look, coming across instead as simply taking a camera to a stage play. It's a fair criticism, as almost all of the film is set in the Younger's small apartment, no room for anything other than closeups or medium shots. But put the blame for that on Columbia Pictures, not on director Daniel Petrie, and especially not on Hansberry. Hansberry was eager to expand the world of her stage play to include greater Chicago, but she was handcuffed by the studio. She had written in scenes that showed the noise and decay of the apartment building and the neighborhood itself; these were cut out by the studio. She had written scenes of the family attacked with hostile looks from white neighbors when they first visited their new house; the studio cut these. Scenes showing Lena at her last day of work shopping for her white employers, contrasting their grocery with the poor offerings at the Black grocers; gone. Any Black vernacular, even among just the family, excised. Any depictions of actual poverty, apart from the size of the apartment, removed. It's a curious, blameless racism the studio insisted on, even as they were eager to exploit the successful play and the rising Poitier. It's only through the power of Hansberry's writing that makes it through to the final cut, and the ability of the cast to breathe life into her words that *A Raisin in the Sun* is as eloquent as it is. We can only imagine the film we might have if Columbia had found the integrity to be true to the play.

In the end, Walter finds the courage to turn down the neighborhood's attempt to buy his family out and will move them into their new home. Music swells as he embraces his family, and we fade to black. But this is not a happy ending, as much as Columbia is trying to sell it. It's not an ending at all, but just the beginning of an entirely new, and more dangerous struggle in the family's life. Lorraine Hansberry grew up in a middle-class family that actually were the first Black family in a white neighborhood. She had not forgotten the hatred and violence her family was assaulted with daily. Hansberry's father needed to hire a security guard for protection; at one point Lorraine herself was narrowly missed by a concrete block thrown through the living room window. Lorraine recalled "being spat at, cursed, and pummeled in the daily trek to and from school." As recorded in an essay included with the disc, "Resistance and Joy" by Sarita Cannon:

> "In a 1964 letter to the editor of the *New York Times*, playwright Lorraine Hansberry wrote about different modes of resistance that she had witnessed within her own family: 'I [...] remember my desperate and courageous mother, patrolling our house all night with a loaded German luger, doggedly guarding her four children, while my father fought the respectable part of the battle in the Washington court.' Hansberry is referring here to the preparations her mother, Nannie Hansberry, made to defend her [B]lack family

from violence after moving into a primarily white neighborhood in Chicago in 1937, and to the suit against the city's restrictive housing covenants that her father, Carl Hansberry, with NAACP lawyers, took all the way to a Supreme Court victory in 1940. She demonstrates a keen awareness of the multiple ways in which people of African descent in the United States have fought for their right to live with dignity, calling into question the idea that there is any difference at all between radical and respectable resistance."[46]

No, there is no "happy ending" to *A Raisin in the Sun*, unless you choose to remain blind to the reality the Younger family faces. Their troubles are about to be intensified and compounded, all for the sake of living with dignity in America.

---

[46] Even the family's Supreme Court victory didn't advance their cause; the Court ruled that they had won essentially on a technicality as the city failed to produce enough signatures on a petition to evict the Hansberry family. No laws were changed as a result of this case.

Rashomon

Japan, 1950. Directed by Akira Kurosawa. 88 minutes, black and white.

All we're really sure of after watching *Rashomon* is a few basic facts. We know that a man, a samurai, has died violently in a forest outside Kyoto in 11th-century Japan. We know that a local bandit is on trial for the death of the samurai, the theft of his horse, and the rape of his wife. *Rashomon* is at once a mystery and a psychological puzzle, a question of the reliability of human truth. *Rashomon* is also one of the finest films ever made, and the film that introduced the world not only to director Akira Kurosawa, but to Japanese cinema itself.

What makes the film so engrossing is the way the story is told. The events of *Rashomon* unfold in anything but a linear fashion; the story is told in flashbacks, and we are given four different descriptions of the crime, each through eyewitness accounts at the bandit's trial. Testimony is offered by the woodcutter who discovers the body (Kurosawa regular Takashi Shimura), the accused bandit (Toshiro Mifune, also a Kurosawa collaborator), the samurai's wife (Machiko Kyo), and - through a spiritual medium - the dead samurai himself

369

(Masayuki Mori). Each version of events is credible. Each version of events contradicts the others. Each narrator appears to be telling the truth. But when each has had their say, we can't be sure even if the samurai was murdered or took his own life.

It's something we've seen since, most recently in Ridley Scott's intriguing 2021 film *The Last Duel*. But this was something that was so new at the time that the studio, Daiei, was hesitant to greenlight the film, fearful that audiences wouldn't understand it. But Japanese audiences took to it eagerly, as it became one of Daiei's highest-grossing films of the year. And when the rest of the world got a look at it - the studio reluctantly agreed to have it submitted as the Japanese entry to the 1951 Venice Film Festival, where it won first prize - critics and filmmakers in both the Old World and the New were astonished at what they saw.

To understand the impact of *Rashomon* on the rest of the film world, it helps to understand two things. The first is how unusually isolated Japan was in the film community up until post-WWII. All other nations - the United States, Europe, Scandinavia, South America, even the Soviet Union - had been exposed to each other's films since 1910. Even as war and censorship temporarily turned off the supply of films from one nation to another, each at least knew the pioneering work of the others, and kept tabs on what was going on abroad. Japan let nothing out and nothing from the west in. Japanese cinema evolved in isolation, using *kabuki* theatre as an influence, not the work of other filmmakers. The world had no idea that Japan had a film history, and until the American occupation following Japan's surrender, only a privileged few filmmakers had any idea what was being seen in the rest of the world's theaters.

Japan, and Kurosawa, caught up fast - Kurosawa credited the films of American director John Ford in particular in teaching him how to film drama, faces, and the outdoors. With the American occupation came American films, as well as access to other films of the west. The Japanese had been more or less teaching themselves their own rules of film grammar from the start, and now they were able to see how other directors approached their craft. Japanese audiences, as well, began to learn how stories were told in other film traditions, and look to their own studios to see how they would respond.

The second thing to understand about how much of an impact *Rashomon* had on the film world is how brilliantly Kurosawa filmed it. It's not just the power of the narration; everything done with the camera, the composition of every shot was crucial in setting the mood and telling the story. Kurosawa's camera moves with a fluidity most directors can't match. Through most of the forest scenes we see three characters, a triangle of husband, wife, and bandit. When he needs to, Kurosawa closes in on just one of the characters, searching faces. When it's called for, Kurosawa will put two of the three in frame, implying understanding between two that the third is not a party to. But most often, all three are in frame, and when one moves, the camera slides around to keep the other characters in frame. It's a way of reminding the audience that the three cannot escape each other, and where another director may cut to different cameras,

Kurosawa orchestrates long unblinking takes that hold us in the scene. No one had seen the camera taken so deep into forests (Kurosawa wrote that cast and crew found themselves covered with leeches during filming until they learned to rub salt on their skin), moving all the while, even shooting up, directly into the sun. Many filmmakers all over the world believed that shooting the sun directly would ruin the film, but Kurosawa did it several times - as the forest canopy dapples the sunlight, deepening the focus, it also creates the idea that the crime will hide from open sunlight itself. Each telling of the story is filmed in a style that best fits the content. When the bandit tells of his duel with the samurai, it is filmed in the tradition of legendary sword fights; when the woodcutter relates the duel he saw, we have a chaotic mockery, two men scared to death, flailing about.

The rest of the world couldn't have discovered Kurosawa at a better time. France was about to rebel against its more formalized past, and the auteurs of cinéma vérité immediately saw in Kurosawa a kindred spirit; so, too, the Italian neorealists. Especially given *Rashomon*'s nonlinear narrative structure, foreign filmmakers recognized it as modernist cinema. Kurosawa showed them (and filmmakers in North and South America, and Scandinavia, and Great Britain, and the Soviet Union...) how crucial shot composition was to a film. During the trial scenes, as the characters are giving testimony the camera is almost always static, facing the witnesses as if the audience is interrogating. But after the first witness offers his testimony, he moves to the background, seated unmoving to hear the report of the policeman who arrested the bandit. Then the policeman joins him for the next witness, so we understand that each witness is forced to consider events from another point of view. All wordlessly, just by keeping the characters in the frame.

And the themes of *Rashomon* are universal. Each narrator is telling the truth as they see it, and we believe that each of them believes that they are being honest. But what *Rashomon* forces us to confront is how fragile human truth may be. Each testimony is designed to put the speaker in the best possible light; each character has themself behaving directly, if not nobly. That even the dead man does this (again, speaking eerily through a medium) suggests it's such a core part of human nature that it remains with us even in the afterlife. Is human reality really this subjective? And if so, does that not point to an ultimate meaninglessness to our lives and actions? Kurosawa would seem to believe so, and when the film ends in an act of generosity and hope, I suspect Daiei of insisting on its addition. No matter. Kurosawa handles it seamlessly.

The film gets its name from the setting that frames the story. The woodcutter seeks refuge with a priest and a common traveler at the decaying Rashomon gate outside the city in a drowning rainstorm (more on Kurosawa's use of weather when we get to *Seven Samurai*). A once regal edifice protecting the city, it is crumbling, and now (in the 11th-century, that is) harbors thieves and the destitute. Since the release of this film, *Rashomon* has come to mean "dispute" in Japan, and I've even heard a translation of the film's title as "truth." It's a mighty film that can change language. If you've never seen a Kurosawa film, this is a great place to start, because it remains as powerful today, across the decades and across the sea.

Red Beard

Japan, 1965. Directed by Akira Kurosawa. 185 minutes, black and white.

Part of the reason I watch and write about these films in alphabetical order is to keep myself fresh; to avoid ruts. Still, I find myself sometimes writing about back to back Ingmar Bergman films (*The Magic Flute* and *The Magician*) and back to back Akira Kurosawa films (*The Hidden Fortress* and *High and Low*). I sighed when I saw I'd follow up last week's *Rashomon* with *Red Beard*; not just another Kurosawa film, but another historical drama. I wasn't prepared to find something fresh and exciting in this 3-hour film, but I did, largely thanks to Stephen Prince's superb and meticulously prepared commentary. Keep reading; you're about to find out how remarkable this film is, and what it is that makes its director one of the greatest the world has seen.

Red Beard marks the close of a chapter for Kurosawa in many ways. This was to be his last film in black and white; a legitimate choice, but not a certain one in Japanese cinema at the time. In other words, deliberate. It was the last film Kurosawa would make in the 2.35:1 Tohoscope widescreen aspect ratio - further films would meet television screens halfway with a 1.85:1 aspect ratio (more on this, and why it matters later). It was the last film with identifiable heroes. After this, Kurosawa's world becomes darker and more ethically muddied. And *Red Beard* was Akira Kurosawa's 16th and final film with the brilliant actor Toshiro Mifune.

The story, boiled down, is deceptively simple, and should not require three hours to tell. Yasumoto (Yuzo Kayama), a young doctor, has just returned to 19th-century Edo after studying at a Dutch medical school in Nagasaki. He has been expecting to take a lofty position with the shogun, but his father has asked him to stop in and pay his respects to the head of the Koishikawa Public Clinic, Kyoiji Niide (Mifune), generally referred to as Red Beard. The clinic serves the poor of Edo, and is understaffed and underfunded by the government. Red Beard, Yasumoto is told, runs the clinic and its staff with an iron fist, sets draconian rules, and the living conditions for the staff are barely above the poverty of the patients (in fact, only the patient wards are heated, not the dormitory-like rooms for the physicians and employees). Yasumoto is incensed to find out he has been assigned to live and work at this clinic indefinitely - his family has had his clothes and belongings sent ahead for him. There will be no position of honor at court for the ambitious young doctor, at least not yet. First, he will have to get his hands dirty with the city's poor. Yasumoto at first refuses to accept his new responsibilities; he will not work, he will not follow any of Red Beard's rules, and he *certainly* will not wear the common uniform Red Beard requires of all his staff. He will go on strike, driving Red Beard to fire him. But an attack by a psychotic patient injures the young doctor, and in his recovery, he begins to see the work of the clinic, and how much he may have yet to learn.

You can see where this is all going, right? "Young, arrogant city doctor has to learn wisdom from the older country physician." Japan was still a closed society in the 1800s, but Nagasaki being a port city was home to a small community of Dutch traders, who had brought Western medicine with them. Japan had a serious medical community at that time, but one that had no real tradition of surgery, instead favoring herbs and medicines as well as therapeutic touch. You can see where a Western-educated doctor might feel superior, perhaps could use a dose of humility. But *Red Beard* isn't a feel-good movie about the simple joys and healing powers of common sense. It's a film about suffering being a central part of the human condition. It is not the young doctor's place to overcome it, but to learn how to work in the face of it. Yasumoto *does* learn humility, but it's not because it will help him to heal, or fix the poverty and abandonment in his patients' lives. It's because kindness and a tender touch are the only things that can ease these peoples' pain - *not* because kindness and compassion are powerful tools, but because they are so rare in daily life.

Again, why three hours? Because only in fairy tales are a character's eyes opened after one exposure to reality, and Kurosawa has a lot to say about suffering in this film. When I wrote about Kurosawa's 1948 film, *Drunken Angel*, also about medicine, I wrote that in that film, disease was a result of the American occupation of postwar Japan, a condition specific to the Japanese people. In *Red Beard*, Kurosawa broadens his field to the human condition, as there is no uniquely Japanese cause of poverty and injustice, these are simply facts of life. In fact, while basing his script on a book of the same name by Shugoro Yamamoto, Kurosawa lifted the character of Nelli from Dostoevsky's novel *The Insulted and the Injured*, as well as scenes involving her directly from the book (now named Otoyo and played by Terumi Niki). The stories these patients tell reveal suffering that is existential and universal. There are no happy endings for them, and we suffer with them knowing that there is nothing we or our communities can do to help them.

Yasumoto's "education" at the clinic is thorough; he requires his arrogance to be broken down in stages. In the first trial, Yasumoto encounters the above-mentioned psychiatric patient, "The Mantis" (Kyoko Kagawa), whom Red Beard has isolated from male staff because of her attacks. Yasumoto believes he can help her, but finds himself no match for her, as she expertly plays on his pride so that she can attack him. Red Beard intervenes just in time, saving the young doctor's life, and cares for Yasumoto as he recovers from his wounds. This at least makes Yasumoto compliant enough to follow Red Beard's orders - though he still won't wear the humble uniform, not yet, anyway. Next, Red Beard simply asks him to sit with an old man as he is dying, not to heal, but to observe, but faced with the reality of hearing the patient's agonal gasps (as a nurse, I tip my cap to actor Kamatari Fujiwara for his realistic performance), Yasumoto proves that he is not yet ready to face the human condition. He abandons the patient to the first staff member who comes along. Red Beard next calls the young doctor to assist with a surgery - it turns out that Red Beard himself is also proficient in Western medicine, perhaps not the simple "country doctor" Yasumoto has taken him for. But the young doctor cannot abide the graphic sight of the barely anesthetized patient (even the Western world hadn't mastered full anesthesia at this point), and passes out as she sluggishly fights the doctors wrestling with her open abdominal wound.

Finally, in the film's second half, Yasumoto tries to care for Otoyo, a traumatized 12-year-old girl rescued from a brothel to which her family has sold her to be a sex worker. Yasumoto is aggrieved that she will not trust him, but at least by now his frustration is with his own shortcomings, and not the girl's behavior. Otoyo will not take necessary medicine from the young doctor, flinging it wordlessly back in his face. Red Beard sits with her and offers the spoon - she flings it back at him. He smiles, and tries again: same result. Again, same result. And again. Finally on the fifth try, she takes her medicine; Red Beard has worn her down with patience and kindness. It's precisely because her life has been empty of kindness - like so many of the poor of the clinic - that she has to learn how to accept it. It is also here that Yasumoto finally understands that he has been wrong about Red Beard. Red Beard is indeed strict, and dictatorial when it comes to patient care. But it is not to serve the older doctor's own ego, but the welfare of his patients. Red Beard is educated, compassionate, and understands the importance of quietly listening to what his patients have to say. He embraces Western medicine - he will embrace anything that helps relieve suffering - but knows that he must treat both the mind and the body. Red Beard's practice is what we would today call "holistic;" he treats the entirety of the human being, not just the disease process. This is what Yasumoto is really here to learn.

After learning how to approach Otoyo himself, Yasumoto falls ill with a fever; the final low point he must reach in order to recreate himself as a healer. Through this, Otoyo will not leave his side, tending to him as he did to her. When Yasumoto recovers, he wakens to a new dedication to his patients and his profession. He will no longer seek a position of prestige with the shogun, he will remain in poverty with Red Beard to alleviate suffering. It's the same place his character may have landed in 100 minutes in a Hollywood film. The difference is, we as an audience have arrived here with him.

How Kurosawa achieved this is not just a story of a talented cast, or a solid script, though he could not have gotten there without them. It's also a story of camera lenses and aspect ratios, the "dry" stuff that only directors and cinematographers and hanky-clutching film writers care about. But here's why they matter in Kurosawa's films, and in *this* film in particular:

Great directors' films often have a "look" about them. You may not be able to put your finger on what it is, but you might be able to point to a scene and say, "That's a Spielberg shot," or, "That's classic Tarantino." Kurosawa owes his look to two things: his use of the film frame (the aspect ratio) and the telephoto lens. Let's take the second one first.

A telephoto lens is exactly what you think it is. It's a lens that zooms in on action from a distance away, like looking through a telescope or binoculars. Kurosawa loves to use telephoto lenses for a number of reasons. First of all, it gets the camera out of his actors' faces, sometimes out of view completely, enabling them to relax and focus more on their performances. It also allows him to cover a scene with multiple cameras at the same time, as the cameras will be far enough away not to be photographed by each other; Kurosawa loves to put them at 90 degree angles to each other. Again, this helps the actors and the crew; a scene can be done in fewer takes, and play out longer because he won't need to reshoot a scene just to get coverage from a different camera that might otherwise be in the shot.

But what shooting from a distance also does is "flatten out" the image on the screen, rendering it seemingly in two dimensions (well, technically seeing a film on a screen is *literally* a 2-dimensional representation, but you know what I mean). A camera lens will focus on people and objects in the foreground, midground, or background, but not all at once, so you've got to pick where the focus will lie rendering the rest fuzzy or out of focus (the human eye actually does the same thing, but adjusts so quickly between distances that we're unaware). When you're shooting from a distance, an entire set becomes "background" so it all comes into focus at once, but in doing so, you lose perception of depth between objects and characters - foreground, midground, and background from the actors' perspective all become smooshed together into what looks like one plane. Kurosawa uses this effect to tremendous advantage. In one scene, two characters are talking behind laundry hanging outside - the camera is elevated, and we can see that we're facing several rows of hanging blankets. The two characters talking are on the left side of the screen, seen exchanging items through a gap in the blankets. On the *right* side of the screen, we see two characters eavesdropping, but two or three rows of blankets ahead of them. It *looks* like the talkers are right on top of the listeners, but because we see rows of laundry, we understand the distance (front to back) is greater than it appears, probably closer to the distance (left to right) that hasn't been foreshortened. Kurosawa has managed to place all of these characters in frame at the same time, no cuts back and forth, to show us the eavesdroppers are close enough to hear, but far enough away to remain undetected.

Filling the frame with visual information was key to Kurosawa. The widescreen aspect ratio he favored, in which the screen was more than twice as wide as it was tall, became his canvas. This was something unique to theaters at the time, as the box-like screens of televisions couldn't accommodate such a wide picture, and Kurosawa liked to use the whole thing. In a scene early on, Yasumoto's first day at the clinic, in fact, four doctors sit at dinner, all in a row, facing the camera. Red Beard is all the way to our right, with Yasumoto on our left, two other doctors between them. Yasumoto is stating his defiance of Red Beard and his rules, the other diners silent, nervously following the developing tension. One long take, no camera movement keeps everyone in shot, maintains tension. You couldn't get this shot in another format, and it's a scene that won't transfer to television without cutting the scene or wildly swinging the shot back and forth. Reluctantly, Kurosawa would switch after this to the 1.85:1 aspect ratio; still wider than the television sets of the time, but easier to edit and manipulate.

Now let's put it all together in the scene in which Yasumoto is attacked by The Mantis. The Mantis has burst into Yasumoto's room, hiding from the staff who are searching for her. Two cameras with telephoto lenses are set up at right angles from each other, back from the scene, and we're shooting in the 2.35:1 aspect ratio.

The Mantis enters, closing the door behind her, crouching by it with her back to Yasumoto, who has been sitting on the other side of the room. He is at the far left of the frame, she is at the far right, and we can see that they are as far apart as they can possibly be in this space. She's frightened, and says that she is not crazy and that no one at the clinic understands her. Yasumoto begins to inch closer, and as he does so, the camera almost imperceptibly zooms in a little: though the distance is shortening between them, Kurosawa wants to keep each actor at the extreme edge of the frame, in their respective "corners." She comments about the staff in uniform (remember, Yasumoto at this point refuses to wear his), and implies that his dress reflects a higher station. She's playing on his vanity, and it's working: he inches closer, Kurosawa's camera again slowly zooming to keep them apart. Now we cut to camera #2, and since it's 90 degrees from the first camera, the distance between the two characters is drastically foreshortened, they look like they could touch each other. The Mantis's back is to us, and we can see her reaching for something in her sleeves. Back to camera #1; they're distant again, but not so far anymore; Yasumoto is being lured in. Still, Kurosawa keeps them at opposite ends of the frame. The Mantis melts in tears, and Yasumoto closes the distance to comfort her, and we cut back to camera #2. Yasumoto hasn't been paying attention to what she's been doing; she's freed her right arm from her sleeve, so while he thinks she's embracing him, she's actually bound him by holding her right sleeve in her left hand. With her freed right hand, she pulls a long hairpin out of her bun and begins her attack. Suddenly, the door slides open revealing Red Beard, and since we're still watching from camera #2, it looks like he's practically on top of them, meaning it seemingly takes him too long to cross the room to get to them. He does just in time, and though Yasumoto has been wounded, Red Beard is able to rescue him.

This is how Kurosawa masterfully builds tension in the scene, using a long take in which actors can build their own pace, can move comfortably, and in which he uses his manipulation of the visual image to focus the viewer's attention on the most important elements of the scene, and play with our sense of distance to convey the psychological distance between two characters. The best directors, like Kurosawa, Bergman, and Spielberg are doing this constantly without the audience even being aware. *Every* frame is planned out, every shot in league with the story and the storytellers to best reach the viewer.

This is why I love films, and even while I'm an avid reader, this is what films can do that books or even the stage cannot. It's why I watch films again and again. The next time you're watching a movie you've seen before, take an actor's performance in a scene, or the camera shots in a scene itself, and ask yourself, "How else could this have been done?" Then ask yourself, "Why did the actor, or director, or screenwriter choose this particular way to do this scene?" That's the beginning of looking at films critically, and actively, not passively. To me, that's the whole fun of the movies. After the emotional experience, figure out the puzzle. It's enjoying the film all over again.

Oh, and I checked. Though there's more Kurosawa to come in, next essay we'll be in the UK, with an entirely different style of film.

The Red Shoes

UK, 1948. Directed by Michael Powell and Emeric Pressburger. 134 minutes, (glorious) color.

This one I owe to my adult son. I raised him on movies, proudly watched his film knowledge and tastes surpass mine, and gratefully accepted his gifts to fill the gaps in my movie collection. He gave me my Criterion copy of *The Red Shoes*, and I can honestly say I discovered this to be essential viewing. It's a love letter to the arts in general, and ballet in particular. Martin Scorsese (instrumental in the film's restoration) and Brian De Palma both cited *The Red Shoes* as getting them into filmmaking in the first place. Did I say it was a "love letter?" Scratch that. As I kept hearing and reading from people connected with this film, Britons had just proved in World War II they were prepared to give their lives for their country. Now they were ready to give their lives for art. This is really what's at stake in this film.

The film centers on a love/obsession triangle in a prestigious ballet company. In the "love" corner of the triangle is Julian Craster (Marius Goring), a fresh-out-of-school composer who grabs an opportunity to become the company's composer/conductor (though he sometimes chafes at his music needing to be subservient to dance). In the "obsession" corner is Boris Lermontov (Anton Walbrook), the dictatorial and demanding director of the ballet, who is so insistent that his company devote their entire lives to dance that he dismisses his prima ballerina for the sin of getting married. Completing the triangle is ballerina Victoria Page (Moira Shearer), driven, vivacious, and talented. She becomes the company's lead ballerina through hard work and genius, but earned an audition because of this exchange at a party:

Lermontov: "Why do you want to dance?"

Page: "Why do you want to live?"

Page is selected to dance a new ballet, for which Craster is commissioned to provide a score. Lermontov has chosen Hans Christian Andersen's dark story "The Red Shoes" as the basis for the new work. A dancer in a small village comes across a pair of red ballet shoes in a shop (in the ballet, we see the shopkeeper has already turned away other prospective buyers - he seems to be waiting for her). She purchases them, and they magically transform her dancing to dazzling heights. She dances with joy into the night. When she finally tires, she tries to remove the shoes. But the shoes are not tired. The shoes never tire, and she can neither remove them, nor stop dancing. "What happens in the end?" Craster asks Lermontov. "In the end she dies," replies the director.

Page trains unceasingly for the new role, and Lermontov orders her to take her lunches in his office, where Craster will sit at the piano and play the music she must learn for the part. Page and Craster talk music and dance over his playing, and develop a respect for each other as artists, even as it leads to a shouting match at a rehearsal over whether he will change his music to accommodate her difficulty with a move, or whether she must learn to dance faster (Lermontov decrees the composer the winner of this argument). Eventually, the two fall in love, though initially hide their relationship from Lermontov. When he discovers it, Craster is fired from the ballet; choosing love, Page flees the ballet and marries him, knowing she'll never work for anyone again who can browbeat greatness out of her the way Lermontov can. Eventually, she returns to the ballet, torn between Life and Art, and as the two men tear at her soul, the Red Shoes finally claim their due.

Melodrama, right? Wrong. One of the first decisions directors Michael Powell and Emeric Pressburger made is that they would cast the ballet parts not with actors who could dance, but dancers who could act, and it shows in the performance and rehearsal scenes. There were to be no "dance doubles" in this film as there were in many Hollywood productions. Shearer herself wrestled with whether or not to take leave from the stage to "slum it" in the movies, and had she known that from then on her film career would eclipse her dance work, she may never have agreed. But Powell and Pressburger in fact created their own small dance company for the film, and even for a ballet novice like me, I was convinced that what I was seeing was real. One small detail that sold me: performers sweating the way I'd never seen in Hollywood musicals. *The Red Shoes* isn't about dancers being transported by their art. It's about dancers working, training, struggling, *suffering* to get the best out of themselves that they can.

The centerpiece of the film is a 17-minute dance sequence of the ballet, and it's like nothing that had been filmed before. In David Ehrenstein's essay for the disc, "Dancing For Your Life," he writes that Gene Kelly screened *The Red Shoes* fifteen times for his fellow filmmakers before taking on *An American in Paris*. It encapsulates the story of the Hans Christian Andersen tale, and it's moving and terrible and fantastical. The camera starts in the audience, facing the stage, but Powell and Pressburger didn't want to tell the story of the audience, they wanted to tell the dancers' story, so quickly the camera goes onstage with the performers, the audience forgotten. And then the performance space is expanded, becoming expressionistic. Suddenly, briefly, images of Lermentov and Craster flash before us, and we understand we are now in the mind of the ballerina, feeding off her personal battles to fuel her dancing. It's all seamless, and it's all simultaneously in service of both the plot of the film and the story of the ballet.

And it's dazzlingly filmed in Technicolor. Even Hollywood was still experimenting with Technicolor, and in post-war Britain *The Red Shoes'* vibrancy announced to the world that British filmmaking would take a backseat to none. Production designer Hein Heckroth created sets not simply lavish, but rich with the colors of passion that elevated the film. No wonder the film is credited with being influential by so many filmmakers - Martin Scorsese still slips *homages* to *The Red Shoes* in films he makes today.

As I said, Scorsese was instrumental in getting this film

restored, and it's worth talking about the restoration journey of *The Red Shoes* and why it's important to restore films in the first place. Film is fragile, degradable, and - in the case of silver nitrate film used at the beginning of the 20th century - highly combustible (as anyone who has seen the Tarantino film *Inglourious Basterds* can tell you). It's why we've lost 90% of the films from the silent era - gone, lost forever, great films that no one will ever get to see. It's best to try to restore films from negatives of course, but if those are gone, you have to gather prints that have been passed from one theater to another, often carelessly; mishandled, scratched, stored improperly, even edited to suit local sensibilities. *All* film is perishable, which is part of the reason the digital revolution - love it or hate it - has become so attractive to the industry; ones and zeros remain ones and zeros forever.

Technicolor made the work of restoring *The Red Shoes* three times harder. Technicolor at the time was a three-strip process, meaning that you didn't just have one strip of film running through the camera. Special Technicolor cameras were designed which included gold mirrors and prisms to direct the image to three different pieces of black-and-white film running through the camera simultaneously, one treated to accept green light, one red, and one blue. It's these three strips together that make up the full color spectrum in Technicolor. So not only are there three negatives to restore instead of one, but when one strip shrinks a tiny bit more than another, it throws the whole color scheme off (think about when you were a kid and the colors in the Sunday comics sometimes didn't line up). Robert Gitt, Preservation

Officer of the UCLA Film & Television Archive, wrote what they were faced with in an included essay:

> "We were provided access to more than two hundred reels of 35 mm nitrate and acetate materials, including... the still extant three-strip Technicolor camera negatives. For quality reasons, we chose these original negatives as our starting point, even though they were afflicted with a daunting number of problems: 65 percent of the film had bad color fringing, caused by different shrinkage and sometimes by misadjustment of the camera during shooting; 176 shots contained color flickering, mottling, and "breathing" because of uneven development and chemical staining; 70 sequences contained harsh optical effects with excessive contrast; and throughout there were thousands of visible red, blue, and green specks caused by embedded dirt and scratches. Worst of all, mold had attacked every reel and begun to eat away the emulsion, leaving behind thousands of tiny cracks and fissures."

To solve these problems, each frame was digitally scanned into a computer, and laborious work began correcting scratches, color problems and contrast issues (in addition, since the soundtrack is also part of the physical negative, pops, crackles, and background hiss was removed from the film). 4K resolution was added at every stage. But "restoring" a film isn't just making it pretty by today's standards. It's remaining faithful to the original filmmakers' intentions, which is why directors, cinematographers, camera operators, and others who worked on an original film are always consulted, if possible. The result:

> "... the entire film was turned into ones and zeros, repaired, and then converted back into a motion picture again. To achieve a proper film "look," we compared the new digital images with those in an original Technicolor dye transfer print and in a new Eastman color test print struck by Cinetech Laboratories directly from the YCM camera negatives. Careful adjustments were made to the final digital version to combine the best qualities of modern color film (greater image sharpness, more sparkle in highlights) with the most pleasing attributes of vintage Technicolor... (bold colors, deep blacks, gentle contrast, with a pleasing range of tones in actors' faces)."

Understand, this restoration wasn't just about prettying up an old film. It was about *saving this film before it disappeared forever.* This is what film restoration is really all about; saving these stories on film for future generations. And you can't just read about *The Red Shoes* to appreciate it, you have to see it. You have to see it to understand how this film exploded across Britain's post-war screens, calling its audience to get back to the vitality and importance of life and the arts.

My boy knew what he was doing when he gave me this film. He wasn't just filling a space in a collection. He knew I needed to see this for myself.

Redes

Mexico, 1936. Directed by Fred Zinnemann and Emilio Gómez Muriel. 59 minutes, black and white.

Redes is a film worth getting into the history of, and for the next few paragraphs, I'm indebted to the essay included with the disc, "El Cine Mexicano" by Charles Ramiréz Berg. While *Redes*[47] was a film produced by an international crew, it jump-started the Mexican film industry, and spoke with a uniquely Mexican voice.

The country at the time was still reeling from a violent revolution, begun in 1910 to overthrow the dictator Porfirio Diaz, but devolved into a brutal civil war, as various factions fought for control. The fighting had ended by 1920, but at the cost of between one and two million Mexican lives (compared to the roughly 620,000 lives lost in the US Civil War), with another 400,000 emigrating to the United States. While Diaz had been exiled, Mexico was still fighting politically to establish the socialist goals of the revolution -

---

[47] Berg offers *The Wave* as the film's translated title, though *redes* more literally translates into English as "nets" or "network."

land and liberty for the peasants who worked the land - and assert independence from the dominance of First World nations.

Mexico's Secretariat of Public Education (SEP) found in the nation's artistic community a political ally, and was particularly eager to resurrect Mexico's film industry. Mexican films had all but vanished in the silent era; only forty feature-length films were released between 1923 and 1930, none of them commercially successful. Mexican audiences preferred foreign films, especially those of their neighbor to the north. But the sound era began to revive national cinema, as Mexicans were hungry to hear their language and their music in the movies they attended.

Mexico in the 1930s was a haven for left-leaning artists from all over the world; even one of the world's most acclaimed film directors, Sergei Eisenstein, shot his unfinished epic *¡Que viva México!* from 1931-1932. Mexican composer Carlos Chávez was head of the department of Fine Arts in the SEP, and invited Paul Strand to Taos. Strand was a celebrated American photographer looking to add social consciousness to his work, and Chávez saw in him an opportunity to bring international prestige to Mexico's film culture, as well as a chance to train Mexico's filmmakers. Chávez planned a series of five short SEP-funded films representing five of the regions and peoples of Mexico - *Redes* to be the first (and sadly, the last). Strand was appointed director of photography and film, and immediately sat down with Agustin Velásquez Chávez to work on a script.

Strand first brought in a New York documentary

filmmaker to direct, Henwar Rodakiewicz, but when the documentarist's previous commitments called him elsewhere, Rodakiewicz suggested bringing in Austrian Fred Zinnemann, who had worked in German films before moving to Hollywood, where he was a bit player and camera operator (Zinnemann would go on to become an accomplished director of his own, helming *From Here to Eternity* and *High Noon*, among other films). Zinnemann would eventually turn to Mexican film artist Emilio Gómez Muriel to co-direct.

Redes was beset with problems from day one. A generous four-month shoot had been planned, but the production time doubled due to problems largely out of the filmmakers' control. The film had to be sent to Los Angeles to be processed as facilities couldn't be found in Mexico, which meant the "dailies" couldn't be viewed often until a month after shooting. Strand (serving as cinematographer) and Zinnemann were at odds artistically; Zinnemann preferring a moving camera, frames filled with motion, Strand believing in the poetry of still life images. The camera used in the production had no sound capacity, so any sound or dialogue in the film would need to be recorded post-production. But in addressing these problems, the filmmakers would create a film of intense power and beauty.

The film tells a simple story. Miro (Silvio Hernández del Valle) is casting a fishing net out into the sea; as he pulls it back, he finds he has caught only one small fish. He and his neighbors are desperate to find work, Miro in particular as his infant son will die without medicine. Reluctantly, Miro approaches local businessman Don Anselmo (David Valle González, the only professional actor in the film) to ask for a loan to save his boy's life. Don Anselmo turns him down, and in the next scene we follow a funeral procession bearing a small casket, Miro's son buried in front of him.

A small man-powered fishing boat has returned filled with a catch. The boat's chief, Mingo (Felipe Rojas) reports the catch to Don Anselmo, who is meeting with a local politician (Rafael Hinojosa) seeking patronage. The businessman instructs his employee to take out the bigger boat, and gives him permission to hire more men. Mingo recruits some men from town, including Miro, whose loss he acknowledges. We follow the crew rowing hard out to sea, casting an enormous net, and struggling to bring in their haul. Proud of their hard work, the men gather for their take after the fish are weighed, but it turns out the money Anselmo is willing to pay them is worth barely a fraction of the value of their catch, which amounts to a subsistence level of pay to the workers. Miro calls for the men of the villages to stand together and refuse to release their future catches until they are paid a fair wage. We see Don Anselmo's politician trying to rally the men in opposition, but as Miro walks off, more and more of the men turn away and follow the fisherman. Miro is shot for speaking out, his funeral procession at the end of the film mirroring his son's.

Long stretches of *Redes* - in particular the sequences showing the fishermen at work - are shot in documentary style, in what Strand called "docu-fiction." The film was shot entirely on location in real fishing villages, using actual fishermen in place of professional actors. If this begins to sound like Italian neorealism, *Redes* has the famous movement beat by a good ten years; given that Luchino Visconti's 1948 neorealist classic *La terra trema* also concerns fishermen standing up to exploitation, I'm comfortable calling it a direct influence.

And those artistic differences between Zinnemann and Strand? They were addressed largely by Muriel in the editing room, in which he seamlessly wove both dynamism and portraiture into the film. The scenes at sea are riveting, and as the men pull at the nets back on shore to wrestle in their catch, the camera moves us around them, as if we're urging them on. But the film is also filled with faces, the weariness of poverty etched into the film's characters. When Miro buries his son, his silent grief is heartbreaking, as is the image of the casket being lowered directly in front of the father. It's a scene so honest that it avoids sentimentality or melodrama; it becomes just another hard fact of life for these people. What Muriel does is remarkable in joining the opposing styles of two filmmakers into a whole that neither might have achieved on their own. Muriel also proves himself a capable student of Eisenstein's theory of montage, as the assassination scene, for example, is a blaze of quick images of Miro, the crowd, a pistol, coins, and political posters, all giving us visual cues to what - and who - is behind Miro's killing.

Redes also makes an asset of the lack of sound on set at the time of shooting. The dialogue recorded later is minimal, and the directors turned to the techniques of silent film to tell the story in primarily visual terms; never a bad idea whether you're using sound in a film or not. That still left the problem of natural background noises - wind, wildlife, and waves, to name a few - which would add time and expense to the project. SEP addressed this by turning to one of Mexico's premier composers, Silvestre Revueltas, for a score to accompany the film. It's a stirring work, which adds a sense of grandeur to the scenes at sea in particular. American composer Aaron Copland wrote in *The New York Times* that "anyone who is interested in the development of music in the Western Hemisphere" needed to hear Revueltas' score for the film.

The expense and difficulty in shooting *Redes* put an end to the five-picture plan the SEP had for its involvement in Mexican cinema, and *Redes* did poorly at the Mexican box office. But the film itself heralded a golden age in Mexican film, and showed the world that *el cine mexicano* could tell its own stories without trying to copy Hollywood films. Mexican filmmakers used *Redes* as a launching pad (Muriel in particular) to establish their own careers. And as the film community grew, Mexican people welcomed the chance to hear their own stories told by their own sons and daughters.

Revenge

Kazakhstan, 1989. Directed by Ermek Shinarbaev. 99 minutes, color.

If, as the ancient Klingon proverb has it, revenge is a dish best served cold, then *Revenge* tells us it's also a dish to be passed down generationally. Additionally, Ermek Shinarbaev's film might be the most beautiful revenge story ever put to celluloid, but we'll get to that later. Right now, we need to talk about Kazakhstan and its Korean heritage to understand what permeates this film.

Kazakhstan is the world's largest (in terms of area) landlocked nation, Russia to the north, China to the south. It's been fought over for centuries, millennia most likely, by nomadic tribes, later to be invaded by both Mongols and Russians. The land, mostly dry steppes and grassland, is harsh, winter temperatures dropping to -40 degrees (both Celsius and Fahrenheit, that spot where the scales converge). It was into this environment that Joseph Stalin dropped the entire Korean population of Sakhalin Island off the Siberian coast, shipped there in the late 1930s in the dead of winter. Why? Probably, as Shinarbaev said in an interview on the disc, to die, along with the Greeks and Germans and other "undesirables" Stalin exiled there.

Sakhalin Island, just north of Japan, was held for centuries by the Chinese, but in the 19th century, Japan and Russia entered into an agreement that allowed citizens of both nations to settle there. After the Russo-Japanese War of 1904-5, the island was split at the 50th parallel; Russia took the north, Japan the south. Screenwriter Anatoli Kim (who also wrote the novel the film was based on) was a child at the time his family was forcibly relocated 3,200 miles inland to Kazakhstan (along with the Soviet share of the 150,000 people of Korean descent on the island), though they were able to return to Sakhalin Island in 1948, after the Soviets had been ceded the entire island at Yalta. This matters because *Revenge* is set in Korea, China, and Sakhalin Island. It also matters because the longing for a homeland by characters set adrift in the world figures prominently through the film.

Revenge begins with a prologue set in 17th century Korea. A king (Oleg Li) watches his young son scrapping with another boy, the prince ending up on the ground in tears. Instead of punishing his son's opponent, the king summons his fiercest warrior, and instructs him to begin training his son. The king tells his warrior that he is to turn the prince into the most feared warrior in the kingdom, by the time the prince turns 21. The warrior may use any means necessary, and may not be interfered with, even if it results in harm or death to the prince. But if he is not successful, the trainer will be executed.

We join the prince as a young man (Yerik Zholzhaksynov). He is about to punish a soldier by having him beaten to death. The soldier's crime is this: While training with the prince, the soldier knocked the prince to the ground, but failed to administer a final blow. The prince's close friend, a poet, intercedes on behalf of the soldier, who is willing to be beaten to death rather than harm or kill the prince. The prince asks for a poem from his friend, but the poet replies he is unable to summon poetry in the face of injustice. The prince tells his poet friend he is free to seek out justice elsewhere, but if he does, he may never return. The poet begins his exile.

Our story proper begins in 1915, when a drunken teacher, Yan (Nikolai Tacheyev), kills a young girl in his classroom with a sickle. Horrified, Yan goes into hiding, and when news of the death reaches Tsai (Kasim Zhakibayev), the girl's father, he swears revenge. Knowing only that Yan was last seen on a boat headed to the Chinese coast, Tsai begins a ten-year journey to track down Yan and kill him.

After years of searching, Tsai finally catches up with Yan in a barn. He is about to kill him with the sickle with which Tsai's daughter was murdered when strangers intervene and Yan escapes. Realizing that he has lost his best chance to exact revenge, Tsai returns to Korea. Tsai's wife, now too old to bear children, tells Tsai that he must take a concubine to bear him a child. He does, a mute simple woman (Zinaida Em), who bears him a son, Sungu. When Sungu is about ten years old, Tsai and his wife summon him to Tsai's deathbed. There, Sungu is told his reason for being: Revenge. Tsai hands him the sickle, and tells him it is now passed to him to execute Yan for killing the sister he never met. Tsai tells Yan that he may not take a wife or father any children, may partake of neither joy nor sorrow until this is done. Sungu solemnly agrees.

What follows is ten years of a life sacrificed, a second victim of Yan's long-ago crime. Sungu (Aleksandr Pan) becomes a poet himself, but has forsaken a life of his own to wander in search of Yan, to carry out his family's bequeathed revenge. His travels take him through Korea, and eventually to Sakhalin Island. He encounters a beautiful young Romanian woman, who wants to begin a family with him; she tells him that all the bond they need is that neither of them are Russian in a Russian land. But like a disease, the burden of Sungu's burden manifests itself physically, as the poet reveals himself to be mysteriously bleeding, unwhole, unable to connect to a human life. Sungu is guided at times by visions of the spirits of his dead father and his slaughtered sister. Everywhere he goes, he is reminded of the family life denied to him. When revenge finally comes, it's not in the form he expects. And like so many others in the film, it leaves him rootless, without a land he can call home.

Revenge, for all its macabre and tragic themes, is shot with great beauty, suffused with light in even (especially) its thematically darkest moments. Shinarbaev worked with cinematographer Sergei Kosmanov, as he had on three other occasions, to illuminate scenes that serve to contrast an open bright world with the prison of our characters' lives. Sungu is not just a stranger, a traveler in every land he passes through, he is a stranger to a human life as well. *Revenge* is one of the most polished of the films in the World Cinema Project collection, probably because it was released just after the breakup of the Soviet Union; Shinarbaev, Kosmanov, and others had had the benefit of learning their craft at Moscow's VGIK film school. But *Revenge* isn't the last gasp of Soviet cinema; it's the first breath of a Kazakh national cinema, a nation full of displaced people, uncertain of whether the future of their new nation - still geographically hard up against both Russia and China - was really in their own hands or someone else's.

Kent Jones writes, in his essay "The Long Road Home" published with the disc, that Kazakhstan filmmakers enjoyed a brief "Kazhak New Wave" in the years following this film's release that dried up in the early 2000s. In recent years Kazhak filmmakers, along with colleagues in Kyrgyzstan, Uzbekistan, Tajikistan, and Turkmenistan have found it increasingly difficult to find the funding - and freedom - to produce their work. Many have had to shut down their careers, turning to other jobs and industries to make a living. One hopes this is temporary, and that artists of these nations may one day find their voices again. Until that day comes, we have films like *Revenge* to remind us that there are important stories in the world crying to be heard.

Rififi

France, 1955. Directed by Jules Dassin. 118 minutes, black and white.

Ready for a good heist flick? How about a classic *film noir*? In *Rififi*, we get both, shot in the streets of Paris; tough guys, dames, and a cool caper.

Tony le Stéphanois (Jean Servais) is a gangster fresh from prison, having served five years to protect his young protégé Jo (Carl Möhner). Jo has spent Tony's prison stretch as a family man, and the closest we see Tony to cracking a smile is playing uncle to Jo's little boy. Through an acquaintance of Jo's (Robert Manuel), Tony is offered an opportunity to participate in basically a smash and grab at Paris's version of Tiffany's, Mappin & Webb, but Tony has something more elaborate in mind. Adding a safecracker to the group (director Jules Dassin himself, acting under the name Perlo Vita), Tony's plan is to sneak into the store at night, crack the safe, and fence the jewels to an associate in London. The robbery itself - as meticulous as it is bold - goes as planned but things begin to fall apart immediately after. When he was released from prison, Tony wanted to pick up where he left off with an old flame, Mado (Marie Sabouret), and took her literally out of the arms of the gangster/club owner Pierre (Marcel Lupovici). In the film's most shocking scene, Tony takes Mado back to his flat, and for her inconstancy, strips her of her jewels and beats her. This doesn't sit well with Pierre, and by leaning on one of the crew, Pierre has learned of their plans. One by one, the jewel thieves find that no matter how clever they were, fate will intervene to collect its due. This is noir, after all.

If this sounds familiar (as it did to some critics at the time), the story had been told before in John Huston's *The Asphalt Jungle* (and would be told again in Stanley Kubrick's *The Killing*). What makes *Rififi* worthwhile is the way Dassin tells the tale, and how engrossed we become, especially in the heist itself. To be able to work on the safe, the crew must first contend with a sound-sensitive alarm system; no bypassing it, as it's designed to trigger if power is cut or rerouted even for a moment. Tony has found a clever way to muffle it, but they need to physically break in and get to it first. That means silence among the crew. The heist itself runs about 30 minutes of the film, and when composer Georges Auric saw in the script that *Rififi* would have a block of that length with no dialogue, he told Dassin, "Don't worry, I'll write something really good for that scene." Dassin told him not to bother, he wanted to do the whole scene without music, just natural sound, and when one of the producers learned this, he told Auric to go ahead and write something anyway. After Dassin played the finished scene for Auric with and without music, even the composer admitted the scene worked better in silence. It works, not only because it helps increase the tension, but demonstrates how thoroughly professional these thieves are. Each man has his job to do and doesn't need to check in with any of the others, doesn't need the encouragement of his colleagues. The men simply get to work, to the point that one of them even slips on ballet shoes before descending into the room with the safe. It's a no-drama crew.

I've never seen Paris look so *noir* before, especially in daylight. Dassin frustrated his producers by refusing to film the streets of Paris on sunny days; he insisted on at least gray cloud cover. Dassin also has a great sense of pacing; in addition to building tension in the relatively static heist scene, there's a harrowing episode at the end involving a car speeding through Montmartre. Pierre has kidnapped Jo's young son against the haul from the robbery, and in rescuing him, Tony has been fatally wounded. Tony, bleeding out and dying, is racing to get the boy home before he succumbs, and he's also trying to hide his condition so as not to frighten his young passenger. It's a scene made even more tense by accelerated editing, and the child laughing at riding in a speeding convertible. It's a scene that stays with you.

Jules Dassin was tapped to direct *Rififi* because of his experience working on films like these - in Hollywood. Despite his French-sounding name, Dassin was an American who grew up in Harlem and moved to Hollywood in the 1940s. Dassin was working in France not just because his talent was recognized in Europe, but because he had found himself on Hollywood's "black list."

Blacklisting (as it came to be known) was a collusion between the major Hollywood studios and the House Un-American Activities Committee (HUAC) during the Red Scare days of the early Cold War. While ostensibly this was meant to rid the United States of Communist influence by investigating its citizens, under the hysteria whipped up by Senator Joseph McCarthy (R-Wisconsin) on the barest shreds of fact, it quickly became a means of trying to homogenize and Christianize the nation under the guise of patriotism. The major Hollywood studios not only cooperated with HUAC, but voluntarily refused to employ actors, writers, directors, and other filmmakers who had been accused of being Communist sympathizers. Dassin was blacklisted in Hollywood because he had been associated in the past with groups HUAC had smeared as "Communist," even if these groups had no clear affiliation. As with other individuals on the black list, Dassin was denied a livelihood in the United States. Dassin was fortunate in that by the time he was blacklisted, he had the resume and resources to work in Europe.

Why did Hollywood go along with McCarthyism? The American film industry always had a reputation among religious groups and social conservatives (as it does today) with promoting immorality in its films, and it was always looking for a way to clean its image.[48] Hollywood also found itself on the

---

[48] Never mind that as perhaps the ultimate capitalist industry in the United States, Hollywood is as careful as any other business not to alienate its customers. Whenever I hear people call Hollywood "leftist" because of positive depictions of LBGTQI+

defensive because most of the major studios had been founded by Jewish men, and many historians have written about the antisemitism underlying HUAC's investigations[49]. But the studios also wanted to fight their unions, and since labor unions were also viewed with suspicion by HUAC, the studio executives smelled a deal of their own with the US government to help rid themselves of unions. Why were they so successful? There were few in Hollywood that had the power to stand up to them. From 1947 to 1952 the president of the Screen Actor's Guild was Ronald Reagan, and he betrayed his responsibility as head of the union by working with both HUAC and the FBI to name his own union members that he suspected of Communist ties and encouraged SAG members to do the same[50].

In an interview on the disc, Dassin talks about his years on the black list. He's gracious about colleagues that cooperated with HUAC, reminding us that staying silent had a terrible cost. He spoke not just of an artist's livelihood, but also the

---

characters, for example, I remember that polls indicate that most of the movie-going public supports inclusivity; people aren't going to buy tickets to films that offend them. Likewise, I wonder why I never hear from these same people when studios release films like *American Sniper* and *Top Gun: Maverick* that practically worship the military and the way our government uses it.

[49] Michael Freedland's book *Witch Hunt in Hollywood* is an excellent place to begin.

[50] Seth Rosenfeld's extensively researched 2012 book, *Subversives: The FBI's War on Student Radicals, and Reagan's Rise to Power*, based on FBI files is illuminating on the subject.

economic responsibilities filmmakers and other artists had to their own families. It's tempting to sort out those who cooperated with HUAC as either heroes or villains, but Dassin pointed out that some people were taking their own lives when faced with an impossible choice (the 1976 Martin Ritt film *The Front* is an excellent place to start learning about this time). It's generous of Dassin, who might be excused for being bitter. Nevertheless, it's interesting that the film's "hero," Tony, has gone to prison for five years rather than give up Jo as an accomplice to avoid his sentence. And when Tony tracks down the member of his gang that talked to Pierre about the job - even though he'd been beaten for the information - Tony kills him for the offense without a second's thought. It's not inconsistent in *film noir* for the main character to adhere to a moral code apart from society's. But this must have felt like a personal choice for Dassin as well.

You can enjoy *Rififi* (the title, by the way, is a made-up nonsense word meaning "a crazy mess," according to J. Hoberman's enclosed essay) as a stylish *noir* or an engaging caper flick without knowing any of Jules Dassin's story, and that's as it should be; a work of art should speak for itself. But it's enriching to me to know something of the human beings behind the work. I'm glad Dassin found work abroad; though he eventually returned to the United States for a few years, he seemed to prefer working in Europe, and returned there. But I can't help but think of the films, and even the lives that were lost, because of a political hysteria that seized our democracy.

A River Called Titas

Bangladesh, 1973. Directed by Ritwik Ghatak. 156 minutes, black and white.

A River Called Titas is a movie about Partition. It doesn't matter that it begins in the 1930s, years before Partition. All of director Ritwik Ghatak's brief oeuvre is about Partition, the pain of separation.

In my youth I fervently believed that art should be judged on its own merits, apart from the artist. I'm grateful for that young man's zeal, and the directions that zeal sent me, just as I'm grateful to be less sure of things as I grow older. *A River Called Titas* can be a bewildering, even a ridiculous film to an unprepared Westerner, but a little background helps put us in touch with the humanity and heartbreak that fills nearly every frame.

Ritwik Ghatak died at a relatively young age, and the only clue I uncovered to the cause of death was in Adrian Martin's enclosed essay, "River of No Return:" "His death at age fifty, in 1976, came at the end of a long string of illnesses." Given that Ghatak suffered from alcoholism and depression, at times requiring inpatient treatment, leads this former mental health professional to speculate that these were at least factors in his death. This film, released just three years before Ghatak passed, is saturated with loss.

Ghatak, like millions on the Subcontinent who lived through the mid-twentieth century, endured a turbulent life. Ghatak grew up in East Bengal, and was subject to the violence of WWII, the Bengali famine of 1943, and the riots and rebellions of the Indian independence movement. After the British Indian Empire dissolved, the Partition of 1947 split India even further, by religion; Pakistan (including East Bengal) became majority Muslim, while India, claiming West Bengal, became majority Hindu. The Partition led to the uprooting of millions on both sides, and many did not survive the transition. The Western world, for the most part, had turned its attention elsewhere, but for anyone growing up in the region at the time (and even for those today), Partition became a defining tragedy. As if that weren't enough, the Bangladesh war for independence began in 1971, during which an estimated 3 million Bengalis died from both atrocities and starvation. Ghatak himself relocated twice in his life. No wonder familial loss and division became central themes in his films.

It's also helpful to understand the role of melodrama in Indian and Bengali culture. The word "melodrama" is understood as a pejorative in contemporary parlance. "Don't be so melodramatic" is a phrase we reserve for toddlers and emotionally immature adults, usually when they're wallowing in histrionics or self-pity. But as a literary term, melodrama refers to a convention where plot and characters are exaggerated or sensationalized to elicit an emotional response from the audience. Modern Western audiences see it as immaturity, but I think that's only true of *bad* melodrama - when it's working, you don't tend to notice it. I think of melodrama as emotional CGI; used wisely, it punches up a scene, and works as a metaphor to establish human connections to larger events. *A River Called Titas* is dripping with the kind of melodrama Bengali and Indian audiences would have come to expect from their films (possibly as they were exposed to so much Victorian melodrama during the British Raj). In Martin's essay, he described melodrama as Ghatak's "birthright."

The movie follows the intertwined stories of several members of a fishing village on the banks of the Titas River. We begin with our principals as children, playing along the banks of the river, already thinking about work and marriage; Basanti follows the two boys Kishore and Subol, and has already selected Kishore as a potential husband. When they are grown, Kishore (Prabir Mitra), traveling to a remote village far across the river with Subol, marries a young girl, Rajar Jhi (Kabari Choudhury). Both are so shy on their wedding night as to barely look at each other, and the next morning set off for Kishore's home village of Gokannaghat, Rajar barely glancing at her new husband. The boatman is worried about bandits on the water, and urges Kishore to place her in the hold, ought of sight. Nevertheless, that night, while the men sleep, pirates board the boat and carry Rajar off with them. Rajar is able to escape her captors by jumping into the water, and the next morning washes up on the banks of the river. Kishore, unaware that she has gotten away, goes mad.[51]

Another ten years pass. Rajar is now living in Gokannaghat with her son from her one night of marriage, Ananta (Shafiq Islam). Basanti (Rosy Samad) has befriended her, though neither woman knows of the other's past. We also find out that Basanti had married Subol when he returned many years earlier, but that Subol had died the day after the marriage, apparently from a fishing accident. Kishore, bearded and half dressed, is wandering the village, still senseless and mute, waving a knife to keep people at bay. Basanti and Rajar have no idea of the other's history, and since Rajar cannot recall her husband's face or name, doesn't connect Kishore with the man she married. Still, she pities him, and begins to care for him, believing that if she cannot find her soulmate, she can become a soulmate to this lost man. Kishore is attacked by the men of the village one night after he accidentally mortally wounds Rajar; as she tends to the dying man, he utters the words, "My wife," seemingly finally breaking through his insanity. But these are his final words, and Rajar dies as well, leaving Ananta a true orphan. The village - including Basanti, to her shame - turn on Ananta, forcing him to take up a homeless existence with the fishermen. But the River Titas is drying up, taking the village with it as farmers fight for the newly-fertile land.

You can see the loss throughout the story, the families being broken apart by events beyond their control. What

---

[51] I know. Melodrama, remember? Just roll with it.

Ghatak did was to take tropes familiar to his audience (the wise - or mad - old man of the village, the mother, the virginal girl, the framework of melodrama) and recast them in a new visual style. Where Satyajit Ray embraced neorealism in his *Apu Trilogy*, Ghatak went further into the avant garde, experimenting with montage in some scenes, but also carefully framing his characters to great effect. There's a terrific scene in which Basanti is speaking to Rajar, but it seems like Basanti is aware that her words are not being received. There's an establishing shot showing Basanti to our left and Rajar across the room on our right, the distance between them accentuated. But then the camera holds Basanti's face in closeup, as if she's really addressing us. As the camera pulls back, the framing keeps Basanti to the far right of our screen, revealing an empty room to our left; we *know* that Rajar is offscreen to our right, but Basanti appears done with trying to reach her. In other scenes, Ghatak will use deep focus to isolate a character even when they're physically present; he'll crowd several characters in focus in foreground, midground, and background, with a character being discussed centrally placed, as if even their presence does not imply belonging.

A River Called Titas may at first glance seem a confounding film for Westerners to appreciate, but I found that a little bit of education easily bridges the gap in understanding. Watching non-Western films is an exercise in stepping back from our own stories and meeting someone else on their own ground. It's why I firmly believe that cinema is neither a mindless entertainment nor an artsy extravagance; it is a medium almost everyone in the world consumes in order to hear and tell their stories. I could watch a thousand Bengali (or Somali or Ecuadoran) films and never really grasp what it is to live as someone else does. But every time I hear a story that isn't my own, I'm at least reminded that my point of view, while valid, is not the only one out there.

Can movies save the world? Yes, I believe they can. All we need to do is be willing to pay attention.

Roma (1972)

Italy, 1972. Directed by Frederico Fellini. 120 minutes, color.

There are filmmakers - like Woody Allen for New York, and the Hughes brothers for Los Angeles - whose films act as very specific tour guides to their respective cities. You may not get the definitive experience of a locale, but you know you're going to share an insider's view that you may not otherwise be privileged to. And you know that view, even if it isn't all-encompassing, will be completely authentic. So it is with *Roma*, Frederico Fellini's love letter to the city of Rome.

Roma lacks a narrative structure; it's loosely about a boy from the provinces who travels to the city, then follows Fellini himself as he films a project in and around the city. While the boy and the young man roughly stand in for Fellini, there are enough biographical details (age and year of arrival, for instance) between Fellini and the youth who steps off the train in an immaculate white suit, to lead us to understand that we are not to literally equate the two. In fact, we really never follow up on what happens to the young man, and in many of his scenes Fellini's camera strays from him, taking our attention with it. Fellini also seems to switch from war-time Rome to the present and back seemingly on a whim, so there's not even a straightforward progression through time. Think of *Roma* instead as someone dumping out a box of old photographs, or having drinks with locals talking about their city, alcohol loosening both lips and remembrances.

Rome is famously "The Eternal City," but Fellini knows her better than that. Throughout we're continually finding the ancient and the modern juxtaposed. In our first glimpse of modern Rome, Fellini's crew is filming along the brand new (in fact, still-unfinished) toll road encircling the city. Interspersed in the cacophony of modern traffic are hand-drawn carts; even a solitary horse is seen negotiating the traffic. A torrential rain works to bring everything to a halt, giving us time to look at the hippie protestors on our right, and the ruins of the Coliseum on our left. Nowhere is Roman past and present more at odds than in the subway tunnels being dug by behemoth machines under the city. As a massive drill penetrates (violates?) subterranean Rome, workers uncover an archaeological site, a home centuries old with painted frescoes on the wall (look closely, and you'll see the face of a tunnel worker duplicated in the artwork, linking past and present). In the film's most potent metaphor, as the 20th-century Roman air pours in through the drill's opening, the images on the walls begin to oxidize and disappear.

There are only two things you need to understand to appreciate this film. The first is that to Fellini, Rome is a beautiful woman. The second is that in Fellini's films, women are exalted and reduced to being saints, sirens, mothers, and whores. None of these roles are exclusive of each other, but we'll begin with Rome as a

Saint, the way we meet her at the beginning of the film, in the eyes of provincial schoolchildren. Rome is introduced to them as a repository of history and as the home of the Catholic Church, from whence faith ripples out. Rome's church dictates every facet of provincial life. Rome's pre-Christian past is deified as well, all part of the holy story of Rome embracing the Church. Even when Fellini delights in lampooning the clergy in the Ecclesiastical Fashion Show, in which neon nuns and roller-skating priests in increasingly flamboyant and outrageous costumes promenade before a wealthy crowd rivaling the excesses of any European fashion house, even then he cannot ignore the sacred center of the city. Fellini may find the clergy comical and hypocritical, but not the Virgin they are in service of. That this woman is also his

Siren or muse takes nothing from that. Rome is also Fellini's call to his art: film and the theater. There are two theater pieces in *Roma*, one in a movie theater in the provinces in the 1930s, another a vaudeville house in the city itself during WWII. In the film theater, a silent movie melodrama about a beautiful woman who seduces Romans into Christianity pulls the audience into what seems to serve as a boisterous town square; it's easy to see the scene as the basis for Giuseppe Tornatore's rural theater in his 1988 *Cinema Paradiso*. The amateur night in the Rome theater is no less rowdy; the predominantly male crowd remains unruly and oppositional to the men onstage. It is when the women perform that the crowd is finally tamed, calmed by their songs and reminded that they are all family in wartime Italy. It's also in this scene of Fellini's Rome of art and performance that we are abruptly reminded of Rome as

Mother, as air raid sirens sound and patrons evacuate to underground shelters. It's Rome protecting her children, age and class distinctions cast aside. But nowhere does Fellini embrace Rome as a maternal figure more than in the youth's arrival to the city in the 1940s. His first stop is a boarding house he has been referred to by relatives back home; it's an enormous set of flats crammed with children, elderly, even a Chinese immigrant cooking (of course) Italian food in his room. The youth is guided through the overflowing abode, finally to be presented to the landlady, an enormous bed-bound woman who both welcomes the youth and establishes the moral code of her home. Following this is one of several outdoor *ristorante* scenes, in which our youth is fought over even by strangers to invite him to join them and encourage him to eat, eat, *eat*. Families, friends, lovers, all intermingle and spill from table to table heaped with pasta, snails, bread, and wine. Rome is a mother who welcomes and feeds all her children. In a city - particularly a 1940s fascist Italy - in which the church and the government maintain a patriarchy, Rome herself will still nurture a matriarchy, even among the

Whores, who serve their male clients, but also keep them in line. Fellini is not content to just give us one look at a brothel, we get two, serving both the lower and the upper classes. The brothels are viewed, at least by their own sex workers, as places where young men can get the "experience" necessary to become good lovers and eventually husbands, and a necessary outlet for all others. In each whorehouse we're exposed (ahem) to both the glamorous and unglamorous sex workers of all ages and sizes. Fellini emphasizes the "working" in "working women." Sex work is seen as one of the few employment opportunities for women, and by the end of the day they're exhausted. In place of pimps are madams that keep the clients in line; they are the gatekeepers to their pleasure palaces, and the men and boys who come to see them know it and respect it. The whorehouses serve as a tacit check and balance to the church, and both sides seem to understand that. Fellini, for his part, seems to need both parties - his city isn't Rome without them.

So *Roma* is ultimately a sort of travelogue, our guide one of her most dedicated children. It's not for everyone (I texted my son after two viewings that I was "Fellini'd out"), but it's worth checking out if you want to see the city portrayed by one who loves her best. (Of course it's also a historical snapshot; Fellini's "modern" sections are at this writing more than fifty years old.) It's also worth seeing if you want to see what an iconic film director can do with such a beloved subject. For example, the city and the camera are always in motion; the film begins and ends with the fluid and energetic camerawork that brings Rome to life, until the moment Fellini wants us to pay attention and it *stops.* But if you're an Italophile there's much here to enjoy. If nothing else, you get the "outsider-insider's" look you won't get from a guidebook.

Roma (2018)

Mexico, 2018. Directed by Alfonso Cuarón. 135 minutes, black and white.

"This was all about memory." - Alfonso Cuarón.

It had been about two years since I'd seen *Roma*, and going into it, I was prepared to compare it with Frederico Fellini's 1972 film of the same name, which I'd written about, well, a chapter ago. But within a scene or two, I was taken in by the unique beauty and heartbreak of Cuarón's deeply personal film. There are some similarities and recalls - you can't have a film that shares a name with a work of one of the 20th-century's most iconic directors and not invite comparisons - but from the same launching pad, Cuarón takes us in an entirely different direction.

Let's get the similarities out of the way: both films recall a specific city that was formative for each filmmaker; Rome for Fellini, and Mexico City for Cuarón, specifically the Colonia Roma neighborhood (hence the name) in which Cuarón grew up and so lovingly recreates. Both films are set in the same era; Cuarón's film covers roughly a year from 1970 to 1971, and the modern sections of Fellini's *Roma* are contemporaneous with the film's 1972 release. Both are haunted by ancient ghosts - ruins and reminders of civilizations that lived before, and in the case of Mexico, the living indigenous people who keep that past alive. But if you haven't seen the film, and are under the impression that Alfonso Cuarón was exploiting the work of a previous director to lift up his own, well, a few minutes in Cuarón's Mexico City will change your mind.

The film opens in an upper middle class home, and we meet Cleo (Yalitza Aparicio) who will be our guide through the film. Cleo is one of two servants who live with the family, and the two speak to each other in Mixtec, an indigenous language apart from the Spanish they speak with their employing family. Sra. Sofía (Marina de Tavira) shares the home with her physician husband Antonio (Fernando Grediaga), her mother Teresa (Verónica García), and her four children, Toño, Paco, Pepe, and Sofi. The family is about to lose Antonio; while Sofía tells the children their father will be away at a conference in Canada, in fact he is simply abandoning them; Cleo will encounter him later in the hospital, and the eldest son will even see Antonio run past him with his mistress on a night in the city.

Meanwhile, Cleo has been introduced to a young man of her own, Fermín (Jorge Antonio Guerrero Martínez), who is learning martial arts as a recruit of the Falcons, a right-wing militia supported by the Mexican government (more on this later). When Cleo tells him in a movie theater that she thinks she is pregnant, Fermín abandons her on the spot; telling her he is buying snacks, he simply walks out of the theater.

When Cleo, fearing dismissal, tearfully tells Sofía she's pregnant, Sofía rallies to her. Cleo and her fellow servant work long, hard hours for the family, cleaning, laundering, cooking, chasing after the children. But in spite of the class differences, the children love Cleo, and Sofía instantly recognizes her responsibility to the girl who is central to the home. Sofía escorts Cleo to the hospital, where she has arranged for her to see an OB-GYN, and later, grandmother Teresa takes Cleo to a furniture store to buy her a crib.

It's during the visit to the furniture store that we are most directly confronted with the political violence that was spilling into the streets of Mexico City, and at this point, it's worth a digression to talk a little about what was going on in Mexico at the time. But to tell the story, we need to back up a few years, and I'm going to turn to historian Enrique Krauze's essay "The Layers of 'Roma'" included with the disc:

> "...[I]n 1968, the regime of the PRI (the Institutional Revolutionary Party), which had governed the country since 1929, had committed a crime that would never be erased from the collective memory. As in other parts of the world then, the young had rebelled peacefully against the established order. Mexico was growing economically, there was order, peace, and stability, but political participation and civil liberties remained severely restricted. I was a part of this rebellious youth, and I marched in the streets. On October 2, 1968, ten days before the opening of the

Olympic Games, the government of President
Gustavo Díaz Ordaz (1964-70) brutally suppressed
a student rally in the old pre-Hispanic square in
Tlatelolco. The celebration of freedom was bathed
in blood. Octavio Paz, Mexico's foremost poet,
who would later win the Nobel Prize in Literature,
saw in this massacre an echo of the human sacrifices
that were practiced in Aztec times on this very same
site."

During the time *Roma* covers, a new president, Luis
Echeverría, had taken office, but as Ordaz's secretary of the
interior, he had been partly responsible for the massacre.
Echeverría had tried to distance himself from those events by
freeing the students who had been imprisoned for two years
when he took office, but these students immediately got back
to work and planned a new protest for June 10, 1971.
Though Echeverría had publicly announced a more open
attitude toward protest, his government had been training
and coordinating with Halcones (Falcons), paramilitary
groups in which they recruited some of Mexico's poorest and
most disillusioned young men by playing on class differences
and economic divides. Carrying rudimentary weapons -
including the bamboo canes the Falcons had been training
with - busloads of anti-protestors attacked the students who
were peacefully marching. This attack, which became known
as the Corpus Christi Massacre - is recreated as Cleo and
Teresa shop for a crib.

Cleo's vantage point is the second floor of the furniture

store, and as the customers begin to hear the noise in the streets outside, they rush to the windows to get a view. (Cuarón's signature camera move is the slow steady pan that offers a detached view of chaotic events around us even as he orchestrates new activity coming into view; think of the debris storm that cripples, then destroys the space shuttle in *Gravity*.) It's bedlam outside, as students and spectators try to flee the militias closing in on them. Protesters seeking refuge burst into the store; one terrified student hides in a wardrobe. They're followed by Falcons, who find the hiding protester, drag him out, and beat him. One of the Falcons pulls a handgun and shoots the protester, then turns the gun toward Cleo and Teresa. It is Fermín. As he's hit with recognition, he turns and flees, and in the stress of the moment the camera tilts down and we see that Cleo's water has broken. Teresa manages to get Cleo back to their car amid the gunfire erupting in the street, but their driver is immediately ensnared in traffic brought to a standstill in the pandemonium. They eventually reach the hospital, but we don't know how long Cleo and her baby have been detained, and as she is examined, the obstetrician cannot auscultate the baby's heartbeat. In one of the film's quietest, loneliest, and tensest scenes, we wait with Cleo to see if her baby can be saved.

There's more - I've brought us a little past the halfway point of the film - but I'm not here to spoil the plot, just to whet your appetite for it. Instead I'd like to talk about the meticulous care Alfonso Cuarón took to film *Roma*, his decision to present the film in black and white (technically it was shot in color to capture the visual tones, but the idea was always to screen it monochromatically), and finally talk about the lengths Cuarón and his team went to to bring the film to the Mexican people.

Cuarón - ironically - seemed to begin his production with a nod to Italian neorealism, and I use the word "ironically" because that's something Fellini all but refuted by the time he was directing. I've talked about neorealism before, so briefly, it was an attempt by Italian post-WWII filmmakers to present "reality" in their films, by using real locations, avoiding camera effects, even in using non actors in the cast. Cuarón began preparations for the film with no script, not even a story in mind. All he thought about was recreating a very specific time in his and Mexico City's past. He went back to the street where he grew up, scoured the city for the old blocks and the old buildings that were there at the time; where he found some had been torn down, he built recreations to the last detail. He consulted family photographs, talked relatives into returning furniture that had been given away and had the art department reconstruct everything else. His team scoured second-hand stores for clothing from the period. He started with the place. He started with memories.

To cast *Roma*, he had his team cross Mexico and photograph Mexicans, thousands of them. Marina de Tavira (Sofía) turned out to be the only actor he turned to; no one else had acting experience, chosen because they looked like the people he remembered. The most astonishing find, of course, was Yalitza Aparacio, the elementary education

427

student who played Cleo, herself the daughter of a single mother who worked as a housekeeper. Born in Tlaxiaco, Oaxaca, Aparacio's father was Mixtec and her mother Triqui, and in her first acting role earned a nomination for an Academy Award for Best Actress, and was named the UNESCO Goodwill Ambassador for Indigenous Peoples. Her performance as the beating heart of this family, the woman who figuratively, and at the end of the film literally saves their lives, lifts this film out of nostalgia and into the hearts of viewers worlds away from her own. I can only imagine how much this film touches people who share her culture if it was able to say so much to me from so far away.

Cuarón found that the best way to work with his cast was to withhold the eventual script from them, only giving them the sections they would be filming that day (de Tavira, the only one with acting experience, found this to be the most challenging way she'd ever worked). Between takes, he'd pull one child aside; "I want you to drop a spoon while you're talking at the dinner table, and make sure you go after it." To another child; "If she drops anything, I want you to go off on your sister that she's too clumsy." In this way, no two takes, while covering the same lines were ever alike, and kept his cast feeling fresh.

Cuarón's attention to detail is exposed in the disc's supplemental documentaries, one produced by Netflix, the others by Criterion. In one, Cuarón tells a story about another filmmaker who was doing a period film, set (I think) in the 19th century. There's a cake in the scene, and it wasn't enough for the director to have the cake decorated as it would have been at the time. He wanted the cake itself baked according to a 19th-century recipe, the same way it would have been prepared during the period. Cuarón smiles as he tells this story, like he understands that the director was being ridiculous, but deep in his heart, he *gets it*. One of the film's producers tells us about a party scene in *Roma*, in which Cleo is surrounded by background chatter, which to be fair, passes in and out of clear audibility as we listen to her own conversation. Apparently, when filming crowd scenes, filmmakers will use Additional Dialogue Replacement (ADR) actors to come into a recording studio, and say the word, "walla" over and over again, as it seems to replicate the vague chatter of background conversations. Also, apparently, there is nothing Alfonso Cuarón hates more than the word "walla." Instead, he brought back the original actors from the scene to do the ADR, and asked them to think about what sorts of conversations these characters might be having over drinks at a party. These improvised conversations, which no one will ever be able to follow, became part of the soundtrack for that scene.

No less fussy is Cuarón over his visuals, and he served as his own director of photography (to stunning effect) on *Roma*. We often think of filming in black and white as an "artsy" attempt by a filmmaker, but I think here it's used to evoke an aura of memory (I think Kenneth Branagh had a similar intent in his 2021 film, *Belfast*); to portray memory as black and white is to strip away a layer of reality, reminding us that we're looking at events through a filter. Cuarón shot digitally because he found that it gave him a wider dynamic range - you get a much, much greater range of blacks, whites, and grays than film will allow, and digital recording also allows for crisper images. The result is something clear, but soft, sharp, but not at all harsh. It's beautiful. When you combine the photography with how carefully Cuarón prepared for this film (set decorators and costume designers were all given charts to show them how different shades of color would show up on black and white film), the result is any frame from this film could hang in an art museum. Indeed, the 108-page booklet included with the Criterion disc is mostly made up of stills from the film.

The last thing I'll say about *Roma* serves as a way to set it apart from Fellini's film. Reading this, you might get the idea that *Roma* was a vanity project for Cuarón, especially in the obsession over the details in recreating a time and a place in his life. Certainly, as great a film as Fellini's *Roma* is, one can be forgiven for suspecting Fellini of making a film for himself alone. But Cuarón knew he was also telling a story of his people, not just in Mexico City, but across the country itself. Despite having made the film for Netflix, a streaming platform, Cuarón wanted Mexicans to have the experience of seeing their story on a big screen. So he and his team set about getting prints of *Roma* into Mexican theaters, and since the film had both audio and visual requirements that exceeded the capabilities of many of these venues, Cuarón's production company (along with some help from Netflix), began to work with theaters in cities to upgrade their speakers, screens, and projectors. Where there were no theaters, Cuarón helped them set up public spaces to screen the film. But much of rural Mexico is without even that much infrastructure, much less access to internet or streaming services. And in those rural areas lived many of the indigenous people that *Roma* celebrated. So Cuaron's team converted a tractor trailer into a 90-seat movie theater, and drove it all over Mexico. They'd park it in the middle of town for a while, and 90 people at a time would get to go to the movies. For free. Popcorn included.

I wrote that Fellini's *Roma* was a love letter to Rome. Cuarón's *Roma* is a love letter to a nation and her people.

The Royal Tenenbaums

US, 2001. Directed by Wes Anderson. 110 minutes, color.

I have a coffee table book given to me by my son of fan art inspired by Wes Anderson movies. Fittingly, the book is titled *Bad Dads*, though my son assures me I shouldn't take the title personally.[52] If it's true that this is something of a running theme through Mr. Anderson's[53] oeuvre - and it is - it is in this week's film, *The Royal Tenenbaums* that we meet Anderson's Worst Dad Ever.[54]

---

[52] Though he may be, albeit subconsciously, retaliating for the occasional glitter bomb I've mailed him over the years. I favor the ultra-fine gold glitter that aggressively adheres to both human and non-human surfaces and seemingly self-replicates. My proudest moment was sprinkling a pinch of it in with my end-of-life advance directives and medical power of attorney. If you find me languishing in a questionable assisted care facility in my final years, you'll know my boy got in the last laugh.

[53] Oddly, "bad dads" could be said to be prominent in the films of another Anderson (and another favorite filmmaker of mine), Paul Thomas Anderson, especially his film *Magnolia*, which features three, no four... honestly I lose count.

[54] If I'm going to pack three footnotes into one essay, I may as well get them out of the way in the first paragraph. *The Royal*

Gene Hackman plays Royal Tenenbaum, the disgraceful - and disgraced - *paterfamilias* of the Tenenbaum family. He is estranged from them, having left the home "at your mother's request," as he tells his three children (in the commentary track, Anderson tells us that the film was originally going to be about his own parents' divorce, but the moment Royal opens his mouth in this scene, the character took the film in a different direction). We're introduced to all of the film's characters as they were perhaps twenty years before, through an ingenious assortment of (invented) book covers. The mother, Etheline (Anjelica Huston), has written a book, *Family of Geniuses*, about raising her three children on her own, as each has shown prodigious talent. The oldest, Chas (Ben Stiller), as a child created, bred, and sold spotted "Dalmatian mice," turning those proceeds into the basis of a modest real estate empire, still as a child. Middle child Margot (Gwyneth Paltrow) becomes a wunderkind playwright - her book is a collection of three plays she's written. And youngest Richie (Luke Wilson) is a junior tennis champion. There's even a neighbor across the street, Eli Cash (Owen Wilson), who the siblings have pretty much taken into their home. Eli achieves fame later in life as the "James Joyce" of Western fiction (*Old Custer* is his alternative historical fiction novel).

Moving to the present day, we find the early promise of

Tenenbaums is Wes Anderson's third film, and the Bad Dad Theme arguably began with his first, *Bottle Rocket*, with James Caan's father-figure to the central characters, Mr. Henry. Bill Murray takes up the mantle as Henry J. Blume in Anderson's second film, *Rushmore.*

the characters in ruins. Chas is now a widower, having recently lost his wife in a plane crash that the rest of the family (including the beagle) survived without a scratch. He has two young boys, Uzi (Jonah Meyerson) and Ari (Grant Rosenmeyer), of whom he has become so overprotective that Chas keeps all three of them dressed in red Adidas track suits, ostensibly the better to find each other in an emergency. Margot is suffering from profound depression, her writing stalled for years, and has left her devoted (and older) husband Raleigh St. Clair (Bill Murray). Richie has been living on his tennis earnings on a cruise ship for the past year. His successful tennis career came to a spectacular end in a match in which he failed to function at all. Not by coincidence, the match came the day after Margot (who is adopted, as Royal unfailingly mentions to everyone he introduces her to) married St. Clair. Richie, it seems, has been in love with his adopted sister for years. Even Eli is going as far off the rails as his mescaline addiction will take him. When Chas discovers his apartment building has no sprinkler system, he takes his boys back home to regroup (Etheline: "But we don't have sprinklers here, either."). The other children return home, too. And Royal senses an opportunity.

Royal has been living in a hotel, and is running out of money. He had been a successful attorney, but Chas sued him for embezzling money from his real estate business, and Royal was subsequently disbarred. Royal was always negligent of his oldest son, favoring Richie, whom he would take on inappropriate outings in the city (like gambling on back-alley dog fights) to which the others were never invited.

Chas harbors the most anger toward his father, still carrying a BB in between two knuckles that Royal shot him with after double-crossing Chas in a childhood air rifle battle. Margot remains bitter over being treated like a second-class child; in the film's opening scenes, as she and her siblings perform her first play at her eleventh birthday party, Royal pans it as "just a bunch of little kids in animal costumes," telling his daughter, "Sweetie, don't be mad at me, that's just one man's opinion." Richie is the only child that looks toward Royal's redemption, but knows how thin the ice is on which his father skates.

Learning the three children are again under Etheline's roof, and feeling threatened by her recent engagement to her long-time accountant, Henry Sherman (Danny Glover), Royal ambushes Etheline outside the home and confesses to her that he's dying of cancer. He has perhaps weeks left to live and wants to set things right with the family. It's a lie of course, and when the family discovers it, Royal is tossed out onto the street. But in his brief "convalescence" at the old house, Royal discovers that he really *does* want to atone to the people he's hurt. But he's just made that an even steeper uphill climb, maybe something he's finally put out of reach entirely.

When I wrote about *The Life Aquatic With Steve Zissou* (Anderson's next film), I wrote about how Anderson uses these odd, quirky people to process the less "cinematic" problems and tribulations we all face in our lives, so I won't rehash that here. But I think in exaggerating the highs of the Tenenbaum clan (seriously, how many of us grew up as part of a home of overachieving geniuses?), their fall from that, and the resulting pain that's come into their lives is easily identifiable. The specifics of how they live may be utterly foreign, but the emotions aren't. When at the end of the film Chas is finally able to admit, "I've had a rough year," it's a simple and heartbreaking line that speaks to each of us.

Stylistically, this is really where Anderson hits his stride, picking right up from where he left off in *Rushmore*, with its fantastic catalog of Max's extracurricular activities. The Tenenbaum home is a character in itself, lovingly and painstakingly created as a space to compartmentalize each of the film's human characters, fleshing them out even more. Anderson's brother Eric did all of "Richie's" artwork we see in the home - including the wall of framed portraits of Margot - and in the supplemental materials there's a foldout floor plan of the Archer Street house, detailed and annotated, which served as a guide to both cast and crew. It's in these plans, for example, that we discover that Margot has been smoking Sweet Afton cigarettes since age twelve - an unfiltered Irish tobacco product discontinued in 2011. In establishing the house, Anderson often will pan from one room to another to give us a sense of how it's all assembled, then meticulously frame each room, along with the characters inside, to give us as complete a view as possible.

Anderson is also known for his soundtracks; instead of going for the obvious, will cultivate music that's a little slyer, a little less conspicuous, but still comments on the scene. Anderson admitted on the chat track that he'll often hear a song and tuck it away for years, waiting for the perfect chance to use it. He loves to take a song we all know and filter it through a different artist, and *The Royal Tenenbaums* is bookended by two songs like this (Anderson also confessed how much he loves ending a film on his characters in a slo-mo exit to music). In the scene in which we're introduced to the Tenenbaum children, Anderson uses a cover of the Beatles' "Hey Jude" performed by the Mutato Muzika Orchestra (and produced by frequent Wes Anderson collaborator and former Devo member Mark Mothersbaugh); our cast exits to Jackson Browne's "Fairest of the Seasons" performed by Nico. It's arty and could fall flat on its face as a gimmick, but it doesn't. I think the secret is Anderson chooses music that has a tenderness about it, which matches the way he feels about his characters.

A tenderness Anderson even extends to "bad dads". It made me think of something Alfonso Cuarón said about the scene in *Roma* where the father drives out of his family's life forever, also a scene from the director's own life. Cuarón remembered telling the actor that his character was free now, that he was finally making an escape from a life that had caged him, and that when he said those words, it was the first time Cuarón had considered what his father was feeling. Anderson doesn't absolve Royal, and he doesn't take his side. But neither will he allow us as an audience the comfort of seeing Royal as inhuman.

The Rules of the Game

France, 1939. Directed by Jean Renoir. 106 minutes, black and white.

"We are dancing on a volcano." - Jean Renoir

The Rules of the Game may be the most challenging film I write about. It's impossible today to view this in the way it would have been seen on its release in 1939. Reports of the film's premiere read like accounts of the opening night of Stravinsky's *Rite of Spring*: audiences rioted. Theatergoers booed, whistled, smashed seats; one report has an audience member calmly unfolding his newspaper and igniting it with a lighter, the intent, it would seem, to burn down the theater. Director Jean Renoir was forced to cut 13 minutes from the film after its opening weekend in an effort to calm audiences (it didn't work), and the film itself was banned throughout the war years for being too upsetting, too negatively depicting France and her citizens. The film's negative was destroyed during a WWII bombing; twenty years later, in 1959 a new version was restored from original prints and footage recovered from filming. Renoir himself would not take part in the restoration, though he gave the project his blessing.

In 1939 the threat of war was hanging over all of Europe. It was becoming apparent that the surrendering of Czechoslovakia to Hitler at Munich, meant to appease the Nazis, would only encourage them. Renoir, who had already commented brilliantly on class divisions in his previous *Grand Illusion*, now wanted to take on the rot in society he believed was responsible for not only the gathering warclouds, but also the economic troubles across Europe. His chosen instrument of attack? A comedy. A farce, à la Musset or Molière, in which Renoir would expose the bourgeoisie as the holders of money and power, but with no sense of consequences to their actions. He would set his film at a country estate, where despite the threat of world events taking over their lives, our central characters occupy themselves with infidelities and assignations. The title of the film hints at the moral code of the wealthy; *The Rules of the Game* address not whether one should cheat on one's partner (and with the partner of a friend), but how it's to be done to minimize social embarrassment and keep good relations intact.

The plot is almost incidental to the film; Renoir admits to creating characters in both the upper class and their servants to fit certain roles, then let the characters themselves dictate to him what they should be doing. He also seems to compare their relationships to variations in a fugue - here a husband and wife "play out" a certain melody, then we find a variation as husband runs to mistress. It gets complicated fast, making it difficult for modern American audiences to follow, but I'm going to have a go at a synopsis, mostly because there are certain plot points that become important in the satire.

We begin at night at an airfield, in which through a clever tracking shot, Renoir follows a reporter announcing the successful completion of a transatlantic flight for French radio (Renoir used an actual French radio personality in this scene). The dashing and heroic pilot is André Jurieux (Roland Toutain); he is met by his close friend Octave (director Renoir himself). André asks if Christine (Nora Grégor) is there to meet him, and is devastated when he learns she has not come, preferring to remain home with her husband, the Marquis Robert de la Chesnaye (Marcel Dalio). When the radio reporter catches up with him for a live interview and asks him how he feels, he responds that it is the worst day of his life - he'd made the flight for a woman and she isn't here to greet him.

It's a clever opening, and not just because the comparison to Charles Lindbergh would have stung especially to French audiences, Lindbergh having been decorated in 1938 by Hermann Göring. But from the darkness of the airfield we cut to posh and brightly-lit Paris apartments, and meet most of the cast as they listen to the broadcast. Christine snaps off the radio, and we find her with her devoted maid, Lisette (Paulette Dubost). Lisette herself is married to the groundskeeper at Robert's estate, Schumacher (Gaston Modot), but is conducting an affair with Octave, who serves as kind of a go-between among the rich, not really in their class himself.[55] Lisette and Robert are both aware of

---

[55] In an interview years later for French television, Renoir said, "My character is in fact a complement to others. He is like a cork

Christine's relationship with André, but Robert has the good taste not to bring this up when he and his wife discuss André's outburst over the airwaves, and husband and wife pledge their devotion to each other. Feeling guilty, Robert phones his own mistress, Geneviéve (Mila Parély) to meet with her the next day to call it off, though he does invite her to a weekend retreat at his country estate, an invitation Geneviéve accepts so that she might win him back. Octave convinces Robert to allow him to bring along a now-suicidal André. And Christine invites her niece, Jackie (Anne Mayen), who is also attracted to André because why not?

Once at the estate, we finally meet Schumacher, who is frustrated trying to rid the grounds of rabbits, and has run across traps set by a local poacher, Marceau (Julien Carette). Schumacher is ready to throw Marceau off the grounds - or worse - but Robert intervenes and allows Marceau to sweet-talk him into his dream of working in an estate as a domestic. Marceau joins the other servants, and immediately begins chasing Lisette (Schumacher's wife, remember?), who seems happy to let him catch her.

A break in the plot synopsis here to talk a little about Renoir's directorial style, which is intriguing. Renoir loves long takes with the camera, and he loves to follow characters around as if the camera is an observer who turns to look when someone new enters the scene. He also likes to keep the camera back from the action, so that we can catch what's

---

that can fit in the neck of different bottles, or like a wedge you use to steady the furniture."

happening in the background as well. When filming in the hallways and passageways of the estate, as Renoir does when "tucking his characters in" for the night, we're focused on a strolling talking pair, brightly lit, usually having an innocent conversation. But behind them, we see other characters moving from room to room, and in one scene a servant gradually extinguishes hall lights, darkening the background in sections. All this implies that it is in the dark, in the quiet in the background, that the real "truth" is being told. And again, long takes allow the scene to be played out.

Which makes Renoir's break in style in the following day's scene so much more dramatic. The guests and servants all take part in a hunt on the grounds, servants beating the bushes for rabbits and pheasants to drive to the awaiting guns of the guests. Renoir (who abhorred hunting) increases the pace of the editing, and dramatically shortens the length of his shots; scenes of rabbits, panicking, racing from the beaters. It's a flurry of movement, quick glances at the prey, working to a crescendo of gunfire, and the camera resting only when an animal flops over dead, in one scene staying on a rabbit as its hind legs stop racing, then the tail trembles, then stillness. It's not a hunt, it's a massacre. It's shocking not just in content, but in presentation, and though our characters seem barely affected by the violence, it's a scene that hangs over the audience for the rest of the film.

That night Robert and Christine hold a masked ball and enlist the help of their guests in musical numbers. With the confusion of masks and musical numbers, the hallways of the estate practically throb with trysts. Schumacher catches

Marceau plotting a meeting with his wife, and begins to run after the couple with a handgun. During the hunt, Robert tells Geneviéve that he no longer loves her and will return to Christine, but as he agrees to a farewell kiss with Geneviéve, the two are spotted by Christine, who assumes the two are still an item. That night Geneviéve is preparing to leave, but Christine finds her and gives Geneviéve her blessing to go after her husband, since it will free Christine up to pursue an affair of her own. But during the ball, Octave *also* declares his love for Christine, something she had not considered. Robert and André get into a woefully ineffective fistfight over Christine, and when Schumacher actually begins to open fire at Marceau (and maybe even Lisette) among the guests, Robert dismisses both the men.

Octave and Christine plan to run off together, and are spotted outside by Marceau and Schumacher, but since Lisette has given Christine her cloak to ward off the chill, both men mistake her for the maid. Schumacher runs off to fetch his shotgun. Meanwhile, running back inside for his bags, Octave encounters Lisette and André, who beg him not to run off with Christine. Having a change of heart, Octave tells André where he can find Christine, and wraps his own coat over André's shoulders. André runs to meet his love, and in a scene reminiscent of the hunt, is shot dead by Schumacher, believing him to be Octave.

The guests gather outside, where Robert informs them that a tragic "accident" has befallen André, offering the fiction that he was shot by the groundskeeper who mistook him in the dark for a poacher. Marcel and Schumacher are immediately hired back, most likely to maintain their silence. Renoir in an interview said that even before he had a script, he knew that the heroic André would die, and would be offered up as a sort of sacrifice. All so that the bourgeoisie could go back to their lives of trifle without dealing with reality. All to keep playing their "game" according to its "rules."

Without the context of the war, *The Rules of the Game* is, for me at least, a hard nut to crack. It's difficult to see the uproar this caused, and the "comedy of manners" is something we're not familiar with today, at least not in the form French audiences of the 1930s would have been. It was also difficult for me to understand, at first viewing, why the film was so adored later on, with many critics describing it as one of the finest films ever made. The casual film viewer isn't going to see that in one viewing, and frankly, neither did I. It wasn't until I'd rewatched the film with commentary, then watched *all* of the many interviews and documentaries included on the disc that I began to see past the surface farce. One thing I noticed, for example, was Robert's fascination with collecting automata - his collection of clockwork birds, a player piano belting out Saint-Saëns *Danse Macabre* during the ball, Robert's excited unveiling of an enormous contraption that seemed to be equal parts calliope and cuckoo clock to serenade his guests. All this seems to reflect not just on the predictable clockwork of the characters through the estate, but of Europe building to war without human intervention. Concentrating less on the surface, I began to see what film scholars saw, and I imagine that as I return to this in a few months or years, I'll see more.

But should it take that much study and concentration to determine a film is "great?" Shouldn't you be able to see it right away, like you do with *Casablanca* or even *Citizen Kane*? In so much of the material I read and watched and listened to surrounding this film, I kept feeling the gatekeeping of film scholars, holding this up as a jewel, but obscuring its brightness with their jargon, like wine writers trying to describe what a certain merlot tastes like, self-consciously aware that other wine writers are reading. That's what I'm hoping to avoid in these essays. My goal is to invite you in, not hold you at arm's length. Maybe it's my frustration at seeing doctors and especially fellow nurses fail to meet patients where they are with common, direct language when educating them. I think *The Rules of the Game* is a great film? Or maybe I'm afraid to disagree. Or maybe I haven't learned enough film history yet to appreciate it. Or maybe it just needs to "percolate."

So I can't recommend this film to someone as an enjoyable entertainment, or especially not as something that will help clarify the wonderful contributions of French cinema. I'd absolutely tell someone studying French film to watch this, or fans of Renoir, or pre-WWII European history buffs. I'm sure I'll come back to this later, myself, especially after writing this essay, which always gives me a chance to process something I've watched. But right now, I'm still wrestling.

Salesman

US, 1969. Directed by David Maysles, Albert Maysles, and Charlotte Zwerin. 91 minutes, black and white.

It's *very* rare for me to buy a movie I haven't seen at least once. But when I saw that the same team that gave us the Rolling Stones documentary *Gimme Shelter* made a film about door-to-door Bible salesmen, I couldn't hit the "Add to Cart" button fast enough. What I got in *Salesman* was a documentary that far surpassed what I thought would be Willy Loman peddling scripture on the road ("Pontius Pilate was *liked*, but he wasn't *well-liked*"). This film is much closer to Eugene O'Neill's *The Iceman Cometh* with a healthy dose of David Mamet's *Glengarry Glen Ross*.

The Maysles brothers[56] never set out to make a "religious"

---

[56] David and Albert Maysles work as a team in this film with Charlotte Zwerin, and the three share the "Director" credit. But the role of "director" gets fuzzy in the documentary genre, and I found out that the brothers did the pre-production and production work - they came up with the idea for the film, found their subjects, and recorded the 100 hours of film themselves, with one operating the camera, the other on sound. But then

film, or even necessarily follow Bible salesmen. They were much more interested in the idea of traveling salespeople in general, men and women "out on their own hook" as they liked to call it. The post-WWII years were the heyday for door-to-door sales, but that era was already ending in the 1960s (the actual filming took place in 1966-67), and they wanted to get a look at shoe-leather capitalism in action. Already, states like New York were passing laws restricting door-to-door sales, and manufacturers were turning to other avenues (like television) to sell their products. It just happened that the Mid-American Bible Company still had people on the road the Maysles could shadow.

The film opens with a quick introduction to our team, four Irish Catholic men banging on doors in the Boston suburbs, their cars and their shoes trying to negotiate snow-covered roads and sidewalks. Each one has a nickname:

---

they more or less turned the editing work over to Charlotte Zwerin, and in documentary, that's where all the heavy lifting is done - with no script, it's the editor's job to piece through the footage and find the story. Zwerin tells us that while the brothers checked in with her and had final approval, they trusted her with their material (which took two years to edit) while they moved onto other projects. All this to say that when I'm talking about the pre-production and shooting, I'll use "The Maysles brothers" as shorthand, but when I talk about the editing, I'll use Zwerin's name. Seems less cumbersome than always mentioning all three, and I think more accurately puts credit where it's due. Especially to Zwerin. Also, I use the term "salesman" when specifically referring to one of our quartet of men - their gender doesn't seem incidental - but I use a gender-neutral term when referring to salespeople outside these four.

there's James "The Rabbit" Baker, Paul "The Badger" Brennan, Raymond "The Bull" Martos, and Charles "The Gipper" McDevitt (later we'll meet their sales manager, Kennie Turner - apparently you retire your moniker when you get off the road). But it's Paul's story we mostly follow, and I'll leave you to make your own comparisons to the New Testament "salesman." Their targets are working-class Catholics, and Kennie has worked out a deal with the local diocese, giving each salesman a handful of leads on index cards; apparently at some point the parishioners filled out a card expressing some level of "interest" in a family Bible. The men travel together and share motel rooms, but for the most part they're out there on their own. Later in the film, they travel south to Opa-locka, Florida, a bizarre suburb of Miami with an Arabian theme, but nary an Arabian in sight; streets bear the names Ali Baba Street, Harem Avenue, Sharazad Boulevard - even a real live "Sesame Street" - and the city hall is architecturally designed to resemble a mosque. But it's Catholic Bibles our heroes are peddling, and it's low-income Catholics they've got in their sights.

The film carries no narration. In a television interview included on the disc, the Maysles bristle at both the terms "documentary" and "cinéma vérité;" both, they feel, are too overt in leading the viewer to where the filmmaker wants to take them. The Maysles insist that their style of filmmaking, which they call "direct cinema," gives the viewer more power to assess the footage on their own, though they do admit that Zwerin guides the audience in deciding where and how to trim 100 hours of footage to 91 minutes. They also acknowledge quickly that the mere presence of a camera changes the dynamics of a sales pitch, but their insistence on a two-person crew minimizes the interference as much as possible. (It also explains why they filmed in black and white; color film requires more lights, more equipment, more intrusion.) The Maysles, after explaining who they are and that they're making a film, simply edge against a wall with the camera and sound equipment. Still, it's amazing how quickly people seem to forget the camera is there; we see women in housecoats and curlers and men in undershirts. Or perhaps, as Albert Maysely suggests, people enjoy the attention. They like the idea that for as long as the camera is rolling, what they say and do is important.

We quickly work out that our salesmen could just as easily be selling encyclopedias or aluminum siding; the sales tactics are just the same. Anyone who has spent any time in sales[57] will recognize the tactics. Potential buyers are asked questions like, "Which payment plan would work out best for you?" or "Can you see the value this brings to a home?" or "It comes in red or white; which color would you pick for your home?" There are no questions that anticipate a "no" answer, and later will remind the target, "You told me how much you liked the white one, and that you want the Catholic Honor payment plan," as if this had already been decided. These aren't cheap Bibles, either. They're designed to be family heirlooms, massive, gilt-edged, and loaded with

---

[57] When I was 19 I spent six months cold-calling people, selling Time-Life books over the phone. It was brutal.

full color artwork. And if the target doesn't want a Bible (or if they do and the salesman feels like he's got a live one on the hook), there's also Catholic Encyclopedias. The value is spoken of as long-lasting value, of moral value, of this being for any children or grandchildren in the home. Time and time again, the first words out of the salesman's mouth after the door is opened is, "I'm from The Church." Difficult for a practicing Catholic to slam the door on that.

The most obvious subtext of the film isn't really religion, though, it's how American capitalism preys on the working poor. None of the people these men visit appear affluent; most seem to be living paycheck to paycheck. And these Bibles aren't cheap; at $49.95 a pop - especially in 1960s dollars - this isn't money these families have lying around. "Can you afford a dollar a day?" our salesmen ask, but the answer clearly seems to be that a spare dollar would be better spent elsewhere. The people who could easily afford these Bibles wouldn't stand for having traveling salespeople invading their neighborhoods. And who are these men interacting with? Who's home during the day? Housewives. David Maysley said that when they screened *Salesman* at a high school, a female student told him this was a film about women, and he said that he discovered she was right. It's not just the religious guilt being laid on these women, as well as the pressure to "make a decision for your family;" there's the pressure to go along with what the nice man is saying, to make him happy, certainly not to stand up to him. All the while considering how to explain to the husband that night that she spent $50 while he was at work. On a Bible.

But as Zwerin weaves together the footage the Maysles shot, another victim emerges - the salesman himself. Capitalism isn't just preying on the customers, but on the employees. These men are all working on commission - if they don't sell, they can't make a living - and the "living" they're making on the road is barely above a subsistence level. There's a scene at a sales meeting at the beginning that's especially eye-opening. Kennie opens by telling his sales team that he's already made cuts in the sales force; not necessarily because of lack of sales, but because of "negativity" in certain individuals. From this they go around the room, each man publicly stating his goal of how much money he wants to make that year. Then it's hammered into each of these men what is hammered into *all* salespeople: The product is great. If you can't sell the product, there's something wrong with *you*, not with what you're selling. It's never that the customer can't afford it, it's that *you* were unable to get your sales pitch across. The Mid-American Bible Company - like all of corporate America - is preying on its sales force by setting them up for failure and then blaming the employee when the inevitable happens.

But it's Zwerin's decision to focus on Paul that makes this the most clear. Paul is in a slump, and his self-esteem is taking even more of a hit than his paycheck. Every time he fails to make a sale, you can almost see the added weight to his shoulders. And it's a lonely life on the road, even traveling with his team. As the men gather at night to play cards, or watch a boxing match on a motel TV, all the talk is about the job, and how they did that day. There seems to be no personal talk at all, and as the men wait for their turns to call home on the motel phone, the others do their best to turn their backs, ignoring the conversations. What's worse is that Paul's teammates are beginning to edge away from him as if a slump were contagious; Kennie told them as much at their meeting when he warned them away from guys who are "negative." They aren't heartless, they do join him on a visit or two for support. But mostly, Paul's colleagues don't want to hear about it, as if facing failure too directly might bring it on them.

All this comes together in a disturbing and heartbreaking scene that Zwerin wisely saves after we've seen both sides. One of the salesmen (I think it was Raymond) has been unable to make a sale, and asks Paul if he will go back to the home that afternoon to try again. When a woman answers the door, Paul introduces himself as the "district manager" and explains that Raymond had already ordered a Bible for this home by mistake (he hadn't). Paul can cancel the order, but the company will force him to discipline Raymond and fine him. Can she help the salesman out by letting the sale go through?

It's astonishing. The woman is in agony, hating to be the "cause" of another human being's punishment, but dreading her husband's response to her purchase (and Paul needs an answer right now). She's in torment. What's more astonishing is that Paul is basically committing fraud in view of the Maysles' camera. Has he forgotten that he's being filmed? Or is he so desperate, and has he been doing this for so long, that he no longer recognizes the ethical breach he's committing, and the emotional pain he's inflicting on a woman who likely can't afford $50 in the first place? The scene doesn't let Paul off the hook, nor should it. But coming as it does at the end of the film, we begin to understand how this happens to a man. How the rot he's had to absorb bit by bit becomes unrecognizable to him.

There are some humorous moments in the film. There's James, trying to make a sale to a Latina woman in Florida, but because of his thick working-class Boston accent, and the fact that he's referring to a Bible as an "order" (which comes out "au-dah"), the poor woman has no idea what he's talking about, and James' solution is just to keep saying "au-dah" louder and slower - there's no language barrier, anyone outside of eastern Massachusetts would have trouble following him. But *Salesman* ends up as a tragedy. Though we never see the impact a successful Bible sale really has on the families, we see the anguish of working-class Catholics feeling like they have to say "no" to their diocese, even their faith. And we see the terrible way in which these companies grind down the people they send out to represent them. In the end it's a heartbreaking film. And a crucial one.

☽ ☽ ☽

One last thing. The extras on this Criterion disc are up to the usual standards. But I found on this one my favorite supplemental feature so far. It's a full episode of the IFC *Documentary Now!* mockumentary series, "Globesman" in which Bill Hader and Fred Armisen parody *Salesman* in their portrayal of door-to-door globe salesmen. It's a gem. It's wonderful.

Seven Samurai

Japan, 1954. Directed by Akira Kurosawa. 207 minutes, black and white.

Well, we've finally come to it. The Granddaddy of Japanese cinema, if not the Granddaddy of World cinema. Certainly the film that Akira Kurosawa and Toshiro Mifune will always be known for. *Seven Samurai* was my introduction to Japan's master of filmmaking, as well as one of the first foreign-language films I remember seeing.[58] To say it's a daunting film for an amateur film writer to tackle is an understatement. So, after a general introduction to the film, I'm going to focus on two manageable pieces of it: Weather as a character in Akira Kurosawa films. And a look at Kurosawa's "other" great actor in his stable, Takashi Shimura.

You've seen *Seven Samurai* before, even if you haven't,

---

[58] My first foreign language film? Technically, it was probably either a *Godzilla* movie or a Shaw Brothers Hong Kong martial arts flick, dubbed and edited near to death for American syndicated television. The first foreign-language film I remember seeing in a theater was probably *King of Hearts* in the Irvine Auditorium on the University of Pennsylvania campus in 1980.

because it's been remade and alluded to hundreds of times. Most famously, it was remade in 1960 by John Sturges (and again in 2016 by Antoine Fuqua) as *The Magnificent Seven*. It was remade in 1998 by Pixar as *A Bug's Life*. Ever seen a recruiting scene in a film, where a commando/master criminal/super spy/government agent assembles a crack team for an impossible mission? That was first done in *Seven Samurai*. That shot where an army appears cresting the top of a hill? First seen in *Seven Samurai*. So much that may seem stale to us now was fresh when audiences saw the film in 1954.

Seven Samurai is an epic by any standard, but particularly by the standards of Japanese cinema at the time. It took a year and a half to film, at a time when most Japanese films were completed in two months or less; for actors, this meant that instead of appearing in three or four films in a year, there would be just this one. The average budget (in US dollars) for a Japanese film was $70,000; *Seven Samurai* ran to half a million. Filming was halted several times while the studio raised more money; Kurosawa didn't sweat it, knowing by this time that his reputation would see him through, and that the studio would be hesitant to pull the plug after investing so much money. The film indeed returned a handsome profit, but studio executives remembered how much Kurosawa's exacting demands as a filmmaker cost them. Later in Kurosawa's career, when productions didn't earn back the studio's investment, that reputation cost him dearly.

Seven Samurai is set in 16th-century Japan, which was kind of a hot mess at the time. The Emperor held only a tenuous control over sections of Japan; most of the rural countryside was fought over by regional warlords, and for common citizens security, as well as social services, were breaking down. The samurai (warrior) class were beginning to rise, but the individual samurai's status was tied to his employment to a lord, and when a lord fell, his warriors were unemployed and wandered the countryside, looking for work.

Teams of bandits seized on the chaos, and *Seven Samurai* opens with the hoofbeats of an army of 40-some marauders approaching a small farming village on horseback. They discuss raiding the village for food, but it's a village they've raided many times before. Better to wait until after the crops have been harvested, so the farmers will have something to give up. The bandits ride off, but their discussion is overheard by a farmer in hiding, and he runs back to the village to report.

This is calamitous news to the villagers, as they're barely able to scratch out a subsistence for themselves. What can they do? None of them know how to fight and they have nowhere to run. The local magistrate can do nothing except possibly after the fact. And they can't spare the food (or the men the bandits will kill or the women they will abduct or rape). They consult Grandad (Kokuten Kōdō), the village elder. He remembers a time when he was a young boy when he was forced to flee his village, ransacked as many others in the area by bandits. He remembered one village that was untouched, a village that had made the unheard-of decision to hire samurai for protection. But the village has nothing they can pay samurai, except handfuls of rice for a few meals.

Grandad's advice? "Find hungry samurai!"

A few head to the closest town to begin their search. It doesn't go well; most of the samurai they approach are offended by their offer. But they run across a curious sight: a crowd has gathered as a samurai cuts off his topknot and shaves his head - an astonishing gesture of self-abasement as a samurai's topknot announces his stature to the world. The samurai, Kambei Shimada (Takashi Shimura), has asked for a priest's robe and two rice balls. We learn that an outlaw is holding a child hostage in a barn, threatening the child's life. Kambei, posing as a priest (hence the haircut) offers the rice balls to the thief. Taking advantage of the distraction, Kambei rushes into the barn and slays the thief, rescuing the child. Impressed not only with his prowess but his humility, the villagers approach Kambei with their offer. Kambei tells them they will need at least seven samurai to give the mission (one that offers a samurai no wealth and no fame, while facing certain death) any chance at success. Kambei reluctantly agrees. He has also attracted the attention of a young man, Katsushiro (Isao Kimura), a youth from a wealthy family eager to learn the ways of the samurai. With Katsushiro, Kambei begins to recruit.

They find five others willing to join them, each for his own reasons. Their first recruit is Gorobê (Yoshio Inaba), a good-natured warrior who agrees because, as he tells Kambei, "Your character fascinates me." One is a master swordsman, Kyûzô (Seiji Miyaguchi), who at first refuses, but later joins them as an opportunity to hone his craft in battle. Another is Shichirôji (Daisuke Katō), Kambei's old right-hand man, who is loyal to his former comrade. Gorobê happens across Heihachi (Minoru Chiaki), a samurai chopping firewood in a man's yard in exchange for a meal; Heihachi, in addition to being humble and affable, applies samurai discipline even to this household chore.

Our last samurai (Kambei reluctantly agrees to include Katsushiro even though he feels he is not yet ready) is "Kikuchiyo" (Toshiro Mifune). He is young, wild, untrained, and carries an enormous chip on his shoulder. The other samurai can immediately see that he is no kind of samurai, which is confirmed when he presents a scroll to Kambei that "proves" his lineage from a samurai family. Kambei laughs when he reads the scroll; illiterate himself, the upstart "samurai" is unaware that the "Kikuchiyo" in the scroll is only thirteen years old. The team rejects him, but undeterred, "Kikuchiyo" follows them to the village anyway. He is to be the seventh "samurai," and the others bestow on him his stolen name when he tells them he has forgotten his true name.

I won't waste any more words on the plot of the film, as you surely have already guessed it: a training sequence, a romance, the climactic battle, in which a heavy human price is paid for the ultimate victory. But for Kurosawa's Japanese audiences, this was something new and daring. Period films like this were generally told with the reverence we might see in a 1950s Hollywood Biblical epic, with formal language and acting. Kurosawa made both farmers and samurai real, relatable people, speaking the kind of language 1950s Japanese audiences were familiar with, including the earthy humor appropriate to both farmers and soldiers. Kurosawa also shot and edited the film as an action picture - while *Seven Samurai* is three and a half hours long, there's not an ounce of fat in the film, no shot or scene that doesn't move the film along. Kurosawa counted himself a student of the great director of American westerns, John Ford, as reflected in Kurosawa's sweeping camera during battle scenes, never content to just passively record action.

Lest you think *Seven Samurai* is "merely" an action picture, Kurosawa makes the excitement of the film integral in telling what turns out to be a morally nuanced story. It turns out that the character of the feral, unschooled, untrained Kikuchiyo is our bridge between the worlds of the farmer and of the samurai. Kambei is the first to figure out that the chip on Kikuchiyo's shoulder was placed there by Kikuchiyo's own father, who was a farmer just like the villagers the samurai are defending. Kikuchiyo understands the farmers better than any of the samurai; when the villagers hide at the first appearance of their protectors, it is Kikuchiyo alone who knows why they're hiding and how to bring them out. But Kikuchiyo also despises them in a way the samurai do not; he holds their meekness in contempt, hates them for choosing servility over standing up for themselves.

When, during training, one of the farmers produces a spear, Kikuchiyo knows where it came from; it was taken from a dead samurai on the run, possibly ambushed by the villagers themselves. Kikuchiyo tells the farmers to bring out more weapons and armor they've collected, and they do. When

Kikuchiyo proudly shows off the haul to the samurai, they are appalled. Shichirôji furiously castigates both Kikuchiyo and the villagers for this obscene display; only Kambei keeps the samurai from abandoning the village when he quietly insists, "only those who have been hunted can understand." That's when Kikuchiyo cracks. Furiously, he denounces the farmers for being cowardly, sneaky, and untrustworthy. "But who made them that way?!" Kikuchiyo cries. It is the samurai, who have preyed on the poor, taken food from them, killed them as collateral damage, and taken their women. There are no purely noble people on either side; both samurai and farmers are both victims and instigators.

Nowhere is this more clearly shown than when a bandit, acting as a scout, has been captured and brought into the village for questioning. The samurai are desperately trying to hold the farmers at bay, who are eager for blood. Kambei angrily insists that this is a prisoner of war, and that he must be treated humanely. This is the code of the warrior, the samurai, and we understand that Kambei is standing for honor. But the farmers don't have the luxury of pretending warfare has civilizing rules and ethics. They don't get to fight on their own terms; for them, warfare means the violent termination of their lives and homes by forces they do not control. They don't seek out conflict, as the samurai do. For them, there is only the rare justice of finally being in a position to punish an oppressor. When an old woman slowly makes her way to the captured bandit with a scythe, Grandad calls on someone among the farmers to help her take her revenge for the family members she has lost to violence. It is a lesson for us and for the samurai that our attitudes toward warfare depend greatly on how it affects us.

๑ ๑ ๑

Now let's talk about the weather, certainly in *Seven Samurai*, but also in Kurosawa films in general. There's a lot of rain and a lot of wind in the film, and none of this is by accident. Whenever you see heavy winds in a Kurosawa film, you can be sure wind machines were brought to the set, and rainfall was often the result of fire hoses. Kurosawa used whatever he could to punch up a scene visually (when I wrote about *Red Beard*, I talked about his use of long lenses and framing), and whenever something especially dramatic or significant occurs, Kurosawa will enlist meteorological assistance. Like Shakespeare, Kurosawa wanted The Heavens to annotate the major events of human life. And with Kurosawa, it's go big or go home. When Kambei kills the thief in the beginning of the film, a whirlwind of dirt and dust whip up the intensity of what we've just witnessed. If there's conflict outdoors in a Kurosawa film, expect to see wind, expect to see characters face physical exterior forces, not just psychological interior ones. Like all great filmmakers, anything Kurosawa can do visually to add to the emotions underlying a shot, he'll do.

Similarly, rain adds not just dynamism to a scene, but lets us know that all is not right in the world. In *Rashomon*, as the characters "narrating" the film gather in an abandoned and decrepit city gate, it is to seek refuge from a torrential rainstorm; only at the end, when the story is told, and a baby is rescued, does the sun come out. So it is with *Seven Samurai*, the final day of the 3-day battle is fought in a deluge. This is no Pacific Northwest drizzle, either; it's a "Keanu Reeves in a *Matrix* movie[59]" monsoon. The rainstorm in this case, adds not just visual motion to the scenes, but plays with the expectations of Japanese audiences. Where they may have been anticipating a form-forward demonstration of martial arts prowess, instead they get a messy and disorganized battle in the mud. We've left the glamor of the noble samurai far behind; we're now witnessing both warriors and villagers in a messy fight for their lives. It's no longer about who has the high moral ground, or who is the more accomplished martial artist. The battle is going to go to who is willing to endure more suffering to get what they want. And at the end, as the villagers plant new rice on a gloriously sunny day, what they've won is sweeter by far.

Always pay attention to the weather in a Kurosawa film. Think about how much extra it cost to bring wind machines or fire trucks to a rural location. Think about how miserable it made the cast and crew, and how many takes had to be redone because an actor got dirt in her eye, or needed to change costumes or dry hair between takes because the scene called them to go from dry to wet. Think about the cameras and recording equipment that had to be protected, and what

---

[59] My son told me once that Major League Baseball should hire Keanu Reeves as a sideline reporter, in character as John Wick during rain delays. Just to stand there without an umbrella and give one-word responses to broadcaster questions.

that may have cost in terms of equipment mobility. Think about visibility on the set of *Seven Samurai* during the final battle, when horses were running next to actors who were doing their own stunts because the Japanese film industry had no stunt performers at the time (especially whenever you see an actor pierced by an arrow; no CGI, no stunt crew, just a trusting actor with a block of wood under their costume and a professional archer shooting at them). Kurosawa's weather was important enough to him to endure all of that.

∩ ∩ ∩

Lastly, it's important to talk about the actor who played Kambei, Takashi Shimura. He tends to be overlooked in this film by the virtuoso performance given by Toshiro Mifune, but I already wrote about Mifune when I wrote about Kurosawa's first film with him, *Drunken Angel*. And since this is the last Kurosawa film I'll write about in this book, it's important to understand Shimura's place in the Kurosawa repertoire.

In almost each of the 21 Kurosawa films in which Takashi Shimura appears (more than any other actor, even Mifune), he represents the calm moral center of Kurosawa's world. If he at times goes unnoticed next to Mifune's fireworks in *Seven Samurai*, it's only because of Shimura's professionalism and generosity as an actor. Watch his Kambei carefully as he moves through this film. There's a gesture he brings that's as simple as it is eloquent. After Kambei cuts his topknot and has his head shaved so that he can disguise himself as a monk, Shimura rubs a hand over his head. It's natural, it's a different feel for a man who has never been bald a day in his life. But Shimura repeats the gesture periodically through the film, even as his stubble begins to grow back in (which must have been a nightmare for continuity). If Kambei is deep in thought, weighing a decision, he'll absentmindedly pass a hand over his scalp. But from the actor, there's nothing absentminded about it at all; it's a gesture that he brings to his character to accentuate an important moment. It's subtle; you may not see it on first viewing if you're not looking for it. But it makes me smile every time.

Takashi Shimura was 49 the year *Seven Samurai* was released. He was born in 1905, and ironically, was actually descended from a family of samurai; in 1868 his grandfather took part in the Battle of Toba-Fushimi during the Japanese Revolution. As a student, I'm pleased to report that Shimura was a fellow English major; in his case, studying (and later teaching) both the English language and English literature (one suspects the conversations he must have had on set with Kurosawa over this shared passion may have added to his job security). His academic experiences eventually led him to try a career in theater, which led to his debut in films in 1934. In 1943, already an established film actor, Shimura appeared in Kurasawa's debut film, *Sanshiro Sugata*.

He was an actor of enormous range; quite possibly more than even Mifune, but whether he was playing a samurai, a peasant, or a police detective, Shimura always portrayed a character at or near the heart of the film. If you wanted to find a character in a Kurosawa film who represented the director's point of view, your best bet would be to look at who Shimura was portraying. Shimura's characters always ran deeper than what was in the script. Yet though he had already established himself as a screen actor before working with Kurosawa, no one else cast him in such prominent roles. The only role this great actor is remembered for, apart from his work with Kurosawa? The lead scientist in *Godzilla*.

෧ ෧ ෧

Sadly, the well-loved DVD edition I have of this film is at least twenty years old, and the supplemental pickings are pretty slim; just a chat track by Japanese film scholar Michael Jeck (informative, if a little fussy in delivery) and a brief essay by film critic David Ehrenstein. Not to worry, though, Criterion has since put together a Blu-Ray edition loaded up with additional commentary and several documentary pieces. It may be time for me to get an upgrade.

The Seventh Seal

Sweden, 1957. Directed by Ingmar Bergman. 96 minutes, black and white.

Before I get into *The Seventh Seal*, the work most consider to be Ingmar Bergman's masterpiece, I need to back up a little. Chances are, if you're my age or older (like Obama, I'm a member of Generation Jones), you have an *idea* of what this film is, but might never have seen it. And if you're younger than me, you might not even be aware of the director, much less the film, which is absolutely fair - you've had enough on your plate with your own generation of superlative filmmakers. My point is, chances are you haven't actually seen this film. And if you haven't, I think you'd be surprised at what you find. For a film that so famously features Death as a character, it's also a celebration of life, an appreciation of the beautiful moments we're given in our brief earthly lives.

The Seventh Seal opens with a knight, Antonius Block (Max von Sydow), having just returned to the shores of Sweden with his squire, Jöns (Gunnar Björnstrand). It is the 14th century, and these men have returned, disillusioned, from the Crusades, where they have been fighting on behalf of Christian Europe to take the Holy Land back from Muslims. They are weary, and the home to which they have returned after ten long years is ravaged by plague, the Black Death sweeping across Europe (by the year 1349, one third of the Swedish population had died of plague). Block has seen little in the Crusades to convince him that God - if he exists - listens to or cares for humanity, and on his return sees the Church using fear of the plague to whip up hysteria and obedience. Block wants answers, and he's determined to find them.

But a figure is waiting for Block on the shore, a figure Block recognizes as having been by his side while he was fighting. It is Death (Bengt Ekerot), who has finally come for Block. The knight, looking for time, challenges Death to a game of chess; if Block wins, he gets more time. Death is agreeable, and the two begin a game they will come back to throughout the course of their journey to Block's home.

Also traveling through the summer countryside are a troupe of players: an actor/director, Skat (Eric Strandmark), and performers Mia (Bibi Andersson) and Jof (Nils Poppe) with their year-old baby (it would have been clear to Swedish audiences that Mia and Jof are diminutive forms of Mary and Joseph). The performers are riding a horse-drawn wagon from town to town to eke out a living, but crowds are often indifferent, and actors held in low esteem; it doesn't help that Skat makes off with the local blacksmith's wife at the first stop where we see the actors perform. Even as Mia and Jof try to entertain the crowd, their merry songs and dances are interrupted by a procession of monks and flagellants[60] from the local church, nearly as ghastly and frightening as the Black Death itself. The procession stops in front of their stage, and a monk seems to take pleasure in castigating the crowd, preaching that their sins have brought the plague on Europe.

Block and Jöns arrive at this town shortly before the procession. The squire, the earthier of the two, visits a small chapel in which an artist is painting a mural with depictions of the plague inside a larger religious motif (Bergman lifted scenes from this film directly from centuries-old religious murals like this, including Death playing chess). Jöns enjoins the artist in a cynical conversation in which he chides the workman for adding to the religious hysteria that created the Crusades. Block heads straight to the main church, and finds inside a cloaked figure in a confessional. Block seeks answers for life's suffering, for answers to what lies beyond this life, and tells his confessor of his chess match with Death and how he hopes to defeat him. But it is Death himself who has been listening behind the screen, and tells the knight he is eager to resume their game.

Meanwhile Jof visits a tavern for a meal and a drink, but a seminarist (a sort of apprentice priest), now turned thief, Raval (Bertil Anderberg), has witnessed Jof's fellow actor run off with the blacksmith's wife, and turns the blacksmith on

---

[60] Ironically, it was the flagellants themselves, traveling from village to village, that were thought partially responsible for spreading plague.

him. Raval leads the tavern clients in mocking, humiliating, and torturing Jof, until Jöns steps inside. Knowing Raval's true nature, Jöns intercedes and punishes Raval, giving Jof the opportunity to escape.

Block himself has also come across the actors, smiling as he sees Mia playing with her baby, Mikael. He talks with her, and they are soon joined by Jof, still scared and smarting from his tavern encounter. But the sight of his wife and son eases his soul, and he invites Block to join them in a meal of the only food they can offer; fresh milk and strawberries. Block joins them, and Jöns as well, who has rescued a seemingly mute girl from Raval.

Block warns the family against traveling south, as he has heard that the plague is much worse in that region. Instead, he invites them to his castle where he can offer shelter for the entire family, an offer they're inclined to accept. But as the knight walks away, Death appears to remind him that their chess match must continue. Block sits with him, and proves himself resilient in reworking the strategy he has given up to his opponent. Death allows Block to journey on before they finish their game, and as they do, they pass through a village where a girl is to be burned at the stake for witchcraft, having first been tortured by the Church in place of a trial. Block stops to talk with the girl; we don't really believe the knight thinks she's guilty, but he's so desperate for answers, he'll speak with her on the chance she has really met with The Devil. The girl tells him all he needs to do is look in her eyes to see The Devil; all the priests and monks seem to see him there, so it must be true. But when his squire asks him what he sees, the knight responds, "Only terror."

As the group is traveling through the woods, Death appears again to finish the game. No one else in the group can see the figure of Death except Jof, who we have learned has visions, and it's then that Block realizes what his game can buy him - time for Jof and Mia and the baby to escape Death. They do, and when Block finally arrives home, and his wife prepares a meal for the knight and his friends, Death finally appears, visible to all, the silent girl Jöns rescued giving her only line of the film, "It is finished."

It sounds grim, doesn't it? There are scenes of great darkness in this film. But Bergman wisely alternates them with scenes of lightness, warmth, and hope, and most of these revolve around the little family of Mia, Jof, and Mikael. When Block sits with them, he seems to find peace, and we suspect that he has found something of life's meaning in the earthly joy the family is wrapped in. There is also something both solemn and reviving in the meal the family shares with their guest, especially in the way the bowl of milk is passed around; there is something paschal about their celebration on a day in the brief Swedish summer. It was always interesting to me to note in this scene that the elements of their eucharist - milk and strawberries - are entirely natural, to be found as gifts of nature. The bread and wine of Christian communion require technology, man's intervention.

But for every scene of suffering and doubt, there is a scene of low humor that not only balances the film thematically, but gives us in the audience a respite. It seems to be no accident that Bergman - whose career in the theater began before his film work and continued after - enjoys using his troupe of actors as both storytellers and the butt of jokes. But they're also a necessary diversion, even if the villagers don't see it, from the Church that is trying to instill obedience in the populace through fear.

What gave this film such an impact when it was released, and why Bergman, of all the gifted Swedish filmmakers, came to be the face of Scandinavian directors, was that it was the first time a director had worked through his own personal doubts and fears through his work. Bergman was reportedly surprised at the international reaction to his "little film," and I don't think that's false modesty. I think Bergman was honestly trying to make a film just for himself in which he could explore these questions, and instead found an audience that was hungry for discussion as well. Bergman knew that the struggle is more real, more human than the answers, and I think he hadn't counted on the fact that *his* struggle would fascinate people more than someone else's preaching. In the end, our knight receives no answers, not even from Death, who seems to know as little as we. But his refusal to stop asking questions is what is heroic about him. There's a wonderful scene where the knight, alone, says to himself, "I, Antonius Block, am playing chess with Death," and then smiles. It's a triumph already that he, one man, has caused the briefest ripple in the Eternal Plan, that he has earned himself at least a chance to ask his questions.

And *The Seventh Seal* is a film rich in imagery, and ripe for people to pick apart, searching for greater meaning. I think Bergman setting his story in the time of the Crusades and the Black Death, filming during a period when Europe was worried about the growing nuclear threat, as well as the threat of authoritarianism, gave audiences plenty of parallels to draw between their lives and the past. But Bergman wisely used a light hand with these metaphors, resulting in a film that speaks across the years. *The Seventh Seal* is a dark film, but it's not just a dark film; it's loaded with Biblical references (the title comes from a passage in Revelations), and it revels in the low humor of a cuckolded husband and a vain traveling performer.

The film is grounded in its humanity. What else do we have in our brief lives? Bergman seems to be urging us to turn to each other for joy and comfort, as God has chosen to remain silent. Look past the gloom as you watch this. Better yet, look into the gloom to understand how we are already equipped to combat it.

Sid & Nancy

UK, 1986. Directed by Alex Cox. 113 minutes, color.

It's useful, in some cases, to consider not just the time period in which a film is set, but also the time in which it is made. *Sid & Nancy* was filmed about ten years after the events it depicts - the rise and breakup of the punk band The Sex Pistols, the volatile relationship of bassist Sid Vicious and Nancy Spungen, and Nancy's death by stabbing, of which Sid was accused. Ten years is enough time (barely) to recognize the punk scene for the movement it was, and the Reagan/Thatcher era of the 1980s gave the anarchistic youth movement plenty of relevance.

Punk rock - or something like it - was inevitable in the mid-1970's. Rock and roll, the defiant music of the previous generation, was entering its own middle age, beginning to be legitimized, sanitized, and worst of all, corporatized. It was a long way from being dead, but a new generation needed its own music. Add to that centuries-old dalliances with anarchy in the United Kingdom, and an economic boom that bypassed the middle classes of both the US and the UK, and you get music and a lifestyle that angrily rejected societal norms. Punk wasn't just saying conservatism wasn't working; it was rejecting entire political systems as hopeless. Punk wasn't about changing the system, it was about smashing it.

That's the setting for one of the most visceral love stories ever captured on film. *Sid & Nancy* posits proof that even the most fucked-up individuals on the planet have a soulmate. That's at the very heart of this film, and that's why I think it will endure.

Sid Vicious (Gary Oldman) is the bassist for The Sex Pistols, the punk band on its meteoric rise, fronted by lead singer, Johnny Rotten (Andrew Schofield). Sid isn't much of a bass player, but then musical ability is beside the point in a punk band; his value is in his stage presence, and the ebullient antagonism he brings even to the band's own fans. He meets Nancy Spungen (Chloe Webb) an American expat living as a sex worker in London. Nancy is stringent and abrasive (Webb described the voice she used in playing Nancy as "audible chainsaw soul pain" softened only by heroin); no one can stand her. Sid and Nancy are at each other ferociously, even as their souls are soldered together with equal parts love and heroin. They cannot live without each other. One wonders how they made it this far in life apart.

The first half of the film is largely set in London; on the eve of the band's trip to the US, their manager insists that Nancy will not be welcome. What follows is the band's disintegration as it attempts to conquer clubs and bars of the American South; the idea being to shake up the expected New York debut, and make the labels come find them. Or, one suspects, let the band's certain confrontation with Bible Belt audiences supply all the free press they could want. Might it have worked? Sure, except The Sex Pistols imploded on the tour, leaving Sid to first try fronting his own band, then hit the road as a solo act. Both end in disaster, but at least Nancy has flown back after Sid is hospitalized following a drug coma. In a scene that's as heartbreaking as it is hilarious, Sid - shirtless, scabbed, and skeletal - tries to pass muster at a family dinner at Nancy's grandparents, but there is no one to accept this pair other than the couple themselves.

The film is told in flashback, beginning and ending with the scene of Nancy's death bleeding out from a knife wound in the bathroom of Sid and Nancy's basement flat (the coroner's report stated the wound was only a quarter inch deep, possibly suggesting problems with coagulation may have led to Nancy's death). That's all we really know about her death. Sid was arrested, then released. He was awaiting trial when he himself died of a heroin overdose. Alex Cox, who directed and co-wrote the film, talked of continually running into people who knew the couple, some who were there that night. Most felt that Sid was unarousable that night and couldn't have stabbed Nancy. Some thought he did, others that the two had a suicide pact that Sid was either unwilling or unable to complete. Some think that Nancy may have surprised someone going through their stash, though if the police thought this, they never followed through after Sid's death. As the film portrays it, Nancy's death was accidental; they were arguing and she jumped on

Sid while he was holding a knife. Both were too drugged to notice her fatal wound, and collapsed in bed together.

The penultimate scene of the film is irresistible. Sid, having been released from custody, is eating a slice of pizza near a dump in Jersey City, NJ, a view of the Manhattan skyline across the river. As he leaves, a trio of little kids are dancing in front of a boom box, and beg Sid to dance with them. He looks around, and joins them, smiling. Were it not for one somewhat incongruous scene to go, we would leave Sid Vicious dancing to KC and the Sunshine Band's disco masterpiece, "Get Down Tonight."

There are a couple things that bring *Sid & Nancy* a notch or more above the usual musical biopic. One is Cox's decision to focus attention more on the couple than on the band itself. The relationship is so intense, so full of *need* that any band drama would pale in comparison. Another is the realistic depiction of heroin abuse. In his commentary track (along with Johnny Rotten portrayer Andrew Schofield), Cox said that he wanted to show not a descent into heroin abuse, but the fact that for a heroin addict, one day is exactly the same as the next. From the time of their addiction, we see Sid and Nancy living in ruin, surrounded by fast food containers they haven't even had the energy to throw away. This is the life of the heroin addict; it's all about getting the next fix. They are pale and bruised, they maintain a relationship only with their dealer (Xander Berkeley), because that is the only relationship that matters to them besides their own.

But along with Cox's talent and devotion to both punk rock and cult cinema - his debut as a writer/director came two years earlier with *Repo Man* - he fell into some extraordinary luck in working with talented people at the beginning of their careers. Cox said that his impetus to getting the film made was learning that another film studio was considering a Sid and Nancy biopic starring Rupert Murdoch and Madonna. Cox said he'd since seen that Murdoch has developed as an actor, but could not see him as Sid at the time, and the thought of pop queen Madonna playing Nancy drove him to get something out quick to prevent that sacrilege from ever happening. He said he was told to check out Gary Oldman, then on the London stage; impressed with his work, Cox cast him over another unknown actor.[61] While this wasn't Oldman's first film role, his ferocious performance launched his film career. This *was* the film debut for Chloe Webb, another actor a friend urged Cox to check out, and who matched Oldman note for note in intensity. Cox also caught legendary cinematographer Roger Deakins at the beginning of his career, and was amazed at what Deakin's camera and lighting added to every scene.

The disc has a ton of extras, lots of interviews and footage of the actual Sid and Nancy. But it also has *two* chat tracks (so, yes, three viewings of the film total for me). One I've already mentioned, a track recorded in 2001 by Cox and Schofield, which is entertaining and educational (Cox

---

[61] Daniel Day-Lewis. Seriously. Can you even imagine? Cox also briefly considered writing a script only loosely based on The Sex Pistols, and casting Sarah Bernhard as a female version of Sid Vicious. Read that again if you need to.

sounds like a genuinely warm and funny person, definitely someone I wouldn't mind chatting with over drinks). But the other commentary track, recorded in 1994, is exceptional. It features a round table of commentary: co writer Abbe Wood, actors Oldman and Webb, cultural historian Greil Marcus, filmmakers Julien Temple and Lech Kowalski (both of whom had worked on punk rock films of their own), and musician Eliot Kidd. While all on this track are respectful of Cox and his choices for the film, some are people who lived through the punk revolution, and are frank in pointing out what they would have done differently in the film. Cox himself admits to making changes from reality for the sake of marketing logistics; the film's Sid wears a T-shirt with a prominent Soviet hammer and sickle in place of the swastika the real Sid wore, and the fictional Sid scratches "NANCY" into his chest with a razor blade in place of the "I WANT A FIX" the actual musician carved to let dealers in the audience know he needed drugs. But the commentators also point out the many places where the film got reality wrong, from the depiction of Johnny Rotten to the important details left out. It's a brave and honest decision to give voice to dissent, even if the dissenters acknowledge things the film got right. If you have access to a copy of the Criterion disc, I recommend it.

I lived through the punk revolution, but I was way too timid (and suburban) to understand it. *Sid & Nancy* helps me appreciate what else was going on at the time. It's worth being aware of, especially if you're not a punk music fan.

Solaris

USSR, 1972. Directed by Andrei Tarkovsky. 166 minutes, color with black and white sequences.

In order to write about Soviet filmmaker Andrei Tarkovsky, and especially to write about *Solaris*, it helps if you know a little bit about Sergei Eisenstein, one of the founding directors of Soviet cinema. And since Criterion doesn't currently carry any Eisenstein films in their collection, we'll talk a little bit about him here.

Sergei Eisenstein (1898-1948) is second only to D.W. Griffith in his influence on world cinema. Eisenstein was a pioneer in film montage - editing together dozens of quick one- or two-second images to describe the action of a scene from multiple viewpoints, as well as to weave symbolic images into the tapestry of a scene. Think of it as the cinematic equivalent of cubism, in which Eisenstein contemporaries Pablo Picasso and Georges Braque combined different three-dimensional views into a single two-dimensional image. Eisenstein dissected and reassembled perspectives of multiple points of view into a scene that no one "narrator" could have viewed. It was a revolutionary technique that commanded the attention of filmmakers all over the world, especially as demonstrated in his 1925 masterpiece, *Battleship Potemkin.*

Battleship Potemkin put both Eisenstein and Soviet cinema on the map, and for a while, Eisenstein was held up as a hero of the Soviet state, and granted extraordinary freedom, even to film in the West. But as Stalin took power, too much attention could be a dangerous thing; the USSR's new dictator didn't generously share the spotlight with anyone. Stalin began to muse that Eisenstein was putting his own fame ahead of the State, and his star began to fade in official circles. The very freedom that Eisenstein was granted to film in Hollywood and Mexico, encouraged by the Soviet government as a way of proving Russian cinema was second to none, now put Eisenstein's loyalties into question. Add to that the fact that in Soviet Russia (as in communist China), any kind of artistic movement carried with it ideological implications, which were also subject to which way the political winds were blowing. The result was that for the rest of his career, Eisenstein would balance the occasional triumph (*Alexander Nevsky* in 1938, which won him both the Order of Lenin and the Stalin Prize) with the threat of banishment from filmmaking, even imprisonment. Eisenstein's career might best be summed up by his planned *Ivan the Terrible* trilogy: *Part I*, released in 1944 was acclaimed, and again won him the Stalin Prize, while *Part II* was criticized by Soviet authorities and not released until 1958 (ten years after Eisenstein's death, and five years after Stalin's passing). *Part III* was never completed, and most of the film was confiscated and destroyed.

Andrei Tarkovsky (1932-1986), another brilliant star of Soviet cinema, shared some similarities with his iconic predecessor. Like Eisenstein, Tarkovsky made only a handful of films (seven in all, along with a few shorts), but even that was enough to bring him to international attention for the quality of his work. Tarkovsky, also filming under the Soviet system, had to contend with official scrutiny and shifting favor; in the case of *Solaris*, dealing with a bureaucracy that demanded frequent changes to the film (and oddly, a bureaucracy as puritanical when it came to sex as American censors under the Hays Code). Both Tarkovsky and Eisenstein died relatively young; Eisenstein of a heart attack, Tarkovsky of cancer.

But a major difference between the two filmmakers was Tarkovsky's rejection of Eisenstein's montage. Tarkovsky preferred long, slow takes of a scene - many critical scenes in *Solaris* are three or four minutes of a single camera following a character, or even held on a character in conversation. Tarkovsky wanted the audience to experience a scene in the same way that a central character would, and rejected the omnipresent and omniscient eye of Eisenstein's montage. And by showcasing this in the science fiction film *Solaris* - often considered to be the Soviet Union's "response" to Stanley Kubrick's 1968 *2001: A Space Odyssey* - Tarkovsky declares his independence from two world film masters.

Solaris is based on the 1961 best-seller by Polish writer Stanisław Lem, though Tarkovsky took major departures from the novel that Lem was never comfortable with. Tarkovsky gambled that a futuristic setting might more easily appease Soviet censors, and was careful not to identify any characters as Russian or foreign by surnames or national identification.

We begin on Earth, meeting Kris Kelvin (Donatas Banionis) about to go on a mission to the space station Solaris, which orbits a planet covered by a global ocean. Solaris is designed to house a crew of 85, but only three souls remain; Kelvin is to determine whether the space station can be salvaged or should be dismantled. But problems on Solaris aren't new; Kelvin watches a film of an interrogation of Berton (Vladislav Dvorzhetsky), an astronaut from twenty years before, in which Berton reports what seems to be hallucinations from a flyover of the planet's ocean. As Kelvin prepares for his journey from his country dacha, we note his uneasy relationship with his father, and the grieving silence from an unspeaking woman who might be his mother or might be a housekeeper.

Cut to Kelvin's arrival on Solaris. The space station, while operating, is in disrepair; the hallways are littered with trash, machinery appears to be broken and neglected. Kelvin is greeted by no one, and tracks down Snaut (Yuri Yarvet), who tells him that one of the three remaining occupants has taken his own life. That leaves only Sartorius (Anatoly Solonitsyn) alive on the station, a brusque and unpleasant scientist that seems to resent Kelvin's presence. But from almost the moment he arrives, Kelvin is aware that they are not the only three on the station - Kelvin glimpses other figures in the quarters of the other scientists, including a dwarf whom Sartorius prevents escaping from his own rooms. These figures the other scientists refuse to discuss or even acknowledge, telling Kelvin he has no idea what life is like on Solaris, and will need to learn for himself. Kelvin sees a young woman who leads him to a cold room where the body of the third scientist has been stored.

Kelvin retreats to his own quarters and, unsure of what's going on in Solaris, barricades himself inside before he goes to sleep. But he is wakened by a woman (Natalya Bondarchuk) whom he recognizes, though she herself is unsure of her identity. She pulls a framed photograph from Kelvin's bag; the photograph is of Kelvin's wife, Hari, who we later learn has died a suicide. The mysterious woman appears to be Hari; a quick check of the door reveals it is still barricaded from the inside. Unnerved, Kelvin has her get into a space suit, and takes her to an escape rocket, launching her into space. But she will return, as he is to learn from Snaut.

It turns out that the ocean covering the planet Solaris is orbiting is thought to be sentient; actually the brain itself of the planet. What it appears to have been doing is manifesting people from out of the minds of the Solaris occupants. But since the other scientists will not speak of their own "visitors" we are never sure if these are reflections of real people from their past, or even manifestations of nightmare figures. Sartorius, for example, has photographs in his room he tries to hide of presumably his children, and we wonder if the dwarf wasn't the planet's early attempt to create a child. Because Hari *does* appear again to Kelvin, and when that iteration kills herself, she regenerates again. But each time she appears, she remembers more, and is closer to the real wife that Kelvin lost. It's possible the planet is learning about humankind as occupants process grief. Or, it is the planet's way of torturing the scientists. No one knows, just that the oceans on the planet swirl and become active with new iterations of the figures. But we can see that Kelvin (who had left Hari before she killed herself) is dropping his cold exterior by degrees as the iterations of Hari become more human in emotions, even apparently capable of loving and being loved. Where the other scientists are becoming more withdrawn, Kelvin is apparently processing his grief, and becoming more human himself. And in the final scene, we suspect this is what the ocean planet may have been seeking all along....

Solaris is a frustrating film to watch, especially on first viewing. I won't lie. A lot of this is by design; Tarkovsky himself said that he wanted people to watch this film several times, so if you see it, be prepared to be baffled on your first pass. Tarkovsky plants clues to different characters who are only explained an hour or more into the film, and that relies on you first noticing and remembering them the first time, which isn't guaranteed. There's another young woman that appears in home movies from Earth and again on Solaris, and I only figured out that she - not the woman we met at the beginning - is Kelvin's emotionally distant mother upon a second viewing. There are odd images - a torn sleeve revealing a pinpoint scar on Hari's first visit - that only make sense later in the film. And a lot that *never* seems to make sense. Even the two Tarkovsky scholars on the chat track -

Vida Johnson and Graham Petrie, who co wrote a book about his films - couldn't explain why Tarkovsky would sometimes switch from color to black and white (except in one instance when they felt the contrast commented on the "reality" of the final version of Hari). It also doesn't help that the space station - wide and spacious - seems to defy our expectations of what astronauts would be able to bring with them from Earth. There's a dinner scene in the Solaris library in which art hangs on the walls, books abound, and a meal is served on formal dinnerware, wine included, by candlelight. I was sure this must be hallucinated, but, no, it's to be taken literally.

But a repeat viewing - if you're up to it - does raise more intriguing questions. Take that library I just mentioned, full of cultural treasures. Tarkovsky felt that cinema, as a "new" art, needed to ground itself in classics of Western art, and so in that scene, Greek sculptures in the background, Bach playing (as it does through most of the film), Snaut asks Kelvin to read a passage from a copy of *Don Quixote*. On second viewing, I noticed that many of these same props appeared in Kelvin's dacha back on Earth. Coincidence? Or is the water planet beginning to change Kelvin's recollections of his home?

Or is this more reflective of Tarkovsky's frustration with the emotional sterility of *2001*? He reportedly appreciated the epic scale and the spaceships of the Kubrick film, but was left cold by Kubrick's refusal to flesh out his human characters. *Solaris* is all about Kelvin's humanity, his growth, as well as Hari's. Bondarchuk was astonishingly only eighteen when she played Hari, a role she would go on to consider her finest. She said the key to playing her character was to base it on the Hans Christian Andersen tale, "The Little Mermaid," a creature who was not human, and felt she had no right to earn the love of an actual human being. It's a restrained and heartfelt performance.

So for a lot of you, *Solaris* won't be your selection off the dessert cart (though now I'm curious to check out the 2002 remake directed by Steven Soderbergh and starring George Clooney). Fair enough. But I can already tell there is going to be something in the background I'll pick up in my next viewing that I haven't seen yet. Which will probably also lead to another theory about what's going on with the planet. If that drives you nuts, fair warning. But sometimes, I like the questions more than the answers.

Swing Time

US, 1936. Directed by George Stevens. 103 minutes, black and white.

For someone who grew up disliking musicals as much as I did, I seem to have an awful lot of them on disc. Before we get to *Swing Time*, let's talk about how I warmed up to the genre.

My ex, Shannon, wasn't into movies nearly as much as me, but was happy to support my addiction. Many is the night when she would send me off to the movies alone, enjoying the peaceful house to quilt, craft, or read. I'd be happy seeing the movies I wanted to see, and when I got home she'd always ask about what I saw, and I'd sit with her and tell her the story of the movie while she worked. She rarely wanted to see something in a theater herself, though when she did, I'd make it a priority; I felt like I owed her. Likewise with watching films on disc.

Somehow, she'd acquired a DVD copy of *Dirty Dancing*, and was mortified on my behalf when I admitted I'd never seen it. Dutifully, I joined her on the couch while we popped it in, and I couldn't believe what I was watching. Halfway through the movie I said, "This is a kung fu flick!" and she laughed at me when I said it. But it was shot exactly like a Hong Kong kung fu movie. In those films, your actors are athletes with incredible skills, and the last thing you want to do is take the camera off a skilled martial artist when they're performing. So you film long takes allowing the audience to marvel at what these performers can do; quick shots rapidly edited together were left to American action films, where the actors, traditionally, lacked technique. Maybe you'd put the camera low so the audience was looking up at the performers, and this is exactly what was going on in *Dirty Dancing*. Dancing is, after all, athletic art. It never occurred to me that physical performers in one genre might be best shot in the same way as physical performers in another genre. That's when I realized; who even watches musicals for the plot, anyway? It's not like I was watching martial arts movies to see the same story I'd been told a hundred times before. I was watching for the performance.

Fred Astaire and Ginger Rogers were elite athletes at the top of their craft when they made *Swing Time*, their sixth of an eventual ten films they would make together. Part of the reason I wasn't looking closely at their dancing was because they always made their routines look so effortless, even spontaneous. But there was nothing either effortless or spontaneous about any of their dance routines; a lot of the grace you see on screen is a result of the muscle memory that comes from practicing a routine for six weeks before filming, working through every step. Both Astaire and Rogers were meticulous in their preparation for a film. They had to be.

Astaire frequently said, "Either the camera dances or I do," meaning that he believed the less camera movement in a dance, the better. An Astaire/Rogers dance number usually runs three or four minutes, and generally they are done in one long camera take, with no cuts away. That means when you're filming a scene, if there's a misstep at the end of a number, you're starting the whole dance all over again from the beginning. The final, complex and syncopated dance number at the end of *Swing Time* that had our performers dancing on two levels of an enormous set was finally completed after 47 takes in a ten-hour day. Ginger Rogers' feet were bleeding by the time they finished. And she *still* made it look effortless.

Ann Richards famously said that Ginger Rogers did everything Fred Astaire did, only backwards and in high heels. Yes and no. It's true that the heels were a challenge; in an interview included with the disc, Rogers said that almost all the surfaces she and Astaire danced on in their spectacular art deco sets were highly polished plastic, treacherously easy to slip on if your weight shifted minutely on landing a heel (only once in their ten films together was she able to dance on a wood floor). She also said that they both rehearsed wearing slacks, and adding a dress complicated the routine, especially if Astaire now had to move to give the skirt room to sway. And if the dress had beadwork? Suddenly, Rogers is twirling with 35-40 pounds of unbalanced weight threatening to take her off her feet. Rogers was also working harder as an actor than Astaire; one of the reasons she was such a good partner was that she fleshed out the delivery in their banter. Astaire was doing about a film and a half a year at the time, all of them musicals. Rogers, because she was being cast in dramas and comedies as well as musicals, was filming about 4.5 productions annually, which meant she was often shooting another film when Astaire was working out the dance moves. Rogers said that it wasn't a fight or disagreements that eventually broke up their partnership; she said she loved working with him. She just needed a break from all that work.

For Astaire's part, he was the choreographer for all their work. He'd work with Hermes Pan, the film's "dance director," who could critique and add ideas, but it was really all Astaire. He described his dancing as "outlaw style," usually a blend of tap, ballroom, and other styles. Astaire loved syncopation, and the dances he constructed were always not just technically difficult, but subtle and complicated. And they *always* advanced the story. There's a terrific scene at the beginning of *Swing Time*; in order to meet Rogers' character (a dance instructor), he signs up for a lesson, and has to klutz his way through her instruction. She tries teaching him a move - three hops on the left foot, three hops on the right, and Astaire has to pretend he can't stay on his feet. But those three left/right hops appear in every subsequent dance in the film, always commenting on the state of their relationship.

The plot of *Swing Time* barely distinguishes it from any other Astaire/Rogers musical. They're *all* the same, just like the plot of any of my beloved Shaw Brothers kung fu movies is indistinguishable from any other. Fred meets Ginger, and is smitten. Ginger finds Fred annoying. Fred woos Ginger and wins her over through his dance. Then they break up, almost always because of a misunderstanding. Then they make up for the triumphant final number. The only thing that makes *Swing Time* a little different is we have three breakups followed by three reconciliations instead of just the one. Honestly - and this is what frustrates me about the majority of movie musicals - the story could be told in ten minutes if the two characters would have a direct adult conversation with each other. But I suppose that would cut back on the dancing. There's a familiar side cast of characters; a rival for Ginger's attentions (Georges Metaxa), a wise-cracking jaded BFF for Ginger (the terrific Helen Broderick - real-life mother of actor Broderick Crawford - who played a similar role in *Top Hat*), and Fred's comic relief buddy (Victor Moore, whose comic inflections are just brilliant). There's also Eric Blore, who occupies the same veiled homosexual "sissy" character he did in *Top Hat*; an attempt, I think, to make the slight Astaire appear more masculine in contrast.

There's also a big elephant in the film, and I'm glad Criterion addressed it directly in a video interview with Mia Mask, a Black film scholar. *Swing Time* is the one - and thankfully only - film in which Fred Astaire does a solo dance number in blackface. It's jarring, and something you want desperately to unsee, even if you're aware that it would be difficult to find a performer from the 1930s who *hadn't* put on blackface at some point. But I learned a lot from Mask, who explained why this happened, and why it's such an affront.

Blackface actually began as early as the 1830s, a hundred years before the film. It was done by traveling "minstrel shows," made up of white performers who wanted to both perform and mock the songs and speech of Black slaves. But blackface wasn't just about darkening white skin; performers would add white makeup around their lips and eyes for contrast, then dress themselves in rags, to further dehumanize the slaves. It was bad enough that they were mocking Black men and women, but making light of the brutality of slavery made blackface and minstrelsy especially egregious.

The offending number in *Swing Time* is called, "Bojangles of Harlem," and it's sometimes excused by saying that this was Astaire's homage to Bill "Bojangles" Robinson (1900-1949), the great Black entertainer best known for his four films with Shirley Temple. But the facts tell a different story: Astaire had met Robinson briefly on the stage, but had never said anything about his dancing. And Robinson never would have recognized this performance as "homage." For one thing, Astaire had a much different style of tap than Robinson, and made no effort to adapt it. He also twice throws his arms out in an Al Jolson "Mammy" pose, something Robinson never did, but would have been true to stereotypes of Black dance. There's also an exaggerated and racist set decoration that opens the scene. Had Astaire really wanted to honor Robinson, he might have danced with him, as Robinson was an acknowledged superstar of Black theater. But the Hays Code - Hollywood's voluntary code of movie censorship - forbade interracial touching in films of the time. All the same, Robinson himself had defied that tenet of the

Hays Code, when he took the hand of the young Shirley Temple to dance with her onscreen.

Mask is generous in reminding us that we need to be prepared to examine the past with an understanding of where norms were at the time, and what audience expectations were. Certainly Fred Astaire did no worse than other white performers of the time. But she helped me to understand where the practice of blackface had come from, and why it was never rooted in humor or mimicry, but used as a means to attack, belittle, and dehumanize people who were already fighting for their very lives.

Taipei Story

Taiwan, 1985. Directed by Edward Yang. 110 minutes, color.

Nearly forty years of military rule was ending in Taiwan when Edward Yang directed *Taipei Story*. Filmmakers were beginning to breathe fresher air, less inhibited in speaking out with authentically Taiwanese voices. For Yang, this meant freedom to film a tale of a disconnected generation, drifting from the values and expectations of their elders into unknown waters.

Chin (Tsai Chin) and Lung (Hou Hsiao-hsien, who also co wrote the screenplay) are a couple passing each other in opposite directions. When we met them, they're walking through a new apartment, talking about its possibilities. A new home means a new beginning, but these two show little excitement, or even affection for each other. We don't know how long they've been dating - only once in the film does Chin bring up marriage - but the lack of excitement or spontaneity in their behavior seems to point to each taking the other for granted.

Chin is looking ahead; part of the reason she takes the new apartment is to flee her father, and the traditional duties of the daughter he wants her to assume. She's eager to take advantage of the new roles Taiwanese society offers women. Chin works as an executive assistant in a property development firm, and has ambitions for an executive path of her own. But the woman executive Chin works with, and believes to be her mentor, soon quits the firm, and effectively ghosts Chin. When Chin is called into a superior's office, she is told that the firm is restructuring, and there is no place for another executive. "We need you to be a secretary," she's told, and quietly resigns rather than face the demotion. She's optimistic, though; Lung is about to travel to Los Angeles to talk with his brother-in-law about taking a partnership in his business, and sees greener pastures in America than in Taiwan.

Lung is looking to the past. His greatest days are far behind him, when he played for the national Little League team as a child. Lung works in his family's fabric shop, and seems to want little more out of life than tending to the friends and family of his past. Upon Lung's return from L.A. (we never see him there), he doesn't talk much about the trip, only to mention vague frustrations before finally giving up on the idea altogether. In fact, the money he has saved up for the partnership stake he instead gives to Chin's father, a lazy and unscrupulous businessman who is in desperate need of cash to pay off some bad loans. Lung also funds an old teammate from his baseball days, who is working nearly around the clock as a cab driver to raise his two children, while also trying to stay on top of his wife's gambling debts. The closest we see to passion in any of Lung's relationships are in his dealings with people from his past.

The film pays unique attention to the urban look of Taipei. Yang had spent more than ten years studying and working in the United States, and upon returning to Taipei, began to see it with fresh eyes. In an interview, he talked about a brightly-lit square he used to drive past, never giving it any notice, but upon his return suddenly spotted the giant picture of Chiang Kai-shek, and realized the political presence that had always been there (in the film we see Chin and her friends riding motorcycles around the monument at night). It's a "new" Taiwan, but it also seemed to be blending into the same blandness that the rest of the world offered, seen best in the city's neon advertisements for both Asian and Western products. "What was Los Angeles like?" Chin asks an architect at her firm. "A lot like Taipei." That same architect, looking out the window tells her, "All the buildings look the same. I can't even remember which ones I designed any more."

Chin is furious that Lung has given away his savings - their future - and begins to look to what the contemporary urban setting can offer. Her younger sister is squatting with friends in an abandoned building, and Chin begins to join them on nighttime excursions to clubs, bars, and restaurants, and out in the streets. She's fleeing the domestic expectations for a single woman of her parents' generation, but is running toward... what? She doesn't know. And it's hard to see, behind the oversize sunglasses she's always wearing, even at night, that do as much to shield her from the city as they do to prevent others from looking in (there's a terrific image early on when she takes off her sunglasses at her new apartment, placing them on the top of a dresser already covered with sunglasses).

Lung, meanwhile, seems to be working harder to assume a traditional role, providing for his friends in need, including an old girlfriend of whom Chin is suspicious. Meanwhile, the two seem to be leading separate lives, barely interacting, not really communicating when they do. For two people who have known each other since they were children, they're fast becoming strangers. It's not that they have secrets to hide, but that Chin and Lung increasingly see little point in unburdening to a partner headed in the other direction.

Yang shoots *Taipei Story* in a way that seems to trap his characters in the city. Much of the action happens in claustrophobic domestic spaces, but even when shooting outdoors, he cages actors in grids; whether against neon billboards, the glass windows of a corporate office, or simply the blocks of city streets. There are some beautiful shots in *Taipei Story* to be sure, but they all work to hem people in, not free them.

Taipei Story was just Edward Yang's second film, and he would go on to become better-known for his later films, like *A Brighter Summer Day* and *Yi Yi*, for which he won the Best Director award at Cannes in 2000. Yang died prematurely of cancer in 2007, but not before he had established himself as a pioneer in the New Wave of Taiwanese cinema.

The Tales of Hoffman

UK, 1951. Directed by Michael Powell and Emeric Pressburger. 133 minutes, color.

In 1951, Britain was still rebuilding from the rubble of WWII, and Britons were eager to look ahead to a time when they could focus again on celebrating the arts, instead of just seeking shelter from Nazi bombs. Michael Powell and Emeric Pressburger, having already given their countryfolk the gorgeous technicolor glory of *The Red Shoes*, now turned to Jacques Offenbach's opera, *The Tales of Hoffman*, for their next project.

Seriously? Opera?

Oh, my, yes.

What Powell and Pressburger did with *The Tales of Hoffman* - a magical, fantastic dreamlike production, à la Mozart's *The Magic Flute* - was present the opera in a way only cinema could, taking it to a level that would have been impossible to present onstage. First, they recorded all the music, conducted and arranged by Sir Thomas Beecham (Offenbach's score was unfinished, so all performances of his opera required some sort of reconstruction from the composer's notes). The vocal roles were all sung by leading operatic singers from three continents. Then the movie was filmed to playback, with ballet dancers lip-synching to previously recorded music. Cheating, you say? Perhaps, but what this allowed Powell and Pressburger to do was convert the opera into a ballet; actors, freed from the breathing demands of their singing roles, were able to convert that lung power into the athletic requirements of ballet. No one could ever meet the respiratory demands of trying to do both at once. Only two roles - that of Hoffman (Robert Rounseville[62]) and Antonia (Ann Ayers) were sung by the people appearing on stage. As it was, the prima ballerina Moira Shearer, first plucked from the stage for her breathtaking film debut in *The Red Shoes*, found even lip-synching to the playback difficult while dancing.

What also made the dual roles a wonderful decision was Powell and Pressburger's decision to give full credit to the voice actors in the film. When Marni Nixon sang in place of leading ladies in films like *West Side Story*, *The King and I*, and *My Fair Lady*, her name - if it appeared at all -was buried in the credits, Hollywood hoping audiences would believe all their actors had brilliant singing voices. *The Tales of Hoffman* presents perhaps my favorite closing credits in all of cinema;

---

[62] In the case of Robert Rounseville, one suspects he was cast (as an actor) for his looks. He is barely required to dance, and his acting is flat, at best. Martin Scorsese, in the disc's chat track, suggests that they got away with this because the character of Hoffman is passive in the opera; he is acted upon rather than a character who moves the story along.

both the physical actor and the voice actor are brought out in a curtain call for each role, each bowing to the other, each accepting applause.[63] There would be no hiding of talent, no subjugating of one half of the performance to another.

Before I talk more about what the playback technique allowed the filmmakers to do, let's touch briefly on the source opera itself. E.T.A. Hoffman (1776-1822) was a German author of romantic fantasy and horror; his novella *The Nutcracker and the Mouse King* served as the basis for the Tchaikovsky ballet, *The Nutcracker*. And that wasn't even the man's day job - he had gone into the family business of law, though one suspects his Gothic heart was more in his writing. Jacques Offenbach (1819-1880) was a French composer of German birth known for over 100 operettas (*Tales of Hoffman*, his final work, was to be his first full-fledged opera). Offenbach was known for lively, rollicking works - like the "Can Can" from *Les brigands* - and chose three of Hoffman's stories for this final work. Together they tell the story of the poet, Hoffman, recalling in a tavern three past loves, each a tale touched by the supernatural, in which the same diabolical older man (brilliantly acted and danced by Robert Helpmann, and sung by Bruce Dargavel) thwarts Hoffman's desires. In the first, the object of Hoffman's attraction is in fact an automaton (danced by Moira Shearer,

---

[63] I was also delighted by the absence of the diminutive "actress" in the closing credits; both men and women are correctly referred to as "actors." Not bad for 1951, and certainly not something that needed to wait until the 21st century's attention to gender-neutral terminology.

sung by Dorothy Bond) created to entice him. In the second, Giulietta (danced by Ludmilla Tchérina, sung by Margherita Grandi) sets out to capture Hoffman's soul for the evil Dapertutto (Helpmann/Dargavel), and in the third and most daring tale (for American censors, anyway), Antonia (danced and sung by Ann Ayars), must choose between her love for Hoffman and her art, as she will die if she sings one last time. As the opera ends, Hoffman's devilish foil has one last time come between the poet and his love, the ballerina Stella (Shearer).

The fantastic plot of the opera allowed the filmmakers to unleash *all* of their creativity, not just on the dance, but on the sets and makeup as well. And the decision to film on playback freed the team creatively in another unexpected way. Because all the "dialogue" and music was already recorded - and sound effects added later in place of natural sound - *The Tales of Hoffman* was actually filmed as if it were a silent picture. All the acting techniques of silent film were drawn on, especially by Helpmann, who choreographed not only his dance moves, but his eye movements and facial expressions in time with the music (if you want an idea of how physical an actor Helpmann was - and how he considered every role to be a dancing role - recall his movements as the Child Catcher in the 1968 *Chitty Chitty Bang Bang*). Another technical problem solved was the movement of then-cumbersome - and noisy - Technicolor cameras, now freed to move since there was no sound being recorded on set. Filmmakers found that not only the dancers benefitted from filming to playback, but the crew as well, especially camera operators who could pan and zoom in time with the score. In a commentary track featuring filmmaker Martin Scorsese and critic Bruce Elder, Scorsese said that he learned from this film to use playback of the soundtrack while filming some otherwise silent scenes in *Goodfellas* (specifically, the montage that reveals the bodies found after the airport heist), so that his own camera operators might film in synch with the Rolling Stones song he would add later.

The film in its entirety is a glorious work of art, with scenes that were designed to show off the saturated colors of the set and costumes, especially refreshing to post-war audiences who had been denied British color films. But the imaginative dance, camera work, and even classic silent-era special effects brought this film to phantasmagorical life even without the color. Both Scorsese and horror filmmaker George A. Romero (the latter interviewed in 2005 for this disc) talked about first being enchanted by this film on black and white television in New York City in the 1950s. There was a station at the time that featured a "Million Dollar Movie" every week, in which the same film would be run twice nightly with an extra matinee showing on weekends; *The Tales of Hoffman* was one of the films selected for broadcast. Both future filmmakers loved the film, even in black and white, and repeated viewings allowed them to figure out how Powell and Pressburger were presenting the story to such effect. Later, Romero said that he would rent a print of the film, along with a 16mm projector, to study it more closely, and to see it in color. He found out later that if the print wasn't available when he wanted it, it was likely checked out by a guy named Scorsese.

Powell and Pressburger had set out with this film to help Britons fall in love again with the arts, having had to simply survive and physically rebuild for so long. They wanted to remind their countryfolk what life was worth living *for*. But they were sometimes criticized for being too European in their cultural tastes, turning to works by German and French artists, casting opera singers and dancers from outside the United Kingdom. But they had a cheeky and wonderful answer for that. In the last scene of the opera itself, just before the performers' curtain call, Sir Robert Beecham is seen conducting an orchestra in the final bars of the opera. Beecham then lowers his baton, and turns his own hardbound score over to the back cover. In brilliant gold ink, against the royal blue of the cover, Sir Robert firmly stamps "Made in Britain."

Tampopo

Japan, 1985. Directed by Juzo Itami. 114 minutes, color.

If you're under the impression that Japanese cinema is all samurai flicks and Godzilla (and I have to admit this book may have contributed to that impression), look no further than director Juzo Itami and *Tampopo*. Itami made films - usually comedies - that poked gently at contemporary Japanese society, and none found a greater worldwide audience than *Tampopo*. According to Itami's spouse, Nobuko Miyamoto - also the actor who played the titular character (the name "Tampopo" also means "dandelion") - three elements were essential in any Itami film. They had to surprise you. They had to be fun. And anyone could understand them.

Itami himself described the film as "*Shane* with ramen." It's a foodie film, a loving paean to Japan's ultimate comfort food, told within the confines of an American western. The widowed mother of a young boy has inherited a modest ramen restaurant (more of a shack, really), through which she scratches out a living. Into her shop wander a pair of truck drivers, Goro (Tsutomu Yamazaki) and Gun (Ken Watanabe, in one of his earliest roles). These are our cowboys riding into town: Goro is never seen without his cowboy hat, both wear kerchiefs around their necks, and their rig is decorated with steer horns. After a brawl outside Tampopo's noodle shop, when Goro objects to the way one of the locals (Rikiya Yasuoka) is berating Tampopo, she asks their honest opinion of her ramen. "It sucks," Gun bluntly tells her, and Goro begins to iterate the problems with the dish; it turns out the two are serious ramen aficionados. Tampopo pleads with them to allow her to become their disciple; suddenly she sees an opportunity not just to make a living from her shop, but to create as much as possible the perfect ramen establishment. Goro agrees and begins the task of training Tampopo, and helping her make over her ramen.

The essential ingredients in a bowl of ramen are broth and noodles; each must be simple, but bold and distinctive. Toppings, like pork, naruto (fish surimi), menma (bamboo shoots), or scallions add flavor and presentation, but the heart of the ramen is in its two core ingredients, and these Tampopo must perfect. Goro begins assembling a team to work on each element. A wealthy benefactor lends out his personal chef to assist Tampopo with the noodles, and the elder statesman of a group of homeless epicurean hobos works with her on the broth. With these guides (and a certain amount of industrial espionage), Tampopo is able to raise the level of her central ingredients. Goro drills her on working efficiently, while concentrating on her customers' reactions to her ramen. And, hilariously, he's "Mickey" to Tampopo's "Rocky," even running her through cardio exercises to whip her into shape for her new role.

Where the film follows the western template is in the stranger coming to town, helping correct an imbalance, and moving on. It's reinforced by flashes of costuming, as in the gang at a rival noodle shop each wearing a different apparel of western clothing, and in Tampopo herself, who Itami wanted dressed "prim, but sexy," like the school marm in a frontier town. But that's just the framework; the film is a glorious celebration of food, not just of ramen, but through various vignettes apart from the main story, the central role of food in life, death, and sex.

There's a wonderful scene in which some high-level Japanese executives take some important clients to a French restaurant, bringing with them a young junior executive, whose role seems to be that of briefcase sherpa and whipping boy. There's a moment of embarrassed silence as the men look over the menu; printed in French, it's possible that none of them can read it. Finally, one asks for sole with consommé and a Heineken, and one by one, each repeats the same order. Until the waiter finally approaches our junior executive, who quietly asks the waiter about the preparation of a few menu items, revealing an astonishing knowledge of French cuisine, right down to the wines.

Take that scene together with one later of our foodie derelicts, who scavenge - and critique - leavings of the best restaurants in Tokyo, and whose senior member will soon assist Tampopo with her broth. When Tampopo's young son isn't interested in the food they've turned up in a late-night visit, one of them asks him what he likes. "Rice omelet," he replies, and a bum sneaks him into the kitchen of an elegant restaurant and whips him up a beautiful dish (the actual restaurant kitchen where the scene was filmed now carries a "Tampopo Rice Omelet" on its menu). The point? Epicureanism is not in the province of only the elite. Just as Tampopo has turned to cowboy/truckers, and not elite chefs to help her reach her goal, great food - and great living - belongs to those who care to reach for it. In a conversation with 21st-century ramen chefs on the disc, they see the film as about finding a way to make the dish your own, while still remaining true to the comfort-food origins of ramen (a dish meant to be noisily slurped, by the way, not daintily picked at, like the finishing school teacher tries to get her charges to do with their spaghetti in another vignette).

Earlier I mentioned that food in this film is connected to life, death and sex, and nowhere do we find that more than in another character - an unnamed gangster the credits only refer to as "The Man in the White Suit" (Koji Yakusho), and his moll (Fukumi Koroda). The film opens with him in a movie theater, his goons setting up a table of fine wine and charcuterie in front of the couple before their movie starts. We also follow their erotic adventures in several scenes of food enjoyed in their lovemaking, including an unforgettable scene of the two passing an unbroken egg yolk from mouth to mouth. As he's gunned down in the street, in his dying breaths he tells his girlfriend about hunting wild boar in the winter, yams being the only food the animals can find, and the intestines immediately grilled on a fire to make yam sausages (the death motif repeated in another vignette as a housewife rises from her deathbed to prepare her family one final meal).

I love this film. It's one of the very few I purchased in a Criterion edition when I already had an imported DVD copy (which in turn, replaced the VHS copy I started off with). One of the reasons the film is so appealing - and why it found an audience far beyond the shores of Japan - isn't just in celebrating the ordinary foodie, but in how it brings the viewer into the film. That first scene in the movie theater, our yakuza speaks to us directly, looking into the camera, and saying, "Oh, you're here for a movie, too? What are you eating?" Throughout, the camera is often held at eye level, as if we the audience were part of the scene, and when two characters talk to each other, note how many times they are filmed in tight frontal close-up, looking and speaking directly into the camera, as if we the viewer are the person they are talking to. It's more than just a clever filmmaker's trick, it actually makes the film a little more personal to watch. It's as if Itami is saying, "This is for you, this is about you."

Tampopo is absolutely necessary viewing for the foodie cinephile; alongside if not surpassing Stanley Tucci and Campbell Scott's 1996 *Big Night* and Lasse Hallström's 2000 *Chocolat*. It's about food being celebrated, appreciated, and created by those of us who love it; not necessarily those of us who make it past the gatekeepers of cuisine. It's about the joy of obsessing over something in life that, well, *feeds* us.

And if you don't want to go out for good ramen after watching this, you need to check your pulse. The thing about this movie? It wouldn't even begrudge you that package of dollar ramen that got you through college - as long as you added something - anything - to make it your own.

The Complete Jacques Tati

Jour de fête: France, 1949. 86 minutes, black and white. *Monsieur Hulot's Holiday*: France, 1953. 87 minutes, black and white. *Mon oncle*: France, 1958. 116 minutes, color. *Play Time*: France, 1967. 124 minutes, color. *Trafic*: France, 1971. 97 minutes, color. *Parade*: France, 1974. 89 minutes, color. All films directed by Jacques Tati.

Jacques Tati, even if he hadn't been 6'1" in all his ungainly glory, would have been a giant in physical comedy. His brief career stands as a landmark among the comic greats. When he came to Hollywood in 1959 and was awarded an Oscar for Best Foreign Film for *Mon oncle*, he was asked who in the room he wanted to meet. "Buster Keaton," he immediately replied, and Keaton rushed over to see him, along with Mack Sennett and Harold Lloyd. Tati, who had developed a talent for mime in the music halls of Europe, hearkens back to Charlie Chaplin in his physical satire of a quiet man caught up in modern times, and to Keaton and Lloyd in the sheer inventiveness of his gags. But to watch Tati perform is to also understand his influence on those who came later - it's impossible not to see the seeds of

Peter Sellers' Inspector Clouseau or of Rowan Atkinson's Mr. Bean in Tati's Monsieur Hulot. Any actor who brings his entire body to his comedy - John Cleese, Steve Martin - owes a debt to Jacques Tati. *Monty Python*'s Terry Jones, who introduces several of the films in this collection, said, "Tati shows us that comedy can be not only funny, but beautiful."

Watching all six of his films in *The Complete Jacques Tati* in one week - including a bonus disc of Tati's short films - is to spend time with not only an artist but a craftsman who obsessed over the details of his own performance, as well as everyone else's. But taken together, the films also describe an arc of tragedy, an artist silenced because he refused to let go of his own vision.

Tati was born Jacques Tatischeff in France in 1907; he shortened his Russian last name to "Tati" to fit on music hall marquees when he began performing. Tati's maternal grandfather ran a framing shop - he'd framed the works of Toulouse-Lautrec and was friendly with Van Gogh. Tati's father took over the framing business from his father-in-law, but after a stint in the army (as well as a place on a local rugby team), Tati found his silent impressions amused his mates, and took to the music halls to develop a routine. By the 1930s, Tati saw that the future of entertainment was in film, and was able to star in some short comedy films, and later direct a few himself. This led him to his first feature film, *Jour de fête* ("Day of the Feast"), released in 1949.

Jour de fête, like most of Tati's work, eschews a storyline for a series of vignettes. The action takes place around a small

French farm community on the day a carnival comes to town. Tati's character is François, the district postman, making his rounds on his bicycle. François is seen as a character who connects the townspeople not only with the outside world, but with each other; he is easily persuaded to run an errand for a merchant or stop and chat (and drink) at the local watering hole. But when he sees a newsreel of some Chicago postal carriers using small helicopters to increase the efficiency of their rounds, François is seized with purpose to deliver the community's mail "American style." His attempts to deliver the mail at top speed allows for a flurry of gags both inventive and hilarious, especially as François' newfound attempt at efficiency doesn't preclude him knocking back one too many when the carnies insist on the postman joining them for drinks.

Jour de fête is by no means a silent film, but Tati begins a technique here he'll become known for over his career. Tati doesn't use much natural sound in his films, because he doesn't like to clutter the soundtrack with audio information that isn't relevant. Instead, he is selective in his sound effects, using them to direct our attention to a gag, or even to provide accompaniment. There's a great scene where François is riding his bike down a road, overlooked by a man on a hill (in the same shot). We hear, rather than see, a bee or wasp buzzing, and François wildly swatting. He then moves on, and as he passes the observer we hear the insect again, and the bystander begins swatting - the visual joke of a bee passing from one victim to another all through sound, and only possible because our ears aren't distracted by dialogue or other noises. It's Tati's way of accenting what are largely mime performances, and it's what makes him so brilliant both as an actor and a director.

Jour de fête was actually to be the first French release filmed in color, which shows you how much of a reputation Tati had built on the basis of his short films. An early French attempt to copy Technicolor - a special film stock known as Thomson-Color - was loaded into cameras, but since a technique for developing it had not yet been perfected, Tati shot with two cameras side by side, one with black and white film, the other in color. It's fortunate he did, because when he finished the film, there was still no lab that could process the experimental color stock, and the film was released in black and white. Tati, never satisfied with his films, released a re-edited version in 1964 with hand-painted highlights (a technique even silent filmmakers dabbled in in the late 19th century). Tati used the occasion to add new scenes, most involving an artist sketching and painting scenes of the carnival. This would be another hallmark of Tati films; many had one or two additional versions released after a film's premiere.

Monsieur Hulot's Holiday was Tati's next work, released four years later. Again, we are treated to a film without a central plot; simply following the escapades of a French gentleman and his lodging mates through a fortnight at a seaside resort. What makes this film unique is the introduction of Monsieur Hulot, a character Tati would go on to play in his next three films. Monsieur Hulot is a well-meaning, affable, somewhat bumbling middle-class-looking chap perpetually dressed in an overcoat, a frumpy hat, and a long pipe, which is never lit, but apparently causes Hulot's tall frame to bend forward. We know nothing about Hulot, not his first name, not if he has family, not if or how he is employed. He is always on the outside of a social situation, even as people invite him in. He lurches, birdlike, in his movements; he never falls, but is always on the verge of falling. His awkwardness leads him to unintentional mayhem, but it's harmless mayhem damaging only propriety; never the physical catastrophes caused by Laurel and Hardy or the Three Stooges. He is charming, and *Monsieur Hulot's Holiday* is charming. In a great body of work, this is my favorite Tati film.

Tati gives Hulot plenty of opportunity to show off physical gags, including some great tennis scenes Tati had previously mimed. Again, Tati uses sound effects to call attention to the comedy; we hear ocean waves in one scene, but only as they are synched to the inhalations and exhalations of holiday-goers practicing calisthenics on the beach. But it's also the first film in which we get a sense of the democracy of Tati's comedy. Tati is democratic in the sense that Hulot does not need to be the comic focus of every scene; one of my favorite scenes is one in which a toddler, burdened with two ice cream cones (one for his sibling), has to negotiate a flight of steps and a closed door, comic tension mounting as we hold our breath waiting for the spill that thankfully never comes. But it's also democratic in the way Tati gently satirizes all his characters. Tati never makes fun of an individual, only a "type," and throughout *Monsieur*

Hulot's Holiday, he gently spoofs businessmen, intellectual students, bourgeois housewives, and stuffy waiters. No one escapes his jabs, but neither is anyone dehumanized.

Tati followed up this success with *Mon oncle*, his first truly color film. Tati reprised the character of Hulot, but placed him in an entirely different setting; this film opens with a jarring scene of urban noise and mayhem. Where Hulot had previously existed in a quaint and nostalgic version of the French countryside, he now is juxtaposed with the ultra-modernity of his sister's family's home, and the plastics factory his brother-in-law manages. The Arpel's home is sleek, cubed, and loaded up with modern "conveniences" and the Arpels are eager to show off their cutting-edge lifestyle. The plot, such as it is, revolves around Hulot's sister (Adrienne Servantie) trying to get her brother to settle down with a job and a family of his own, and the fish-out-of-water comedy comes from Hulot trying to surmount the obstacles the home and the plastics factory present to him. (Hulot himself lives in a delightfully thrown-together apartment building, the entirety of which he must meander through to reach his third-floor flat.)

Again, Tati uses sound to accentuate the comic scenes, but here he uses spare dialogue more as sound effect than to drive the plot. The Arpels speak minimally in their home, the human audio track as sterile as the design. Contrast that with Hulot talking with his neighbors; we only pick up snippets of dialogue (as a bystander might in real life), but the characters are more open and animated, as if speech is equated with human connection. Nowhere do we see this more than in Hulot's relationship with his nephew, Gerard (Alain Bécourt). Gerard himself seems unable to relax or open up to his parents in their home, but loves the unstructured jaunts into town with Hulot (the film is titled, "My Uncle" after all), as well as the simple connection of holding Hulot's hand - physical contact we never see extended by his own father (Jean-Pierre Zola) until the final scene of the film. Tati also insists this connection transcends class boundaries, as we see Gerard getting his pristine school uniform filthy with his ragamuffin friends,[64] the only bond that matters is joining in the merry gang's pranks.

Mon oncle was a success internationally - Tati's films appealed to international audiences partially because his mime translated universally - and won the Academy Award for Best Foreign Film. But in France the film received some criticism for Tati's perceived attack on modern architecture. Tati said repeatedly that he wasn't criticizing modern design, but the Arpel's glorification of it, to the point where they had lost the rhythms of a more natural life. But France (Paris especially) was going through a critical housing crisis at the

---

[64] Tati mirrors this theme in the opening scenes of the picture, following a pack of stray dogs (dogs are *everywhere* in Tati's films) as they forage through the trash cans of the town. But wait - one of these "strays" is a dachshund, and is wearing both a collar and a plaid sweater. It is the Arpel's dog, who has found a pack in the street dogs of the neighborhood. The introduction ends with a delightful shot of the dachshund wriggling under the Arpel's gate to go home - the only dog of the pack short enough to do so - and the mutts staring for a minute outside the gate watching their friend return home before they move on.

time, and modern design was seemingly a solution to the problem of providing clean, affordable shelter to the unhoused citizens of France. Tati, nostalgic for a less structured past, appeared to oppose progress.

Play Time is the film Tati himself considered to be his masterpiece, a film he worked on for nearly ten years following *Mon oncle*. The film opens with a scene of construction in Paris; even the opening titles are presented as signage at the site of a building going up. The film itself is a masterwork of design in relation to theme; through the first half of the movie we find lines and grids *everywhere*, into which Tati plops Monsieur Hulot, a man incapable of coloring inside the lines. The entire design of the film moves toward circles in the second half, the idea being we must break out of the order in which our lives try to keep us in order to find human connection. The plot, as usual, is incidental, as Hulot enters a modern glass office building in an attempt to interview for a job, then to a friend's apartment, finally getting swept up in the opening night of a new restaurant. Tati doubled down on the theme of *Mon oncle* that modern design was keeping us apart, and doubled down on his defense that he was commenting on the public's obsession with modernity, not modernity itself. Hulot is literally unable to connect with an interviewer in the labyrinthine glass lobby of the office building he enters, and an early glimpse of "cubicle culture" shows us workers isolated from the people who can assist them. When Hulot runs across an old army buddy who invites Hulot to his apartment for a drink, we find that he is living in a posh, but spare apartment on the first floor with a huge plate glass window exposing the living space to passersby. As the camera pulls back, we see an identical flat next door and two directly above, and the entire visit plays out only to the sounds of street traffic, like cels in a newspaper comic strip. Only when Hulot finally arrives at the restaurant opening - another nightmare of lines and design proscriptions - does the contemporary structure literally begin to collapse, the physical setting unable to contain the rush of guests. And only when the interior does fall apart, are guests free to spontaneously enjoy the company of their fellow diners.

Play Time was Tati's most ambitious film, and in many ways his most brilliant use of the Hulot character to comment on urban life. But it was filmed at tremendous cost. Tati built a huge set dubbed "Tativille" in the Paris outskirts, unable to find a contemporary setting that suited his needs. A producer suggested Tati actually build an office building, one that might be resold after production in Paris's booming real estate market, but Tati insisted on a layout of smaller buildings and façades that the city could use as a film school and studio after *Play Time* was complete. Before filming even began, Tativille was destroyed by a gale, needing to be rebuilt entirely, and as the film's financiers had forgotten to make payments to the insurance company, Tati's production company took the economic hit. Tati insisted on filming in 70mm, the most expensive film stock, generally reserved for Technicolor widescreen Hollywood epic. Tati wanted viewers to access every subtle gag Tati slipped into the frame, despite the scarcity of 70mm projectors in France at the time. The film's budget ballooned from 2.5 million euros to 15 million euros, making it the most expensive French film to date. To raise the funds, Tati mortgaged his home and persuaded his family to put up his and his sister's inheritance. All the while, Tati's perfectionism and need for control slowed production to a crawl.

The film bombed in France, and was unable to recoup losses abroad. Part of the problem was critics' claim that Tati was against modernism, and despite Tati's defense, *Play Time* seems to bear that out. Nothing goes right on the opening night of the ultra-modern restaurant, but in the film that's more due to the inexplicable incompetence of the contractors, waiters, and management - who only prepare for 50 meals to be served on the grand opening - than on design flaws in the architecture. But if that's the case, why insist on a cutting-edge design and menu? There are long Hulot-less stretches of the film (and Tati never cast famous stars, often filling his roles with non-actors, such as the officers wives he recruited from a nearby NATO base to fill out the female cast), frustrating to filmgoers who wanted to see their beloved "uncle." As clever and inventive as the film was, it simply wasn't as entertaining as Tati's previous works. And with a running time of over two and a half hours - soon to be cut to the two-hour version that survives - it was too much for audiences to endure.

Tati's grand vision had brought him financial ruin. His production company folded, and Tati lost the rights to all his previous works. Tati - and his sister - lost the inheritance they had planned on. Tati lost his home, and he and his wife were forced to relocate to an apartment. The city of Paris - in more need of housing and office space than a film studio - razed Tativille to the ground.

Tati was able to find backers for his next film, *Trafic*. The film reflects a chastened, but still unsuppressed filmmaker trying to reconcile his vision with hard economic realities. Tati would bring back Hulot one final time, this time employed as a car designer trying to get a "camping car" prototype to an Amsterdam auto show, beset by obstacles all the way through. No elaborate sets were constructed, and much of the filming is done on location. There's a subdued tone to the film, but Tati produces some gems regardless both in Hulot's visual gags, and in the traffic scenes, as Hulot tries to get the car to the expo before it closes. But the star of the film is Hulot's car itself. When he is stopped at the border by customs officers, he has the chance to show off the car's gadgetry to the police. Everything has a dual use, from the car's horn that conceals an electric shaver to the coffeepot/cigarette lighter. Events conspire to keep Hulot from getting to the expo before it closes, mostly involving events outside his control, like the breakdown for the truck carrying the prototype and the flighty behavior of the auto manufacturer's wife (Maria Kimberly) whose entitled disregard for regulations gets him in trouble with customs in the first place. The film ends with Hulot being fired, but as the common people of Amsterdam gather around Hulot's creation outside the exhibit hall, we suspect that our favorite Frenchman might find salvation with the masses after all.

Tati's final film, *Parade*, signals a bittersweet return to his music hall origins. Originally commissioned as a special for Swedish television, *Parade* is presented as a circus, with Tati as ringmaster and performer. As such, it's mostly filmed on video; a Tati biographer suggested that Tati wanted to prove his expertise with a new medium, but we suspect he wasn't given much of a choice. But Tati also filmed some scenes in both Stockholm and Paris on 16mm and 35mm, and the completed project was given a theatrical release in 1974. The resulting film is intimate and delightful, and the closest contemporary audiences will get to seeing Tati as the great mime artist live audiences discovered in the 1930s. Silver-haired, and perhaps a little slower, Tati is as graceful as ever, and his silent portrayals of a boxer and a soccer goalkeeper remain fresh and funny, and it's wonderful to see, for the first time, the response from a live audience. *Parade* also shows Tati at his most democratic as an artist. In a welcoming speech to the audience, Tati says that they will all perform and witness together, and the film is filled with audience members - some genuine, others clearly planted professionals - joining the cast in the circus-style acts. Tati is also generous in showcasing the talents of a new generation of performers, stepping out of the limelight to let his young colleagues shine. As the audience files out at the end of the show, the camera lingers on two young children wandering backstage and playing with the props and art materials of the circus. The camera, and we, linger on their play. This is clearly Tati passing on the baton to a new generation, watching to see what they will make of his work.

Jacques Tati died in 1982. In 1995, his daughter,

filmmaker Sophie Tatischeff, was finally able to find a lab that could process the Thomson-Color film stock from Tati's first film, and *Jour de fête* was finally seen in color.

The Testament of Dr. Mabuse

Germany, 1933. Directed by Fritz Lang. 121 minutes, black and white.

Dear Reader, doubt not my commitment to you! When I learned that *The Testament of Dr. Mabuse* was a sequel (actually a double sequel, but we'll get to that), I tracked down a (non-Criterion) copy of *Dr. Mabuse, the Gambler*, Fritz Lang's 1922 silent film. "Why not?" I figured. What I didn't realize was that Lang's original film was released in two parts, totaling four and a half hours in run time. *Testament* tells its tale in a comparatively brisk two hours, but add to that a second full viewing with commentary, plus the 90-minute French version of the film Criterion gave me. That's ten full hours with a madman (Mabuse, not Lang), and that's not even including the hours of interviews and documentaries included with both titles. It was fascinating, but at the same time, well, you're welcome.

It wouldn't have been necessary for German audiences to be brought up to speed on the character of Dr. Mabuse (pronounced mah-BOOZ-uh), since he was already fully residing in popular consciousness, but some background will help the rest of us. The character had been first introduced in 1921 by novelist Norbert Jacques, and the criminal mastermind quickly took hold. Lang turned the book into a film, in which Dr. Mabuse, a psychologist, hypnotist, and master of disguise, runs a criminal enterprise worthy of any James Bond villain. Based on Frederich Nietzsche's archetype Übermensch (Superman), Mabuse was a man who believed in power for its own sake, and was far more interested in controlling human beings than in amassing wealth. Mabuse was also created at a time when the practice of psychoanalysis was in its infancy, and his supernatural ability to control the minds of men merely through his thoughts would have played on the skepticism of the public over this new "science." At the end of *Dr. Mabuse, the Gambler*, Mabuse (Rudolf Klein-Rogge) is eventually discovered, and being apprehended, goes mad.

The Testament of Dr. Mabuse works beautifully as a psychological thriller, a police procedural, and as social commentary, though how much the film anticipates the rise of the Nazi party in Germany is something of a debate which I'll address at the end of this essay. I mentioned that this film is a double sequel. That's because Lang had brought back his police inspector Lohmann (Otto Wernicke) from his first sound film, *M*; Lohmann is the one who pursued Peter Lorre's child murderer in that film. *Testament* begins arrestingly, as do all Lang productions. We open in an industrial space, possibly the basement of a factory, to a man hiding behind a workspace. There's a rhythmic, cacophonous din hammering the soundtrack; what machinery is producing it or where it's coming from, we don't know. He's spotted by two men who enter the scene, but escapes; two attempts on his life later he circles back and places a phone call to Inspector Lohmann. We learn his name is Hofmeister (Karl Meixner) and he's a disgraced cop, but he's been staking out the industrial space for the past four days to try to work his way back into the good graces of the force. But before he can relay his message, the lights are cut, there's a shot... and Hofmeister begins eerily singing into the phone. Whatever has happened, it has driven him mad.

That opening scene establishes quite a few themes for the rest of the film. The first is that Lang will use sound to full effect in his films, not just as a means of reproducing speech or playing music. In a scene later, worthy of Hitchcock, Lang's villains will use the sounds of car horns in traffic to cover up the sound of a gunshot in an assassination - in a later scene the ticking of a bomb transitions to a character tapping on a poached egg at breakfast. This scene also begins what will be the first of messages sent but not received, miscommunication which will plague both cops and criminals throughout. It also lets us know that Lang plans on keeping us, the audience, on edge throughout. We also get information piecemeal, trying to follow crumbs that will eventually lead us in a grand circle.

We learn that Mabuse has spent these eleven years catatonic, in an asylum run by Professor Baum (Oskar Beregi, Sr.). He has not uttered a word, but after making motions with his hands in the air, was given paper and pencil, and has been filling pages with scribblings in his cell.

Baum has been collecting these, and when another doctor at the asylum has a look at them, he recognizes details of a plan for robbing a jewelers that matches the report of a burglary in the newspaper. Baum dismisses this as coincidence, but his colleague (Theodor Loos) rushes to report this to the police. En route, he is shot in traffic.

Lohmann, meanwhile, is trying to figure out what happened to Hofmeister, who is now at the asylum. Hofmeister is unable to communicate, but Lohmann begins to uncover signs of a unified criminal ring in Berlin with the help of Kent (Gustav Diessl), an ex-con and reluctant gang member who is being pushed too far. Kent and his gang report to an unnamed leader - a figure behind a curtain - who orders the men to commit crimes with no seeming gain. They are ordered to break into a bank vault and replace all the currency with counterfeit bills, and to kill the guards to make it look like a failed robbery attempt, but the money from the bank, as well as from jewelry heists, goes to purchase narcotics the gang will flood the streets with. None of them know why they are doing this or who they work for, only that those who attempt to find out are killed.

Meanwhile, at the asylum, a toe tag is placed on the body of Dr. Mabuse, who, having apparently finished his writings, has quietly expired. But in his study, poring over Mabuse's screeds, Baum is visited by - and seemingly inhabited by - a ghostly phantom of the dead doctor. Is this Mabuse continuing his work from beyond the grave? Or has Baum, seduced by the writings of Mabuse, imagined himself as the villain's successor, destabilizing the society of lesser men to rule himself in the "empire of crime" to come?

It's all the stuff of pulp fiction, which is of course is exactly where Lang's story came from. But Lang (and Thea von Harbou, Lang's wife and go-to screenwriter until their marriage blew up) keep us grounded in Lohmann, a smart, tough, beefy, no-nonsense cop who's trying to make sense of the whole affair. Nothing makes sense, especially not that the case always seems to circle back to the asylum, back to a man who spends the first half of the film catatonic before he dies. When Baum is himself discovered at the end, like Mabuse, he goes mad, and is confined to the very cell in which he'd imprisoned his predecessor in crime. Is Baum really possessed by the spirit of the great hypnotist? Or does he only believe he is? And does it matter? As Lohmann discovered during his investigations, the answer to the question, "Who is leading the criminal network?" is "Mabuse." But when he asks, "Who is Mabuse?" the answer is "the criminal mastermind behind it all."

All of this led to speculation that Lang and von Harbou were forecasting the rise of the Nazi party in this film, in an organization led by an autocrat who sought to conquer the will of the common people. It's an observation that I think makes more sense in retrospect, especially as Lang himself eventually fled the Nazis and von Harbou enthusiastically joined them. The original 1922 iteration of Mabuse seems to arise more from the post-WWI loss of ideals in Germany, rising, as he does, from the gambling dens. But between pre production on the film in 1932 and the film's French release in 1933, the Nazis had risen to power, and Joseph Goebbels himself had banned the film in Germany, whether because the Nazis recognized themselves in Mabuse and his gang, or because the film seemed to hint at the fragility of the government isn't clear. And Fritz Lang himself, as I discovered, isn't much help.

There's an interesting interview with Lang conducted in 1964, in which he recounts the story that's generally associated with Lang leaving Germany. Lang attended a meeting of German filmmakers in which Nazi propaganda minister Joseph Goebbels spoke excitedly about German films, including some that Lang himself had made. It was at the end of this talk that Goebbels mentioned - without explanation - that the next day he would ban *The Testament of Dr. Mabuse*. The ban was indeed announced the next day, and Lang received a summons to Goebbels' office. He arrived, was kept waiting, and finally directed in. Lang said that Goebbels was charming, and told Lang he wanted to place him in charge of all films produced under the Third Reich (Lang and Hitler - though for vastly different reasons - had both decried German Expressionism of the early 20th century, so this isn't as crazy as it sounds). Lang knew he couldn't refuse Goebbels, and simply told him it was an honor to be asked. Lang knew he had to leave Germany, but as he nervously watched the clock, he realized that the banks were closed and that he'd have to leave Germany only with what he could take with him. He packed a bag and left that night for France, then on to Hollywood.

But Lang's own passport, and records recovered after the war don't back up this story. Lang's passport shows several trips in and out of Germany after the *Testament* ban, plenty of time to clear out his bank account and move a great deal of his possessions out of the country before he came to America. Lang was known to change stories over the years on other topics, and he may have been attempting to acknowledge the many German artists who *did* have to flee at a moment's notice. And no records have ever been found of Lang meeting with Goebbels, or of Goebbels offering Lang such a position. And in watching the 20-minute interview, I saw Lang - if you'll indulge me in some amateur armchair psychology - betray himself through body language.

In the first half of the interview, the interviewer (Erwin Leiser) is seated behind a desk with Lang in a chair across from him. Nothing unusual. But as Leiser asks about Goebbels, Lang rises from his seat, walks behind the desk, and replies to his interviewer while standing over him. It clearly spoke to me of the body mechanics of a man trying to control and sell a response, not just reply. After a few minutes, Lang sits down *on the desk* facing Leiser, in his space. When Leiser asks about Lang's journey to the United States, Lang walks over to a bookshelf, breaks eye contact with Leiser, and tells the story almost to himself, gesticulating, as if this were an often-practiced anecdote. His demeanor and tone of voice never changes. But it's clear that his chair has gotten a little too hot for him.

I don't begrudge Lang telling his story his way, and the man certainly found himself in a precarious situation. But the interview, along with information from Lang historians in the written and supplemental materials, tell me to be careful in taking at face value Lang's own views on the Nazi response to *Testament*. It's important, however, only if you're trying to establish Lang's motives in making the film. But watching the film today, it's impossible not to take a larger lesson from it, intended or otherwise. For me, *The Testament of Dr. Mabuse* will always point to the fragility of our institutions, and how susceptible they are to manipulation. When Baum, in conversation with Lohmann, turns to the camera and says, "When humanity, subjugated by the terror of crime, has been driven insane by fear and horror, and when chaos has become supreme law, then the time will have come for the empire of crime," it's difficult not see an attack on democracy, not just in 1930s Germany, but in present-day America. In the end, it doesn't matter what Fritz Lang set out to say with *The Testament of Dr. Mabuse*. The film still speaks to our susceptibility to fear.

The Thin Red Line

US, 1998. Directed by Terrence Malick. 171 minutes, color.

"This great evil, where's it come from? How did it steal into this world? What seed, what root did it grow from? Who's doing this? Who's killing us?"

Here's the thing about *The Thin Red Line*, Terrence Malick's nearly three-hour war epic. I watched it through, then the following night, reran it for the commentary track with director of photography John Toll, production designer Jack Fisk, and producer Grant Hill, as I normally would. But twenty minutes into the movie, I turned off the chat track and cued the film up from the beginning. It wasn't that the commentary wasn't interesting; it was, and I'd return to it later. But suddenly I needed to see and hear this remarkable film all over again.

Terence Malick was returning to directing from a two decades absence; his last film had been *Days of Heaven* in 1978. Malick had established himself as a director of poetic, enigmatic films, featuring graceful, balletic photography. Malick chose as his subject the 1962 James Jones novel of the same title (Jones had also written *From Here to Eternity*).

The novel was a fictionalized account of the Battle for Guadalcanal in 1942; the book's author had drawn on his own experiences as a soldier in the Pacific Theater. Included in the written material with the disc is an article Jones had written for the March 30, 1963 *Saturday Evening Post* entitled "Phony War Films," in which Jones angrily criticizes Hollywood for sanitizing, glorifying, and redeeming warfare. Looking at just the cast of Malick's film - John Travolta, George Clooney, Nick Nolte, Sean Penn, Woody Harrelson, John Cusack, among others - you'd think this would be another star-studded epic for Jones to shake his fist at. But Jones needn't have worried. It's true that actors were knocking on Malick's door eager to work with him, and that Malick's financiers were placated by his casting of bankable Hollywood names. But Malick mostly cast them in small roles, turning a deeply philosophical story over to unknown actors.

The campaign to seize Guadalcanal from Japanese forces was an early turning point in the Pacific during WWII; from that tiny island, strategically located in the Solomon Islands, just northwest of Australia, either army could send bombers for thousands of miles. There's a patriotic film to be made from that, sure, but Malick recognized the deeply personal accounts and the suffering Jones wrote about in his book, and chose to tell stories of the effects this battle had on the individuals charged with fighting it. And Malick chose to tell their stories in his own visual way, with cutaways, usually beautiful cutaways, to scenes of nature. The film begins and ends with pregnant images; a crocodile sliding into a river, and at the end a coconut embedded in sand, lapped by surf. We may or may not have ideas what these images mean (and I'll be the first to admit I'm not the sharpest clam in the chowder). But clearly the questions these images raise have little to do with a geopolitical conflict, or warring ideologies.

The plot is driven by a march uphill. GIs having landed on the beaches of the tropical paradise, now must ferret out the Japanese troops. To take the island means to take a hill in the middle, and that hill is fiercely defended by Japanese bunkers with a clear field of vision for the machine gunners hunkered in at the top. Lt. Col. Gordon Tall (Nick Nolte) sees something else at the top of that hill: the general's star that's eluded him his entire career, and he's ready to browbeat Capt. James Stards (Elias Koteas) and company C into a suicidal frontal assault that will win him his promotion. Stards isn't held in much esteem by his men, but as he gets closer and closer to defying his commanding officer, all eyes are on the besieged captain. Private Witt (Jim Caviezel) begins the film AWOL, communing in a seeming Eden with Solomon Island natives. Thrown out of the outfit to a disciplinary unit by Sgt. Welsh (Sean Penn), Witt's relegation to stretcher bearing seems to awaken an empathy in him for his brothers in arms, and a desire to shoulder more of their burden. And there's Private Bell (Ben Chaplin), the only character to whom the film gives a backstory, as we're given glimpses of the wife he left behind, to whom his life is devoted.

The ugliness of war is set against some of the most beautiful natural photography I've ever seen in a film. Malick's camera keeps us in the middle of a patrol or a battle, but also gives us quick glimpses away, as if into the eyes and thoughts of the soldiers. But as often, Malick steps back with the soundtrack, as if to put the action in a larger perspective. Natural sound is replaced with a subtle, yet sweeping Hans Zimmer score, and dialogue is often replaced by voiceover. I know, I know, voiceover is supposed to be the antithesis of good screenwriting. But it's beautiful in *The Thin Red Line*, and used in a way I've never heard before. Generally, as in the passage I quoted above, it takes on a philosophical quality, as if the character is looking back at the scene through a long lens, perhaps of time. Or, as if there's another part of the soldier's awareness speaking to the terrified combatant. It's also impossible sometimes to pick out which character is speaking the lines, as if these thoughts are being kicked from soldier to soldier. The result is a film that's brutally realistic about warfare and soldiering, and also asks questions about warfare's place in both human nature and biological nature. "This great evil," where did it come from, indeed? What does it do to us? Is it from the earth, or against it?

One of the things I love about movies is learning about the craft of filmmakers; how they do what they do, especially intriguing filmmakers like Terrence Malick. I have to say, Malick himself is a ghost throughout the supplemental materials; he's spoken of with reverence and affection by all who worked with him, but we never catch a glimpse of him or hear his voice. I was curious to hear how such an "artistic" director worked. Despite the dreamy nature of his films, I'd read he brought in this war epic in on time and on budget.

One of the actors (I forget which one, might have been Dash Mihok) said he'd never been on a film set like it. He said that on most outdoor film sets, you sit around waiting for the weather or light to get right, and that makes sense. If you start a scene in sunny daylight, you need to make sure the sun is always out as you cover multiple angles or sections of a scene. He was amazed that Malick would shoot all day, every day, regardless of what the sky looked like: bright sunlight, overcast, even golden hour (that hour before sunset where the fading light saturates everything in a warm glow). He finally asked Malick about that, and Malick told him that having scenes done in different kinds of light gave him more options in the editing room. If he had takes of a conversation between two characters in daylight, cloud, and overcast, that gave him more options where he could drop that scene in the finished film. Malick had a script and a vision of his final product, but also the flexibility to work with what he'd shot. It also gave him the freedom to run with an actor's performance on set, as he did when expanding John Savage's portrayal of a soldier driven mad, past what was originally scripted.[65]

---

[65] Speaking of acting, I saw something in *The Thin Red Line* that I'm just going to go ahead and put down to great acting. I saw a clip of Michael Caine and Morgan Freeman on *The Graham Norton Show* where Freeman said he had learned something valuable from Caine's master class on film acting. Caine had said that when you're talking to another actor in a closeup, pick one eye to look at and stick with it. Otherwise, your eyes will flit back and forth trying to look at both eyes, and you'll end up looking shifty to the camera. Well, there's a scene in which John Cusack's

The Thin Red Line is a beautiful, remarkable film that both respects and transcends the typical war picture. Like *Saving Private Ryan* (which was being filmed at the same time, though on the other side of the world) it is a war film that respects the sacrifices of the citizen soldier without glorifying or sanitizing the suffering they endured. It's a film that allows the combatants to ask their questions aloud (even if rarely to each other). It's also a film that allows us to ask of ourselves, of each other, whether we've been in battle or not:

"Is this darkness in you, too? Have you passed through this night?"

---

character volunteers to lead the charge to the Japanese bunker, and Nick Nolte's general is excitedly giving him a pep talk. You can see Cusack's eyes going back and forth, and I thought, "Aha! John Cusack didn't take Michael Caine's acting class!" But later in the film, Cusack's character has realized that the general is just wasting his men for his own glory, and has grown cynical. In *that* scene, the general is excitedly telling Cusack's soldier that if they keep up the momentum, they can take the whole island that night. And Cusack just stares at Nolte through the whole scene, and Cusack's stare is *dead steady*. Maybe it's a coincidence. But I choose to believe that John Cusack just showed character growth through eye movement.

The Threepenny Opera

Germany, 1931. Directed by G.W. Pabst. 110 minutes, black and white.

I'm going to lean heavily on Tony Rayns' great essay enclosed in my disc of *The Threepenny Opera* in my opening paragraphs because the story of how this play and film came about is just too good to pass up. It starts in the 18th century with Jonathan Swift, author of *Gulliver's Travels*, who urged English poet and dramatist John Gay to pen a "Newgate pastoral," a sort of scamp's answer to high-minded opera of the time, by setting one in London's main prison. Gay came up with *The Beggar's Opera*, a romp based on real-life villain Jonathan Wild, and full of cynical commentary about corruption both in government and among the police. First staged in 1728, it became so popular that authorities banned a performance license for its sequel, *Polly*, apparently because it was hitting a little *too* close to home. But the cat was out of the bag, and "ballad opera" became a cheeky favorite of English audiences.

Cut to a couple hundred years later, when a popular revival of *The Beggar's Opera* was being staged in London. It was a huge hit, news of which spread to The Continent, and a German woman named Elisabeth Hauptmann ordered a copy of the text and translated it into German for her employer (and boyfriend) Bertolt Brecht. Brecht himself was a piece of work, full of revolutionary zeal, but had yet by that point fully embraced Marxist ideology. He also had yet to write a successful play, though apparently that hadn't humbled him, as he was already said to have a "strong personality." Brecht had lots of fingers in lots of pies in those days, but when he was approached in April of 1928 by Ernst Josef Aufricht, a wealthy newcomer to Berlin who had just purchased a new theater and wanted Brecht to come up with something he could stage at the grand opening on August 31, Brecht turned to *The Beggar's Opera*. Brecht approached composer Kurt Weill with a nonnegotiable offer for the music: Weill would get 25% of any royalties, Hauptmann would get 12.5% (as translator), and Brecht himself would receive the remaining 62.5%. Brecht told Weill if he refused, they'd just use the music from the English play, and Weil - a Jew who possibly suspected which way the political winds were blowing - reluctantly agreed. Such was the beginning of a partnership which, though brief (the two only worked four years together), would come to define German theater for a generation.

The play was an enormous success, thanks largely - it was roundly observed - to Weill's score, incorporating elements of jazz into more traditional music hall dance music. As has always been the case since sound films were born, if a musical is a hit on stage, a film version is certain to come along. The production company, Nero - a small up-and-comer in the German film industry - shelled out 40,000 Reichsmarks for the film rights and specified that Brecht and Weill would have creative control. But the creative team came up with an outline that altered the plot of the stage play to create a much more politically controversial - and leftist - vehicle. Whether they were frightened by this or just needed to recoup their investment, Nero sold the rights to Tobis-Klangfilm, a giant in German cinema as well as the German subsidiary of Warner Brothers. The new owners tried to buy Brecht's contract, but he refused, and he and Weill took them to court when they learned production had started under Austrian director G.W. Pabst, already a leading force in German cinema. Weill won, and Brecht lost, though Brecht later claimed that he had really "won" because all he wanted to do was showcase the oppression of the artist. But Pabst (a leftist himself) had preserved the political content of the script, and both Weill and Brecht found the production honored their intentions, though in a more humanistic way. Pabst also dropped much of the music, retaining only the most popular (and dramatically effective) songs.

The Threepenny Opera centers on three powerful London figures. Mackie Messer (Rudolf Forster) is an organized crime figure, and runs the docks, if not all of London - he's introduced with the song "Mack the Knife," later made famous to Americans by Bobby Darin. Jonathan Jeremias Peachum (Fritz Rasp) runs London's beggars; if you want to work the street, you pay him for a license, and "The King of Beggars" will issue you a costume and backstory. Our third figure is Tiger Brown (Reinhold Schünzel), London's chief of police, and Mackie's former war comrade; whether out of friendship or fear, Brown seems to give Mackie free rein over the city. Mackie, upon leaving his favorite brothel, spots Peachum's daughter, Polly (Carola Neher) strolling with her mother (Valeska Gert). He takes Polly out for drinks and she agrees to marry him that night. Mackie has his men steal the necessities for a 2:00 AM wedding, officiated by a nervous priest and witnessed by Tiger Brown, whom Mackie has summoned to the warehouse that serves as his headquarters. When Peachum discovers this the next morning, he's furious, both that his daughter would marry without his permission, and that she'd align herself with a powerful rival.

Peachum and his wife go to Brown, demanding that he arrest and hang Mackie immediately. As leverage, Peachum points to the upcoming queen's procession and threatens to unleash his army of beggars to ruin the event. Brown agrees, but tips off Mackie so he can lay low, which he does at a brothel. But the jealous Jenny (Lotte Lenya), Mackie's favorite sex worker, betrays him to Mrs. Peachum and the police, and he is arrested. In his absence, Polly runs the gang, and she takes over a local bank, installing Mackie's henchmen as officers. Impressed, Peachum has a change of heart and tries to recall the mob he has unleashed, but they refuse to listen, and in the beggars' protest, both Peachum and Brown lose their authority. They both end up before Polly at the bank, joined by Mackie, who has escaped. The three decide together they will run the bank, as it's a safer and more lucrative form of stealing. How can Peachum count on the support of the poor even as he works to fleece them? "They don't know we need them."

You can see the cynicism in the story, as well as the attack on the rise of global capitalism. Brecht rather neatly sides with the proletariat, depicting them as the victims of capitalism, while at the same time despising them, in showing their willingness to be duped. But taken together, we're painted a picture of government, as corrupt as the criminal element, colluding with them to grow rich on the backs of the poor. In the end, the respectable banking system is simply thievery in better clothes, and with better manners.

Pabst is a skilled director, and his experience in silent film serves him well. Pabst understood the importance of sound in cinema, and not just as a means of conveying music or dialogue. The opening credits are terrific; white titles against a black background with a chorus singing over it, plenty of pauses in between titles to let the entire theater go dark, the audience holding onto the music in the absence of light. He also complements the cynical themes of the story with his direction. When Mackie and Polly sing a love song, it's on the docks, with their backs to us, no closeups, the camera held at a distance. Because it isn't a love song, not really, it's a business alliance between two people, each with something to gain. It isn't a naturalistic approach to musical theater. Songs are set apart, bracketed, calling our attention to them as an audience. They're there to do a job, and the characters know it as well.

The time was right for this film, though it wouldn't be for long. The Twenties roared in Europe as well as the

United States, and audiences were ready for not just a new sound, but to make fun of propriety and the status quo. And both the London revival of *The Beggar's Opera* and Brecht and Weill's stage play were hugely popular, putting songs from the production in the air, even before the film premiered. But times were also about to get darker, and by 1933, the film was banned by the Nazis as anti authoritarian.

The Criterion disc also includes a second version of the film, shot for French audiences. It was typical for German filmmakers to shoot a second release of a film for foreign markets; 40% of German films at the time were exports. In this case, Pabst recast the principal characters in the film with French actors, and after shooting a scene for the German production, would then bring in the French cast and film the scene again, same script, same camera setups. But the differences between the two are telling. French studios wanted a more upbeat film, and Pabst cast Albert Préjean as Mackie and Florelle as Polly Peachum - two performers who were known for a lighter stage presence, and brighter singing voices. Pabst made a few editing changes in the French version - titled *L'opéra de quat' sous* - including a scene of mechanical dolls dancing over the opening credits. But his two leads make for a much less cynical pair, and Pabst even lights the set more brightly throughout this production. In addition, the French version is a few minutes shorter, mostly because the tempo of the songs is more upbeat. Where the German Mackie is dangerous, the French Mackie is dapper, and Florelle's takeover of the gang seems like a gay lark in comparison to Neher's steel will. It's an interesting commentary by Pabst on what he believed the two audiences wanted from the film.

∩ ∩ ∩

There's something else about the Criterion version of this film I feel like I have to address. The commentary track on this edition sucks.

I have no idea how many people listen to commentary tracks on DVDs or Blu-Rays, anyway. I suspect few do, and I think as people move to streaming their films, they'll listen to them even less. I was enamored of them when I first made the switch from VHS to DVDs and replayed every new film almost as soon as I'd seen it with the normal soundtrack. Gradually, not so much. An informal polling of my friends seems to reveal that when people *do* listen to a chat track, it's for entertainment purposes. They want to hear stories told about the production from their favorite actors. I think that's a great thing, and can especially recommend the commentary track from Kevin Smith's *Clerks* as one of the funniest.

But part of the deal with *Criterion Tuesdays* was to jump into *all* the features in a Criterion disc, commentary tracks included. With these older films, that usually means chat tracks from film scholars or critics. That's not a bad thing, not at all, and I've learned to be especially grateful when Peter Cowie clocks in for a commentary shift on an Ingmar Bergman film. He's clear, prepared, insightful, and you learn a great deal about the film that enriches viewing. I despise the anti-intellectual, anti-scholar bias that has always been present in the United States, but seems to be particularly aggressive right now. You can learn a lot from professionals who have devoted their minds and their education to film, literature, music – any topic.

But, Lordy. The commentary track on *The Threepenny Opera* is dreadful, and I can't take the chance that some poor hopeful soul will stumble across this one and think that it represents *all* scholarly commentary. Trust me, this one is an outlier.

I won't mention here the names of the two film professors that present the commentary; you're free to look that up for yourself. The first problem is that I think they assume that the viewer is a graduate student in either film or literature. Either that, or they're so used to lecturing their beleaguered students that they no longer know how to communicate with normal people. I've never heard such dense, opaque talk in my life, not even when I was an English major. No concept is presented with clarity, no term defined, we are presumed to be up to speed on all things Brechtian, and all permutations of the word "space." The person who can follow what these men say doesn't need a commentary track to begin with. I suspect one of them might have gone easier on the elitespeak if it weren't for the bullying of the other, and this is where I really lost it with these two. One of the professors was constantly - and I do mean *constantly* - talking over the other. Clearly waiting only for his turn to speak, and eager to interrupt his colleague mid-sentence if he thought a point had been missed or required correcting. The other professor started talking more hurriedly, I think just to be able to get an entire point in, and I expect he was cowed into not using more elementary terms because his "partner" would be ready to jump on him. It stood in particular contrast to the last commentary I listened to - that of *The Thin Red Line* - by three people who had worked together on the production, and were used to a collaborative relationship. These two were just children, and one was a bully. By the time I was literally yelling, "SHUT UP!" at the television, I knew it was time to bail.

So please. Pretty please. If you happen to stumble on this commentary, or if someone close to you does, I beg you to keep in mind this is *not* typical of scholarly critique. This was children in a sandbox. In need of a time out.

Touki bouki

Senegal, 1973. Directed by Djibril Diop Mambéty. 89 minutes, color.

It's interesting how films can expose our own biases. *Touki bouki* is the first film I watched from Criterion's *Martin Scorsese's World Film Project* collection, and really the first African film I'd seen.[66] I had expected something less sophisticated, forgetting that just because filmmakers in less affluent countries lack the resources and the distribution networks wealthier countries have doesn't mean they haven't been studying film all along. It's not that they aren't making films, it's just that their films have little chance of being seen in the West. From its opening shots, *Touki bouki* slapped that ignorance (and arrogance) out of me. Hopefully for good.

---

[66] I'd seen the dubbed version of *The Gods Must Be Crazy* when it was released in the US in 1984, but it's difficult to hear Black voices in that coproduction of South Africa and Botswana (released in Africa in 1980). It's a funny film, but there's more than a whiff of the White Savior motif, and the movie is suspiciously free of any sign of apartheid.

Touki bouki (*The Journey of the Hyena*) is one of the most kinetic films I've ever seen, its style fully supporting the story of a young couple running from poverty, from complacency, from Senegal, to an imagined better life in Paris. Mory (Magaye Niang) and Anta (Mareme Niang) are nearly always in motion, whether on foot, on Mory's motorbike festooned with a bull-horned skull, or a stolen car bespangled with American stars and stripes. But director Djibril Diop Mambéty supports the couple's unease by never resting on a particular style of filmmaking. In the opening scene we see a slow procession of cattle moving out of the savanna, led by a young boy on the back of a bull (Mory as a child, in flashback, perhaps?). It's a stately scene, and typical of the slower pace of African filmmakers of the 1950s and '60s. But we cut to the end of the journey; a horrific documentary-style scene of cattle sliding across the blood-soaked cement floor of a slaughterhouse, their throats being slashed. We're definitely into more French New Wave territory, though Mambéty won't rest there, either, as the camera begins to assume the points of view of Mory and Anta, and we begin even to enter into their fantasy world, in an imagined triumphant return from Paris, flushed with wealth and fame. The soundtrack won't be pinned down either, as Mambéty samples from African music, jazz, and even cabaret.

Touki bouki takes a hard look at the poverty burning through Senegal, from the vast shantytown housing to the incessant search for potable water to the crime that flourishes under these conditions. Mory and Anta see no future for themselves; Anta, as a university student, is even criticized by her family for attempting to better her condition. The two are convinced Paris holds the answer, stubbornly clinging to this dream even as we overhear wealthy French tourists cast slurs on both the country and its people. As they travel to the port of Dakar, Mory stops at the home of a wealthy acquaintance, and while their host showers, Mory steals his clothes, money, and car. The two make it to Dakar and buy passage on a ship, but as they are boarding, Mory hears himself being paged to the captain. Realizing his theft has been found out, Mory leaves Anta on the ship, running off himself in search of the motorbike the couple had abandoned.

The film is a bitter commentary on the state of Senegal government and society, but I think Mambéty is attempting to show us Senegal as both oppressor and victim. He does not forgive his nation for abandoning her children, but he also wants outsiders to see the inevitable human cost that comes from the Western world treating Africa as something to be plundered. The film doesn't let his fellow Senegalese off the hook for their plight, but there are moments of real affection as well, as in a genuinely funny scene where children laugh at the spectacle of two adult women getting into a fight. When Mambéty films women working in the marketplace to scratch out a living, he seems to be both contemptuous of their naivete and respectful of their work ethic. Sometimes you feel the weight on the filmmaker of trying to speak both to his own people and to a wider audience.

Martin Scorsese, in a brief introduction to the film, called it a "cinematic poem," and that may be the best way to describe it. *Touki bouki* was made on a budget of just $30,000, partially funded by the government, and Mambéty reportedly hated to work from a script, preferring to film on the fly. That points to an artist brilliantly improvising, finding his story in circumstance. I think, like all great poets, Mambéty was much smarter than that. Two images in the film stand out to me as the product of thoughtful planning, or of editorial savvy when putting the film together. Both are moments of rest from the frenetic pace.

The first is a scene of Anta and Mory taking a break in their travels, resting to eat and gather their thoughts. Mambéty frames them facing each other at the far ends of the picture, sitting in empty bleachers. They're together, but there's a distance between them, and I think it establishes that while they have the same goal, they are different people, and while they are together now, that may not last. I think that scene also looks ahead to the end of the film, when Anta alone remains on the boat to France, while Mory must stay behind.

And then there's the ocean. As much as Mambéty forces us to look at an urban Senegal, the film is interspersed with beautiful, loving shots of the waves of the Atlantic crashing on Senegal's shores, then gently pulling back to sea. The ocean is both a barrier and an invitation for our couple. In the context of the film, I think the waves are both a dream and a harsh reality, and the camera, while it doesn't stop there too often, lingers when it does. There's poetry in these images, and it's anything but accidental. I don't think these scenes are afterthoughts. I think Mambéty was sophisticated enough as a filmmaker to understand their value in an otherwise fast-paced film.

As Westerners, we might have been forgiven for missing the stories we were never given access to in the past. It's hard to even be aware of films from outside the US, Europe, and Japan when they don't make it to our theaters, aren't written about, and never made it to our television screens. But that's no longer an excuse in the age of digital streaming platforms. Take some time to seek out the films from marginalized nations. Watch them, and then talk about them with your friends. Post about them on social media. There's a world of stories out there. Go find them.

Trances

Morocco, 1981. Directed by Ahmed El Maânouni. 88 minutes, color.

Trances was a surprise when I pulled it out of Volume 1 of Martin Scorsese's World Cinema Project collection; it's a concert film and documentary of a Moroccan pop band. Scorsese discovered the film on late-night New York television while he and Thelma Schoonmaker were editing *The King of Comedy*;[67] the film had been brought to a NYC film festival by Susan Sontag, where it had been picked up by a local station. Scorsese was... well, he didn't say *entranced* by the film, but certainly taken with it, so much that he and Peter Gabriel used the band's music as reference for the soundtrack to *The Last Temptation of Christ*.

The group at the heart of the film is Nass El Ghiwane, which translates as disciples of El Ghiwane, which itself refers to a chanting musical tradition, one based in theater.

---

[67] Scorsese said that in those days he and Schoonmaker liked to edit from about 11 PM to 7 AM because no one would bother them. Having done more than my share of graveyard shifts as a nurse, this hit me right in the feels.

Morocco had won its independence in 1956, and the nation, led by its nascent home-grown film industry, was searching for authentic Moroccan voices, voices not coerced by Western governments or culture. Producer Izza Génini, after seeing the band onstage and its effect on the crowd, knew she - and the Moroccan youth - had found that voice.

What's extraordinary is how much of a following Nass El Ghiwane had picked up, even as Moroccans - like the rest of the world - were listening to ubiquitous Western pop music. Take away the crowds, the arenas, and the microphones, and Nass El Ghiwane is essentially a folk quartet, singing old Sufi poetry to traditional acoustic instruments, drums and strings. At the time of the film, the band members were Omar Sayed (percussion), Larbi Batma (percussion), Allal Yaâla (a fretless banjo), and Abderrahman "Paco" Kirouche (guembri, a three-stringed bass lute). Kirouche (the others were founding members from 1969) stepped in after the death of Boujemâa H'gour; in a section honoring H'gour, we learn it was he who convinced the group to abandon its early Egyptian pop sensibilities (full of love songs in Classic Arabic) to take up *bssat*, Moroccan street theater. And in a polyglot nation, H'gour convinced his bandmates to also cover the struggles of daily life in Moroccan Darija, a dialect of Arabic that has no written form, but is the street language of Casablanca. They became the first group to embrace the common tongue. But Kirouche also made a contribution to the band as a trained *maâlem*, or Gnawa music master, reaching centuries back into the Moroccan past for a music tradition that inspired ecstatic trances in its adherents.

Which leads us to the audience participation in the band's concerts. Whether Nass El Ghiwane is performing in theaters and arenas in Morocco, Tunisia, and France, or with other street musicians in the poorer sections of Casablanca, people come to dance. In the larger venues, they often join the band onstage, and as they ease into the music, begin to enter trances of their own, writhing and gyrating, often falling to the ground insensate. Part of me wanted to be cynical about these audience displays; like Evangelicals speaking in tongues, it comes across as a kind of performance art, fans wanting to prove their devotion by out-trancing or out-babbling their neighbors. Or maybe I'm wrong (on both counts), maybe there's a legitimate spiritual loss of self going on. Either way, there's *something* going on here audiences find worth connecting to, if not actually being swept away, then desperately attempting it.

As a Westerner, accustomed to the scales and rhythms of western music, I have to say that the music is not hard to get into. Even hand-operated drums[68] like the bendir and derbouka (Google them) lend a surprisingly rich and complex sound, perfectly accompanied by the acoustic strings. Honestly, it feels like if the band had even accented the music with contemporary instruments, you'd lose something in the translation. The quartet's clear, but workmanlike voices help to remove the ego of the musicians from the equation, as if they recognize that their job is merely to carry the music to the people. Everything about Nass El

---

[68] Drums without drumsticks. My own term. You're welcome.

Ghiwane seems egoless, which I think is also part of their appeal. Their music is not in any way a barrier to the public, but an invitation.

All this came at the perfect time for the Moroccan film community. Interestingly, Morocco was present at the birth of film, when the Lumière brothers filmed a goatherd there in 1897. But Morocco was used as an "exotic locale" by Western filmmakers from then on, or at least an *idea* of Morocco was; even *Casablanca* was filmed on California studio lots. After WWII, as filmmakers began seeking realism by shooting on location, Morocco became a destination for Alfred Hitchcock and David Lean, among others. But once Moroccans had achieved independence, they were eager to take back their country from foreign voices, and the film community saw documentary as a way to do that. There were fiction films, of course, but Morocco's regulatory film board, the Centre Cinématographique Marocain, began to fund newsreels, so that current events could be covered by Moroccans, not foreigners. Director Ahmed El Maânouni, who had been studying film in Belgium, returned home to make movies, and his debut film, *Alyam alyam* (which featured a song by Nass El Ghawane) became the first Moroccan entry at the Cannes Film Festival. Once producer Génini heard the band perform, and realized the power of a film about them, her choice for a director was clear.

Trances is also far more than just a concert film. The camera follows band members around their home neighborhoods in Casablanca, where we're surprised to find poverty-stricken areas

Western filmmakers ignored. As they walk or drive around town, we're mostly struck by how successfully the band has dodged the kind of groupie-laden pop star fame of their counterparts in the West; they relate to friends and merchants as part of the neighborhood. El Maânouni also cuts in newsreel footage of the suffering and violence of Morocco's past over the music. It's no accident - part of what Nass El Ghiwane is doing is using old music to comment on current political strife, and the director's montage accurately translates that commentary to film.

All that makes for an eye-opening documentary, and is partially the reason when Martin Scorsese founded the World Cinema Project in 2007 to preserve and highlight films from marginalized nations that he selected *Trances* as the first film to be restored. But there's another reason Scorsese - who has directed documentaries on The Band, The Rolling Stones, and Bob Dylan - was attracted to this film. The music.

When you watch this, watch it loud.

Trouble in Paradise

US, 1932. Directed by Ernst Lubitsch. 82 minutes, black and white.

"The Lubitsch Touch."

You keep hearing that term when people talk about the films of Ernst Lubitsch. Other directors are known by weightier terms; "Hitchcockian," "Spielbergian," "Tarantinoesque." With Lubitsch, you just need a touch, a light, winking caress for this auteur to make a film all his own. Something "Hitchcockian," brilliant though it is, can be broken down, analyzed. A 'touch," on the other hand, is pleasantly mysterious, impossible to duplicate. With *Trouble in Paradise*, considered to be among Ernst Lubitsch's most sparkling creations, I'll do my best to get across a sense of his magic.

Lubitsch was the first of the wave of German filmmakers to arrive in Hollywood, which he did in 1923. It isn't an exaggeration to say that he changed the course of American films, turning movies away from the 19th-century melodrama of D.W. Griffith, and showed us that comedy in particular could be lighter and wittier than the Mack Sennett slapsticks. If America is truly a melting pot, Lubitsch's

European sensibilities added spice to the stew. And by "spice," we're of course talking about sex.

Trouble in Paradise is a romantic comedy, perhaps the first non-musical romcom Hollywood produced. At its heart is a love triangle; dashing thief Gaston (Herbert Marshall) is torn between his partner in crime, Lily (Miriam Hopkins), and his mark, wealthy widow Mariette (Kay Francis). Mariette is also hilariously pursued by two ineffective would-be suitors. The first, François (Edward Everett Horton), is told early on in the film, "Marriage is a beautiful mistake, which two people make together." In the very next scene, Mariette tells her other suitor, The Major (Charlie Ruggles), not to take her rejection personally. "Don't be so down-hearted, Major. You're not the only one I don't love. I don't love François, either." Nevertheless, the two men, even as they must know they're hopelessly outclassed, can't seem to bring themselves to give up on the chase. One suspects that each is less afraid of not getting the girl, than of the other actually succeeding.

The way that Lubitsch is able to add tension to the plot is that all three characters in the triangle are immensely likable. The usual stereotype (continued to this day) is to make it clear that one of the pursuers is unsuited to the chased, whether male or female.[69] Both women are tough cookies with their hearts in the right place. One imagines

---

[69] Though not the most current example, I keep thinking of Bill Pullman's Walter gracefully bowing out in *Sleepless in Seattle* to make room for Tom Hanks. Seriously, just naming the character "Walter" is the screenwriter's kiss of death.

that Mariette, while she would enjoy a little romance in her life - from the right man - has given her business and her independence priority. And though she's the wealthy owner of a perfume conglomerate - surely an easy target to Depression-era audiences - she stands firm against her board by refusing to lower worker salaries. Lily is an absolute hoot: blonde, seemingly flighty, but whip smart, especially in matters of human nature. Lily and Gaston work European cities by posing as aristocrats, and Lily seems to relish the game even more than Gaston, who has lived the act so long he probably couldn't drop the role if he tried. And Gaston himself is charming, smart, respectful of competence in any class or gender in which it's to be found, and dismissive of fools of all types. What the three have in common is that they're all aware of the games being played in society and never lie to themselves about their role in those games. The minute characters begin to assume they matter more than they do (as do Mariette's hapless suitors), they become prey. Gaston and Lily are hardly the only thieves in the story; they're just the ones who are honest to themselves about their roles. One way in which Lubitsch establishes his "touch" on the story is that while the three principals are certainly cynical about the world they live in, they're not disillusioned by it. To truly love life, you must look at it head-on.

The way Gaston and Lily work their way into Mariette's confidence tells you a lot about the characters. Early in the film, we find Mariette shopping for a purse:

Salesman: "This one, Madame Colet, is only 3,000 francs."

Mariette: "Oh, no, that's entirely too much! How about that one?"

Salesman: "Oh, this one, Madame. Well, that's 125,000 francs."

Mariette: "But it's beautiful. I'll take it."

When the purse goes missing at the opera (stolen by Gaston, of course), Mariette offers a reward for its return.[70] Gaston, in character as an aristocrat, tells Mariette he found it behind a statue at the opera. There's a pause, and Gaston gallantly comes to the rescue:

Gaston: "It embarrasses you to offer me the 20,000 francs reward?"

Mariette: (gratefully) "Yes."

Gaston: "Don't be embarrassed. I'll take it. I need the money. I wish I were in a position to ignore

---

[70] In a scene that Lubitsch left out of the final cut, a down-and-out woman brings a purse to Mariette - clearly not the right one - and seeing the woman's circumstances, Mariette tells her it's the missing purse and gives her the reward. She then tosses the purse on a chair, atop a pile of other returned purses.

the whole matter, but you know, madame, the stock market, a bank crash - to make a long story short, I'm a member of the nouveau poor."

Mariette finds Gaston's "honesty" refreshing, as Gaston, a keen judge of character, knew she would. She hires Gaston as her personal secretary, and Gaston brings Lily in as an assistant. But Mariette begins to fall for the elegant and able Gaston (he thoughtfully increases the burglary premium on her insurance to cover the amount he and Lily plan to steal from her), and Gaston begins to fall for her, too. Gaston, in the end, is forced into not a "romcom" choice, but a choice of adult life, between two women he loves.

Lubitsch released *Trouble in Paradise* just in time. The Hollywood studios had created the Production Code two years earlier - a rigid set of guidelines designed to sanitize and censor their own films to appease religious groups - but it would be two years until The Hays Code (as it came to be known, after the former US Postmaster General who ran the office) really developed any sort of teeth. It would be the last time Lubitsch would be able to so flagrantly flaunt the sexuality in the film. It was bad enough that the film featured an unmarried couple who lived in sin, much less that the couple were lawbreakers who remain unpunished for their crimes. But from the opening titles, Lubitsch winks at us broadly, the words "Trouble in" appearing over a graphic of a bed (with two pillows!), holding for a second or two to imply "trouble in bed" before finally adding the word "Paradise." A scene with Gaston and Lily kissing on a couch in their suite ends in a dissolve to an empty couch, implying the two have moved onto the bedroom to finish what they started. And there's this exchange between Mariette and Gaston as the sexual tension between them is mounting:

Mariette: "When a lady takes her jewels off in a gentleman's room, where does she put them?"

Gaston: "On the - on the night table."

Mariette: "But I don't want to be a lady."

But it wasn't just the European ease with sexuality that Lubitsch brought to Puritan America. Lubitsch refused to shoot any scene in a way he thought boring or conventional. Everything had to be fresh. Take the opening of the film, after that wonderful title sequence. The film opens in Venice. What every other filmmaker did - and most still do - is establish a shot of a famous landmark in a city, the Eiffel Tower for Paris, say, or Big Ben for London. Then cut to a middle shot establishing a building, then to a character. Lubitsch does it backwards. Our opening shot is of a man picking up a garbage can. He then carries it to a gondola, and dumps the contents onto a pile of rubbish in the craft, then boards, pulling away into the canals, singing as he goes. Only then does the camera sweep over to Lily and Gaston's suite. It's perfect: we know where we are, and we have a cheeky image of the urban reality of a romantic city. When working with screenwriter Samson Raphaelson, Lubitsch would always look for a different way of presenting a scene than the tired way it had always been done. In the commentary track, Lubitsch biographer Scott Eyman tells us that whenever the two were stuck, Lubitsch would say, "Write the scene dull," and then they'd pick apart the standard approach, often finding novelty from that starting point.[71]

Trouble in Paradise is an absolute, sparkling gem. If you take American cinema before and after this film, you can see the influence Lubitsch commanded, especially in what would come to be called the "screwball comedy." Lubitsch gave us films that dripped with wit, both visually and in dialogue. Most people have never heard of him, which is a shame. But if you enjoy a particularly smart romantic comedy, take a moment to thank Ernst Lubitsch for freeing American films, even if it was to be only briefly, from their melodramatic and puritanical roots.

---

[71] It's good advice, applicable to many other fields. Including writing. Lubitsch seems to be telling me to just get something down on paper, monkey with it later. I suspect he would have little patience with "writer's block."

Two-Lane Blacktop

US, 1971. Directed by Monte Hellman. 103 minutes, color.

There was a period of time in American film, beginning around 1967 with *The Graduate* and lasting only four or five years, when the youth counterculture had their say. It wouldn't take long for the Hollywood studio system to take notice and wrest control back, returning to exploiting this audience instead of listening to them. But for a brief flash as the 1960s matured into the '70s, we had a series of beautiful and urgent low- to mid-budget films. *Easy Rider. Vanishing Point. Harold and Maude. Medium Cool. Billy Jack.* And this week's film, *Two-Lane Blacktop*.

If you haven't heard of this film, or director Monte Hellman, it's because Universal never gave *Two-Lane Blacktop* the release it deserved. In a documentary on the disc, Hellman writes this off to studio politics, the one executive who believed in the project running into a studio head who preferred to see it fail. It's the only explanation that makes sense, and it's a pity.

There's not much of a plot; the movie can be summed up as a coast-to-coast race between two cars. The cars themselves even appear as part of the cast in the credits: The Car (1955 Chevrolet) and The GTO (1970 Pontiac). But the human cast (no character in this production is referred to by name) is a snapshot of early '70s pop culture. Singer/songwriter James Taylor, in his only screen appearance is The Driver. Beach Boys drummer Dennis Wilson is The Mechanic. And you know what? They're pretty good, particularly Taylor as a quiet, alienated (and alienating) soul. Warren Oates is GTO, one of the only established actors Hellman cast in the film (along with a brief appearance by Harry Dean Stanton as a hitchhiker). And Laurie Bird as The Girl, a model at the time, only 17, her career cut short by suicide only eight years later.

In fact, my plot summary falls apart because it implies a resolution; there is none. Not only is the race never completed, it becomes irrelevant nearly as soon as it has begun. Couple that with the fact that the reason none of these characters have names is because none of them (apart from GTO) talk that much[72], and it sounds like the makings of an awful film-school project. There aren't even any set pieces of exciting drag races. But surprisingly, we find

---

[72] Although James Taylor gets one of the coolest lines of the film. While negotiating a race with a hot rod driver (played by screenwriter Rudolph Wurlitzer), The Driver says, "Make it three yards, motherfucker, and we'll have an automobile race." His delivery is so cooly casual, that in re-watching it twice, with each of two different commentary tracks, it's the only place in the film where both sets of commentators (Hellman and filmmaker Allison Anders on one and Wurlitzer and author David N. Meyer on the other) pause their commentary to appreciate Taylor's delivery.

ourselves in good hands, and not just because of the naturalistic performances of the cast, and a tight script. Hellman talks of filling *Two-Lane Blacktop* with what he calls the "connective tissue" of film, the scenes in between the action where characters process and react to the events filmed stories usually focus on.

That also keeps the film from becoming just another disposable look at the male-dominated street racing world, authentic though it appears. The Driver and The Mechanic never speak to each other except in coded motorhead jargon, which is also true of their interactions with GTO. It's a closed community, one that literally doesn't have the language to discuss relationships outside the racing world. The Girl not only changes the dynamics of these interactions, but she becomes the catalyst for all of the film's motion, as she introduces something the men are missing from their car culture. She's also the only truly free character in the film. When she enters *Two-Lane Blacktop*, The Driver and The Mechanic are eating in a diner, and we see her get out of a van pulling up outside the window. She unloads a couple bags, spots their Chevy, and then simply gets in the back, apparently unconcerned about who's driving the car or where it's going. When she leaves the film, it's just as quick, on the back of a motorcycle, and when she can't find a place to put her army surplus duffel bag, she simply leaves it on the side of the road.

The American Road, thanks in part to Jack Kerouac, is supposed to be a romantic place. It's not for these trio of men; it's a place that offers no solutions, only constantly reminds our characters of what's missing. Both The Driver and GTO talk to The Girl about taking her to Florida, but without her, they just don't seem to see the point of settling anywhere. And GTO, though he first comes across as confident and assured, picks up every hitchhiker he encounters, desperate for human contact, even as he does all the talking (and his stories keep changing). We suspect he is finally telling the truth when he begins to open up to The Driver about his loss of a career and a family, but the Driver abruptly cuts him off with a curt, "I don't want to hear it. It's not my problem." Without The Girl, even The Driver can't seem to handle human connection.

I think the key to *Two-Lane Blacktop* working so well is in Hellman's editing, in stitching the film together. Hellman spent his early years as a filmmaker working with the man who seems to be responsible for a generation of great filmmakers, director and producer of B movies, Roger Corman. Corman used to make the awful kind of low-budget horror, science fiction, and exploitation films that would show up on drive-in screens across the country, and he was always pushing his filmmakers for something - fast! - he could get into circulation. The second film for a drive-in double feature - the "B" movie - usually ran about 60 minutes long; longer than that and a filmmaker couldn't produce the film a week Corman needed. But when Corman sold these films to independent television stations, they needed to have a run time of 70-75 minutes. So Corman initially hired Hellman to go through footage Corman and others had shot for the B films, and find 10-15 minutes of extra story. It sounds like a great hands-on way to learn editing, the kind of rote-sounding craft that filmmakers need to learn.

Hellman also had a good eye for the "happy accidents" that come from the filming constraints of a low-budget feature. The filming of *Two-Lane Blacktop* - like the movie itself - was a road trip that needed to be shot in sequence. At one Oklahoma service station, rain clouds were gathering the day of shooting, and Hellman needed to decide whether to start shooting in the rain and hope it would continue, or wait a day or two for the rain to pass through. Hellman shot in the rain, and noticed that the weather added movement to the film, as characters had to run from cars to buildings and back. As the rain let up, rather than reshoot, he talked the local fire department into turning their hoses onto the set so he could keep that scene in the film.

All that to say, where *Two-Lane Blacktop* might have become something navel-gazing and intolerable, it actually moves with a quiet yearning that I found relatable and beautiful. It also never hurts to fill your movie with scenery moving past car windows.

Hellman at one point quoted the poet Marianne Moore, talking about why she avoids air travel. He recalled her saying something like, "You can get on a plane in New York and five hours later you're in San Francisco, and you don't know any more when you got there than when you left." It's a great statement about seeing this country at eye level. I think every American ought to have the opportunity to travel coast-to-coast, or border-to-border, or at least 1,000 miles by car or bus, or even train.

Road trips have always been a part of my life, and my own Great Road Trip happened in 2016, when I drove with my dog, Hugo, from Danville, Pennsylvania to my new "forever" home in Olympia, Washington. 2,828.8 miles in five days. I had to take the interstates because of time constraints, but that didn't even matter. Sure the same fast-food and chain restaurants and motels dot the entire route, and people read the same books, watch the same movies, and (often) listen to the same music across America. But the people change. And the skies change. And the land changes, especially as you see plains corduroy into hills, hills heighten into mountains. And you can find spots of individuality, like the guys at the Indiana rest stop I bought a plate of shawarma from, their stand planted between a McDonald's and a Sbarro's. You get a sense of something bigger than yourself, different from yourself that air travel can't give you, because you *experience* the change as it's happening.

This is what *Two-Lane Blacktop* gives us a feel of. We may or may not find answers on the road, but the getting out of our environs forces us to see what's different, and to compare. It's a pity Universal shelved the film after the briefest release (oddly, Hellman found the film banned in the Soviet Union, sort of pleased he'd managed to offend capitalists and communists alike with the same movie). I think this film sums up the poetry and bittersweet emotions of the road trip, and is one of the few that doesn't lock us into a specific era. Watch this film. And go on a road trip. As GTO tells us:

"Those satisfactions are permanent."

Ugetsu

Japan, 1953. Directed by Kenji Mizoguchi. 97 minutes, black and white.

Here's the thing about Kenji Mizoguchi, the thing I can't get out of my head: On the one hand, he's an elder statesman of Japanese cinema, his formative work done in Japan's silent era in the 1920s, a filmmaker Akira Kurosawa looked up to, and a man who was known as being particularly gifted in telling the stories of women. On the other hand, according to *everyone* who knew him, he was an enthusiastic patron of brothels. In fact, at some point in his career he was attacked by a prostitute, and either stabbed in the back with a knife, or slashed with a razor. Tokuzo Tanaka, the first assistant director on *Ugetsu*, talked in an interview about going out for drinks with Mizoguchi one night, and after a few, Mizoguchi took off his shirt to show off the scar. The legendary director, so demanding on set, was grinning. "You can't make films about women," Mizoguchi pronounced, "if you don't have one of these!"

I don't know what to make of that. In reading what I wrote just now, I make him sound like the Bill Clinton of

Japan; a man whose love of women was both his greatest asset and his greatest liability. Maybe that was the case with Mizoguchi. Maybe his relationship with sex workers wasn't about exerting power. Or maybe it was, and he developed empathy in spite of himself, or in atonement for his behaviors. Or maybe his reputation as a voice for women only holds up in comparison to other male filmmakers. Mizoguchi describes his specialty in telling women's stories as a "commercial decision"; when he got his start, there was already a director at his first studio who had a reputation for making "men's movies," and Mizoguchi was told to balance out the other man's films. "But over time," Mizoguchi said, "my interests deepened."

Let's look at *Ugetsu* together, and you can tell me.

Ugetsu is based on two stories published in 1776 by Akinari Ueda from his nine-story collection *Tales of Moonlight and Rain*: "The House in the Thicket" and "A Serpent's Lust." But Mizoguchi also flavored his film with a tale from the West: "How He Got the Legion of Honor" by Guy de Maupassant.[73] The three stories are combined and set in 16th-century Japan, a chaotic time of civil war, in which society had all but broken down, and a time that Mizoguchi often revisited in his films. Genjuro (Masayuki Mori) and his brother-in-law Tobei (Sakae Ozawa) are poor farmers in Nakanogo, a village on the shores of Lake Biwa. Genjuro also has a pottery kiln, and when he's able to sell

---

[73] All three stories are reprinted in a booklet included with the disc.

some pieces in a nearby village, the silver he earns fills him with ambition to sell his goods in a larger town across the lake so that he can better the lives of his wife, Miyagi (Kinuyo Tanaka) and his toddler son. Tobei also has dreams of his own, to take advantage of the war spreading through the land to become a samurai, much to the contempt of his wife, Ohama (Mitsuko Mito). When a rogue army sweeps through Nakanogo, both families are forced to flee and cross Lake Biwa in an abandoned boat. But halfway across, a derelict boat appears out of the fog, and its lone boatman, dying, warns the families of pirates on the lake. Alarmed, they return to their village shores, but only briefly - the plan is to drop the women off while the men continue on to sell Genjuro's pottery. Ohama, however, refuses to part with Tobei, and Miyagi begs Genjuro not to leave his family. Genjuro swears he'll return when he has sold his pottery and leaves his family by the shore, with Tobei and Ohama to cross the lake with him.

The three are able to cross without incident, and Tobei immediately approaches a lord asking to join his army. Tobei is ridiculed and dismissed; clearly no samurai, he is told that he will at least need armor and a spear for them to consider his offer. The three set up in a marketplace, and begin to sell Genjuro's pottery; it's a wartime economy, and Genjuro finds plenty of business, with Tobei and Ohama helping him. But the moment Tobei receives his share, he runs off to an armorer, eluding Ohama, and purchases the necessary equipment. Once procured, he runs off, Ohama searching for him.

Meanwhile, noblewoman Lady Wakasa (Machiko Kyo) stops by Genjuro's stall with her servant. She orders several pieces and asks him to bring them to her at the Kutsuki mansion that night. Genjuro does so and finds himself in a luxurious estate. Lady Wakasa explains to Genjuro that she and her servants are all that are left of a great house; her father was killed by a marauding army. She dances, charming Genjuro, and the ghostly voice of her father is heard approving of the match. Lady Wakasa seduces Genjuro and convinces him to marry her.[74]

Back in Nakanogo, invading armies are once again laying waste to the village, and as Miyagi flees with her son on her back, she is robbed and wounded by rogue soldiers, staggering away with her child. Ohama, still on the hunt for her husband, is likewise attacked by soldiers near a Buddhist temple, where she is taken inside and raped.

Tobei, now part of a lord's army, is out in the field, and witnesses an enemy general, mortally wounded, asking a vassal to behead him. The vassal does so, and Tobei ambushes him, killing him with his spear. Tobei returns to his lord with the general's head, claiming he (Tobei) had killed him. Tobei's lord doesn't believe him, but says he will reward him anyway. Tobei asks for a horse and soldiers of his own, and receiving them, finally has what he has sought from the war.

---

[74] This wasn't the first time these two actors appeared as a couple on screen. Three years earlier, both appeared in Kurosawa's *Rashomon* as the ill-fated samurai and his wife.

Genjuro finds himself living a life of ease and pleasure with Lady Wakasa. But returning from town one day to the estate, he is stopped by a Buddhist priest, who is alarmed at Genjuro's appearance. The priest tells Genjuro that Lady Wakasa is in fact a ghost, and is in the process of stealing his life and soul. The priest paints Sanskrit texts on Genjuro's skin, and Genjuro travels back to the mansion. When the writings on his body are discovered by Lady Wakasa and her servant, they reveal themselves to be spirits, and flee from him as he attacks with a sword from the house. The next morning, he is discovered by townspeople in the middle of the ruin of the Kitsuki mansion. With nothing but the clothes on his back, Genjuro begins his journey home.

Tobei is also making his way home to show off his new status. His men convince him to stop at a brothel for the night. Inside, Tobei finds Ohama, now a fallen woman, working there to survive. Tobei, heartbroken, buys her freedom and promises to take her home.

Genjuro has finally returned to Nakanogo and finds Miyagi and their son (now a few years older) eager to welcome him home. Genjuro is ashamed of his absence from them, but Miyagi, delighted to finally have him home, will not hear of his sins. They fall asleep as a family, but in the morning Miyagi is nowhere to be found. Instead, a village elder stops by, relieved to find Genjuro's son safe, but surprised to see Genjuro. When Genjuro asks if he's seen Miyagi, the elder replies that she was killed by soldiers years before and that he has been caring for their son all this time. The film ends with Genjuro rededicated to his rural life and his son placing an offering on Miyagi's grave.

Is Mizoguchi telling us that the men should have listened to their wives all along? I don't think it's that simple. Mizoguchi recognizes that these two men aren't wrong to be ambitious, especially if it means providing for their family; Miyagi is at first quite pleased with the silver Genjuro earns with his pottery locally but is also quick to tell him that there are more important things than riches. The men seem to think it is their responsibility to rise higher in this world, and I don't think Mizoguchi is telling us that they're wrong. But what they're failing to do is understand how their ambitions affect the women in their lives. They cannot see past their own aims and will not face the consequences for the people they leave behind, people who do not have the means to chase dreams of their own. *Ugetsu* is not about the dreams of men, it's about the suffering of the women they will not consult, will not hear.

And yet, there's no melodrama in the film. This isn't about women needing to be *protected*, it's about women needing to be *considered*. The women of *Ugetsu* aren't trying to avoid life's suffering, they're trying to manage it and do their best under it. There's a moment when Miyagi (who we now know to be a spirit) turns away from her prodigal husband with a bittersweet smile. It isn't that she's forgiven him; we'll never know whether she has or not. But even as she stands on the threshold of a world beyond, a world without her son, she knows that she has arranged - even from beyond the grave - that her son will grow up with his father. The smile is for herself, knowing she has fulfilled her duty as a mother.

Whether Genjuro has fully realized his transgression or fully appreciates her sacrifice is beside the point.

The women are the stronger characters because they are the ones looking at life clearly. They do not seek to elude suffering in this life, they seek to manage it and to shepherd their families through it. Where the men (and Genjuro in a very literal sense) seek escape in fantasy, it is the women who know they can't afford not to look at the world as it is.

Kenji Mizoguchi made a career out of telling stories from a feminist standpoint. Whether that was a perspective forced on him or whether it's something he brought with him - whether to his films or his brothels - is something I can't answer. But I hope to call this film to the attention - even if just the attention of my friends - because I think it begs a larger discussion. I would love to benefit from the insights of the women in my own life who have seen this film.

This is why I write these essays. If it's just me talking, I won't learn a thing. If it's just film scholars talking, I'll only learn so much. The purpose of these films - the purpose of all art - is to get us folks on the ground talking to each other. *Ugetsu* is a great film for getting this discussion going. And if it comes from a flawed, human filmmaker, so much the better.

Vivre sa vie

France, 1962. Directed by Jean-Luc Godard. 83 minutes, black and white.

It's okay not to like great films.

Sorry, I was talking to myself.

I need that reminder from time to time because you can get - "bullied" is maybe too harsh a word, maybe not - *compelled* to think there's something wrong with you if you're not enjoying a film or a director that is universally praised. And the praise heaped on Jean-Luc Godard is voluminous. As it should be; the man is a giant not only in French cinema, but across the globe. There isn't a filmmaker alive who hasn't been influenced by him in some way. Before we get into *Vivre sa vie*, it's worth spending a little time on Godard and the French New Wave.

The French New Wave refers to a new style of filmmaking that came out of France, beginning in the post-WWII period, when the French were freed from Nazi oversight and when a flood of Western film - held back while the Germans occupied Paris - deluged French shores, in particular the *film noir* of Hollywood. It took a while for

French filmmakers to digest all this, but in the late 1950s, a new generation of filmmakers appeared who rejected the safe, historical stories of the past, along with their attention to aesthetics. These new filmmakers, of whom Godard was the most prominent (and productive), began to espouse realism in film and take a low-budget, almost guerilla-style approach to their work. These films weren't about beauty, or about audiences being comfortable; they were full of ideas - personal essays - and they began to experiment with the relationship between filmmaker and viewer. Many of the New Wave filmmakers, notably Godard himself, had come from a background not of film or painting, but of writing. It was in many ways a case of film critics taking over the medium.

Now, here's why that's so important: Every art form, from painting to literature to music - *every* serious art - has a moment when its artists step back and look at not only what they are saying, but *how* it is being said. This is where art theory, or music theory, come in. It's "meta" - it's when an art form looks into itself and asks itself basic questions. What makes my art different from the others? What "truths" does my art address more directly than others? Why am I expressing myself in a symphony and not a novel? What can I say with a short story that I can't say with a poem? That may all sound well and good - and very intellectual. But I believe that is the moment when an art form *becomes* an art form, evolving from the popular entertainment it had been. And I believe this was cinema's moment.

It wasn't the dawn of film theory exactly; Sergei

Eisenstein had dabbled in it with his theory of montage, and the whole Italian neorealist crowd was having their own movement. But the French took it to a whole new level, and then they wrote about it, incessantly, in articles in the new (in 1951) film magazine *Cahiers du cinéma*, and (being French) audiences talked and talked and *talked* about what they had seen. I credit the New Wave filmmakers with being unafraid to stand up and proclaim movies to be Art, at a time when Hollywood (perhaps in deference to American anti-intellectualism) was terrified of the term. The New Wave directors not only felt that their films deserved greater intellectual rigor; they felt film in general demanded it.

In *Vivre sa vie* (*My Life to Live*), we're going to see those influences in a number of ways. The film is set in twelve "tableaux," small scenes of a Parisian shop girl and aspiring actress, Nana (Anna Karina, who was married to Godard at the time), as she descends into prostitution. There's almost no actual sex in the film; most of it is the transactional uneasy negotiations with clients and cafe conversations with pimps, fellow prostitutes, and her former husband. Most of the film involves Nana desperately trying to hold onto some control over her life, even as she is ceding control of her body to men. Godard opens the film with a quote from Montaigne - "Lend yourself to others, but give yourself to yourself" - but it's clear that Nana has little of her own to hold onto.

Part of New Wave filmmaking was to never lie to yourself or to your audience, meaning that you should never let the audience forget that they are watching not reality, but a filmed version of it. The film opens with a closeup profile of

Nana, then a shot of her facing the camera, then the other profile, over snippets of a melancholic minor theme that will play sparingly over the film. It looks like mug shots. But it also looks like an actor's screen tests. Whichever, it's far from a naturalistic opening, and the film is continually calling attention to itself *as* a film, as in the moments when Nana looks directly into the camera. I mentioned that the film is full of conversations, and each one is filmed in a different style, Godard seemingly experimenting with film's most pervasive convention. The first time we see Nana after the opening credits she's in conversation with a man sitting next to her at a counter, and the camera moves from the back of one head as they talk to the other. Godard might be bringing us into the scene, as if we're standing behind them in a crowded restaurant, unable to see their faces. The next conversation is done with an entirely different camera angle and editing style, Godard reminding us that we aren't watching two people talking, but a *film* of two people talking.

And then there are the moments, without explanation, where *Vivre sa vie* becomes a silent film. Nana actually attends a silent film early in the movie, a viewing of *The Passion of Joan of Arc* in a Paris theater when she has nowhere else to go. It's a beautiful scene, as Nana's tears mirror Joan's. But the intertitles in the silent film suddenly become subtitles, and later in *Vivre sa vie* all sound cuts out of the film in two spots and the characters' conversation appears subtitled. It's as if Godard is constantly interrogating us in the audience to see if we're keeping up with what he's trying to do. Or at least keep us aware of the artificial nature of film.

This was all radically new filmmaking, and no matter how you reacted, it couldn't be ignored. Godard was challenging filmmakers all over the world, and for many, it was liberating. It opened up an entirely new dry of expressing ideas, freeing directors (and actors, screenwriters, cinematographers and the rest) from the genre conventions that dictated how stories were to be told. Even if you went on making films the way you always did, that became a choice in itself. And in the United States, young filmmakers, like Martin Scorsese and Brian De Palma and Frances Ford Coppola, were emboldened to consider the art they served beyond merely its commercial possibilities. Really, the New Wave was a seismic shift, a turning point for movies as Art.

But that doesn't necessarily make them entertaining. *Vivre sa vie* has moments of great beauty and tenderness, to be sure. There are moments as I watch how Godard frames Karina, lingers on her, when I think, "This is a man in love with a woman, given an excuse to just stare." But, honestly, a lot of it is mystifying. It's like attending Stravinsky's *Rite of Spring*, or wandering into a museum of modern art without having studied the works. You don't know what's going on. I appreciate *Vivre sa vie*. But watching it is like feeling locked out of a film I'm trying to understand. It becomes too easy to classify Godard, or Truffaut, or Resnais, as "filmmakers that make me feel stupid."

That's a mistake, but it's a mistake that can be forgiven when no one else seems to be writing about how frustrating it can be to watch New Wave movies. It's not that you or I are stupid, it's that clear communication isn't happening. Part of that, honestly, is by design of the filmmakers who wanted to keep audiences off-balance, to shake them out of comfort and complacency. Part of that was these filmmakers admittedly flying by the seats of their pants, using the process of making movies to help *them* get a handle on ideas that weren't fully fleshed out. It's okay for each of us to like what we like. It's okay not to get it.

But the one thing I won't do is dismiss Godard. I value my jaunts outside my comfort zone; they keep me on my toes, and they keep me humble, reminding me that I will always have something to learn. And as a fan of Scorsese and Tarantino and Anderson and a dozen other directors, I have nothing but gratitude for the New Wave influences that enrich their films. So every few months I'll return to *Vivre sa vie*, or *Breathless*, or Truffaut's *The 400 Blows* to see if distance will show me anything new. Likely not. But I never know when I'll see an echo of these films in a contemporary picture, which might be a key to unlocking one or both. At the very least, it'll give me the chance to turn to my dog and say, "That's an homage to Godard."

She, at least, thinks I'm brilliant.

The Wages of Fear

France, 1953. Directed by Henri-Georges Clouzot. 147 minutes, black and white.

The Wages of Fear has no right to be as good as it is, not with a running time of nearly two and a half hours. At its heart it's a suspense thriller, and the rule with them seems to be you get in, you get out, you don't give your audience too much time to relax. In an interview on the disc, assistant director Michel Romanoff quotes American director John Frankenheimer as saying that the car chase is cinema in its purest form. That's essentially what this movie comes down to: two trucks carrying nitroglycerine over 300 miles through the Mexican jungle. But director Henri-Georges Clouzot gives his actors plenty of room to shine, and his mise en scène is....

Crap. I'd made it this far without using the term "mise en scène," but the damned thing was going to pop up sooner or later, anyway. Fine. Let's get in the mud with this most elusive film term, even harder to pin down than "film noir" (and *of course* this film has plenty of noir elements in it, too).

Mise en scène literally translates to "placing on stage." It refers to literally everything that appears in front of the camera. Actors, props, sets, lighting, composition, costumes, hair and makeup... everything, even sound. Basically it's all the stuff you see and hear in a movie scene apart from the script itself. It's all the visual cues that support the mood or the themes of a film. Good mise en scène supports what the filmmakers are trying to communicate in their film, bad mise en scène ignores it. Great films (and great filmmakers) use mise en scène to bring you into the film, make it real for you while you're watching.

Clouzot was terrific at mise en scène. He was obsessive about every detail of his films, and he wasn't above bullying his actors and crew on set for those details - a documentary included with the film is entitled *Henri-Georges Clouzot: The Enlightened Tyrant* if that gives you any clue as to his temperament.[75] The reason the whole mise en scène discussion comes up on this movie is that the story takes place in the wilds of Mexico, when in fact the entire thing was filmed in the south of France. Clouzot had made a honeymoon trip to Brazil with the intention of making a

---

[75] Clouzot had an amazing gift for pissing people off. One of his early films, *Le Corbeau*, released in 1943, managed to piss off both the Vichy regime *and* the left-wing Resistance, as well as the Catholic Church. In a trial after WWII, Clouzot was banned from going on a movie set or even holding a film camera *for life*. Eventually, letters from other filmmakers got his sentence reduced to two years. I was unable to find out if any actors he had worked with rallied to his support. Also, you gotta love the French for taking their movies so seriously they might put you on trial for yours.

documentary that never panned out,[76] but returned to recreate the town of Las Piedras largely from memory. And it seems like he got every detail, from the casting to the costumes to the light spot-on.

Consider the opening scene. Our first glimpse isn't of the town, but of some cockroaches tied together by string in some rocky soil. The camera pulls back to reveal a filthy child - dressed only in a grubby shirt - pulling at them, torturing them. We hear the call of a shaved ice vendor and the kid gets up and takes a few steps in the direction of a mule-drawn cart, then stops, apparently realizing he doesn't have any money, anyway. When he returns to the cockroaches, there's a vulture standing over them.

The scene, filmed in harsh glare, tells us many things without a word. It's hot and dry. We're in a place of poverty, no paved roads, the children without clean attire or proper playthings. And life is cheap. As the camera moves through the town, we see other things: men sitting idle, seeking shade. A man, bored, pelting a tied-down dog with pebbles. No motion, except for a woman on her knees in a cafe, scrubbing the floor.

Las Piedras is a town of waiting, where life has come to a standstill. I'm reminded of Casablanca from the 1942 Michael Curtiz picture, except the politics that holds the people here is poverty. It's a Mexican town, but most of those trapped seem to be European and American expatriates. There's a Frenchman, Mario (Yves Montand), soon to be joined by a

---

[76] Guess why? That's right! He pissed off the Brazilian authorities, this time for filming people in poverty! Ding ding ding ding!

countryman, Jo (Charles Vanel), who arrives on the daily plane. Jo has to bribe the local customs agent for a visa; he's arrived from Paris under mysterious circumstances, and apparently with little more than the clothes on his back. Later, we'll meet Bimba (Peter Van Eyck), a German, and the Italian Luigi (Folco Lulli). All want to get out of Las Piedras, all dream of getting home. But that takes money (the roads are bad and there is no train, making the plane the only means out). And there is no work in the town.

But just outside the town is an American oil facility - Southern Oil Company. It's run by Bill O'Brien (William Tubbs), and the workers there are unionized Americans who stay close to each other. The film was attacked by American critics as being anti-American, but I think Clouzot is painting with a broader brush, attacking colonialism and capitalist exploitation no matter where it originates. It turns out that Jo and O'Brien have some questionable past together, but when Jo tries to use their history to blackmail a job out of O'Brien, it seems the financial might of the Southern Oil Company has washed away his sins.

The plot gets going when three hundred miles away, a fire breaks out at another SOC facility. The only way to get it under control is by concussing it with an explosion of nitroglycerin (no, I don't know how that works, either), which the distant plant doesn't have. The Las Piedras site has more than enough of the stuff, but none of the safety riggings or coolers required from keeping the highly volatile explosive from going off if dropped or mishandled. Because of that, the SOC can't use their own unionized employees to transport 200 gallons of NTG in jerry cans, so they turn to the desperate locals offering four men $2,000 each to drive two trucks spaced thirty minutes apart over bumpy roads, around hairpin turns, over dilapidated bridges, and through the jungles. Why two trucks? Because the odds of even one of them making it through are slim. Why the locals? Because no one will miss them if they're killed. No one who matters, anyway. And suddenly, we're reminded of the boy with the cockroaches in the first scene of the film.

For an hour and a half, we follow Mario and Jo in one truck, Luigi and Bimba in the other, white-knuckled as they encounter obstacles along the way, all the while never knowing when a single pothole will end their existence before they even know what hit them. It's a test of nerves, as well as a testament to their desperation (when one man fails to make the cut after a driving test, he hangs himself, knowing this was his last best chance out of Las Piedras). But Clouzot has used the hour leading up to the journey well. There's a scene before the news of the fire reaches the men, where a bored and nasty Jo confronts Luigi and his friends in a bar. We know Jo has a gun, and Clouzot plays out the scene, building tension, following the footsteps of Jo pacing to Luigi's table in the silenced bar. Luigi is set to go after Jo with a bottle, but stops when he sees the gun, and Clouzot doesn't let Luigi or us off the hook for a while. Jo talks about the gun not being lethal, but a man's nerve, and suddenly pushes the pistol into Luigi's hand. It takes the astonished Luigi a moment to decide he doesn't have what it takes to shoot a man face-to-face (and later we learn Jo has done exactly that to another man who had been chosen as a driver ahead of him). The scene reeks of tension and gives us a preview of what we'll be feeling as the trucks begin their journey. It also prepares us for what fear does to a man, as it's Jo who cracks under the pressure.

All of this done in a noirish palette of black and white, filmed in a realistic style that allows for no sentimentality, which makes the men's suffering all the worse. None of these drivers are saints - Luigi is really the only one with likable qualities - but their suffering is what earns them our compassion. No one deserves to have their life treated so carelessly, no matter what they've done. Though he's filming a journey, Clouzot keeps the camera inside the truck cabs for long periods, claustrophobic. We're trapped with these men as they're trapped in their circumstances, and after a while you can practically smell the sweat and grime and fear on the characters.

The Wages of Fear is a terrific film, losing none of its punch over the years. A simple, direct conflict and scrupulous attention to every detail of the production will give this film a shelf life as long as there are desperate people and others willing to exploit desperation. Now that you're familiar with mise en scène, keep an eye out for it, in the movies and television you watch, even ads. Look at what in the picture supports the mood a director is trying to create, or look for the things that distract from it. Look at costumes, look at the walls or the scenery behind a character. This is why I buy movies and watch them more than once. This is the fun part, once the story has been told, in figuring out what tricks the filmmakers use to tell their tales.

War and Peace

USSR, 1966-67. Directed by Sergei Bondarchuk. 422 minutes, color.

Let's address the elephant in the cineplex and get it out of the way: That's not a misprint, the running time of *War and Peace* is just over seven hours. But no one expected audiences to take in the whole film in one sitting - it was released in four parts over two years (similarly, the Leo Tolstoy novel was originally published serially). So I didn't sit down for a marathon, instead watching the film over three days. Actually, not a lot different from binging a season of *Game of Thrones*, or the extended cuts of *The Lord of the Rings* films, as at least two of my friends like to do on Christmas Day. Still, I was kinda glad there wasn't a commentary track to double my viewing time.

Tolstoy's novel has been embedded in the Russian soul and psyche so thoroughly that it's hard to believe it was written "only" in 1867, and yet, this was the first attempt to film the book since the beginning of the sound era of Russian film. There had been several versions in the silent era, but that was pre-Soviet, and while the book was fine, Leo

Tolstoy had run afoul of the state with his spiritual and political beliefs later in life; nothing official was said, but under Stalin, Soviet artists had enough on their plates without taking chances. So it wasn't until the "Khrushchev Thaw" beginning in the mid-1950s (a period of relaxed censorship under Nikita Khrushchev) that Soviet filmmakers began to breathe a little easier. And the timing couldn't have been better, because Hollywood was about to drop a bomb of its own on the Russian film industry.

In 1956, Producer Dino De Laurentiis and director King Vidor released their own version of *War and Peace*, starring Henry Fonda as Pierre Bezukhov and Mel Ferrer as Prince Andrei Bolkonsky. The film flopped in the US, but Russian filmmakers were appalled that the West had appropriated the Great Russian Novel. Worse, Soviet audiences flocked to the film, not because they appreciated the stripped-down Tolstoy interpretation (they didn't), but because they were smitten by Audrey Hepburn as Natasha Rostova. The Soviet state-sponsored film community knew it was time to reclaim their birthright. And while they were at it, prove to the world that Soviet cinema stood second to none in producing grand historical epics.

Mosfilm studios - more or less an organ of the state - made a surprising choice to helm the project in Sergei Bondarchuk. Bondarchuk, barely into his forties when production started, had spent most of his film career as an actor, and had only one film under his belt as a director, a film well-received, but much smaller in scale. The old guard of Soviet cinema, many of whom *had* proven themselves capable of films on a more epic scale, were incensed that they had been passed over for the honor. Bondarchuk, not one to mend fences, only added fuel to the fire by casting himself in the lead role as Pierre Bezukhov, a man twenty years younger, for whom Bondarchuk definitively could not pass. The new director saw no virtue in either humility or teamwork, and apparently was demanding on set of both actors and crew; he seemed to go through cinematographers faster than Spinal Tap went through drummers. By all reports, the set of *War and Peace* was not a happy place, and Bondarchuk himself suffered two heart attacks during the seven years of production, one of which required resuscitation.

But Bondarchuck had a powerful ally behind him in Mosfilm, and the Soviet government was determined to let no ruble go unspent in support. The reported budget at the time was the equivalent in US dollars of $9 million (or $60-$70 million today), but that was meaningless as the state picked up the tab - or simply provided gratis - expenses that would have bankrupt any other production. The government opened all 58 state-sponsored museums to provide jewelry and artifacts to the production during the entire shoot, never remunerated. The army provided planes (for aerial shots), fifteen thousand troops, and three generals (as advisors), also for the entire shoot, also never billed. An estimated 120,000 extras were used, tons of explosives and smoke grenades, and costumes created from scratch. Historian Denise J. Youngblood, in an interview on the disc, conservatively estimates the true "budget" of the film at $700 million, acknowledging some estimates at up to $1 billion (in 2023 dollars). It's not difficult to imagine Bondarchuk feeling the burden of that kind of "support" on his shoulders, as well as the expectations of every Russian who had grown up with the book and knew it by heart.

The novel itself[77] is a sprawling, over-achieving, soaring, sometimes messy affair, and *War and Peace* the film is no different. Honestly, the best summary I've ever seen is in the title of the essay contributed to the disc by scholar Ella Taylor: "Saint Petersburg Fiddles, Moscow Burns." Let's burn through a plot summary, film by film:

Part I (*Andrei Bolkonsky*) begins in 1805, where we meet Pierre Bezukhov, the illegitimate son of a St. Petersburg nobleman. Bezukhov is indecisive about his own future, whether it is to be in the army or the diplomatic corps. He falls in with a bunch of hard-partying wastrels, but his heart's not really in it. Pierre's father eventually recognizes him, and Pierre is more or less bullied into marriage with Hélène Kuragina (Irina Skobtseva, Bondarchuk's wife), who fairly quickly turns to other men to liven things up. Meanwhile, Pierre's friend, Andrei Bolkonsky (Vyacheslav Tikhonov)

---

[77] I actually read the Leo Tolstoy novel, years ago, when I was trying to catch up on classics I felt like I should know. It's not a difficult read at all, and I don't think anyone needs to be intimidated by it. The chapters are relatively short, and that turned out to be my downfall. I figured I would read a chapter or two on each of my 30-minute lunch breaks at the hospital, getting through it in a year or less. But that turned out to be too intermittent for a novel with so many characters and subplots, especially the (to me) long and unfamiliar names. I got through it, but it didn't take.

has joined the army and is wounded in a campaign against Napoleon in Austria, and taken for dead. Though he recovers in health, his enthusiasm for the glory of war is a casualty, replaced with a firm sense of reluctant duty. He returns to his father's home just in time to witness his wife die in childbirth.

Part II (*Natasha Rostova*) introduces us to a young girl who will find herself pursued by several men in the saga, and come to embody the Russian ideal of womanhood. Natasha (Ludmila Savelyeva, a ballet dancer with one acting credit to her name, and cast in part for her resemblance to Audrey Hepburn) is the daughter of a count, and attends her first ball at age 16. There, Andrei asks her to dance, and the two fall in love. Andrei asks Natasha's father for her hand, but he insists they wait one year, during which Andrei must travel abroad with the army. During that year, Natasha is overwhelmed by Hélène's brother, Anatole (Vasily Lanovoy), and agrees to elope with him, even though he's already married. At the last minute she comes to her senses and refuses to run off with him, but by this time, word has reached Andrei, who releases her from the engagement. Despondent, she turns to Pierre for counsel, who lets slip that he's in love with her, too. Great. Thanks for that.

Part III (*The Year 1812*) is when the war really begins to heat up, as Napoleon's army invades Russia. General Kutuzov (Boris Zakhava), for whom Andrei had previously served as aide-de-camp, is promoted Field Marshal by the czar, despite being nearly blind (along with all the symbolic baggage this implies). He asks Andrei to serve as a staff officer, but Andrei asks to be given a command in the field, as he's instilled with a sense of loyalty toward his men. Kutuzov, in a rare flash of good sense, agrees. But even though his unit is in reserve, they are hit by a shell, and both Andrei and Anatole are gravely wounded. Meanwhile, Pierre (now a full Count, after his father's passing) feels he can no longer cavort with the wealthy away from the war, and finds himself at the battle, where he assists an artillery battery, first ignored by the troops for his aristocratic clothes, then earning their respect as he gets in the mud with them. But the Russian army is forced into retreat, leaving Moscow unprotected.

Part IV (*Pierre Bezukhov*) opens with Moscow ablaze. Natasha and her family are forced to flee, but they hastily unpack most of their possessions from their horse-drawn carts and leave them behind, as they learn that the army is desperate for any conveyances to serve as ambulances for the wounded. But Pierre will not flee. Learning that Napoleon himself will be arriving in Moscow, Pierre disguises himself as a humble peasant with the idea to get close enough to Napoleon to assassinate him. But he is taken prisoner by the French, avoiding execution by the grace of a French officer who'd taken a liking to him. Still, Pierre is marched along with the retreating French army, witnessing the horrors of war, until he is at last rescued by partisans. The French are driven out of Russia, apparently defeated more by the will of the people (along with an assist from the Russian winter) than by the czar or his generals. Andrei is returned to his estate, and on his deathbed, forgives Natasha. Natasha returns to Moscow, and as it's being rebuilt, reunites with Pierre, both now maturer, wiser, and with a renewed sense of duty to Mother Russia and her people.

For all the bridges he burned with the Soviet film community during this production, Bondarchuk came through, probably because of his love of the source novel and zealotry in seeing it done right (qualities that may have earned him the job of directing in the first place). And even though his middle-aged appearance belies the youth of the character he's playing, his soulful eyes and experience as an actor serve him credibly as our guide through this period of Russian history. There are a few distracting experiments in style in Part I a more experienced director probably would have avoided, but when it comes to filming on a grand scale, it's impossible to imagine better. The battle scenes, at times filmed from the air to give the viewer an idea of their scope, are both sweeping and chaotic. None of this could be done today, not in these days of CGI, just as no other studio had the resources to pour into this at the time. As characters are traveling, the Russian countryside becomes a character of its own, lulling the viewer with a pastoral beauty that makes even a foreigner understand why the Russian people hold their land so dear. The burning of Moscow - the sets blanketed in a blizzard of black ash and smoke - is both heartbreaking and obscene. One begins to understand how suffering also takes root deep in the chambers of the Russian heart.

Equally as grand are the ballroom scenes; I literally gasped at the sight of Natasha's debut. The wealth of St.

Petersburg society is as impressive as the vistas of warfare, otherwise we could never appreciate how much the aristocracy dined and danced while the rest of the country bled. Bondarchuk famously put his camera operators on roller skates among the dancing couples to get the graceful shots he wanted. And the ballrooms go on and on and *on* bejeweled with actual paintings and art objects from the 19th century.

Sixty million Russians bought tickets to see Part I and Part II when it was released, double the Soviet box office for the Hollywood 1956 version. The film was a success all over Europe (and in Japan), but in 1969, the Mosfilm and the Soviet government got the validation they had sought all along, when *War and Peace* won the US Academy Award for Best Foreign Language Film, the first Soviet film to bring home an Oscar. The Russians had reclaimed Tolstoy, and in the bargain, claimed their seat at the table of international film.

When We Were Kings

US, 1996. Directed by Leon Gast. 87 minutes, color.

In the early 1970s, I was a kid living in Pottsville, Pennsylvania, a coal town in Schuylkill County that had seen better days come and go. One day my oldest sister was driving us somewhere on Rte. 61, and as we passed through the borough of Deer Lake, she pointed to a turnoff. "That's where Muhammad Ali trains," she told me. I couldn't help myself; I stared down the road, knowing there was no way I'd catch a glimpse of him, even as five years earlier I'd stared at the moon, even then knowing there was no way to make out the Apollo 11 spacecraft. But I had to look, in both cases, as if seeing the place might connect me to the people.

I don't think I'd ever seen a boxing match at that point, and except for maybe a few Olympic matches, I haven't seen one since. It's not something my mother would have approved of, and later, as a health professional, I couldn't see anything but the downside of the "sweet science." And Ali! Gracious! All that crowing and boasting *certainly* ran counter to the sensibilities of a white introvert of Swedish Lutheran upbringing! But you couldn't ignore the man. He battled his way into white consciousness whether we invited him there or not. Ali, even then, was the once-in-a-generation athlete who transcended his sport.

When We Were Kings is a documentary made about the heavyweight fight in Zaïre in 1974 between the reigning champ, George Foreman, and his challenger, Muhammad Ali. The fight - "The Rumble in the Jungle" - was arranged by the up and coming boxing promoter, Don King. He was determined to put Ali and Foreman in the ring together, and got commitments from each of the boxers if he could guarantee a paycheck of $5 million to each. An enormous expenditure like that frightened off US sponsors, and King started looking overseas for a venue. Mobutu Sese Seko, dictator of Zaïre (now Democratic Republic of the Congo), saw in the fight an opportunity to bring the world's attention to his nation (and legitimize his regime), and agreed to put up the $10 million. Once it was settled that the fight would happen in Africa, King set about organizing a three-day music festival to run concurrently with the fight, a celebration of Black culture in which African American musicians would join African musicians onstage.

But four days[78] before the fight, a sparring accident in the Foreman camp threatened to bring the whole thing crashing down. Foreman suffered a cut over his right eye that would require eleven stitches and five weeks to heal before he could enter the ring. There was no delaying the music festival, acts

---

[78] Four days, according to an interview on the disc, but eight days according to other sources.

were locked in and the organizers had to pay them whether the concert went on or not. US acts like B.B. King, James Brown, and The Spinners were already en route, if not already there, to be joined by African artists Miriam Makeba, Manu Dibango, The Pembe Dance Troupe, and others. Without the draw of the fight, musicians played to a mostly empty stadium the first two nights, until promoters opened the venue for free the final night of the concert. Mobutu, fearing he'd lose the fight altogether, prevented either fighter from leaving the country. The fight was rescheduled from September 25th to October 30th, and in order to accommodate US television audiences, it was held at 4:00 AM local time.

While a disaster for promoters, this was a boon for director Leon Gast, and the documentarians of *While We Were Kings*. Suddenly, both Foreman and Ali had five extra weeks of training time, providing filmmakers with more opportunities to follow the fighters around and film their training and interactions with locals. Ali is the star of the film, but only because he provided Gast and crew with greater access. In an interview on the disc, Gast says he approached both camps with the idea of filming, and while Foreman agreed, he was all business, and did none of the showboating his opponent reveled in. Gast said Ali would frequently call him and let him know that if Gast could get a camera crew to a certain road at 5:00 AM, for example, he could get a great shot of Ali running by.

It's amazing to see Ali with the crowds. Early on, he'd hear locals chant, "Ali, *bomaye*!" ("Ali, kill him!") and Ali himself would whip up crowds with this chant whenever he saw them. Ali spoke at every opportunity about feeling at home as a Black man in Africa, marveling that Black Africa had achieved something the US never had - freedom for Blacks to operate at all levels of society. He reiterated at every chance that America is where he lived and worked, but Africa was where he felt at home. He was so good at portraying the quiet Foreman as a Christian American that many Africans didn't realize Foreman was Black until they saw him.

Foreman was heavily favored to win the Rumble in the Jungle. He was 25 years old at the time of the fight as opposed to Ali's 33 years, and Ali's age wasn't his only problem. Foreman was undefeated at the time, and his success was attributed to his size and physical dominance in the ring. Ali had lost two bouts in his career, in which he had gone a full fifteen rounds before losing to both Ken Norton and Joe Frazier. Foremen had demolished both boxers in two rounds. Even Ali's own camp was secretly pessimistic, and worried what a humiliating loss would do to Ali's ego. It was said that Ali's own training staff had grown pensively quiet in his locker room just before the fight, and it was Ali himself who rallied their enthusiasm.

Norman Mailer appears in the film and describes Ali's strategy in the first round, the right hand lead. Boxers turn to the side when facing an opponent, Ali leading with his left shoulder, meaning Ali's left hand had less distance to travel than his right. That's a miniscule amount of time for you and me (well, for me, anyway), but to a professional like Foreman, it's practically an eternity to see a punch coming.

No opponent would be stupid enough to give Foreman that much time to prepare for a punch (or to leave himself open), and neither would Foreman's sparring partners; it would be so ineffective as to be perceived as an insult. Ali was banking on the fact that Foreman would not have trained against the tactic, and that he could surprise Foreman into an early beating. But after the first round, all it seemed to do was annoy the younger, stronger man.

That's when Ali turned to the "Rope-a-dope." It's unclear whether this was a strategy Ali had devised going into the fight, or whether it was a desperate improvisation when the right hand lead failed him. But Ali allowed Foreman to maneuver him against the ropes - a purely defensive position - and put up a guard in the hope that Foreman would tire himself out using Ali as a punching bag, in a barrage of powerful (but non scoring) blows. Ali could conserve energy, but it was a near-suicidal tactic against a man who hit so hard. But it worked. Whether because of Ali's incredible conditioning, or the fact that Foreman was unused to fighting this far into a match, Foreman visibly began to tire. And in the eighth round, Ali came off the ropes and began a barrage against Foreman that ended with the heavyweight champion of the world on the mat. Ali had won.

So why wasn't *When We Were Kings* released in 1974 or 1975? Gast had lost his own funding following the unexpected death of one of his producers, and it took 22 years to raise the money to transfer the film to videotape, edit the footage, and find a distributor. There was so much footage, in fact, that Gast needed to make a decision whether to focus attention on the fight, the music festival, or both. In the end he stuck mostly to the fight, but there was so much footage left over that a second documentary was released in 2008, *Soul Power*, directed by Jeffrey Kusama-Hinte, covering the Zaïre 74 music festival. *Soul Power* is also included on the Criterion disc, and runs just a few minutes longer than *When We Were Kings*. Keeping the cameras pointed toward the stage to hide the lack of crowds, it's a terrific concert documentary and celebration of Black music (if you've never seen James Brown on stage, it's worth it for that performance alone).

When We Were Kings won the 1996 Academy Award for Best Documentary Feature, and is widely considered to be the greatest boxing documentary ever made. It's not hard to see why. I think the film is masterfully edited, giving us a feel for the setting and the people, and an insight into Ali and what this trip to Africa meant not only to him, but to African Americans. Spike Lee tells us in the film, "There's a time, if you called a Black person an African, they'd be ready to fight," and the documentary shows us how much pride a new generation of African Americans found in their African heritage. And the "talking heads" Gast consults do a great job of walking a novice like me through boxing strategy, helping me to understand the story of the match.

But those same talking heads add a discordant note when watching the film in the Black Lives Matter era. Though Spike Lee and Malik Bowens were interviewed for their perspectives on the fight, far more screen time is given to writers Norman Mailer and George Plimpton, both of whom were ringside in

Zaïre, both of whom were interviewed years later, closer to the 1996 release date. I'm grateful that Gast, a white man, had the resources to film the trip in 1974 when others didn't. But apart from Don King, the American side of the fight promotion are all white men, and it's hard not to feel some sense of appropriation that more Black commentators weren't telling their own stories. If Gast was interviewing people in the 1990s for the film, why not turn the camera toward contemporary Black boxers or athletes, who might talk about what the Rumble in the Jungle meant to them?

I think the film does a great job in showcasing the cultural pride wrapped up in a sporting event, and I don't doubt Gast's commitment to the participants. It's also an illuminating look at one of the icons of American sport and American civil rights. I just think we've learned a lot since 1996 about the importance of *who* is telling a story, not just whose story is being told.

Young Mr. Lincoln

US, 1939. Directed by John Ford. 100 minutes, black and white.

We hunger for origin myths. When it comes to things we cherish, we want grand stories for how it all began, stories that point to the greatness that lies ahead. We wanted to know our place in the world, so we created Adam and Eve in the Garden of Eden. We wanted to crown baseball as an American invention, so we resurrected Abner Doubleday, a deceased civil war general, and laid creation of the game at his feet. Neither of these myths are literally true, but they don't need to be. Mythology isn't about historical, factual truth. It's about our values and our aspirations. If we need certain figures in our past to be larger than life, then we will fashion them that way. But our myths are always about getting after fundamental truths. As Joseph Campbell pointed out, we don't go to the trouble of creating myths about things that aren't important to us.

John Ford's *Young Mr. Lincoln* serves as such an origin myth; a look at one of our most iconic presidents while he was still "human," before the tide of history turned him into something like a god. Henry Fonda (not at the time under contract) said that he at first turned down the role, as he couldn't see himself playing "The Great Emancipator." Ford called Fonda into his office, and in an f-bomb-laced tirade (that closing scene in *The Fablemans* was apparently not an exaggeration) informed the young actor that he would *not* be portraying Lincoln as president, but as a "young jackleg lawyer." The film, true to its title, follows Abraham Lincoln during a period of roughly ten years, most of the film tied up with a murder trial in which Lincoln defends two brothers.

Of course the film is haunted with allusions to the Civil War, and previsions of the man to come; the French title of the film was *Toward His Destiny*. But Ford wisely keeps a light touch with these, saving his grandest image for the last scene, when Lincoln walks up a hill, alone, as storm clouds gather. What Ford and Fonda instead concentrate on is the young man finding himself, testing his voice, working through the strategies writ small that he will later rely on to guide a divided nation.

The film opens in New Salem, Illinois, with pompous political oratory preached from the front of Lincoln's store. But the speech is coming not from Lincoln, but from a local politician, and when young Abe is called on to say a few words, Fonda rises awkwardly, unsure of what to do with his hands. Shortly after, a family passes through in a covered wagon; unable to afford supplies, Lincoln offers to extend them credit at his store. The matriarch of the family, Abigail Clay (Alice Brady) tells Abe there's a barrel of books he's welcome to, which peaks the shopkeeper's interest. On the top of the barrel is a copy of Blackstone's Law Commentary,[79] and in the next scene we'll see Lincoln studying the book on a river bank, lying on the ground, his long legs perched halfway up a tree trunk. The next we see Mr. Lincoln, he is arriving in Springfield, Illinois, in 1837 on the back of a mule, his feet almost dragging on the ground, about to set up practice with his friend John Stuart (Edwin Maxwell).

But first there's a July 4th celebration to attend, and Ford uses the celebration to build on the budding Lincoln mythology. It starts with Abe watching a parade go by, and as we see him acknowledging the veterans of the War of 1812 and even a few old-timers who fought in 1776, we're reviewing American history up to that point. There is of course a rail-splitting competition which Lincoln wins - it's the only time we see Fonda play the character with physical grace. Lincoln is asked to judge a pie contest, and as he alternates between a hunk of peach pie and a slab of apple pie (fruits of the South and North, respectively), he seems unable to reach a decision. But the most telling event of the day is a tug of war between two teams, and Lincoln slips in to assist the underdogs after the contest has begun. Lincoln

---

[79] Up until the 1890s, the way to become a lawyer in the United States was to literally "read law." This was usually done under the apprenticeship of an attorney, but even that was optional; Lincoln himself never studied under a lawyer. Law schools existed, but were seen as a complement to apprenticeship and not a replacement for it. Once you felt you were ready, you took an oral or written bar exam, and if you passed, you could hang up your shingle as a lawyer.

brings his team to victory by cheating; he ties the end of the rope to a wagon, letting a horse team do the work! It's funny, but it's also an important scene. As a political pragmatist, President Lincoln was not above pushing the limits of the Constitution to keep the country together.

It's later that evening that we again encounter the Clay family (though oddly, Lincoln never seems to recall the family as the source of his law book, nor do they seem to recognize him). The two Clay brothers, Matt and Adam (Richard Cromwell and Eddie Quillan) are confronted by a man who had been bullying them earlier. As they fight, the man pulls a gun, and one of the brothers pulls a knife; the attacker drops to the ground with a knife wound. But the gun has gone off, and though no one was shot, the noise attracts the attention of J. Palmer Cass (Ward Bond), a friend of the attacker, who after examining the victim, pronounces him dead and the brothers murderers. The brothers are arrested and taken to jail, but a gathering crowd begins to turn into a lynch mob. Lincoln, alarmed, tells Abigail that she needs to follow him to the jail. When she asks Lincoln who he is, he replies, "I'm your lawyer."

Lincoln alone stands between the mob and the Clay brothers at the door to the sheriff's office. He talks the crowd down, and in the scene uses every tactic available to him. He starts by offering to fight any man who thinks he's able to make it through him; none take him up on that. Then Lincoln switches to self-deprecation and humor, telling the crowd that with him as their lawyer, the boys are as good as dead anyway and that it would be unfair of the mob to cheat him out of his first clients. Finally, he turns to shame, singling out members of the crowd, and reminding them that as they open their Bibles when they return home, they'll feel differently about this than they do right now. It's a powerful scene, one Fonda sells by cutting back on the grandstanding, as Lincoln seemingly reaches into his heart to speak to the crowd (though we realize the lawyer's mind is in play through the entire speech).

For the remainder of the film, *Young Mr. Lincoln* turns into both a courtroom drama and a mystery. Both Matt and Adam claim to be the brother that did the actual stabbing, each to protect the other from hanging. The only witness is Abigail, who at one point is browbeaten by the prosecuting attorney (Donald Meek) to reveal which brother did the killing, so that only one will be hanged rather than both.[80] Lincoln steps in to prevent Abigail from having to make this Sophie's Choice, and in the end is able to save both brothers with the timely help of a Farmer's Almanac. I don't think it's a coincidence that *Young Mr. Lincoln* chooses as its central conflict a story about trying to keep a family together.

The entire film, though touching on historical points in Lincoln's early career, is a fabrication. The trial is loosely based on a case the historical Lincoln tried, but only loosely, and screenwriter Lamar Trotti has assembled a story to highlight what he imagines to be the nascent qualities of the

---

[80] I found this plot point - that both defendants would be hanged if the jury couldn't determine which one held the knife - to be the least believable part of the trial. But apparently, there was precedent for this in actual case law at the time.

future president. You could sift through the historical record all you like and never find transcripts of any trial as presented here, or of Lincoln defusing a lynch mob. But as mythology, the film works brilliantly. We're there to witness the young man's fascination with law, specifically law as a tool to pursue justice. We find an earthy, physical man who turns to his mind as he takes up his life's work. We see the beginnings of an intellect that will not be overtaken by intellectualism; Lincoln the pragmatist will never lose sight of the common man, nor let an ideology handcuff him. And Ford frames Lincoln throughout as a man apart from the people; note how often the camera finds him alone. Lincoln is for us, but not for himself. He is already on the road to his destiny.

Young Mr. Lincoln is fascinating for another reason. Soviet filmmaker Sergei Eisenstein wrote an essay in 1945 (included with the disc) in which he praised this film as the one American film he wished he had made. It made me think of the great patriotic films of other nations, usually depicting battles for freedom or great military commanders. The hero of *Young Mr. Lincoln* is the rule of law, and the ungainly and humble bumpkin that stands up to become its greatest champion. In the setting of the film, the nation is barely over fifty years old, our current midwest then The West, and our democracy not yet assured, as the ugliness of the lynch mob demonstrates. It's at this teetering moment in the young nation's history that our greatest hero stands for our greatest virtue: Justice. As a declaration of an ideal, *Young Mr. Lincoln* stands as a uniquely American point of view.

I write this at a time when democracy in the United States is very much in doubt. I live in a time when voices we've ignored for so long are rising, reminding us of all those we've buried in our attempts to better the lives of some. Our country is bitterly divided between those who want to shout down those voices and those who want to include them. Perhaps a nation founded on the twin sins of genocide and slavery is ultimately unsustainable; it's harder these days to see a way past that. That's when I think we need the mythology of *Young Mr. Lincoln*. Not to fool ourselves that there was a time that was pure, or that our heroes were unblemished, or that we literally ever lived the way we promised to. But the ideals expressed in the myths are so strong that they challenge us to look at our own lives in comparison. If we use our myths to say, "Look what we did! Look who we are!" we're lying to ourselves. But if we use them to say, "Look who we must be!" they can act as signposts to a better society. Our myths are not our history. Our myths are our dreams.

Our movies are our collective dreams. We dreamt better once. We need to keep dreaming better.

Acknowledgements

I had no idea.

It turns out that writing the book was the easy part. Getting me to the point of conjuring up the confidence and the wherewithal to publish this book was the loving work of a whole team. Many, many good people have had a part in this.

First, I need to thank D. Margaret Hoffman, without whom *Criterion Tuesdays* would simply not exist. She has been my friend, mentor, cheerleader, confidant, the works, and saintingly patient with me as I mustered the fortitude to actually believe I had something of value to say. She walked me through every step of the process, endured an *epic* Zoom panic attack, and took time from her own writing to answer my questions. If you have any desire to write, be it journaling or publishing, or anything in between, I beseech you to seek out her *Saving Our Lives* series, wonderful books to launch the writer in you. *Beseech*. Please visit her website at www.dmargarethoffman.com.

Thanks to Barth Keck, who read and commented on almost all of my essays while they were still in blog form. Barth's knowledge and erudition gradually convinced me I might have a wider audience out there. Barth, you may have thought I wasn't listening, but you're too valuable a friend to dismiss. Thanks. Look up Barth at www.ctnewsjunkie.com.

Thanks to my crack team of proofreaders: Mike Czarkowski, Tina "T-Bird" Forgey, Beth Hollinger, Sam Johansson, Barth Keck, Cheryl Meinschein, Liz Smith, and Roxanne Tucker. They were lifesavers. If you find any errors in grammar, punctuation, or spelling, it is to their homes you should descend with pitchforks and torches. I'll bring the cabbages.

Thank you to Andrea Griffith, owner of Browsers Bookshop in Olympia, WA. Andrea helped me find a road to publishing that bypassed Amazon and led straight to independent booksellers. Shop local, wherever you are!

Thanks to Shannon McShea, who taught me by example that you can support someone's jam even when it isn't *your* jam. You helped me to value myself.

Thank you, Sam Johansson... for *everything*. You always believed in me even when I didn't believe in myself. You'll never know how much that meant, and continues to mean.

Finally, thank *you*, dear reader. I'm astonished that you - or someone you know - would plunk down cash for my words. I'm honored that you chose to spend some time here, what with everything else going on in your life. We writers, we think about you. You fuel us. You make all the difference.

About the Author

Peter Johansson (he/him) got this way by not listening to his mother when she told him to play outside. Peter is an RN who lives in Olympia, Washington with his Wheaten terrier, Jonesey Peaseblossom. When not at the movies or at the ballpark (Go, Mariners! Go, Rainiers!), Peter and Jonesey can often be spotted at the bookstores, cafes, taprooms, and dive bars of downtown Olympia. Peter has a grown son who is a hoot and a half, and whom he loves with his whole heart.

Comments or feedback on *Criterion Tuesdays*? Peter can be reached at peterjohansson@criteriontuesdays.com.